W9-DBV-139

'GROOMING' AND THE SEXUAL ABUSE OF CHILDREN

CLARENDON STUDIES IN CRIMINOLOGY

Published under the auspices of the Institute of Criminology, University of Cambridge; the Mannheim Centre, London School of Economics; and the Centre for Criminological Research,
University of Oxford.

General Editor: Lucia Zedner
(University of Oxford)

Editors: Manuel Eisner, Alison Liebling, and Per-Olof Wikström
(University of Cambridge)

Robert Reiner, Jill Peay, and Tim Newburn
(London School of Economics)

Ian Loader and Julian Roberts
(University of Oxford)

RECENT TITLES IN THIS SERIES:

The Multicultural Prison: Ethnicity, Masculinity, and Social Relations among Prisoners
Phillips

Breaking Rules: The Social and Situational Dynamics of Young People's Urban Crime
Wikström, Oberwittler, Treiber, and Hardie

Tough Choices: Risk, Security and the Criminalization of Drug Policy
Seddon, Williams, and Ralphs

Discovery of Hidden Crime: Self-Report Delinquency Surveys in Criminal Policy Context
Kivivuori

Serious Offenders: A Historical Study of Habitual Criminals
Godfrey, Cox, and Farrall

'Grooming' and the Sexual Abuse of Children

Institutional, Internet, and Familial Dimensions

ANNE-MARIE McALINDEN

OXFORD
UNIVERSITY PRESS

OXFORD

UNIVERSITY PRESS

Great Clarendon Street, Oxford, OX2 6DP,
United Kingdom

Oxford University Press is a department of the University of Oxford.
It furthers the University's objective of excellence in research, scholarship,
and education by publishing worldwide. Oxford is a registered trade mark of
Oxford University Press in the UK and in certain other countries

© Anne-Marie McAlinden, 2012

The moral rights of the author have been asserted

First Edition published in 2012

Impression: 1

British Library Cataloguing in Publication Data
Data available

ISBN 978-0-19-958372-0

Printed in Great Britain by
CPI Group (UK) Ltd, Croydon, CR0 4YY

Links to third party websites are provided by Oxford in good faith and
for information only. Oxford disclaims any responsibility for the materials
contained in any third party website referenced in this work

For your love and support:
Stephen, Ben, and Luke

General Editor's Introduction

Clarendon Studies in Criminology aims to provide a forum for outstanding empirical and theoretical work in all aspects of criminology and criminal justice, broadly understood. The Editors welcome submissions from established scholars, as well as excellent PhD work. The *Series* was inaugurated in 1994, with Roger Hood as its first General Editor, following discussions between Oxford University Press and three criminology centres. It is edited under the auspices of these three centres: the Cambridge Institute of Criminology, the Mannheim Centre for Criminology at the London School of Economics, and the Centre for Criminology at the University of Oxford. Each supplies members of the Editorial Board and, in turn, the Series Editor.

'Grooming' and the Sexual Abuse of Children addresses an under-researched but very important topic of criminological concern, namely the ways in which potential perpetrators of child sexual abuse identify and gain the trust of the children they target. The author, Anne-Marie McAlinden, deliberately adopts the commonly used short-hand term 'grooming' while recognising the wide variety of activities that this spans and the dangers of employing such an emotive term. One reason for this choice is that a central aspect of McAlinden's endeavour is to explore the lack of a settled meaning and the diverse ways in which the term grooming is constructed in popular as well as in official discourses. Her contention is that the varied construction of grooming is vital to understanding the nature of political debate, the development of public policy, and the formulation of legislation.

McAlinden demonstrates that the ways in which grooming is conceived has the consequence of determining which kinds of activity are targeted and which are neglected. In particular, a common tendency to equate grooming with online approaches by strangers diverts attention from the many other settings – public, institutional, and private - in which grooming occurs. By identifying areas of neglect, the book makes a vital contribution to identifying systemic weaknesses in child protection, not least as regards family members and others known well to children, who are shown to be the most common perpetrators of child sexual abuse. Unsurprisingly, the book proposes a new definition of grooming that better captures the complex, multiple forms of activity and the range of situations in which it occurs.

McAlinden's research is based upon in-depth interviews with criminal justice officials and a range of other professionals who work with child sexual abuse cases. These interviews yield rich and informative insights into the complexities of the phenomenon. Most troublingly, they reveal the acute difficulties faced by professionals who seek to identify grooming and to develop effective means of protecting children against predation. Particularly disturbing are the discussions of institutional grooming in religious, educational and other closed communities; of the complex power relations within these institutions that serve to perpetuate and conceal; and of the consequent difficulties of devising effective strategies to prevent, combat, and prosecute abuse.

Throughout, this book provides insightful analysis of the construction of sexual grooming, political debates, and the development of policy and legislative responses in the United Kingdom and the Republic of Ireland. It furnishes illuminating data on the nature, forms and extent of grooming that make clear just how serious are the challenges faced by legislators, policy makers, and, not least, by professionals working on the ground. The final part of the book makes interesting proposals for reform that go beyond resort to criminalization to suggest a public health approach based upon social and institutional initiatives directed at the twin aims of prevention and protection. McAlinden sets out how such a change in approach to grooming might be achieved, yet she acknowledges the continuing difficulties faced, not least in fostering wider recognition of the prevalence of sexual offending against children within, as well as outside, the family home. In so doing, she makes a significant contribution to larger debates about sexual offending, child protection, risk assessment and risk management, penal populism, the role of the media, and penal politics more generally.

This important, if disturbing, addition to the *Clarendon Studies in Criminology Series* fills a notable gap in our criminological knowledge. Its findings are of considerable importance to students and scholars of criminology, as well as to criminal justice and child care professionals. It will certainly be of interest and concern to those working in contemporary criminal justice, social work, and child protection.

For all these reasons, the Editors welcome this new addition to the *Series*.

Lucia Zedner
University of Oxford
September 2012

Acknowledgements

Examining a complex topic such as the grooming of children for sexual abuse within the context of the legal and policy frameworks of four jurisdictions and a multi-disciplinary theoretical framework has proved a daunting but ultimately rewarding task. I hope that the book adequately reflects this experience. In researching and writing this book I have received much help and support along the way. I am extremely grateful to the British Academy for awarding me a small research grant to conduct the primary research (Grant Ref: SG10187) and to the School of Law at Queen's University Belfast for granting me one semester of research leave during the 2010–11 academic year to conduct the fieldwork. My sincere thanks go to friends and colleagues within the School of Law, and in particular Professors Kieran McEvoy, Shadd Maruna, and Phil Scraton for constructive feedback on draft chapters. I would also like to thank Professor Jill Peay, as peer reviewer for the Clarendon Series, for her insightful and very helpful feedback on the draft manuscript, and all at Oxford University Press, including my editor Lucy Alexander, for support and guidance throughout. Special thanks are due to the 50 or more professionals in England and Wales, Scotland, Northern Ireland, and the Republic of Ireland who gave generously of their time during interviews and shared their invaluable knowledge and experience with me.

Thanks, above all are due to my family: To my sister Patrina and her family, and my parents, Maria and Pat, for their enduring faith and encouragement; and my husband, Stephen, for his unwavering love and support. My greatest debt of gratitude is to him and our two boys, Ben and Luke, for providing much needed diversion from the intensity of research and writing and who put up with this book as a guest in our home for much too long.

Anne-Marie McAlinden
June 2012

Contents

PART I

The Theoretical Context

1

Introduction

After creating at least eight fake 'profiles', Michael Williams targeted youngsters he met on his post round, on school runs as a taxi driver, and in his role as secretary of a football club. He dyed his hair different colours to hide his identity and pretended to be a young boy called 'James' and a teenage girl called 'Gorgeous Charlie' to meet children aged between 11 and 16. Many victims were tricked into performing sex acts on a webcam but he convinced others to meet him in parks, on beaches and at his home, where he abused them.[1]

One of the most contentious debates in the area of sexual offences against children has centred on behaviour known as 'grooming'. This term has been used to describe the offender's actions during the initial stages of sexual abuse where a potential perpetrator sets up opportunities to abuse by gaining the trust of the child or others in order to both facilitate abuse and subsequently prevent disclosure (Salter, 1995, 2003). It is thought that children themselves may be groomed or prepared for abuse either directly (Salter, 1995) or, as is the case more recently, through internet chat rooms (Gillespie, 2001, 2004a; Gallagher et al, 2003). The term 'grooming', however, much like other terms within popular discourses on sex offending (including the word 'paedophile'), should be used in a measured and considered way. There are dangers attached to the deployment of such pejorative terminology which relate to the effects of labelling (McAlinden, 2007a). In particular, in the current public and penal climate around sex offending, especially against children, such labels tend to promote stereotypical images of predatory sex offenders. As such, they have the potential to contribute to 'moral panics'

---

[1] M. Seamark, 'Paedophile Postman used Facebook and Bebo to Groom up to 1,000 Children for Sex', *Daily Mail*, 29 May 2010, <http://www.dailymail.co.uk/news/article-1282157/Facebook-grooming-How-pervert-postman-used-site-groom-hundreds-children.html> (accessed 30 March 2012).

(Cohen, 1972), to pathologize harmless or benign behaviours towards children, and to obfuscate rather than illuminate the realities of 'risk' concerning individual patterns of offending behaviour.

Moreover, use of the word 'grooming' to describe 'what are ostensibly courting behaviours' fails to acknowledge that many of the behaviours covered by the word would be considered appropriate if they were used outside the context of abuse (Fernandez, 2006: 191). In this respect, the use of such labels may also signify to the offender that 'the problem is the behaviour rather than the inappropriateness of the target person' (Fernandez, 2006: 191). It is for this reason that the term 'grooming' is often set aside by commentators as euphemistic in favour of other stronger terms such as 'entrapment' (eg Howitt, 1995: 176; Gallagher, 1998, 2000). Having acknowledged these caveats, however, such difficulties should not preclude critical academic discourse about the subject. For the purposes of this study, therefore, and in order to retain the integrity of the term, I use the term 'grooming' throughout, at first instance in relation to how it occurs within the existing literature and, subsequently, as I define it.

It has been claimed that 'grooming is a ubiquitous feature of the sexual abuse of children' (Thornton, 2003: 144). However, despite the purported significance of this process in the onset of sexual abuse and the recent prominence of the term in public and official consciousness, it is a notion insufficiently understood in the relevant sociological, criminological, psychological or, indeed, legal literature. The main purpose of this book is to critically examine contemporary popular and state-led constructions of grooming within the comparative context of the four jurisdictions in the United Kingdom and Ireland—England and Wales,[2] Scotland, Northern Ireland, and the Republic of Ireland. Other jurisdictions, such as the United States, Canada, Australia, and several Western European countries are also included for comparison and illustration. Comparisons are made in particular with regard to the criminalization of grooming, vetting and barring schemes, inter-agency frameworks, and current penal policy on the regulation of sexual crime. In par-

---

[2] England and Wales, although two separate countries within the United Kingdom (along with Scotland and Northern Ireland), have an integrated legal and criminal justice system. Therefore, both jurisdictions are discussed as a single entity throughout the course of this book.

ticular, there are a range of stereotypes and assumptions surrounding grooming as encapsulated in the introductory quotation. This book aims to deconstruct the term, to challenge and confront common misunderstandings concerning grooming within academic, official, and public discourses, and to examine its actual role within the highly complex processes of sexual offending against children.

Public and Official Discourses on Grooming

Contemporary public and official discourses on grooming have been framed predominantly within the context of two governing paradigms—one, the internet and 'on-line abuse' committed by strangers (Gillespie, 2001, 2004a), the other, child care organizations and 'institutional abuse' committed by those in positions of trust (McAlinden, 2006a). These social and political constructions of potential risks to children, however, tend to underplay the exclusion of other sources of harm, particularly those within intra-familial settings—an issue to which I shall return.

In relation to the first context, cases of sexual exploitation of children involving the internet have received widespread international official attention within the last few years (Gallagher et al, 2003). Of these cases, those involving child pornography, or 'child abuse images', have received the greatest amount of attention (Jenkins, 2001; Gallagher et al, 2003; Taylor and Quayle, 2003; Akdeniz, 2008).[3] In contrast, internet-initiated grooming and subsequent sexual abuse of children has lagged some way behind. While many jurisdictions currently criminalize this form of 'grooming' via more generic child pornography legislation,[4] several jurisdictions have explicitly recognized the extent of the dangers of 'on-line grooming' for some time. The United States,[5] Canada,[6] and Australia[7], for example,

[3] One of the most high profile of these cases was the 'Wonderland' investigation—an international operation involving several police forces in different countries. See eg 'Paedophiles Jailed for Porn Ring', *BBC News On-line*, 13 February 2001, <http://news.bbc.co.uk/1/hi/uk/1168112.stm> (accessed 18 February 2011).

[4] See eg Austria, Belgium, the Czech Republic, Denmark, Finland, Germany, Greece, the Netherlands, and Poland: Kierkegaard (2008).

[5] For US Federal Law, see 18 USC 2422: Coercion and Enticement. See also various state laws, eg Georgia State Law: Ga Code Ann. § 16-12-100.2 (1999). For a brief overview see also Gillespie (2005: 5).

[6] The Criminal Code, s 172.1, enacted by The Criminal Amendment Act 2001.

[7] Australian Criminal Code Act 1995, ss 474.26–474.27; see also various state laws, eg the Northern Territory of Australia Criminal Code Act, s 201, para 3.4.2.

have various offences to cover on-line grooming based on either coercion, enticement, or luring a child via electronic mediums with the intention of committing sexual abuse (Nair, 2006: 183–4; Davidson and Martellozo, 2008a: 278–9; Kierkegaard, 2008; Choo, 2009: 50–69). For the most part, however, grooming in these jurisdictions remains firmly linked to the internet and, at the time of writing, legislation has not been enacted to cover grooming behaviour which takes place off-line.[8] Aside from the United Kingdom and Ireland, Norway,[9] Sweden,[10] and the Netherlands[11] are the only other Western European states to enact specific legislation on grooming.

In England and Wales and Northern Ireland, the term 'grooming' has more recently found expression in section 15 of the Sexual Offences Act 2003[12] and article 22 of the Sexual Offences (Northern Ireland) Order 2008 respectively, which cover the offence of 'meeting a child following sexual grooming etc' (Ost, 2004; Craven, Brown, and Gilchrist, 2007). Scotland and the Republic of Ireland have enacted the respective offences of 'meeting a child following certain preliminary contact'[13] and 'meeting a child for the purpose of sexual exploitation'[14] which are couched in similar legal terms. New policing units have been created such as the UK-based Child Exploitation and Online Protection Centre (CEOP) and the associated Virtual Global Taskforce (VGT) to protect children from the dangers associated with the internet and related communication technologies (Gillespie, 2008) (see Chapter 6). Moreover, the gravity and potential dangers of sexual grooming, particularly via on-line methods, have also been recognized by the judiciary as

---

[8] See also New Zealand (Crimes Amendment Act 2005, s 131B) and Singapore (Penal Code Amendment Act 2007, s 376E) which have modelled their provisions on s 15 of the Sexual Offences Act 2003.

[9] The General Penal Code ('Straffeloven'), s 201a.

[10] The Swedish Penal Code, ch 6, s 10a.

[11] The Dutch Criminal Code, art 248e.

[12] As amended by the Criminal Justice and Immigration Act 2008, s 73 and Sch 15, para 1.

[13] Protection of Children and Prevention of Sexual Offences (Scotland) Act 2005, s 1.

[14] Child Trafficking and Pornography Act 1998, s 3, as amended by the Criminal Law (Sexual Offences) (Amendment) Act 2007, s 6.

an aggravating factor in the commission of sexual offences against children.[15]

In relation to the second context, in England and Wales in particular, serious failures in pre-employment vetting have provoked public outcry and acted as a catalyst for legislative and policy change. A series of public inquiries into 'institutional abuse' from the early 1990s onwards highlighted the link between institutions, such as care homes, and the sexual abuse of children (Reder, Duncan, and Gray, 1993; Corby, Doig, and Roberts, 2001).[16] Similarly, in Scotland,[17] Northern Ireland,[18] and the Republic of Ireland,[19] there have also been a number of public inquiries and reviews into institutional child abuse. The major themes to emerge from these inquiries across jurisdictions are indicative of the existence of the grooming process within an institutional context—what I have previously termed 'institutional grooming'[20] (McAlinden, 2006a)—and its effectiveness in making such abuse possible and, ultimately, preventing its exposure. These include delays in disclosure, initial disbelief of victims, the 'conspiracy of silence', and denial and minimization of allegations of abuse (see Chapter 5).

---

[15] In *Re Attorney General's Reference (No 41 of 2000)* [2001] 1 Cr App R (S) 372, the Court of Appeal increased the defendant's sentence for indecent assault and making indecent photographs of children due to the fact, inter alia, that he had sexually groomed a child with special needs. See also *R v T* [2005] EWCA Crim 2681; *R v M* [2007] 1 Cr App R (S) 16.

[16] See eg, the Warner Report (1992) on the selection, development and management of staff in children's homes; the Utting Report (1998) on the safeguards for children living away from home; and the Waterhouse Report (2000) into the abuse of children in care homes in North Wales.

[17] See eg the Edinburgh inquiry (Marshall, Jamieson and Finlayson, 1999); the Fife inquiry (Black and Williams, 2002); and the Kerelaw inquiry (Frizell, 2009). See also reviews of residential care for children: Skinner (1992); Kent (1997); and Shaw (2007).

[18] See eg Kincora (DHSS, 1982; HMSO, 1985; Moore, 1996), and the Martin Huston case (DHSS, 1993).

[19] See the Ferns Report (Murphy, Buckley, and Joyce, 2005); the Ryan Report (Commission to Inquire into Child Abuse, 2009); the Murphy Report (Commission of Investigation, 2009); and the Cloyne Report (Commission of Investigation, 2011).

[20] I have used this term to describe the process whereby sex offenders make unique use of the organizational environment as a cover to target and sexually abuse children and to groom organizational systems and professionals, which may act as the gatekeepers of access, into viewing them as posing no danger to children (McAlinden, 2006a).

In England and Wales, key recommendations arising from the inquiries and reviews have resulted in a plethora of legislative developments in the area of pre-employment vetting and barring. Most recently, the Report of the Bichard Inquiry (Bichard, 2004) following the conviction of Ian Huntley for the murders of Holly Wells and Jessica Chapman in Soham, resulted in the Safeguarding Vulnerable Groups Act 2006 and a new regulatory framework on vetting. Scotland and Northern Ireland have formulated broadly equivalent measures.[21] Many inquiries, however, have made similar recommendations to enhance child protection which have not been realized (Parton, 2004). This is due to a complex interplay of factors including the increased resource implications and new statutory frameworks required to give legislative effect to such recommendations. It can also be related to a broader process of political expediency, whereby the state seeks to demonstrate its power and resolves to curtail a problem (Garland, 1996), which then diminishes once the issue becomes less prominent in public consciousness. Indeed, these policy and legal discourses have usually been reactive in nature, often emerging in the immediate aftermath of high profile child abuse cases. Such was the expansive remit of the Safeguarding Vulnerable Groups legislation, that the coalition government announced plans to scale back the legislation in England and Wales to 'common sense' levels (see Chapter 6).[22]

Despite governments and civil society generally becoming more focused on the concept of grooming and its role in sexual abuse cases, significant difficulties remain in understanding the dynamics of the offending process. A core task of the analysis is to unpack and critically explore the complexities and subtleties of the role of grooming behaviours within the often multi-faceted process of the onset of sexual offending against children, including how they might be addressed more effectively within political and policy-making discourses. In particular, in countering conceptualizations of grooming within the two key contemporary constructs of the internet and institutional abuse, the book also seeks to critically

[21] Protecting Vulnerable Groups (Scotland) Act 2006; Safeguarding Vulnerable Groups (NI) Order 2007.

[22] Protection of Freedoms Act 2012, Part 5. See also 'Nick Clegg Reveals End of Vetting Scheme', *The Independent*, 11 February 2011, <http://www.independent.co.uk/news/uk/politics/nick-clegg-reveals-end-of-vetting-scheme-2211567.html> (accessed 14 February 2011).

examine the role of grooming behaviours within the context of intra-familial as well as extra-familial abuse.

Contextualizing the Debates

The assessment, treatment, management, and offending patterns of sex offenders have generated an abundance of academic and practitioner literature (see eg Sampson, 1994; Soothill et al, 2000; Friendship and Thornton, 2001; Matravers, 2003; Kemshall and McIvor, 2004; McAlinden, 2007a, Boer et al, 2011). While sexual offending encompasses a broad spectrum of offending behaviour, the focus of recent official and public discourses on the subject has been sexual offending against children in particular. Concerns about the presence of 'predatory' sex offenders in the community have generated a constant flurry of media activity and intermittent waves of public panic (Ashenden, 2002). At the same time, a surge of legislative enactments in a range of jurisdictions, including most notably the United States and England and Wales, have placed increased emphasis on offender management and public protection (Home Office, 1996, 2002; Hebenton and Seddon, 2009; McAlinden, 2010b). Within this broader context, a key issue for contemporary discourses on child protection and sex offender management is how to identify and manage those who may pose a risk to children prior to the occurrence of actual harm (Room, 2004; Ost, 2009).

In common with contemporary public and official discourses, the majority of recent academic work on the sexual exploitation of children has focused on the broad spectrum of issues involving sexual abuse and the internet (eg Calder, 2004; Powell, 2007; Sheldon and Howitt, 2007; Sher, 2007; Livingstone, 2009; Davidson and Gottschalk, 2010, 2011). Within this context, scholars have focused specifically on the issue of child pornography and the internet with passing reference to its role in the grooming process (Taylor and Quayle, 2003; Quayle and Taylor, 2005; Kierkegaard, 2007; O'Donnell and Milner, 2007; Akdeniz, 2008). Others have explored the legal and social response to the sexual grooming of children involving child pornography (Ost, 2009). The use of pornography or sexually explicit imagery often has a role to play in the sequential process of grooming. This is but one element, however, of a broader and more complex process (see Chapter 4).

Regarding grooming in particular, there is a body of work on how sex offenders are known to operate in the manipulation of children and, to a lesser extent, families or communities prior to the onset of sexual abuse (Salter, 1995, 2003; Wyre, 2000; van Dam, 2001). This literature, however, is restricted and over-simplistic in focus, neglecting a specific consideration of the institutional context. Earlier psychological studies, for example, have explored the role of grooming in targeting children with obvious vulnerabilities, such as those with emotional or learning difficulties or from dysfunctional families within the context of England and Wales (Gallagher, 1998) and the United States (Salter, 1995, 2003) in particular. Many such texts are written as practical guides to help parents and carers identify risk and protect their children (van Dam, 2001; Salter, 2003; Sanderson, 2004; Powell, 2007). Earlier research has been carried out from the perspective of victims (Berliner and Conte, 1990; Hunter, Goodwin, and Wilson, 1992; Watkins and Bentovim, 1992), of offenders in treatment programmes (Budin and Johnson, 1989; Conte, Wolf, and Smith, 1989; Elliott, Browne, and Kilcoyne, 1995) and of both together (Phelan, 1995). Cases of institutional abuse also establish that sex offenders may seek employment that enables contact with children (Barter, 1999; Gallagher, 2000; Sullivan and Beech, 2002). There is no empirical work, however, on grooming from an institutional perspective.

Indeed, currently there is no empirical data available which examines all aspects of grooming, involving children (both on-line and in face-to-face contacts), families, communities, and institutions, in a multi-jurisdictional context. Moreover, as noted above, existing work has also tended towards psychological or legal analyses, often within a specific jurisdiction, lacking a clear critical, theoretical foundation. As the first comparative, interdisciplinary, thematic study of the role and impact of the grooming process in sexual abuse cases, this book is also intended to broaden contemporary discourses beyond their rather narrow positivist and legalistic focus and better capture the complexity of this important subject.

A central contention of this book is that dominant contemporary discourses on grooming—particularly in terms of the restricted focus on the grooming of children by strangers, either via on-line methods or within organizations—neglect other important facets of the behavioural pattern of sex offenders and, therefore, provide only a limited representation of the breadth of offending behaviour, including the potential role of grooming. This book seeks to present a more nuanced, multidimensional understanding of grooming and the ways in which such efforts may be countered. In this respect, the sociological process of sexual grooming may have resonance in terms of not only extra-familial sexual abuse by strangers but also within the course of intra-familial abuse committed by those known to the child in a range of social settings including within families, community, and organizations.

Indeed, grooming may also occur in face-to-face situations as well as on-line where children may be persuaded that inappropriate sexualized relationships are 'both natural and commonplace' (Ost, 2004: 148). As others have argued, current discourses neglect the fact that sex offenders also groom not just the child but also their family or the wider community as an integral part of their offending behaviour, often as a necessary prerequisite to gaining access to the child (Salter, 2003). Sex offenders often seek to gain and exploit trust to bypass individuals or procedures which would otherwise protect children. In addition, these discourses fail to recognize the significance of 'institutional grooming' (McAlinden, 2006a)—that offenders may have a nuanced grasp of, what Douglas (1986) termed, 'how institutions think' and are able to navigate around safety measures and exploit system weaknesses in order to abuse children and avoid exposure (see Chapter 5).

Towards a New Definition of 'Grooming'

Within this study, primary research also identifies, for the first time, new and emerging forms of grooming which have not previously been highlighted in the existing literature, including the grooming of professionals. Based on extensive reading of the subject, this book espouses a new definition of grooming which better captures the complexity of the process and the multiple manifestations of grooming: *(1) the use of a variety of manipulative and controlling techniques (2) with a vulnerable subject (3) in a range of interpersonal and social settings (4) in order to establish trust or normalize sexually harmful behaviour (5) with the overall aim of facilitating exploitation and/or prohibiting exposure.* This is the broad working definition of grooming adopted throughout the study. Given the current public and political controversy which contextualizes 'grooming', the significance of the term within the range of sexual offending against children will be examined in relation to the primary research and revisited in the concluding chapter.

In critically examining the problems intrinsic to recent social and legal responses to 'grooming', I will also argue that there are uncertainties and misconceptions about what sort of behaviour is covered by the term (Gillespie, 2004a). As noted above, there is a lack of academic research on the subject, especially regarding behaviours which occur off-line and there is no universal or commonly accepted definition of the term. Contrary to the tenor of popular, official, and academic discourses on grooming, it has been well documented that children are most likely to be sexually abused by family members or someone well known to them (Grubin, 1998),[23] where grooming can also occur. Indeed, many more offenders make contact with victims and gain acceptance via off-line methods—through care homes, churches, schools, or clubs or by getting to know particular families. The ambiguities surrounding what amounts to sexual grooming, which have become embedded in the legislative and policy responses, also have implications for the criminalization of such behaviour (Gillespie, 2002a).

This analysis will contend that because of difficulties of drawing clear boundaries between innocent and more sinister relationships with children, particularly at the early stages of the offending process, criminal law and policy are limited in their response to pro-offence behaviours which occur before the manifestation of actual harm. Recent legislative activity concerning grooming, common to many jurisdictions, reflects a reactive response after specific problems or cases have occurred rather than an effective proactive and anticipatory response to managing potential risk. No system can eliminate risk entirely or protect children from the infrequent and unusual. The limitations of current pre-emptive approaches to managing sex offender risk (McAlinden, 2010a), however, creates a moral, social, political, and practical imperative to be innovative, to question accepted wisdoms, and to draw, as appropriate, from the theoretical, policy, and practical experiences of other

---

[23] Home Office research by Grubin (1998: 15), for example, indicates that approximately 80 per cent of offenders sexually assault children well known to them, with many of these offences taking place in the home of either the victim or the offender. Irish research also attests that in four-fifths of cases, the perpetrator was known to the victim (McGee et al, 2002: 177).

jurisdictions, in order to devise a more effective response to sexually harmful behaviour towards children (McAlinden, 2007a: 6).

Background to the Primary Research

Theoretical and policy arguments on grooming in this book are informed and illustrated by original primary research derived from interviews with professionals in the fields of child protection, sex offender assessment, treatment and management, and victim support in the four jurisdictional case studies in England and Wales, Scotland, Northern Ireland, and the Republic of Ireland. This material informs the discussion in Part II of the book.

Comparing the jurisdictions

While there is an abundance of academic literature on comparative criminal justice and criminology (see eg Downes, 1988; Ruggiero, Ryan, and Sim 1993; van Swaaningen, 1998; Newburn and Sparks, 2004; Nelken, 2007; Reichel, 2008), the preponderance of this work has tended to focus specifically on Continental Europe and the United States as well as England and Wales. As Croall, Mooney, and Munro (2010: 6) have argued, even within British texts, the focus is predominantly on England and Wales, with scant mention of Scotland and Northern Ireland notwithstanding differences in regional approaches. These authors regard this as an 'unjustifiable and curious omission' and advocate that a 'wider consciousness of what is both shared and diverse within and across all the UK juris-dictions…would contribute to a richer, more complex and more challenging British criminology' (2010: 6).

With this challenge in mind, this book is distinctive in focusing on key points of convergence and divergence within penal policies on sex offending more generally and grooming specifically, not only between the respective regions of the United Kingdom but also the neighbour-ing Republic of Ireland. Each jurisdiction has broadly similar legal and policy frameworks for sex offender management and child pro-tection, but with some unique characteristics that make for important comparisons (Chapter 3). Points of notable difference relate chiefly to variations in inter-agency frameworks, vetting and barring systems, and the scope of the offence of meeting a child following sexual grooming/certain preliminary contact/for the purposes of sexual exploitation. While Northern Ireland has largely emulated England and Wales, Scotland has had its own but related momentum. The Scottish Executive has also introduced some innovative measures for managing sex offenders such as orders for lifelong restriction which have not been replicated elsewhere. The Republic of Ireland, however, at the time of writing, has a narrower framework on vetting with no disqualification lists and no provision of 'soft' intelligence during criminal record checks, and no formal inter-agency structure.

In addition, the geographical, land border between Northern Ireland and the Republic of Ireland, and the relative proximity of these jurisdictions to Great Britain, becomes important when considering the modus operandi of sex offenders—that they may be extremely mobile often moving outside the jurisdiction in which they reside in order to escape notice or seek targets elsewhere (Hebenton and Thomas, 1996: 107–8; Hughes, Parker, and Gallagher, 1996: 34; Criminal Justice Review Group, 2000: ch 17). For the purposes of clarity, throughout this book the legislative and policy framework in England and Wales is highlighted and discussed first and then linked to more nuanced discussion of parallel or alternative policies in the other jurisdictions.

A brief methodological note

In total, 51 in-depth confidential and anonymous interviews were conducted (England and Wales: $n = 14$; Scotland: $n = 11$; Northern Ireland: $n = 14$; Republic of Ireland: $n = 12$) in or close to major cities in each jurisdiction—Birmingham, Edinburgh, Belfast and Dublin—in the course of spring–summer 2011 (May–September).[24] The overall sample size was determined by 'saturation' (Glaser and Straus, 1967)—when the collection of new data did not shed any further light on the core themes of the study. Participants included criminal justice and other professionals from police, probation, social services, prisons, independents, such as forensic or clinical psychologists, and advocacy groups who work daily with child sexual abuse cases. Such a diverse range of professional voices was necessary to ascertain the views of the multiple stakeholders who are integral to the assessment, management, treatment, and reintegration of sex offenders against children, and the protection and support of victims. It was

---

[24] Interview participants are identifiable only by a two-letter code for each jurisdiction (ie EW, SC, NI, RI) and the interview number within that jurisdiction.

also considered appropriate to understand the broader and multifaceted processes of offending against children and to examine the complex role of grooming in such cases. Further details of the methodology are provided in Appendix 1. The interview schedule which sets out the primary themes of the research is included as Appendix 2.

Recurrent Themes

The book will consider the principal themes and debates concerning popular and state-led responses to sexual offending in general as well as the grooming of children for sexual abuse specifically. As a predominant theme, the book locates debates about sex offenders and child protection within the context of broader concerns in the area of crime and justice such as risk (Parton, Thorpe, Wattam, 1997; Kemshall, 2001; Matravers, 2003), regulation and preventive governance (Ashenden, 2002). The central importance of risk to social and political theory (Beck, 1992; Ericson and Haggerty, 1997) has become a dominant theme in contemporary penal policy and in criminal justice discourses more generally (Feeley and Simon, 1992, 1994; Braithwaite, 2000; Shearing, 2000). The assessment and management of risk has also been evident in relation to concerns over the dangers posed by sex offenders, particularly within the context of post-release control (Kemshall and Maguire, 2003; Matravers, 2003; McAlinden, 2007a). The most recent manifestation of these concerns is the explosion of risk-averse policies which have attempted to apply the logic of precaution (O'Malley, 2004; Ericson, 2007) and respond pre-emptively (Zedner, 2009) to all potential risks posed by sex offenders (Seddon, 2008; Hebenton and Seddon, 2009). A primary example of this is the enactment of expansive legislative frameworks on pre-employment vetting which extend to all those who work or volunteer with children or vulnerable adults. Such situational approaches to the prevention of child sexual abuse (Wortley and Smallbone, 2006) also seek to locate the risk posed by sexual offenders firmly in the public sphere.

The book also examines the populist approach to penal policy (Bottoms, 1995; Johnstone, 2000) which has resulted in 'hyper innovation' (Moran, 2003; Crawford, 2006) in the area of sexual offending and an array of legislative and policy developments within a relatively short period.[25] This facet of penal policy on sex

[25] It has also been argued, however, that there has been an exaggerated focus on punitiveness in recent times, since the use of punitive sanctions has historically been an endemic feature of the criminal justice system. See Matthews (2005).

offending is particularly relevant in relation to two spheres which have witnessed a flurry of legislative and policy activity over the last decade—sex offender notification and related orders as well as pre-employment vetting (McAlinden, 2010a). The trend is the most marked in England and Wales which to a large extent has provided the lead on such developments, being influenced by similar crime control polices derived from the United States (Christie, 2000; Garland, 2001; Newburn, 2002; Jones and Newburn, 2006). The other jurisdictions in the United Kingdom as well as the Republic of Ireland, however, have also followed suit. It is well documented that public perceptions about sexual crime are most often displaced by empirical realities (Levenson et al, 2007; McAlinden, 2007b; Willis, Levenson, and Ward, 2010). Indeed, a central contention of this book is that the cyclical enactment of such legislation, often in response to public clamours following high profile cases of child sexual abuse or murder, displaces the focus on perceived sites of danger away from the private sphere.

A further related theme is the role of the media in creating myths and misconceptions about sexual crime, and the consequences of this for child protection (Silverman and Wilson, 2002; Greer, 2003). The media have been instrumental in propagating a number of myths about sex offending, not least in terms of over-representing the danger posed by predatory strangers (Sampson, 1994; Greer, 2003). As discussed further in Chapter 7, other potent public myths about sex offending include that sex offenders typically offend in networks or 'rings'; that sexual abusers are an homogeneous group—adult male 'paedophiles' who prey on young children; and that all sexual offenders pose the same degree of high risk. As noted above, this need to control the risk posed by predatory strangers in particular has also become embedded in much of the legislation on sex offending in the United Kingdom and Ireland from the late 1990s onwards. Measures such as sex offender notification and the offence of meeting a child following sexual grooming feed into and perpetuate the stranger danger fallacy and, therefore, fail to protect children adequately.

Indeed, unlike much of the existing research which concentrates on the role of the internet and child pornography in the sexual grooming of children by strangers, this book also focuses on the process of off-line grooming and its role and significance in both intra- and extra-familial contexts. By adopting this more holistic approach, the book is able to include within its remit not just known offenders who have been convicted of sexual offences, but also a consideration of how to manage the potential risk posed by offenders who may never have come to notice. This issue of how also to respond to the hidden nature of sexual crime is crucial and must be addressed if the problem of identifying and managing those who pose a risk to children is to be dealt with in a positive and proactive way. In particular, developing social education and public health approaches offers the opportunity to probe this category of 'unknown risk' (Soothill, 2005; Soothill et al, 2005a, 2005b), which is vital in terms of breaking cycles of offending and reducing the overall incidence and prevalence of child sexual abuse.

Structure of the Book

The book is divided into three parts, the first of which provides the theoretical and policy context. Chapter 2 elaborates more fully on some of the themes raised within this introductory chapter. The chapter primarily examines what is currently known about the nature and extent of sexual grooming and its role in both facilitating abuse and preventing its discovery. Initially it outlines the lack of settled meaning of the term and the consequent problems associated with a criminal law response. Drawing on the work of Ben-Yehuda (2001) and others, the chapter also examines the sociological literature on abuse of trust as a key variable in the grooming process. Broad typologies of grooming as they relate to a number of overlapping classifications are set out briefly as a prelude to fuller discussion of the dynamics of grooming in subsequent chapters. The chapter concludes with an analysis of studies to date on the extent of grooming behaviour.

Chapter 3 critically examines the central components of the legislative and policy responses to sex offending against children in England and Wales, Scotland, Northern Ireland, and the Republic of Ireland as a necessary backdrop to a fuller discussion of issues and practices in later chapters. The assessment, management, and reduction of risks posed by sex offenders, particularly those who offend against children, has dominated public and political discourses on penal policy since the late 1990s. Important similarities and differences in approaches to penal policy between the four jurisdictions are outlined as well as possible explanations for the broad convergence in approach. The chapter also provides a critical overview of the framework for multi-agency working in relation to sexual crime and acts as an introduction to the empirical data which is set out in subsequent chapters.

Part II seeks to critically examine the range of specific issues presented by the role and significance of the grooming process in the onset of child sexual abuse as well as current legal and policy responses to grooming behaviour within the United Kingdom and Ireland. This includes a critical analysis of the dynamics of grooming as it occurs with children and within particular families, communities and child care institutions, as well as a detailed examination of measures to control would be sex offenders within on-line and institutional environments. Chapter 4 considers the manipulation of children for sexual abuse, as well as the grooming of families and communities who may act as the gatekeepers of access. This includes consideration of a number of variables such as the establishment of trust, the process of victimization, the selection of particular targets, and the use of various deception techniques to facilitate abuse and prevent detection.

Typical access methods also include choosing a career or volunteering for work that will place offenders in close proximity to children. Chapter 5 examines the new and emerging issue of 'institutional grooming'—that sex offenders may target and groom entire organizations, as well as individual children, and those who work within them. Evidence has emerged primarily from public inquiries into cases of institutional physical and sexual abuse of children in care homes in a range of jurisdictions and also from recent studies of the grooming process more generally, including my previous work (McAlinden, 2006a). These have demonstrated how offenders may make use of the pervasive features of organizational contexts such as power, anonymity, opportunity, secrecy, and trust to both facilitate abuse and prevent disclosure. Primary data will be examined to highlight how offenders may also seek to extend grooming behaviour to criminal justice and other professionals.

Chapter 6 considers pre-employment vetting and barring schemes and the respective offences of meeting a child following sexual grooming/certain preliminary contact/for the purpose of sexual exploitation as the primary legislative responses to institutional and on-line forms of grooming respectively. In relation to the latter, it will be argued that there is a range of evidential and practical difficulties intrinsic to legislative and policy attempts to anticipate harmful behaviour to children. In relation to the former, the chapter also underlines problems with the recent expansion of the legislative and policy framework on vetting, which stem largely from pre-emptive or preventive approaches to risk, as well as the problems inherent in the vetting process at the more general conceptual level. The chapter concludes with a broad overview of transnational policies and protocols implemented to combat grooming behaviour.

In challenging contemporary public and official discourses on grooming as well as the prevailing academic and policy rationales on which they are based, there is a need to promote a new paradigm of grooming and its role in child sexual abuse. In consequence, social, cultural, and political responses to such behaviour must be reconfigured. The final part of the book puts forward a constructive solution to the problems associated with the underlying limitations of current legislative, policy, and social responses to grooming highlighted throughout the book. It advances the case for the development of a broader social response to child sexual abuse to complement the current regulatory framework. As argued above, given that the criminal law may be somewhat limited in its response to grooming, concerted efforts are required to foster social and institutional awareness of how sexual abuse occurs and how in turn it may be prevented.

The penultimate chapter of the book will outline the central tenets of a future approach to identify and manage potential risks to children, in particular reducing the offender's opportunity for abuse. This would be founded on the twin pillars of prevention and protection. It would be comprised, inter alia, of a public health or education campaign at the primary level of prevention to promote cultural awareness of the realities and dynamics of child sexual abuse, as well as a continuum of services engaging victims, offenders, and families at the secondary level of prevention aimed at early intervention. The concluding chapter pulls together the major themes discussed in previous chapters, highlights the implications and challenges for discourses on grooming and risk-based public policy concerning the early identification and management of those who pose a risk to children.

2

The Nature and Extent of Sexual Grooming

'Jailed, the PC Caught Grooming a Girl of 14 on the Net'[1]
'Teacher to be Sentenced for Sexual Grooming'[2]
'Pervert who Groomed Teenage Girl on Internet is Jailed'[3]
'Dinner Lady's Child Grooming Warning Over Biscuit'[4]
'Police Probe into Claims of Gang Grooming Girls for Sex in Rochdale'[5]
'Man Charged with Sexually Grooming Girl (14) on Internet'[6]
'Organised Child Sex Abuse "Growing Problem" in Wales'[7]
'Up to 50 Children May be Victims of Internet Sex Ring in Torbay'[8]

Consider the above samples of recent newspaper headlines. These are broadly reflective of the nature of media coverage of 'grooming' in sexual abuse cases which have routinely appeared in British and Irish, tabloid and broadsheet, newspapers over the last few years. Such captions speak to the dominant contemporary paradigms of grooming and to the nature and image of grooming as commonly propagated by the media and understood by the public. These news snippets relate to three broad scenarios, the first two of which have been highlighted in the introductory chapter: the grooming of children via the internet ('on-line grooming' or 'internet grooming'); would be sex offenders who utilize their employment

[1] *Daily Mail*, 4 April 2009.
[2] T. Pugh, *The Independent*, 1 February 2010.
[3] G. McIlwraith, *Daily Record*, 12 August 2010.
[4] *Belfast Telegraph*, 8 October 2010.
[5] *Manchester Evening News*, 11 January 2011.
[6] G. Jackson, *Irish Times*, 11 January 2011.
[7] *BBC News Wales*, 17 January 2011, <http://www.bbc.co.uk/news/uk-wales-12204559> (accessed 18 February 2011).
[8] K. Storrar, *Mirror*, 18 February 2011.

situation as a vehicle for abuse ('institutional grooming' (McAlinden, 2006a)); and, more recently, predatory street gangs who will prepare young girls for sex trafficking and exploitation ('on-street grooming' or 'street grooming'). These vignettes of abuse might be very different, not least in terms of the mode of initial approach and the number of offenders or victims involved. What they have in common, however, is the idea of the alien yet omnipresent sex offender ready to prey on unsuspecting teenagers and young children. This social and cultural construction of the sex offender as 'outsider' (Becker, 1963) or 'other' (Garland, 2001) is well documented in the literature (eg Ashenden, 2002; Silverman and Wilson, 2002; McAlinden, 2005: 378–80; 2007a: 130–1). As Ost (2009: 168, 178) has argued, however, the contemporary media focus on 'stranger grooming, and on online grooming in particular' may ultimately 'endanger' rather than 'protect' children. Given the prevailing 'societal perception that grooming is predominantly an internet issue', there is a social, cultural, and political imperative, however, 'to understand more clearly the nature of grooming, the processes involved and the nature and extent of the problems that arise from it' (McLaughlin, 2009: 14).

While 'on-line', 'institutional', and 'street' forms of grooming tend to pervade public consciousness, I would argue, as a minority of other writers have (eg Craven, Brown, and Gilchrist, 2006), that there are other equally prevailing strands of preparatory behaviour which may precede abuse. The core task of this chapter, and indeed the book as a whole, is to underline the common misconceptions about grooming behaviour, which have become embedded in public and official discourses, and to provide a fuller more nuanced account of this multi-layered process. The purpose of this chapter, therefore, is two-fold: to provide an overview of the broad typologies of grooming as a precursor to more detailed discussion of the full complexities of the offending process which will be undertaken in the next part of the book; and to examine, from published studies and official statistics, what is currently known about the extent of grooming within the context of child sex abuse cases.

Lack of Settled Meaning

The social and cultural ambiguities surrounding the grooming process say something of the process itself. While grooming is not a new concept, the area has been under-researched and there is a good deal of uncertainty as to the precise meaning and scope of the term. The verb 'to groom' has been defined as 'to prepare, as for a specific position or purpose',[9] or 'to prepare for a future role or function'.[10] Within the context of sexual offending against children, however, 'grooming' has been the subject of multiple definitions and there is no universally accepted understanding of the term which fully captures all aspects of the process.

Grooming has variously been described as 'emotional seduction' (Salter, 1995: 274) or as a 'tactic' used by would-be abusers to 'entice' children to engage in sexual behaviour (Kierkegaard, 2008: 42). Kierkegaard's full description, for example, is 'where paedophile criminals contact children and gain their trust for the purposes of meeting them and engaging in sexual behaviour' (2008: 42). Other writers have also unhelpfully chosen to frame their conceptualization of grooming around paedophilia. Howitt (1995: 176) suggests that 'Grooming…is the steps taken by paedophiles to "entrap" their victims'. Similarly, O'Connell (2003: 6) in her typology of on-line grooming practices describes the process as 'a course of conduct enacted by a suspected paedophile, which would give a reasonable person cause for concern that any meeting with a child arising from that conduct would be for unlawful purposes'. This definition acknowledges the potential longevity of grooming which may involve a series of stages as well as the difficulties of recognizing harmful behaviour particularly at the early stages of the process. The influence of such definitions has also become embedded within official discourses on grooming. The Home Office (2002) definition was also centred on grooming as 'a course of conduct enacted by a suspected paedophile', and subsequently informed the legislative drafting of the offence of meeting a child following sexual grooming in section 15 of the Sexual offences Act (SOA) 2003.[11] These references to paedophilia, however, are problematic in masking the realities of sex offending behaviour and in helping sexual abuse to remain hidden.

Not all sex offenders are 'paedophiles' in the strict clinical understanding of the term—a sexual attraction to pre-pubescent children (Stelzer, 1997: 1677–8; American Psychiatric Association, 2000: 528). These explanations, therefore, do not accurately capture the nature of

---

[9] See *The Oxford Illustrated Dictionary* (1975).

[10] Web Dictionary, at <http://dictionary.reference.com/search?q=groom> (accessed 18 February 2011).

[11] This provision has been amended by the Criminal Justice and Immigration Act 2008, s 73 and Sch 15, para 1 (see Chapter 6).

sexual grooming which can also occur with older children and young adults. If a sex offender does not fit the stereotypical public image of 'paedophile', people known to the offender may be slow to recognize the signs of grooming behaviour (Craven, Brown, and Gilchrist, 2006: 288). The failure to recognize that most sexual abusers are 'ordinary people' known to the child can leave children more vulnerable to abuse (Sutton and Jones, 2004: 21). Moreover, as Craven, Brown, and Gilchrist (2006: 288) have argued, such media and public characterizations may also prevent some sex offenders from identifying and acknowledging their own grooming behaviours.

The description put forward by Kierkegaard (2008), cited above, and other sources are also focused singularly on the grooming of children to the neglect of other dimensions of the process. The Council of Europe's Convention on the Protection of Children against Sexual Exploitation and Sexual Abuse defines grooming as 'the preparation of a child for sexual abuse, motivated by the desire to use the child for sexual gratification'.[12] Gillespie, as one of the leading academic writers in this field, also provides an account of grooming which is centred on the child as direct victim: 'The process by which a child is befriended by a would-be abuser in an attempt to gain the child's confidence and trust, enabling them to get the child to acquiesce to abusive activity' (2002a: 411; see also Wyre, 2000; van Dam, 2001). On the positive side, this depiction does at least provide some guidance about the overall purpose of sexual grooming, underlining the pivotal role of trust in the process.

Craven, Brown, and Gilchrist's (2006: 297) more recent description as 'a process by which a person prepares a child, significant adults and the environment for the abuse of the child' is fuller in terms of the scope of who may be targeted. These authors at least acknowledge, as this book also contends, that grooming may extend well beyond the physical and psychological coercion of the child as direct victim to encompass the psychological manipulation of adults or the immediate social environment as part of the preparatory stages of abuse. Their classification, however, omits the second and arguably equally important purpose of grooming—to not only make the abuse possible but also to avoid detection by others or prevent the child from making a disclosure (Salter, 1995,

---

[12] Explanatory Report to art 23 of the Convention on the Protection of Children against Sexual Exploitation and Sexual Abuse, para 156, <http://conventions.coe.int/Treaty/EN/Reports/Html/201.htm> (accessed 15 March 2011).

2003). More recently, Craven and colleagues have argued, rightly in my view, that grooming includes three central elements: gaining *access* to the child; ensuring the child's *compliance*; and maintaining the child's *secrecy* to avoid disclosure (Craven, Brown, and Gilchrist, 2006: 297) (emphasis added). What most of these authors have neglected to discuss, however, is *how* access, compliance, and secrecy are secured and maintained prior to, throughout, and following sexual abuse. In this respect, I would endorse the view of Salter (1995, 2003) who argues that the creation and subsequent abuse of trust emerges as a pivotal construct in the grooming process. Some of the key themes from the literature on 'trust' and 'betrayal' are examined below.

The most comprehensive definition of the grooming process perhaps to date and the one that comes closest to capturing the multiple contexts as well as the dual consequences of grooming, although it neglects any specific mention of 'trust', is the one put forward by Sutton and Jones (2004: 6, n 2) in the context of a Save the Children position paper:

> ... the strategy used by sexual abusers to manipulate the child, and potentially protective adults, so abuse can take place in a situation where the abuser has total control over the victim. It is a process where the abuser gradually overcomes the child's resistance through a sequence of psychologically manipulative acts. It is also used to silence the child after the abuse has taken place.

Given the absence of a clear, all-encompassing narrative of sexual grooming which fully captures the complexities of the process, this chapter also works towards developing its own working definition. This is based on an overview of the dynamics and nuances of the grooming process, including the centrality of trust, as well as the purpose of grooming behaviour. As discussed below, the current lack of consensus and clarity about the parameters of the expression is also reflected in the wide range of evolving terminology which is often used interchangeably within the literature.

The problems of definition associated with the term 'grooming' may be due to a number of factors: First, as Gillespie (2004a: 586) argues, grooming is a transient process that is difficult to capture and virtually impossible to pinpoint when it begins and ends. These difficulties stem from the fact that it may be very difficult in practice to make a clear distinction between friendly behaviour towards a child and something that has a more sinister motive, especially at the outset of the process. In this sense, '"Grooming" is the new word to describe activities which in themselves are legally (and indeed socially) innocuous but which are carried out with malign intent' (Norrie, 2005: 21). As Craven, Brown, and Gilchrist (2006: 292) put it, '[t]he only difference may be the motivation underlying the behaviour'. Some of this uncertainty is in part attributable to the fact that since only a relatively small amount of research has been carried out, especially into the minutiae of off-line or face-to-face methods, professional as well as social understanding of the area is still fairly rudimentary.

Secondly, as noted above, a related problem is that within popular and even official discourses, grooming is immediately linked to the internet and is used mainly to refer to on-line behaviour.[13] This is contrary to the reality that the vast majority of abuse takes place by someone known to the victim rather than a predatory stranger (Grubin, 1998; McGee et al, 2002) and where the grooming is most often off-line. This latter misconception in the common usage of the term is due largely to media portrayal of the risk of sexual abuse and recent public education and awareness campaigns on the dangers of chat rooms and safe use of the internet. As Jackson and Scott have argued, media coverage of the risks posed to children by adults tends to 'reverse the order of danger' in that cases involving 'stranger danger' far outweigh those involving intra-familial abuse (1999: 92–3). In much the same way as the depiction of 'stranger danger' in the media impacted upon the public's views about child sexual abuse and sexual offenders in the past, recent media reporting of 'internet grooming' seems to be having the same effect, namely moral panic and increased fear of such crime (Craven, Brown, and Gilchrist, 2007: 66).

Thirdly, the enactment of recent legislation on grooming in several jurisdictions has not done anything to remove these ambiguities from the debate over the sexual grooming of children. In fact, it may even be said to have added to the confusion. Section 15 of the SOA 2003, which applies in England and Wales, and equivalent legislation in Scotland, Northern Ireland, and the Republic of

---

[13] Grooming was also associated primarily with on-line behaviour in parliamentary debates on the SOA 2003. See eg Baroness Blatch, *Hansard*, HL Debs, cols 788–9 (13 February 2003); Lord Alli, *Hansard*, HL Debs, col 795 (13 February 2003).

Ireland,[14] create the offence of meeting a child following sexual grooming/certain preliminary contact/for the purpose of sexual exploitation. Within the respective pieces of legislation, however, the term grooming is nowhere defined. Although the legislation has been criticized for its failure to provide any definition of grooming (McLaughlin, 2009: 13), this is perhaps not surprising given the lack of settled meaning of the term even with professional and academic discourses. Moreover, this provision continues to be known as 'the grooming offence', even though it is not intended to be so. In fact, it is the behaviour following grooming that is to be captured by the offence, and not the grooming process itself (Gillespie, 2004a: 586). The inherent ambiguities surrounding the term grooming have implications for not only establishing the extent of grooming but also for the criminalization of such behaviour (see Chapter 6).

An Abuse of Trust

Over the last few decades, the topic of trust has captured the attention of a number of scholars. Friedrichs points out that although trust is a central cultural concern, there is no single meaning of the term (1996: 11–12). Many of the available definitions, however, can be related specifically to the behaviour of sex offenders as they groom both people and institutions (McAlinden, 2006a: 344–6). Luhmann (1988), Johnson-George and Swap (1982) and Coleman (1990) all define trust as a behaviour, or attitude, which permits risk-taking behaviour. The level of faith placed in sex offenders by parents or carers allows them to take risks with their children's well-being which in turn provides the offender with opportunities to undermine this trust. Luhmann (1988) and Cook and Wall (1980) centre their definitions on the concept of confidence, while both Dasgupta (1988) and Good (1988) focus on predictability. Similarly, Gambetta (1988) and Kee and Knox (1970)

---

[14] The offence of 'meeting a child following sexual grooming etc' was amended and re-enacted in Northern Ireland under the Sexual Offences (NI) Order 2008 (art 22). Scotland has enacted the offence of 'meeting a child following certain preliminary contact' (see the Protection of Children and Prevention of Sexual Offences (Scotland) Act 2005, s 1), while the Republic of Ireland has the corresponding offence of 'meeting a child for the purpose of sexual exploitation' (see the Child Trafficking and Pornography Act 1998, s 3, as amended by the Criminal Law (Sexual Offences) (Amendment) Act 2007, s 6).

suggest that trust is inversely related to the willingness to become vulnerable to the actions of another person or group. All of these concepts are evidenced by the often unquestioned faith placed in sex offenders by children themselves, as well as parents, the local community and staff in institutions and their unwitting cooperation with the offender's deviant agenda. Moreover, the totality of these factors—confidence, predictability, and the willingness of others to take risks—allow the offender to deliberately suspend suspicion and facilitate the continuum of abuse.

Ben-Yehuda is one of the most notable of the recent scholars in the area of betrayal and trust. In this respect, it is useful to consider some of the themes highlighted by his work and examine how they might aid an understanding of the dynamics of grooming. First, trust is influenced by social structures and societal institutions and violations of trust and loyalty—betrayal—can appear in varied social contexts including inter-personal, group, organizational (and even national) contexts (Ben-Yehuda, 2001: 6–7; see also Luhmann, 1988; Friedrichs, 1996; Kramer et al, 1996; Oliver, 1997). This factor illustrates that trust has resonance not only at the micro-level within inter-personal relationships—such as those between offenders and children and their carers—but also at the macro-level in terms of how relationships operate between the offender and wider society and the institutions within which they may work (Coleman, 1990).

Secondly, trust invokes the concepts of reliability, faithfulness, and responsibility and assumes such relationships as loyalty, friendship, and belief (Ben-Yehuda, 2001: 11–13). These are the necessary pre-conditions that the offender must construct in order to establish intimate and social relationships with those he wants to groom. The offender pretends to be friendly and trustworthy to the specified relevant audience and manages to deceive them into believing that his or her falsified presentation of self is true (Ben-Yehuda, 2001: 6–7). The offender tries to create shared interests and identities on a personal level and an imagined sense of community at the collective level. It is this sense of belonging or shared membership of the same group that makes betrayal possible (2001: 27–8).

Thirdly, there are a few basic characteristics of a culture that masks reality and which facilitates betrayal. A breach of trust typically involves deception devices such as secrecy, manipulation, lying, cheating, or concealment and the specific and deliberate motivation to do so (Ben-Yehuda, 2001: 6–7). As discussed in Chapters 4 and 5, sex offenders employ a range of techniques within the grooming process. They may use their position or status in the local community, including their work with children, to facilitate and disguise their sexually abusive behaviour. Within the institutional context in particular, they are able to make use of organizational features such as secrecy, power, and anonymity to both initiate abuse and keep it hidden.

Finally, trust is not only morally but also socially constructed. Even though trust may have different meanings in different contexts, because trust is considered sacred, its violation amounts to an infringement of a moral code which may be deeply engrained within society (Ben-Yehuda, 2001: 6–7). This argument may help explain why society has such a strong emotional and often punitive reaction to sex offenders. These reactions are typically more severe, however, towards those offenders who commit institutional abuse, such as clerical abusers, where the very act of betrayal becomes a form of deviance in itself (Ben-Yehuda, 2001: 311). As will be discussed in the second part of the book, many of these themes are reflected in the process of grooming at the personal, familial, social, and institutional levels.

Typologies of Grooming

In tandem with the broad slant of existing academic work which tends to focus almost exclusively on internet grooming, some studies have espoused typologies of 'on-line grooming' (see eg O'Connell, 2003). There is, however, a dearth of corresponding research on modes of grooming which take place off-line or on types of grooming as a whole. In order to counter this specific fissure within the literature, I would argue that there are three principal overlapping modes of grooming which are differentiated and unpacked here as a cursory framework for the purposes of more in-depth critical analysis of the dynamics of grooming in the second part of the book. These include differences in the context—where it may happen (intra-familial and extra-familial); the subject—who may be targeted (children, families, communities, and institutions); and the mode of grooming—the means of approach (face-to-face contacts, internet or on-line based activities, 'street grooming', and 'peer-to-peer grooming').

The context: intra-familial and extra-familial grooming

Extra-familial grooming occurs where children themselves are abused by strangers or those previously unknown to them. This is the concept of grooming which has captured the popular imagination and, as noted at the outset, has also fed into recent international legislative and policy responses. The grooming of a child within an extra-familial context may take place either on-line, in face-to-face situations, within organizations, or on the street. Intra-familial grooming occurs within the context of intra-familial abuse—that is where children are abused by intimates within their families or at the very least those previously well known to them. As noted above, intra-familial abuse accounts for the vast majority of sexual offending against children. An earlier UK study, for example, found that 74 per cent of victims already knew their abusers and, of those, 58 per cent were abused by a family member (Mrazek, Lynch, and Bentovim, 1983). Similarly, in the United States, one study of 530 female college students, reported that 17 per cent had been abused before puberty and, of these, approximately 50 per cent had been abused by a relative (Finkelhor, 1979). More recent studies have produced higher figures—that between 80 per cent of sexual abuse victims, in England and Wales (Grubin, 1998) and the Republic of Ireland (McGee et al, 2002), and 98 per cent, in Northern Ireland, know their abuser (Leggett, 2000).[15] Within the context of intra-familial grooming, although children themselves are the ultimate target, their parents, carers, or others who would protect them may also be groomed in order to gain access to the child. These, however, are the currently neglected facets of the grooming process as commonly understood.

The subject: child grooming, familial and social grooming, institutional grooming

Children may be groomed in a lengthy process which begins with befriending the child, establishing an exclusive relationship, gradually increasing intimacy with the child, and culminating in sexual contact (Salter, 1995, 2003). Similarly, the child's family, the wider community, and those within child care or other organizations may also be manipulated and primed in similar ways to children,

---

[15] A similar figure of 93 per cent has been produced by the StopItNow! organization: *Who Sexually Abuses Children?*, <http://www.stopitnow.org/csa_fact_who_abuse> (accessed 5 March 2011). See also Chapter 7.

particularly in terms of their acceptance of the offender's self-presentation as posing no risk to children. While the previous forms of grooming have received some attention to varying degrees within the existing literature, the notion of 'institutional grooming' has been almost totally overlooked. This concept has emerged from my own previous work (McAlinden, 2006a) and from anecdotal conversations with professionals in the field. The notion can be used to convey the grooming of children within an institutional context, where sex offenders appear to make use of the unique features of the organizational environment to facilitate abuse and avoid detection (see Chapter 5). I will also argue that the notion can be extended to the grooming or manipulation of professionals who work with sex offenders into viewing them as posing no risk to potential victims.

The mode of grooming: face-to-face, 'on-line', 'street', and 'peer-to-peer' grooming

The phrase 'face-to-face' grooming is used within this book to refer to off-line grooming behaviours. This type of grooming may be used by the offender usually within the context of intra-familial or quasi-familial abuse where the offender seeks to establish an intimate relationship with the child, their family or the wider community. Both on-line and street grooming are targeted at children themselves whereby would-be offenders seek to establish a relationship with the child either via the internet or other mobile technologies or via approaches to young girls on the street as a prelude to sexual offending. As argued throughout this book, while the latter forms—on-line and street grooming—are among the most prolific modes of sexual grooming, face-to-face contacts represent the often overlooked but most statistically significant form of grooming behaviour.

While there are numerous challenges to protecting children on the internet, including, inter alia, bullying and harassment, and exposure to pornography, the issue of grooming has arguably become the most prominent (Gillespie, 2002a). Although 'on-line grooming' is the preferred term which is adopted most often throughout the course of this book, within this category there are a variety of umbrella terms which cover various forms of on-line contact between potential offenders and victims and which are often used interchangeably within the literature. These include 'entrapment' (Gallagher, 1998), 'cybersexploitation' (O'Connell, 2003), 'online child sexual abuse'

(Martellozzo, 2012), 'internet child abuse' (Davidson and Gottschalk, 2011) or 'internet exploitation' (Gallagher et al, 2003, 2006), and 'internet grooming' (Craven, Brown, and Gilchrist, 2007: 63) or 'electronic grooming' (Davidson and Martellozzo, 2008a: 278). These labels cover the situation where an offender has used information and communications technology (ICT) to engage in grooming behaviour with a child through, for example, social networking sites (Choo, 2009), chat rooms, or via e-mail or instant messaging (McLaughlin, 2009: 12).

The label 'street grooming', also referred to as 'on-street grooming', denotes a further classification of grooming behaviour which has more recently emerged—that of the grooming of potential victims by groups of offenders as part of organized gangs for the purposes of illicit enterprises such as child prostitution or the production of child pornography. Other labels include 'localized grooming' and, in its most serious and complex form, 'domestic' or 'internal trafficking' (Barnardo's, 2009: 16, 2011: 6). In a similar vein, 'peer-to-peer' forms of grooming occur where children or adolescents may groom other children for the purposes of sexual exploitation or abuse. This form of grooming, which does not feature strongly in the literature, can take place with an older child grooming a younger sibling as a precursor to abuse as well as within extra-familial contexts (eg Leclerc, Beauregard, and Proulx, 2011).

The foregoing analysis establishes that there are a number of commonalities within each of these contingencies of grooming. What these occurrences have in common, as highlighted in the introduction, is a number of sequential elements: (1) *the use of a variety of manipulative and controlling techniques (2) with a vulnerable subject (3) in a range of inter-personal and social settings (4) in order to establish trust or normalize sexually harmful behaviour (5) with the overall aim of facilitating exploitation and/ or prohibiting exposure.* This is the definition of grooming which is adopted throughout the course of this book which, I would argue, better captures the complexity of grooming and its multiple processes and manifestations, their actual role in the onset of offending against children, as well as their underlying purpose.

'Self-grooming'

A further dimension of grooming which emerges from the literature is that of offenders 'grooming themselves' in terms of the process of either justifying or denying their inappropriate sexual tendencies (van Dam, 2001). This term is worth inclusion here in the definitional context, and in subsequent chapters, for two principal reasons. One is its relationship with other forms of grooming. Self-grooming, for example, is likely to be affected by the response from the community and the child and, in particular, the success or failure of their efforts to abuse the child (Craven, Brown, and Gilchrist, 2006: 292). The other is the fact that justification and denial may ultimately have an impact on the effectiveness of treatment or other interventions with sex offenders.

The Extent of Grooming

The covert nature of sexual grooming makes it difficult to pinpoint yet alone quantify such behaviour. While the scale and extent of grooming locally, nationally, and internationally is ultimately unknown (Kosaraju, 2008), a range of both quantitative and qualitative sources collectively provide some representation of the nature and extent of sexual grooming. These have included studies of the disclosure process in children who have been abused (eg Hunter, Goodwin, and Wilson, 1992; Watkins and Bentovim, 1992; Berliner and Conte, 1990, 1995; Sas and Cunningham, 1995), of offenders in treatment programmes (eg Budin and Johnson, 1989; Conte, Wolf, and Smith, 1989; Christiansen and Blake, 1990; Elliott, Browne, and Kilcoyne, 1995; Smallbone and Wortley, 2000; Beckett et al 2004; Hudson, 2005) and of both taken together (Phelan, 1995).

In addition, a number of more recent studies have also emerged which detail the percentages of children who have received an unwanted sexual contact or solicitation over the internet (eg National Center for Missing and Exploited Children, 2000; Internet Crime Forum, 2001; Hasebrink, Livingstone, and Haddon, 2008). Moreover, many of the public inquiries and official reviews into child physical and sexual abuse, particularly in England and Wales and the Republic of Ireland, but which are common to all four jurisdictions in the study, also provide insights into the extent of grooming within an organizational environment (Corby, Doig, and Roberts, 2001; Sullivan and Beech, 2002). This section will provide a critical overview of the available quantitative data on grooming, while analysis of qualitative studies with both victims and offenders on the actual process of victimization will be undertaken in the second part of the book.

Before undertaking an examination of quantitative data on the extent of sexual grooming, a number of methodological caveats emerge: First, sexual offences remain one of the most under-reported forms of crime (Gillespie, 2007b: 6) and most cases are never reported to child protection agencies or the police (Baker and Duncan, 1985; Finkelhor, 1988; Finkelhor et al, 1990; Cobley, 2000: 36–9).[16] Given the nature of child sexual abuse, victims may feel a particular sense of fear or embarrassment in coming forward and reporting the offence (Lewis and Mullis, 1999; Cobley, 2000: 30–6; Maguire, 2007). This problem may be even more manifest when the abuser is a trusted intimate of the child or their family (McAlinden, 2007a: 4). Moreover, some children, especially adolescents, may be reluctant to admit engaging in potentially dangerous activities online such as discussing matters of a sexual nature or giving out personal information about themselves (European Commission, 2007: 9). In addition to the deeply personal impact which sexual abuse may have on victims (Talbot et al, 2002), the fact that not all reported incidences result in arrest, let alone prosecution, may have a deterrent effect in undermining the victim's willingness to report the grooming or abuse (Wolak, Finkelhor, and Mitchell, 2005). Indeed, the attrition rate for cases of child sexual abuse, including grooming offences, means that the numbers of eventual prosecutions may represent only a fraction of such offences committed against children (Choo, 2009: 24).

Secondly, inducing feelings of shame and guilt in the child victim about their complicity in the abuse are hallmarks of the abusive process (McAlinden, 2006a: 346–8) and are likely to be primary reasons underlying delays in disclosure (McGee et al, 2002: 178–80). Studies of the disclosure process by children, which are discussed below, demonstrate that grooming is a fulcrum in inhibiting and delaying child disclosure of sexual abuse (Sas and Cunningham, 1995). As Gillespie has argued, 'we know that all sexual abuse

---

[16] The 2009/10 BCS self-completion module, for example, showed that only 11 per cent of victims of serious sexual assault told the police about the incident (Smith et al, 2011). This rate of reporting to the police is the same as the 2007/08 BCS figure (Povey et al, 2009). Evidence from self-report studies also suggests that those convicted often reveal the commission of many more offences than are reported to authorities by their victims (Groth, Longo, and McFadin, 1982; Abel et al, 1987).

is under-reported and there is no reason to believe that the same is not true of grooming' (Gillespie, 2004b: 10).

Thirdly, there are not only discrepancies and disagreement concerning the precise meaning of grooming as highlighted above, but definitions of sexual abuse itself are inconsistent and the surveys reveal considerable divergences in approach (Haugaard and Repucci, 1988: ch 2; La Fontaine, 1990: 40; Itzin, 2000: 71). Baker and Duncan (1985), for example, reported that 12 per cent of women reported contact or non-contact abuse as a child. This contrasts sharply with a much higher figure of 30 per cent of women who had experienced contact or non-contact sexual abuse in childhood (McGee et al, 2002: 67). The shift in cultural appreciation of child sexual abuse as a serious social problem in the intervening 20 years between these two studies will account for much of the discrepancy in figures. Nonetheless, definitional difficulties may also make direct comparisons between studies problematic.

Fourthly, as discussed further, there are differences in legislative and policy frameworks on grooming, particularly in terms of the precise scope of sexual behaviour towards children captured by the criminal law. Such differences mean that there may be substantial variations in the numbers of reported cases of on-line grooming between countries (Choo, 2009: 24). For example, while all of the offences which criminalize grooming for sexual purposes within the United Kingdom and Ireland require the offender to have met the intended victim or travelled with the intention of meeting the victim, this is not a legislative requirement in Australia or the United States. There may also be differences in the organizational priorities of the police or other law enforcement agencies (Choo, 2009: 24), which can have an impact on the practices of recording grooming offences within and across jurisdictions.

Fifthly, the different age parameters of children and youth surveyed, in studies of on-line victimization in particular, make it difficult to estimate accurately the incidence and prevalence of on-line grooming behaviours and to make comparisons between studies. Taken together these difficulties mean that the true extent of child sexual abuse, or indeed the role of grooming in the process, remains relatively unknown. Leaving these caveats aside, it is generally accepted, however, that the danger of on-line solicitation by a stranger is thought to be much lower than off-line risk from someone known to the victim.

The disclosure process

Since secrecy is axiomatic to child sexual abuse, most cases become known through accidental disclosure where external circumstances conspire to interrupt the 'secrecy phase' (Sgori, 1982), and alert authority figures that the child is being abused. The clandestine nature of grooming and child abuse means that there are rarely any witnesses or corroborative evidence (Sas and Cunningham, 1995: 9). In many other cases, therefore, identification of the abuse depends on 'purposeful disclosure'—on the ability of the child to come forward and tell someone, and also on the capacity of that person to respond effectively (Sas and Cunningham, 1995: 8). The grooming procedure is extremely effective as the vast majority of children do not disclose the abuse at all and many others delay reporting the offence for months or even years. One NSPCC study, for example, showed that three-quarters of children who had been sexually abused did not disclose the abuse at the time and, of this group, a third claimed to have never spoken of the abuse (Cawson et al, 2000).

In relation to the former category, as acknowledged above, a complex range of emotions, including fears of admonishment or abandonment, and feelings of embarrassment, guilt, and shame, many of which are central to the grooming process, all conspire to silence children and inhibit their disclosures of abuse. In a study of 156 sexual abuse victims in a Family Crisis Program in Boston, only 55 per cent of children ever disclosed the abuse (Sauzier, 1989). A later study of 116 confirmed cases of child sexual abuse which were referred to a treatment facility, found that 74 per cent of children had never given purposeful disclosure (Sorenson and Snow, 1991). The SAVI report found that almost half of those surveyed (47 per cent) in the Republic of Ireland had never disclosed until the time of the research. This figure, however, was higher for young men where 60 per cent of those who had experienced childhood sexual abuse had told no one prior to the study (McGee et al, 2002). Similarly, in the context of Northern Ireland, the 2010 Young Life and Times Survey found that almost two-thirds (63 per cent) of the 786 teenagers surveyed did not tell anyone about the grooming—only 15 per cent told a parent or other relative and 21 per cent told someone else in authority.[17] Moreover, the effectiveness

---

[17] See <http://www.ark.ac.uk/ylt/> (accessed 14 April 2011). See also Beckett (2011: ch 5).

of grooming with the child's family, the local community and within organizations may also mean that the person chosen by the child to whom they reveal the secret of the abuse may not always believe them. In particular, the family, the community, or child care organizations may be either unwilling or unable to countenance the offender, who may be a trusted relative, friend, neighbour, or colleague, as a danger to children.

In relation to the latter category, many children experience delays in disclosing the abuse. Studies demonstrate that between 46 and 69 per cent of victims do not disclose their abuse until they are adults (Allnock, 2010). This has been attributed, inter alia, to the relationship with the offender (Hanson et al, 1999; Smith et al, 2000), the consequences of disclosure (Sorenson and Snow, 1991; Berliner and Conte, 1995; Hershkowitz, Lanes, and Lamb, 2007), the age or development stage of the victim (Keary and Fitzpatrick, 1994; Sas and Cunningham, 1995), and grooming behaviours (Sas and Cunningham, 1995; Pryor, 1996) as well as the unequal status between victims and offenders (Erooga, Allnock, and Telford, 2012). A child who has been sexually abused, particularly by someone in a position of trust, may be emotionally and psychologically unable to report the abuse until many years after the initial abuse occurred (Sas and Cunningham, 1995). In this respect, the study by Sas and Cunningham undertook a comprehensive examination of factors pivotal to disclosure either through discovery by adults or reporting to the police. The qualitative analysis of over 500 cases of child sexual abuse, including interviews with 135 children and young people, aimed to identify 'immediate disclosers' from 'delayed disclosers' and the factors associated with each.

One of the key findings was that children who were at risk for on-going abuse included those who had experienced pre-abuse grooming, had been young at the time of first sexual contact, and who were abused in their homes by someone they lived with and with whom they had close emotional bonds. Grooming was a prominent feature of what they termed 'father-figure abuse', where it was observed in two-thirds of such cases. It was also a feature of cases where the abuser knew the victim in a professional capacity (38 per cent). From these findings it may be inferred not only that children who are groomed at a young age and within the context of intra-familial sexual abuse are the most likely not to disclose the abuse, but also, by extension, that this group may be the most susceptible to grooming behaviour. Indeed, younger children are often unable to recognize the inappropriateness of the offending behaviour and so do not disclose immediately (Howard, 1993; Finkelhor and Dziuba-Leatherman, 1995). In a similar vein, grooming may also account for the delay in prosecution for childhood sexual abuse due to the feelings of betrayal, powerlessness, guilt, and self-blame concerning child sexual abuse which inhibit immediate disclosure (Lewis and Mullis, 1999).

Studies of on-line grooming

Studies of on-line grooming by far account for the majority of statistical information which is currently available on the nature and extent of grooming. Data on the extent of on-line grooming stem from two primary sources—victimization surveys which involve asking children or young people about their use and experience of on-line technologies, as well as official statistics on reported cases of 'on-line sexual abuse' or recorded offences of 'meeting a child following sexual grooming.'

Victimization surveys

Although statistics regarding the extent of on-line grooming are difficult to establish and evaluate, there have been some country specific surveys of children's experiences of using the internet. These studies tend to suggest that the risk from grooming which takes place in an on-line environment is quite low, at least certainly in comparison with off-line risks.

An earlier American survey, the first Youth Internet Safety Survey, found that approximately one in five youths (19 per cent) aged between ten and 17 'received an unwanted sexual solicitation or approach over the Internet in the last year' and 3 per cent had received an 'aggressive sexual solicitation' where the offender had attempted to contact the young person off-line (Finkelhor, Mitchell, and Wolak, 2000: 14). This study, however, found that no youth was assaulted as a result of a contact made over the internet (Mitchell, Finkelhor, and Wolak, 2001) which indicates that not all on-line risks actually manifest themselves in physical or sexual abuse. A similar figure, of approximately 20 per cent of a sample of young people receiving unwanted sexual approaches on-line, has also been produced in the United Kingdom (Internet Crime Forum (ICF), 2001). More recent figures generally reveal mixed results with some producing lower and others slightly higher estimates of on-line approaches. Moreover, recent studies also provide a more nuanced picture of on-line grooming practices and include estimated numbers of unwanted on-line sexual approaches as well as numbers of subsequent meetings between children and would be offenders.

In the United Kingdom, a more recent 'cybercrime' survey estimated that 850,000 cases of unwanted sexual approaches were made in chat rooms on-line during 2006 and that 238 offences of meeting a child following sexual grooming were recorded (cited in Choo, 2009: xi). In the United States, the second Youth Internet Safety Survey reported frequent exposure of young people aged between ten and 17 years to unwanted sexual material, sexual solicitation,[18] and general harassment on-line (Wolak, Mitchell, and Finkelhor, 2006). In comparison with the first survey, proportions receiving unwanted sexual solicitations had declined from 19 per cent to 13 per cent. Reports of sexual solicitations of a distressing or aggressive nature, however, which involve off-line contact through telephone or in person or requests for such contact, stayed roughly the same between the first and second surveys at 3 and 4 per cent respectively. Another US study found a similar figure of one in seven (14 per cent) of youth receiving on-line sexual solicitation, with 89 per cent of these approaches being made in chat rooms (Ropelato, 2007; see also Ybarra, Espelage, and Mitchell, 2007).

A 2006 Irish survey of children's use of the internet revealed a number of interesting findings (Webwise, 2006).[19] Almost one-quarter (23 per cent) of the 848 children aged between nine and 16 who were surveyed reported that they had received unwanted sexual comments on-line, where boys were twice as likely to be subject to such comments compared to girls (Webwise, 2006: 15). Of this figure, 9 per cent reported having received such remarks more than five times. Seven per cent had met someone off-line and, of this group, 24 per cent indicated that the person who had presented themselves as a child on the internet later turned out to be an adult (Webwise, 2006: 17). Moreover, while

[18] This was defined in the study as requests to engage in sexual activities or sexual conversations, or to give out personal sexual information that were unwanted, or whether wanted or not, made by an adult.

[19] Available at <http://www.webwise.ie/article.aspx?id=4526> (accessed 15 March 2011). Webwise is the Irish model of Insafe, a pan-European internet safety initiative funded by the European Commission. See also <http://www.saferinternet.org/web/guest/home> (accessed 16 March 2011).

the meeting was a positive experience for most children, 11 per cent reported that the person they had first met on-line had tried to physically harm them in person (Webwise, 2006: 17).

The EU Kids Online Project (2006–09), funded by the European Union as part of the Safer Internet Action Plan, undertook a comprehensive examination of a range of issues relating to children's use of the internet and new technologies in 25 Member States (Livingstone and Hadden, 2009).[20] The study utilized nationally representative samples of 1,000 children aged between nine and 16 and their parents, representing an overall sampling figure of 25,000 children. The report found that approximately one-quarter of the teenagers surveyed within the European Union had received unwanted sexual comments on-line, with significant disparity between countries (Hasebrink, Livingstone, and Haddon, 2008: 29). In Poland, teenagers had received the highest number of unwanted sexual contacts on-line, with over half (56 per cent) of the 12 to 17-year-olds surveyed admitting to being subject to such comments. Approximately one-third of nine to 16 year olds in Sweden (32 per cent) and of nine to 19 year olds in the United Kingdom (31 per cent) also stated that they had received unsolicited comments while on the internet. At the lowest end of the spectrum, were Ireland and Portugal with only 9 per cent and 6 per cent of eight to 18-year-olds respectively having been the recipient of unwanted sexual remarks on-line.

While on an initial reading of these statistics some of these figures might appear to be quite high, it is highly probable that any statistical increase may have as much to do with increased use of the internet by children and young people as with increased risks of their sexual victimization. We are living in an age of global information and communications-based technologies characterized by widespread use of the internet for a range of business and leisure activities (Kierkegaard, 2008: 41) and where large numbers of children regularly use the internet for social networking purposes, including blogging, gaming, and instant messaging (Vogelstein et al, 2005; Lenhart and Madden, 2007; Choo, 2009: 8–11).[21] It perhaps would have been reasonable, therefore, to expect an increase, rather than a decline, in such figures.

[20] See <http://www2.lse.ac.uk/media@lse/research/EUKidsOnline/Home.aspx> (accessed 15 March 2011).
[21] See eg UK CEOP figures which show that 41 per cent of children aged 8–11 regularly use the internet (CEOP 2007: 3). Similarly, a US study estimated that 70 per cent of all American teenagers visit social networking sites on a monthly basis (eMarketer, 2007), a figure that is likely to have increased.

As noted above, the dangers attached to sexual crime are 'particularly prone to mischaracterization' (Wolak, Finkelhor, and Mitchell, 2004: 425). In particular, there is a dominant social, cultural, and political emphasis on the internet as a tool of deception, which allows much older adult predatory offenders to strike up relationships with young children and lure them into sexual encounters. The issue of internet-related grooming, however, is considerably more complex than either media portrayals or some statistical studies might suggest (Gallagher et al, 2006: 9). Indeed, a deeper reading of these and other statistics on on-line grooming practices reveals that the purported risk to children from on-line strangers is significantly misplaced if not overstated on a number of important levels.

First, the image of the devious offender who uses the ruse of the internet on the pretext of befriending children as a prelude to abuse has perhaps been overplayed. Wolak, Finkelhor, and Mitchell (2004: 425), for example, in a US national study of internet-initiated sexual crimes against minors found low rates of deception violence on the part of offenders. Only 5 per cent of offenders represented themselves on-line as peers of their intended victims. Most (79 per cent) had taken the time to develop relationships with victims in multiple ways including by telephone, and were open about wanting sex from their victims (Wolak, Finkelhor, and Mitchell, 2004: 428) (see also O'Connell, 2003: 7). Much smaller numbers of offenders posed as 'friends' first or devised 'elaborate ploys', such as claiming to run modelling agencies, before assaulting their victims (Wolak, Finkelhor, and Mitchell, 2004: 428).

Secondly, not all on-line approaches actually translate into face-to-face meetings where a potential contact sexual offence may take place. According to two of the recent studies on children's use and experience of the internet cited above, only 7 per cent of children in Ireland (Webwise, 2006: 17) and 9 per cent of children overall within the European Union (Hasebrink, Livingstone, and Haddon, 2008: 29–30) have arranged to meet someone they first had contact with on-line in an off-line setting. In the US study by Wolak, Finkelhor, and Mitchell (2004: 430), however, most cases progressed to face-to-face meetings (74 per cent), where nearly all (93 per cent) involved illegal sexual encounters between offenders and victims. Of those cases that did not eventually result in an off-line meeting, this was due, inter alia, to victims reporting the on-line approaches to parents, other adults, or the police, or to the early intervention of 'observant' family members. As Gallagher et al (2006: 9) note, the generally low percentages of children who 'succumb' following on-line approaches may suggest that children are mindful of the risks of the on-line environment and are able to protect themselves (see also Webster et al, 2012: 16, 100–1). These findings also reinforce the need for public education and awareness programmes aimed at both children and their parents to reduce opportunities for on-line grooming and the commission of potential contact and non-contact sexual offences.

Thirdly, the numbers of children abused following on-line contact are much fewer than the number of those who are abused by family members or those known to them in face-to-face contacts which, as detailed above, has been placed moderately at 58 per cent in early studies (Mrazek, Lynch, and Bentovim, 1983) and more recently as high as 80 to 98 per cent (Grubin, 1998; Leggett, 2000; McGee et al, 2002). Most studies of on-line sexual behaviours tend to minimize the role of family members or acquaintances and even other children in the commission of such offences. Finkelhor, Mitchell, and Wolak (2000) found that 19 per cent of offenders claimed to be women and a rather high figure of 48 per cent were under 18. Indeed, the 2010 Young Life and Times Survey conducted with 16-year-olds in Northern Ireland found that a total of 47 per cent were approached in a more 'intimate' setting—17 per cent through a friend or sibling; 7 per cent at a house party; 6 per cent through a hobby, activity, or organization; and a further 17 per cent at a pub or club. [22] This figure can be contrasted with the 27 per cent of approaches made via on-line methods. These more recent figures also demonstrate that approaches made by would-be sex offenders for the purposes of sexual grooming occur more often in the context of face-to-face inter-personal or social settings as opposed to on-line.

Fourthly, the image of the 'predatory paedophile' is also not sustained when one examines the ages of targeted victims. Indeed, the term 'paedophilia' has been the subject of multiple, legal, societal, and clinical definitions (Harrison, Manning, and McCartan, 2010).[23] From a medical standpoint, as noted above, paedophilia is

---

[22] See note 17 above.

[23] The American Psychiatric Association (2000: 528) identifies paedophilia as a subclass of paraphilias, sexual disorders involving 'recurrent, intense sexually arousing fantasies, sexual urges, or behaviours generally involving sexual activity with a prepubescent child or children (generally age 13 years or younger) over a period of at least 6 months'.

a recognized clinical term which generally refers to a diagnosable psychiatric syndrome characterized by sexual attraction to pre-pubescent children or gratification from sexual intimacy with them (Stelzer, 1997: 1677–8; American Psychiatric Association, 2000: 528). In the study by Wolak and colleagues, however, the majority of victims were young teenagers, rather than children. Seventy six per cent were between 13 and 15 years old and none were younger than 12 (Wolak, Finkelhor, and Mitchell, 2004: 428). This picture is also confirmed by some of the range of other studies cited within this chapter. In the EU Kids Online Project, for example, 'on line risks' which were deemed to include bullying and harassment, as well as exposure to pornography and unwanted sexual solicitation, were found to increase with age. While only 14 per cent of nine to ten-year-olds have encountered one or more of these risks, this figure rose considerably to 63 per cent of 15 to 16-year-olds (Hasebrink, Livingstone, and Haddon, 2008: 3). Similarly, a 2003 UK-based study of the various forms of international and internet-related child sexual abuse, including child trafficking and pornography, as well as grooming behaviours, demonstrated that the large majority of victims, albeit out of small sample sizes, were adolescents, specifically aged 12 to 16 years (Gallagher et al, 2006: 41). In the Northern Ireland 2010 Young Life and Times Survey, 56 per cent of those who reported having been groomed were aged 15 to 16 when the grooming first happened, and only 16 per cent were under 13 years.[24]

As will be discussed in the final part of the book, the contemporary public and official fixation with the internet as the primary vehicle for initial deception and later actual abuse have a number of important implications for prevention (Wolak, Finkelhor, and Mitchell, 2004). In particular, the key critiques outlined above point to the need to reframe current analytical frameworks on grooming and, in particular, to develop more effective social and policy responses to combating the dynamics of sexual grooming and abuse in all of its various permutations.

Official statistics

The official crime statistics in some countries denote an increase in the number of cases of 'online sex abuse' being recorded by the police or adjudicated by the courts, a number of which involve grooming activities carried out in social networking sites (Choo,

[24] See note 17 above.

2009: xi). In Australia, there have been over 130 prosecutions under state and territory legislation as well as Commonwealth legislation for on-line procuring, grooming, and related exposure offences (Griffith and Roth, 2007). In the United States, the annual reports of 'on-line enticement of children for sexual acts' made to the National Center for Missing and Exploited Children (NCMEC) via the anonymous on-line or telephone reporting service, Cyber-Tipline, demonstrate substantial increases in figures from 707 reports in 1998 to 6,384 in 2006 (NCMEC, 2007). This increase has been attributed to a number of factors, however, including the ease with which child pornography can be accessed on-line and the opportunities that exist for grooming children via a range of internet-based media, as well as the introduction of a mandatory reporting obligation on the part of internet service providers (ISPs) to report child pornography to the NCMEC (Choo, 2009: 26).[25]

In the United Kingdom, the number of police investigations into on-line grooming has risen considerably over the last few years. Although the number of offences of 'sexual grooming' recorded in England and Wales fell to 310 in 2010/11, a figure of 397 in 2009/10 (Taylor and Chaplin, 2011: 16) represents a 23 per cent increase from 322 in 2006/07 and a 113 per cent increase from 186 in 2004/05 (Nicholas, Kershaw, and Walker, 2007: 168), when the offence was first introduced. There are much lower numbers of prosecutions and convictions, however, and sanction-detection rates for England and Wales are around 40 per cent (Taylor and Chaplin, 2011: 16) (see also Chapter 6).

Figures collated by the Child Exploitation and Online Protection Centre (CEOP) also indicate an increase in the sexual exploitation of children. The organization received 6,291 reports of exploitation and abuse in 2009/10 which represented an increase of 16 per cent (from 5,411) from the previous year (CEOP, 2010: 9). The largest increases in figures were attributed to reports relating to on-line grooming, particularly via instant messaging (such as MSN and IRC), followed by social networking sites (such as Facebook and Twitter). A quarter of all reports (1,536) related to grooming, and of this figure, 434 reports involved an abuser inciting a child to perform a sexual act, 389 involved suspicious contact with a child, and 135 involved making arrangements to meet a

---

[25] See USC 13032(B)(1).

child (CEOP, 2010: 13–14). Furthermore, grooming which took place on-line heavily outweighed that which took place in an off-line environment (CEOP, 2010: 14). As the report acknowledges, however, the increase in figures could be attributed to recent media and public drives concerning the issue of on-line grooming. Moreover, the increase in reports of on-line grooming could also be due to public perception that CEOP tends to receive reports concerning on-line grooming rather than sexual abuse in general (CEOP, 2010: 14).

The overall number of known internet grooming cases, however, may be relatively small in relation to the total number of reported cases of child sexual abuse. As Choo points out, major police investigations such as Operation Wonderland[26] and Operation Ore[27] have led to substantial increases in UK prosecutions for on-line child exploitation, which would include a range of illegal sexual activities such as child pornography, as well as grooming (2009: 24). Even allowing for the fact that all data compiled by law enforcements agencies, whether the police, or the courts, are not indicative of actual victimization rates, the total number of cases of on-line grooming still appears to be quite small. In this respect, a 2003 study of international and internet child sexual abuse and exploitation cases, referred to above, examined child sexual abuse (CSA) related reports to Computer Examination Units (CEUs) in three police forces in England and Wales over a four-year survey period (1999–02). The study found that one metropolitan police force had seven known cases of grooming which accounted for only 2.3 per cent of all CSA-related reports to the CEU. In one of the two shire county police services, there were only five grooming cases (0.5 per cent) out of the total number of 984 recorded cases of CSA offences during that period (Gallagher et al, 2006: 40–1). Extrapolating these findings to cases known to UK police forces as a whole, the authors estimated that these figures would equate to 0.8 cases per police service per annum. Similarly, in the Republic of Ireland, figures from the Irish Internet Hotline site, an anonymous reporting service for members of the public who encounter suspected illegal

---

[26] See Chapter 1 at note 3.

[27] Operation Ore was a British police investigation, commencing in 1999 and lasting several years, carried out in conjunction with US law enforcement agencies which was aimed at prosecuting on-line users of a website featuring child pornography.

content on the internet, reveal a drop in on-line child grooming activities. While there were five confirmed reports of cases where a person was attempting to procure a meeting with the child for the purposes of sexual exploitation in 2007, this fell to just one case in 2009.[28] Further official statistics on grooming will be included in Chapter 6 in relation to the effectiveness of legislative and policy frameworks.

Data on street grooming

While there is a sizeable international literature on sex trafficking of women and children in particular across international boundaries (eg Gallagher et al, 2003, 2006; Obokata, 2006; Scarpa, 2008; McCabe and Manian, 2010; Shelley, 2010), much less is known about the use of grooming for trafficking purposes particularly within more localized and nationalized contexts. Indeed, given the relative newness of the phenomenon there is very little data available on 'street grooming'.

One notable exception is a 2009 study by Barnardo's (Barnardo's, 2009) which revealed that organized networks of adults may be grooming hundreds of children, some as young as ten, to be trafficked within the United Kingdom for sexual exploitation. The report, *Whose Child Now?* showed that of the 609 children and young people the charity was working with at that time in various projects across the United Kingdom, 90, or one in six, children were trafficked into the country and had been subjected to this form of child sexual exploitation. In England and Wales, however, there were only 25 proceedings on the grounds of trafficking for sexual exploitation (a figure which also includes adult victims), with only 15 guilty verdicts and accompanying sentences (Barnardo's, 2009: 6). In the 2010 Young Life and Times Survey, 18 per cent of grooming approaches to young people in Northern Ireland occurred on the street, either hanging around in town or in the local community,[29] demonstrating that 'street grooming' is a growing phenomenon.

The inherent limitations of official statistics on sexual crime and grooming in particular have been acknowledged above. The true extent of street grooming may be difficult to measure as

---

[28] See Hotline.ie Annual Reports 2007 and 2009 respectively <http://www. hotline.ie/hotlinepublications.php> (accessed 15 March 2011).

[29] See note 17 above.

victims may be either too afraid or ashamed to make a formal complaint or have been groomed not to recognize themselves as victims (Barnardo's, 2009: 9; Beckett, 2011: 46–8). A Barnardo's study of the 'Sexual Exploitation of Children and Young People in Northern Ireland', comprised, inter alia, of survey data as well as interviews with professionals and with children and young people themselves, confirmed that although there are very few reported cases, 'what we are aware of is only "the tip of the iceberg"' (Beckett, 2011: 48).[30] Nonetheless, the low number of prosecutions for this form of sexual exploitation of children, of which grooming is an integral part, also endorses the difficulties of policing this type of behaviour as well as the general assertion of this book that the criminal law is somewhat limited in its response to grooming behaviours. Concerted policy responses to grooming are also in their infancy. Figures from the NWG demonstrate that only around 20 per cent of the local authorities in England (40 out of the 209) currently provide any kind of specialist service for dealing with the sexual exploitation of children and young people (Barnardo's, 2009: 7).[31]

Currently, most knowledge in the public domain about the nature and extent of street grooming comes from a handful of high profile cases in England and Wales which made news headlines beginning in the early part of 2011. In one such case, following what became known as 'Operation Retriever', two men from Derby were jailed indefinitely for abusing up to 100 young girls aged mostly between 12 and 18.[32] In another case, which emerged only a few days later, nine men aged between 20 and 40 from Rochdale in Greater Manchester were investigated over allegations that they had groomed teenage girls for sex and were arrested on a number of charges including, inter alia, suspicion of rape and conspiracy to engage in sexual activity with a

---

[30] This study identified a number of types of sexual exploitation: abuse through prostitution; the 'party-house' model; sexually exploitative relationships (where young people perceive the abuser to be their boy/girlfriend); internet exploitation; and trafficking (Beckett, 2011: 26–8, ch 6).

[31] The National Working Group (NWG) is an umbrella organization for services which provide support to sexually exploited children and young people.

[32] T. Symonds, 'Derby Sex Gang Convicted of Grooming and Abusing', *BBC News On-line*, 24 November 2010, <http://www.bbc.co.uk/news/uk-england-derbyshire-11799797> (accessed 18 February 2011).

child.[33] A further case involved an investigation of organized sexual exploitation and abuse involving multiple child victims in Torbay.[34] Similarly, eight Asian men from Telford in Shropshire also appeared in court charged with a number of serious sexual offences including trafficking young girls within the United Kingdom.[35]

Following these cases, CEOP commissioned a thematic assessment of 'localized' or 'on-street grooming' in the United Kingdom and in particular whether there were patterns of offending, victimization, and vulnerability of children outside the home. This study found that out of over 1,200 offenders, the vast majority are men (87 per cent), almost half are aged between 18 and 24 and many operated in networks ranging from just two people to much larger numbers (2011a: 9). Twenty per cent were of Asian origin, although the data on the ethnicity of offenders was inconclusive due to the small number of areas with agencies reporting. Of over 2,000 victims, the vast majority are female (69 per cent), aged between 14 and 15 at the time of first contact with a statutory or non-statutory agency, and white (61 per cent). A significant number of victims had been reported missing (842), and many other victims (311) were in care at the time of the exploitation. The study noted, however, 'very few cases are known in areas where agencies do not routinely engage victims and collect data...As a result, the majority of incidents of child sexual exploitation in the UK are unrecognised and unknown' (CEOP, 2011a). As will be discussed further in the next part of the book, 'street grooming', therefore, is perhaps one of the most high profile forms of grooming, but remains one of the hardest forms for justice and support agencies to detect and target.

In the aftermath of these cases, there were also claims from children's charities that the grooming of teenagers has been previously overlooked as social workers are instead preoccupied with younger

[33] 'Police Probe into Claims of Gang Grooming Girls for Sex in Rochdale', see note 5 above. These men were eventually sentenced in May 2012: 'Rochdale Grooming Trial: Nine Men Jailed', *BBC News Online*, 9 May 2012, <http://www.bbc.co.uk/news/uk-england-17993003> (accessed 14 May 2012).

[34] 'Up to 50 Children May be Victims of Internet Sex Ring in Torbay', see note 8 above.

[35] E. Sefton, 'Ground-breaking Cases Alleges Girls were Transported to Various Locations for Sex', *The First Post*, 22 January 2011.

children.[36] While these cases demonstrate that there is a clear danger to children and young people from organized criminal gangs, the recent public prominence of such cases serves to detract attention from other potential risks or sources of harm, including that from within the home. As discussed further in Chapter 4, the media emphasis on the racial element of these cases also furthers the 'othering' process (Garland, 2001).

Data on peer-to-peer grooming

A minority of studies have shown that children may also be groomed by other children, particularly in an on-line environment which affords them anonymity. As noted above, Finkelhor, Mitchell, and Wolak (2000), found that 48 per cent of offenders were under 18. This also accords with research evidence on child sexual abuse as a whole which shows that a growing number of sexual assaults against children are committed by other children (Grubin, 1998). Studies estimate that approximately one-third of all reported cases of child sexual abuse are committed by those under 18 (Richardson et al, 1997; Grubin, 1998; Masson, 2004). According to the Northern Ireland 2010 Young Life and Times Survey, while in almost half of cases (46 per cent) the offender was at least 17 years older than the victim, 12 per cent of 16-year-olds who took part in the survey reported that the person who tried to groom them was 'about their age', that is not more than two years older than them.[37] Almost a further quarter (20 per cent) were only three to four years older than the intended victim. A similar figure of one in four perpetrators of child sexual abuse being 17 years or younger has also been produced for the Republic of Ireland (McGee et al, 2002). As a whole, therefore, the recurrent pertinent public image of the predatory much older adult offender who seeks out young victims to abuse is once more undermined by the statistics. In the recent large-scale research undertaken by Barnardo's in Northern Ireland, referred to above, peer grooming emerged as 'an increasing issue of concern' where almost 24 per cent of cases of sexual exploitation involve

---

[36] 'Children as young as TEN are being used, abused and thrown away by British sex gangs', *Mail On-line*, 17 January 2011, <http://www.dailymail.co.uk/news/article-1347864/Sex-gangs-grooming-children-young-10-says-leading-charity.html> (accessed 17 January 2011).

[37] See note 17 above.

peer exploitation (Beckett, 2011: 96, 22). Similarly, research conducted by the University of Bristol on behalf of the NSPCC found that one in three girls and 16 per cent of boys reported some form of sexual partner violence (Barter et al, 2009).

The issue of peer-to-peer grooming in off-line contexts has also emerged from anecdotal conversations with professionals in the field of sex offending against children and will be explored further in the second part of the book. Moreover, some of the recent cases on 'street grooming' also highlight a cross-over with 'peer-to-peer' grooming where young girls in particular are used to groom others into sex trafficking rings. It can also take the form of 'sexting' (Lenhart, 2009; Lounsbury, Mitchell, and Finkelhor, 2011; Ringrose et al, 2012) as discussed further in Chapter 4.

Conclusion

In sum, there may be multiple manifestations of grooming in a range of inter-personal as well as societal and organizational settings. This may involve children, in both on-line and face-to-face situations, as well as their families, the local community and even organizations. The common denominator, in all manifestations of grooming, however, is the degree of 'trust' placed in the offender and its subsequent betrayal. The establishment of trust, in whatever form, makes abuse possible and simultaneously masks disclosure.

This chapter has also argued that there are many misconceptions concerning sexual grooming as commonly understood by the public and reflected in the popular press. Misunderstandings concerning the real nature and extent of child sexual abuse in general have also spilled over into the area of sexual grooming specifically. In particular, the danger to children has been constructed as emanating primarily from a devious, male, predatory, adult offender who is ready to prey on children and young people who are previously unknown to them. In reality, however, grooming, much like sexual abuse itself, is a considerably more complex occurrence, involving family and acquaintances of the child or young person where an intimate relationship has already been established and even involving growing numbers of women and young sexual offenders.

The lack of settled meaning of the term grooming in both the popular imagination as well as academic and official discourses, together with the problems of early identification of grooming behaviour, means that such behaviour is not easily captured by a legislative response. As will be argued further, the difficulties of proving intention and the particular problems of trying to apply the legislation on grooming to non-internet-based situations and within intra-familial or quasi-familial contexts, mean that the legislation will not be applicable to the majority of sexual offending perpetuated against children. As Finkelhor and colleagues have argued in relation to the risks associated with on-line grooming in particular but which could equally be applied to grooming as a whole, '[t]he diversity of those making sexual solicitations is an important point for prevention planners to recognize. A too narrow construction of the threat was a problem that hampered prevention efforts in regard to child molestation a generation ago, and those responding to internet hazards should be careful not to make the same mistake' (Finkelhor, Mitchell, and Wolak, 2000: 7).

3

Legislative and Policy Frameworks on Sex Offender Risk Management

> Sex offenders have always found ways of gaining the trust and confidence of children, all too often to sexually abuse them at a later date. Deceit is their stock in trade...Liberty has raised the concern that restrictions will be placed on people displaying inappropriate sexual behaviour before an offence is committed...Of course there must be proof of intent before action is taken but that has to be balanced by protecting the child before actual sexual activity takes place.[1]

The respective legislative and policy frameworks which have been designed to address sexual grooming in England and Wales, Scotland, Northern Ireland, and the Republic of Ireland have not emerged in a vacuum. Rather, each can be viewed individually and collectively as the pinnacle of a general trend of regulatory initiatives on sex offending which are designed to pre-emptively govern the risks posed by sexual offenders. This upward trajectory of retributive policies on sex offending is perhaps most marked in England and Wales which has usually been the first jurisdiction in the United Kingdom and Ireland to enact such measures, with the other jurisdictions generally following suit. In order to provide some context to the respective legislative responses to grooming, which will be discussed in Part II of the book, the chapter also provides an overview of the historical and political relationships between the respective legal systems and traditions in the United Kingdom and Ireland.

Although there are many points of convergence, there are also subtle differences in regulatory approaches to sex offending between these jurisdictions. Various explanations for key policy differences are

---

[1] Sexual Offences Bill [HL]: Baroness Gould, *Hansard*, HL Debs, col 786 (13 February 2003).

explored below. It must be acknowledged, however, that there are a number of caveats which underpin the comparative method (Zedner, 1995; Roberts, 2002; Nelken, 2007). These relate, inter alia, to differences in legal frameworks and cultures, socio-political ideologies, and penal cultures and infrastructures which make direct comparisons difficult; the volume of data generated by meaningful comparison; and differing explanatory frameworks adopted by academics and practitioners. With these challenges in mind, the core task of this chapter is to highlight the broad trends within criminal justice policies on sex offending as well as the variations and nuances which are 'embedded within changing, local and international, historical and cultural contexts' (Nelken, 2007: 148).

Risk, Regulation, and Preventive Governance

The politics of 'risk', 'regulation', and 'governance' (Beck, 1992; Ericson and Haggerty, 1997; Braithwaite, 2000; Shearing, 2000) have come to dominate international debates on security and justice and responses to crime and anti-social behaviour (Crawford, 1997, 2003; Christie, 2000; Shearing, 2000; Loader and Walker, 2007; O'Malley, 2010). In an era of 'governing through crime' (Simon, 2007), a range of social problems have been reconceptualized as crime with an associated focus on attributing blame and imposing consequences for deviant behaviour. The upshot is an inevitable flood of regulatory activity designed to pre-emptively manage risk and treat wider social ills, as well as the inflation of public anxiety about crime and the erosion of trust at the inter-personal level within civil society.

Recent initiatives range from preventive detention and restrictions placed on dangerous offenders on release from custody to the development of multi-agency panels to assess and manage risk (Rose, 2000). This relatively 'new penology' (Feeley and Simon, 1992) and its links with 'actuarial justice' (Feeley and Simon, 1994), has formed the basis of targeted intervention with selected 'at risk' groups such as sexual offenders (Simon, 1998; Kemshall and Maguire, 2001), for whom exceptional forms of punishment and control are thought necessary (Zedner, 2009). As Stafford et al (2011) argue, these are potent ingredients which unite to bind policy together across the United Kingdom.

The management of dangerous or 'risky' individuals, such as sex offenders against children and persistent violent offenders, has generated enormous popular and official concern (McAlinden, 2010a; Harrison, 2011). The state's prioritization of such dangers over other forms of deviant behaviour is driven in large part by media-fuelled popular discourses concerning the ominous and omnipresent sex offender (Edwards and Hensley, 2001a). Consistent with broader academic discourses, the notions of risk management (Parton et al, 1997; Parton, 2006; Kemshall and Maguire, 2001) and, more recently, preventive governance (Ashenden, 2004) have become the touchstones of sex offender management and child protection. Within this broader context, the specific question of how to identify and manage those who may pose a potential risk to children prior to the occurrence of harm (Room, 2004) has emerged as a key issue for contemporary discourses on sex offending against children.

While the majority of work has focused on developments within the United Kingdom as a whole and within England and Wales in particular, other writers have noted the 'rise of prevention and proactivity' in Scotland (Norrie, Sutherland, and Cleland, 2004: para 499) and the marked 'shift of emphasis from reaction to prevention…aimed at both offenders and potential offenders against children' (Norrie, 2005: 20). As the opening quotation conveys, this 'shift in sentencing and offender management' policies, however, is based on 'the perceived "riskiness" of the individual offender in terms of what they *might* do as opposed to simply what they have done', and as a result there is little or no attempt to differentiate between levels or types of risk posed by sex offenders (Weaver and McNeill, 2010: 274–5).

A related area of debate concerns the emergence of a policy of 'radical prevention' (Hebenton and Seddon, 2009: 2; see also Seddon, 2008). Scholars have charted the development of criminal justice policy which has shifted 'From Dangerousness to Risk' (Castel, 1991) towards a framework based on 'precautionary logic' (Ericson, 2007; see also McSherry and Keyzer, 2009: ch 2). This pre-emptive approach to penal policy is characterized by the search for security and certainty via the imposition of reactionary risk-averse policies which seek to govern 'worst case scenarios' and prevent all possible connotations of future risk before they become manifest (Zedner, 2009). Legislative and policy measures which seek to criminalize the act of meeting a child following grooming, prior to the commission of a contact sexual offence, as well as the expansion of the legal framework on pre-employment vetting, have attempted to respond to both *known* and *unknown* risks posed by sex offenders. In effect, the desire to pre-emptively govern risky behaviours or situations, rather than simply risky individuals (O'Malley, 2004: 318–19) has led to the development of a range of precautionary regulatory policies on sex offending in general, and grooming in particular, which privilege anxiety over risk (Hebenton and Seddon, 2009: 354).

During the last ten years or so, the government has come under increasing pressure to be seen to be actively 'doing something' in the face of glaring media focus and heightened public fears concerning the presence of sex offenders in the community (Simon, 1998). There are usually two polar responses of the state in the face of its limitations to control crime: a politics of denial of responsibility (Cohen, 2001), or a politics of punishment as demonstrable evidence of its strength and commitment to controlling the problem (Garland, 1996). In relation to sex offenders, although there is some evidence of the former, particularly where loopholes or weaknesses subsequently emerge in current policies, the state's response to the regulation of sex offenders can more clearly be related to the latter. As Zedner notes 'the mentality of precaution feeds on existing insecurities and gives sway to the exercise of fevered bureaucratic imagination' (2009: 58).

As noted above, there have been two particular yet inter-related 'moral panics' (Cohen, 1972) about sexual offending as related to grooming behaviour. One is the scandal of long-term institutional and institutionalized abuse of children in care in both church and state settings. The other is the paedophilia 'stranger danger' phenomenon which occurs on a seemingly random basis. While the first of these panics has been reflected in a range of legislative measures to control pre-employment vetting, the second is reflected in the offence of 'meeting a child following sexual grooming' which is common, in one form or other, to all of the jurisdictions in the United Kingdom and Ireland.

The specific issue of how to prevent sex offenders from using their employment as a cover to target and sexually abuse children, however, has perhaps become one of the most contentious and politicized in the recent debates on sexual offending and has been the subject of a spate of legislation for more than a decade (Sullivan and Beech, 2002). In England and Wales in particular between 1997 and 2006, no fewer than five primary legislative reforms were introduced to strengthen vetting procedures and to criminalize those who abuse their position of trust in order to offend against children (McAlinden, 2010a: 29). Expansive forms of state regulation often lead to increasingly volatile, contradictory, and incoherent penal policies (Garland, 1999a; O'Malley, 1999; Crawford, 2001). Using a purely legal framework, such as vetting, to try to pre-emptively manage potential risks or harms can do little to protect children from grooming activities and sexual abuse in an intimate environment where they may be most at risk from unknown dangers. Moreover, the range of evidential and other operational problems surrounding the enactment of the offence of meeting a child following sexual grooming, and reciprocal offences throughout the United Kingdom and Ireland, also has implications for the identification and criminalization of grooming behaviour (see Chapter 6).

An Overview of Legal Systems and Traditions

The legal systems of the various constituencies within the United Kingdom and Ireland, although now quite separate, have shared legal histories and traditions which have also impacted on policies relating to child care and protection and the regulation of sex offending. Criminal justice policies in each of the jurisdictions have not emerged in isolation from developments in the United Kingdom as a whole and indeed internationally. The discussion places each jurisdiction within the context of its political relationship with England and Wales in particular. This section will also serve as a preface to detailing the individual legislative frameworks which relate to the management of sexual offenders in the community and to sexual grooming in particular which will be undertaken later in this chapter and in Part II of the book.

Until fairly recently, criminal justice policy enacted for Scotland was the same as that for England and Wales. Devolution occurred in Scotland under the Scotland Act 1998 which re-established the Scottish parliament at Holyrood in Edinburgh in 1999 and transferred justice issues to the legislative remit of the new Scottish government. As a result, older pieces of legislation relating to sex offending enacted in Westminster, which pre-date Scottish devolution, extend also to Scotland as well as Northern Ireland. A primary example of this is Part I of the Sex Offenders Act 1997 which enacted the original provisions on sex offender notification and which has since been replaced by Part 2 of the Sexual offences Act 2003. Even though the 2003 Act post-dates devolution, the notification provisions in Part 2 of that

Act also extend to Scotland.[2] For the most part, however, the majority of the recent measures on sex offending in Scotland, including most notably the offence of 'meeting a child following certain preliminary contact'[3] which relates to grooming, as well as provisions on pre-employment vetting,[4] have been legislated for separately. Indeed, since 1999, crime and criminal justice issues in Scotland have spawned a burgeoning academic literature, particularly within the last few years (Duff and Hutton, 1999; McAra, 2008; Croall, Mooney, and Munro, 2010; Drake, Muncie, and Westmarland, 2010).

The legislative relationship between Northern Ireland and England and Wales is a rather more intricate one (McLaughlin, 2005). Local legislative policies in Northern Ireland have had a 'consistent' and 'shared' relationship with those adopted by the British government but have also been modified to meet Northern Ireland's 'own strategic political needs' (Pinkerton, 1994: 29). Although the formal break from England and Wales began when Ireland was first partitioned in 1920, the devolution of Executive powers was not formally legislated for until the Northern Ireland Act 1998.[5] Full devolution of criminal justice and policing from the House of Commons in Westminster, London, to the Northern Ireland Assembly in Stormont, Belfast, however, did not take place until March 2010. In the interim, there have also been periods of direct rule. In consequence, for the last number of years, criminal justice policy in Northern Ireland has been strongly influenced by and tended to track developments in England and Wales (Birrell and Muncie, 1980: 65; Dickson, 2001: 5), particularly in relation to safeguarding children (Northern Ireland Assembly Research and Library Service, 2010a: 1). Pinkerton argues that while it is generally accepted that in matters of social policy the step-by-step or 'parity principle' has held sway, in the case of child care legislation, or policies relating to children and young people, however, it is something of a mixed picture (1994: 28; see also Kelly, 1990: 78).

---

[2] Section 142 of the Sexual Offences Act 2003 provides that for the purposes of the Scotland Act 1998, this Act is to be taken as a pre-commencement enactment.
[3] See the Protection of Children and Prevention of Sexual Offences (Scotland) Act 2005, s 1.
[4] See eg the Protection of Vulnerable Groups (Scotland) Act 2007.
[5] This Act repealed the Government of Ireland Act 1920 which partitioned Ireland.

Several pieces of legislation pertaining to the post-release control of sexual offenders enacted in Westminster—such as Part I of the Sex Offenders Act 1997 and later Part 2 of the Sexual Offences Act 2003, referred to above—extend also to Northern Ireland. Where this is not the case, reciprocal legislation first enacted in Westminster was later adopted in Northern Ireland in comparative form in the ensuing months or years. An example of this latter approach in the field of sexual offending is the legislative provision for sex offender orders, first enacted in England and Wales by the Crime and Disorder Act 1998[6] and later adopted in Northern Ireland by the Criminal Justice (NI) Order 1998.[7] This process has been termed one of 'delay and quasi-imitation' (Pinkerton, 1994: 28). As Dickson suggests, under the period of direct rule between 1974 and 1999, following the first reintroduction of the Stormont government in the aftermath of 'the Good Friday Agreement',[8] and indeed until full devolution in 2010, 'the process of assimilation between the content of the law in Northern Ireland and that in England was, if anything, fortified' (2001: 8).

With reference to the legal and political relationship between England and Wales and the Republic of Ireland, until partition in 1920, Ireland was part of the United Kingdom of Great Britain and Ireland. As a result, until this point, legislation enacted in Westminster applied also to the Republic of Ireland.[9] After partition, however, particularly after the formal formation of the Irish State in 1948,[10] there was a deliberate halt to progressive reforms relating to the care and protection of children and a general unwillingness

---

[6] See s 2. Note also that sex offender orders, together with restraining orders (the Criminal Justice and Courts Services Act 2000, s 66 and Sch 5) have also been replaced with a new and extended measure under Part 2 of the Sexual Offences Act 2003—sexual offences prevention orders (see ss 104–13 of the 2003 Act).

[7] See s 6. See also previous note: sexual offences prevention orders now also apply in Northern Ireland.

[8] 'The Good Friday' or the 'Belfast Agreement' was signed by most of Northern Ireland's political parties on 10 April 1998 (Good Friday).

[9] The legislation dating from this period relates to two controversial areas of sexual offences or child care and practice—the Punishment of Incest Act 1908; and the Children Act 1908 which regulated, inter alia, the establishment of juvenile courts and the committal of children to industrial schools.

[10] The Republic of Ireland Act 1948 established Ireland as a Republic by ending the constitutional role of the British monarchy and vesting in the President the power to exercise the executive authority of the state.

to follow the same legislative route as Great Britain (McAlinden, 2012b). As will be discussed further below, this has been attributed to two main factors. The first relates to the adoption of conservative social policies which were based on a rigid Catholic morality, the safeguarding of its new found national identity, and the aspiration of complete political independence from Britain (Arnold, 2009: 13, 38; McAlinden, 2012b). The other relates to the formidable influence of the Catholic Church on law making and political processes in general and to the Church's patriarchal and moral monopoly of public discourses on issues concerning sex and sexuality in particular (Inglis, 1998, 2005).

The latter issue was pivotal to the systemic nature of institutional child abuse in Ireland and the suppression of 'the truth' about the scale of such abuses by Church and state for many years (see Chapter 5). The Republic of Ireland is a jurisdiction which remains to some extent in its infancy in relation to the regulation of sexual crime. It could also be considered, to some extent at least, to lag behind the jurisdictions in the United Kingdom, often enacting legislative or policy measures relating to sex offender risk management some years later (Northern Ireland Assembly Research and Library Service, 2010a: 7).

A final point of comparison is the relationship between Northern Ireland and the Republic of Ireland as two distinct yet adjacent legal jurisdictions on the same island which are separated by a land border. The Criminal Justice Review Group, set up as part of the Good Friday Agreement, recommended an element of 'structured co-operation' between Northern Ireland and the Republic of Ireland and 'mutual recognition and harmonisation' of a range of criminal justice policies, including 'dangerous offender registers' (Criminal Justice Review Group, 2000: ch 17). In addition to informal cooperation and information sharing between key criminal justice agencies on both sides of the border regarding high risk sex offenders, a number of initiatives have been set up. These have included the 2006 Memorandum of Understanding between the Gardaí and British police forces on the sharing of information about sex offenders, and the North-South Child Protection Network, which allows professionals to share expertise, policies, and best practice (Northern Ireland Assembly Research and Library Service, 2010a).

Such developments are also broadly in line with those within the European Union as a whole where there has been a growing emphasis on enhanced judicial and police cooperation (Ramage, 2007; Constantin, 2008; Jacobs and Blitsa, 2008), including exchanges of information between Member States about dangerous offenders. It seems, however, that recent cross-border police cooperation between the Republic of Ireland and Northern Ireland has thrived 'at the micro-level of engagement' among police officers on the ground based on 'personal relationships and ad hoc arrangements' (Walsh, 2011: 302, 327) rather than the implementation of formal EU mandates. This issue will be revisited in Chapter 6.

Within this broader context, a further issue concerns the possibility of sex offenders leaving one jurisdiction in which they reside and entering another close by in order to commit a sexual crime or avoid detection. There have been a number of such cases involving a cross-border dimension where released sex offenders have left Northern Ireland or the Republic of Ireland and travelled to England and Wales or Scotland and even Continental Europe,[11] or the other way around.[12] These cases and the overall danger of this occurring perhaps remain more acute, however, for Northern Ireland and the Republic of Ireland because of the relatively small size of the respective jurisdictions and the ease with which individuals may access and cross the border.[13] Indeed, the potential difficulties concerning standardized criminal record information and vetting arrangements as well as policing the offence of meeting a child following sexual grooming when the offender lives in one jurisdiction and the victim in another will be examined in Part II of the book.

In sum, Northern Ireland has a legal system which broadly replicates that of England and Wales and is governed by many of the same legislative measures on sex offending or has ratified reciprocal measures of its own soon thereafter. The Republic of Ireland,

[11] See eg 'Sex Offender Ernest George Finlay has Sentence Reduced', *BBC News Northern Ireland Politics*, 1 April 2011, <http://www.bbc.co.uk/news/uk-northern-ireland-politics-12941040> (accessed 19 April 2011).

[12] See eg 'High Risk Sex Offender Paden "May Be in NI"', *BBC News Northern Ireland*, 26 June 2010, <http://www.bbc.co.uk/news/10422284> (accessed 19 April 2011); 'Sex Offender Fraser McLaughlin Arrested in Dublin', *BBC News Northern Ireland*, 3 September 2010, <http://www.bbc.co.uk/news/uk-northern-ireland-11176260> (accessed 19 April 2011).

[13] See eg 'Sex Beast Paul Redpath Recaptured', *Belfast Telegraph*, 28 July 2009, <http://www.belfasttelegraph.co.uk/news/local-national/sex-beast-paul-redpath-recaptured-14435872.html> (accessed 19 April 2011).

on the other hand, has had a completely different legal system, traditions, and legislative measures since at least the late 1940s. Scotland has had a distinct but related momentum on sex offending particularly following devolution of justice issues in 1999. There may, however, be a number of unique problems relating to formulating responses to sexual crime and to the management of sexual offenders in the community which occur within a particular jurisdiction.

In Northern Ireland, for example, there are some local variations in relation to police legitimacy and paramilitary involvement in sexual offender issues. Such problems have manifested themselves in the form of 'punishment beatings' of suspected sex offenders by paramilitary groups (Leggett, 2000; Knox, 2002: 174). These groups may play on the fears of the local community concerning the presence of sex offenders and consequently present themselves as protectors and alternative law enforcers in stark contrast to what they see as the failure of the local authorities to deal adequately with the problem (McAlinden, 2007a: 91). As will be discussed in the last part of the book, the legacy of political conflict in Northern Ireland in terms of segregation, sectarianism, fear and mistrust of the authorities may mean that issues around sex offending are not easily raised within public discourses. This, therefore, also underlines the importance of developing a coordinated social response to combat sexual grooming and abuse which is tailored to localized contexts.

Explaining the Convergence of Penal Policies on Sex Offending

Within the wider international context, England and Wales has developed one of the most stringent penal policies for protecting the public from the risk posed by sex offenders based on a punitive, managerialist framework. This broad approach has been reflected in the general legal and policy framework on sex offender risk assessment and management, particularly within the context of post-release control, as well as in the enactment of recent measures to combat the risk of sexual grooming.

Despite the prominence of risk within penal policies as a whole, there are various permutations of risk within specific societies (Tonry, 2001; Cavadino and Dignan, 2006a). A range of theoretical frameworks delineate the development of regulatory state policies in general (eg Majone, 1994; Braithwaite, 2000; Moran, 2001;

Crawford, 2006). There is much less work, however, which seeks to explain individualized accounts. Risk may be 'a key idea in understanding contemporary penality' (Sparks, 2001: 159), what is less clear, however, is how constructions of risk actually come to dominate official and popular discourses on particular crime problems in specific national contexts and so become 'the structuring principles of penal systems and penal politics' (Sparks, 2001: 159).

In addition to shared political, legal, and historical traditions and cultures, there are several other factors which may help to explain why penal approaches to sex offending in general, and to grooming in particular, in Scotland, Northern Ireland, and the Republic of Ireland broadly converge with those of England and Wales. These relate to three broad factors: the 'policy transfer' (Newburn, 2002; Jones and Newburn, 2006) of punitive crime control policies on sex offending derived from the United States; the dominance of neo-liberalist political economies (Cavadino and Dignan, 2006a); and the alignment of the social and political construction of risk and its control by various stakeholders—media, public, professionals, and government—within localized, individualized contexts (McAlinden, 2012a). Elsewhere, I have applied this framework to a critical explanation of penal policy variation between England and Wales and other Western European states, which have generally resisted retributive measures on sex offending in favour of inclusionary therapeutic interventions (McAlinden, 2012a). I will argue here, however, that these factors can also usefully explain why, in turn, Northern Ireland and Scotland and, to a lesser extent, the Republic of Ireland, have also followed the same path as England and Wales and implemented broadly exclusionary, regulatory approaches to sexual crime. While there are acknowledged nuances and contradictions in contemporary configurations of penal policy within a given nation state (Muncie, 2005; Pratt, 2008a, 2008b), this analysis concentrates predominantly on policy trends at the broader macro-level.

Policy transfer

Many of the recent punitive crime control policies on sex offending enacted within the United Kingdom as a whole derive from similar regulatory policies enacted in the United States (McAlinden, 2006b; Hebenton and Seddon, 2009). A large body of work on comparative penal reform has generally highlighted the spread of penal policies which appear to have originated in the United States (eg Christie, 2000; Garland, 2001). The work of Newburn and Jones (Newburn, 2002; Jones and Newburn, 2006) has pinpointed the process of 'policy transfer' between the United States and the United Kingdom in relation to crime control. Their central argument is that a range of factors including ideological proximity, shared political discourses and vernacular, and the dominance of symbolic and rhetorical politics, have contributed to harmonization in the regulatory concepts and substantive legal frameworks adopted. As Muncie argues in relation to youth justice, policy transfer is 'one of the most tangible drivers' in promoting retributive responses to offending behaviour (2009: 358).

A number of UK initiatives have been closely modelled on American responses to the risk posed by sex offenders. One obvious example is the use of preventive detention with dangerous offenders (McSherry and Keyzer, 2009, 2011). Perhaps the clearest example of this, however, is notification. Indeed, the United States, the United Kingdom and Ireland, and France are among only a handful of countries in the world which have a system requiring sex offenders to notify their details to the police (Fitch, Spencer Chapman, and Hilton, 2007: 53). In the United States, a body of state and federal laws, known collectively as 'Megan's Law',[14] require certain classes of sex offender to register their personal details with law enforcement authorities and permit various forms of notification of this information to the community. Some of the key differences between the schemes in the United States and the United Kingdom have dissipated over the last few years particularly in terms of the degree of notification permitted to the local community.

In England and Wales, there has been an ongoing campaign for a similarly styled 'Sarah's Law' which also calls for the authorities to make public the identities and whereabouts of known sex offenders.[15] A community disclosure scheme allowing parents to check the backgrounds of those with unsupervised access to their children was

---

[14] At the Federal level, sex offender registration and community notification are now governed by the Adam Walsh Child Protection and Safety Act 2006.

[15] 'Sarah's Law' was named after eight-year-old Sarah Payne who was abducted and murdered by a known sex offender, Roy Whiting, in Sussex in July 2000. The campaign was led by Sarah's mother, Sara Payne, and backed by the *News of the World*'s 'Name and Shame' campaign which called for the authorities to publicly identify all known sex offenders. This campaign was also accompanied by public protest and vigilante activity in Paulsgrove (Ashenden, 2002; Williams and Thompson, 2004a, 2004b).

piloted in four areas in England (Kemshall et al, 2010) with a parallel pilot in the Tayside area in Scotland (Chan et al, 2010). The scheme was implemented in all 43 police forces in England and Wales by April 2011, and across Scotland from October 2010, bringing policies on notification even more closely into line with those in the United States.[16] At the time of writing, Northern Ireland has yet to implement a public disclosure scheme. As Croall, Mooney, and Munro have argued, 'devolution has also thrown up the possibility of policy transfer across the different constituent countries of the UK. Transnationalism, in this respect, works within the UK as it does on a global level' (2010: 13).

The transfer of criminal justice policy on sex offending is also evident in relation to legal approaches to grooming. The United States along with a range of other jurisdictions has configured the risk of sexual grooming as occurring primarily within the context of on-line environments (Davidson and Martellezzo, 2008b: 339). As noted in the introductory chapter, there are various offences at both federal[17] and state[18] levels to cover on-line grooming based on either coercion, enticement, or luring a child with the intention of having sexual relations. Such developments have undoubtedly directly informed policy developments on grooming in England and Wales, and in particular the implementation of the offence of meeting a child following grooming, which the other jurisdictions within the United Kingdom and Ireland have replicated. As will be discussed further, although this offence was not designed with the express intention of being applied solely to the on-line environment, a range of inherent limitations means that it will be difficult to use in practice within the context of intra-familial or quasi-familial abuse which takes place in off-line settings (eg Gillespie, 2004b: 11; Ost, 2004: 152–3; Craven, Brown, and Gilchrist, 2007: 65; McLaughlin, 2009: 12).

Reasons put forward for such parity in approaches to the regulation of sexual crime between the United States and the United

---

[16] Section 327A of the Criminal Justice Act 2003 (inserted by s 140 of the Criminal Justice and Immigration Act 2008) places a duty on each MAPPA to consider disclosure to particular members of the public of an offender's convictions for child sexual offences where there is a risk of serious harm to a particular child or children. At the time of writing, there is no statutory footing for the scheme in Scotland.

[17] See 18 USC 2422: Coercion and Enticement.

[18] See eg Georgia State Law: Ga. Code Ann. § 16-12-100.2 (1999).

Kingdom include high profile cases of sexual abuse or murder of young children, which have acted as 'precipitating events' (Lieb, 2000: 423), related campaigns involving 'co-victims' or the immediate family, and the pivotal role played by the media in garnering public support for these policy campaigns (Jones and Newburn, 2005). In particular, such 'memorial laws' (Valier, 2005) are often named after particular victims and are used symbolically to 'lever up punitiveness' (Zedner, 2002: 447). As argued throughout, particular cases of sexual offending against children involving the medium of the internet or within the context of institutional care have played a pivotal role in shaping public attitudes towards sex offenders and official policies on the risk posed by sexual grooming. In addition, as discussed further below, the neo-liberal turn of recent penal policy in both jurisdictions (Cavadino and Dignan, 2006a) also helps to account for this alignment of regulatory policies on sex offending.

The tentative progress of implementing 'Sarah's Law' throughout the United Kingdom, however, is indicative of the limitations of policy transfer. As Muncie notes, the process is not 'one-dimensional' (2005: 37) but is instead subject to important socio-cultural differences in the way in which policies are reformulated and reconfigured within national and localized cultures (Muncie, 2005: 44, 2009: 359; Crawford, 2006). While the policy transfer thesis may help to account for the partial convergence of penal policies on sex offending between the United States and the United Kingdom as a whole, and to a lesser extent the Republic of Ireland, in terms of scope, it does little to explain material differences in the substance of local policies on grooming in particular among the individual jurisdictions of the United Kingdom and Ireland. An analysis of the underlying differences between the individual legal frameworks on vetting and barring and grooming respectively will be undertaken in Part II of the book.

Political economies

While there has been a global trend towards punitiveness and increasing rates of imprisonment,[19] this tendency has perhaps been most marked in relation to the United States and the United Kingdom (McAlinden, 2012a). Although the United States is the world leader in terms of incarceration rates, with a figure of 756 per 100,000

---

[19] In recent years, over three-quarters of all countries worldwide have increased their rates of imprisonment (Council of Europe, 2011: 41).

(Walmsley, 2009), England and Wales and Scotland have relatively high prison populations which are among the highest in Western Europe. Council of Europe figures demonstrate that England and Wales imprison more people per 100,000 (152) than most other Western European nations (apart from Scotland (156) and Spain, including Catalonia (173)), and approximately 50 per cent more than Belgium (101), France (103), Germany (89), Italy (106), the Netherlands (99), and Sweden (77) (Council of Europe, 2011: 38–40). Such figures were undoubtedly given impetus by the Criminal Justice Act 2003 and the introduction of an indeterminate public protection (IPP) sentence,[20] which have now been abolished.[21] Similarly, Scotland introduced risk assessed orders for lifelong restriction (OLRs) for sexual or violent offences or those which endanger life under the Criminal Justice (Scotland) Act 2003.[22] These may be imposed by the High Court following conviction for an offence for which a life sentence is not otherwise available and effectively amount to a sentence that allows for lifelong risk management of individuals. The number of OLR cases is very small, however, in comparison to the former IPP sentence in England and Wales (Darjee and Russell, 2011).[23] Northern Ireland and the Republic of Ireland had corresponding lower rates of imprisonment of 88 and 81 per 100,000 respectively (Council of Europe, 2011: 38).

Cavadino and Dignan (2006a) argue that differences in both the mode and severity of punishment can, at least in part, be attributed to differing political economies of late modern societies. According to these authors, in 'neo-liberal' societies, such as the United States and England and Wales, the demise of the 'welfare state' (Garland, 1985, 1996) has resulted in an ethos of individualism, and penal and social policies which are fixated upon forms of segregation and stigmatization

[20] See Part 12, ch 5. See also corresponding provisions on life/indeterminate and extended sentences in the Criminal Justice (NI) Order 2008, Part 2, ch 3.

[21] Part 3, ch 5 of the Legal Aid, Sentencing and Punishment of Offenders Act 2012 repeals IPP sentences and extended sentences and replaces them with provisions for life sentences to be imposed on conviction for a second serious offence and new provision for extended sentences.

[22] See s 1, which inserts s 210F into the Criminal Procedure (Scotland) Act 1995. As of June 2011, no sex offenders had been released under an OLR (Darroch, 2011).

[23] There were 49 OLRs imposed in Scotland in the first four years since their introduction in 2003 (Darjee and Russell, 2011), whereas there have been well over 6,000 IPPs between 2005 and 2010, where fewer than 100 individuals have been released (Jacobson and Hough, 2010).

of those on the margins of society (Petrunik and Deutschmann, 2008). Law and order or incapacitation is the dominant penal ideology which is shaped by the social exclusion of deviants and high rates of imprisonment (Wacquant, 2001) and an emphasis on punishment rather than correction. The forces of neo-liberalism, it seems, have also spread to Scotland and Northern Ireland (Horgan, 2006) as related jurisdictions which share 'broadly similar standards of living and constitutional arrangements' (Grimshaw, 2004: 3). As Garland argues (1999b), small jurisdictions may be especially susceptible to global influences.

The significance of the neo-liberal framework lies in the modes of governance employed. Social regulation is linked to a community protection model in which the reformative welfare agenda has been displaced by a concern with controlling the 'dangerous classes' (Pratt, 2000a; Garland, 2001) and punishment is justified as the primary response to offending behaviour (Kemshall and Wood, 2007). This argument also links to the notion of 'criminalisation as regulation' (Lacey, 2004), where in the face of a heightened sense of insecurity about sexual crime, the state attempts to assert its authority via the penal system and ever expanding forms of regulatory activity (O'Malley, 1999; Ericson, 2007; McAlinden, 2010a). As noted above, this politics of severity has been particularly evident in England and Wales in relation to the risk regulation of sex offenders since at least the late 1990s (McAlinden, 2012a).

In Scotland, the distinct civic and political culture, based on a 'commitment to communitarian, collectivist and egalitarian values' (Croall, Mooney, and Munro, 2010: 9), has historically ensured that it remained immune from populist concerns (Cavadino and Dignan, 2006b: 231; McAra, 2008: 493; Croall, Mooney, and Munro, 2010: 9). More recently, however, it seems that Scotland has been affected by the same neo-liberalist turn that is evident in social and justice policies in the rest of the United Kingdom and elsewhere (Croall, Mooney, and Munro, 2010: 9; see also McAra, 2007; Davidson, Miller, and McCafferty, 2010). The traditional notions of welfarism and social democracy in particular (Duff and Hutton, 1999; McCrone, 2001; Law, 2005; Keating, 2007) which had helped to resist the neo-liberal policies of British governments (Garland, 1999b) have been undermined by the politicization of criminal justice issues and increasing levels of populist penal discourses, particularly since devolution (Mooney and Poole, 2004; Croall, 2006; McAra, 2007; Tata, 2010; Munro and McNeill, 2010). This has been reflected in the erosion of welfarism, the augmentation of managerialism and privatization, and the significant rise in social inequalities which have impacted upon the criminal justice sphere in particular (Croall, Mooney, and Munro, 2010: 10; see also Davidson, Miller, and McCafferty, 2010).

The core priorities of criminal justice agencies such as criminal justice social work[24] have moved from supervision as an alternative to custody, and rehabilitation and welfare values, towards an emphasis on responsibility, public protection, and risk management (Weaver and McNeill, 2010: 272; see also McNeill and Whyte, 2007; McAra, 2008: 491). Many punitive crime control policies were enacted between 1997 and 2007 under a New Labour government in England and Wales (Tonry, 2003), and a new Labour dominated government in Scotland which has contributed to policy convergence (Croall, 2006; Croall, Mooney, and Munro, 2010: 10). McAra labels this 'detartanisation' (2008: 494)—the weakening of Scotland's political identity and the concomitant decline in distinct Scottish criminal justice policies.

Although the Republic of Ireland has also experienced a period of rapid social and economic change since the late 1990s (Nolan, O'Connell, and Whelan, 2000; Fahey, Russell, and Whelan, 2007), a 'culture of control' (Garland, 2001) has not manifested itself to the same degree. As O'Donnell argues, 'criminal justice agencies have been slow to embrace a culture of performance management and evaluation' (2005: 99). Indeed, despite a recent programme of prison expansion (O'Donnell, 2008), Ireland has traditionally low crime rates (Adler, 1983; Kilcommins et al, 2004; O'Donnell, Baumer, and Hughes, 2008) and relatively low rates of imprisonment. These have been attributed to a strong social commitment to the Church and the family, strong inter-personal networks and high levels of confidence in the police and other criminal justice agencies which enhance a communitarian ethos and informal social controls (O'Donnell, Baumer, and Hughes, 2008: 126).[25]

---

[24] In Scotland there is no centrally co-ordinated probation service but the responsibility of offender supervision and treatment in the community is undertaken by criminal justice social workers employed by local authorities (see generally McIvor and McNeill, 2007).

[25] See also Braithwaite's (1989) theory of 'reintegrative shaming' which contends that such societal features result in low levels of crime at both the micro- and macro-levels of offending.

In this respect, the Republic of Ireland seems more akin to Cavadino and Dignan's (2006a) model of a 'conservative corporatist' society or what they have also termed a 'Christian Democracy' (Cavadino and Dignan, 2006b: 129) which lies in the middle of the spectrum between a neo-liberalist model at one end and a social democratic corporatist model at the other. Such societies feature 'mixed' modes of punishment, medium rates of imprisonment and rehabilitation/reintegration as the primary sentencing rationale.[26] The Republic of Ireland has generally grappled with the tension between the two extremes of neo-liberalism and 'social democratic corporatism', the latter of which is distinguished by inclusionary social and penal policies, generous social rights, and low rates of imprisonment deriving from a 'rights-based' ideology and a focus on 'penal welfarism' (Garland, 1985) rather than punishment (Cavadino and Dignan, 2006a).[27] Ireland has recently enacted more punitive, exclusionary penal policies on sex offending including sex offender notification and the offence of meeting a child following sexual exploitation. The existence of a written constitution in the Republic of Ireland may be posited by some as a possible explanation for political and social reluctance to enact retributive penal policies, as has been argued in the case of other Western European countries such as France or Germany (see eg Zedner, 1995; Prosser, 2005). This argument would not hold true, however, for the United States which also has a strong constitutional mandate for challenging the legitimacy of legislation yet simultaneously harsh penal policies on sex offending. Further possible explanations for such differences between the Republic of Ireland and the other jurisdictions in the study will also be undertaken further below.

While Cavadino and Dignan's (2006a) framework usefully classifies the societal features which have a bearing on penal policy, arguably it does not engage with the crucial question which is why societies such as England and Wales have seemingly entrenched cultural and political intolerance to sex offenders, and resulting penal policies based largely on an exclusionary, precautionary approach to risk. In this respect, an additional factor which helps to explain the convergence of penal policies on sex offending

---

[26] According to the authors, examples include Germany, France, Italy, and the Netherlands (Cavadino and Dignan, 2006a).

[27] Classic examples include Sweden and Finland. See also Pratt (2008a, 2008b).

across the United Kingdom and Ireland is the social construction of risk and its control.

The social construction of risk

Punishment and crime control are culturally conditioned (Garland, 1990; Nelken, 2000; Sparks, 2001). Penal policies on sex offending in the United Kingdom and Ireland are 'an index of culture' (Nelken, 2007: 153) and are in themselves shaped by a complex interplay of social, political, and cultural factors. Similarities or differences in approach between England and Wales and the other jurisdictions in the study can be attributed principally to the complexities of the construction of risk which appears to be socially, politically, and culturally embedded. Sparks, drawing on the work of Garland (1990), argues that risk is a 'mixed discourse', encompassing 'moral, emotive and political as well as calculative' dimensions (2001: 169). In this respect, the convergence of punitive discourses on sex offending across the separate jurisdictions of the United Kingdom and Ireland can be explained in terms of the conflation of penal attitudes, policies, and practices concerning risk. As Hebenton and Seddon argue, it is the 'cultural background' to legislative and policy formulation on sex offending which 'informs risk selection' (2009: 355).

There are a number of inter-related factors which may account for the shared social intolerance of sex offenders and common retributive penal policies on sex offending (McAlinden, 2012a: 180–2). The first of these relates to media coverage of violent and sexual crime and resultant punitive public attitudes which become part of the wider process of populist penal policy (Simon, 1998). New forms of state regulation are often precipitated by scandals in 'times of crisis' (Moran, 2003: 28; Agamben, 2005). 'Signal crimes' (Innes, 2004) in the form of high profile cases of sexual offending against children, have been instrumental in cementing social and political interpretations of the perceived threat posed by sex offenders and increasing levels of punitivity.

As I have noted above, there are a number of dominant themes in recent media coverage of high profile cases of sexual abuse within the United Kingdom and Ireland (McAlinden, 2006b, 2007a: 18–23). These themes have been assimilated to a greater or lesser extent into specific debates on sexual grooming and how to protect children from this particular risk that sex offenders may pose. They include revelations about organized abuse in environments traditionally considered secure such as children's homes, clubs, and schools—discussed separately in Chapter 5 in relation to institutional grooming and abuse; the prevalence of 'stranger danger' cases which highlight the dangers posed by released sex offenders living in the local community who were previously unknown to the victim—a theme which was discussed in the previous chapter and which reoccurs throughout the book; and the media-led cry for a more punitive criminal justice response—which has ultimately come to fruition by the widespread adoption of regulatory penal policies based primarily on public protection, risk management, and preventive governance.

The overall effect is to convey the impression that sex offenders are living on every street corner, potentially threatening the safety of all children (Wardle, 2007). Intense media coverage of violent and sexual crime means that penal policy is subjected to increased public scrutiny and debate (Pratt, 2008b: 286). Media coverage may suggest that such crime is more ubiquitous or threatening than is actually the case and that harsher punishment is required in response (Greer, 2003; Roberts et al, 2003; Pfeiffer, Windizio, and Kleinham, 2005). As the number of high profile cases of sex offending increases, so too does the demand for tougher penal policies. Certainly the range of headlines on grooming outlined at the beginning of the previous chapter is indicative of the fact that the risk of grooming has also been subsumed within this populist rubric.

Secondly, levels of punitivity may also have their roots in prevailing religious cultures and traditions. Awareness of child sexual abuse was first heightened among professionals and the public in the United States in the 1970s (Kempe, 1978; Finkelhor, 1979) and later in Great Britain (Parton, 1985). Catholic cultures, however, such as France and Southern Germany were slower to recognize sexual abuse as a moral, legal, and social problem, compared to Protestant or secularized cultures such as the United States, England, Canada, Sweden, Norway, the Netherlands, and Northern Germany (Bagley and King, 1990: 25–37). Melossi (2001) also affirms that social, economic, and political relationships and conditions which shape leniency or forgiveness on the one hand and punitivity on the other have their roots in religious traditions. His comparison of Protestant societies such as the United States or England and Wales and Catholic societies such as Italy in relation to differential rates of imprisonment reveals a juxtaposition of 'a rhetoric of strong penal repression' and 'soft authoritarian paternalism' (Melossi, 2001: 412). According to these arguments, other predominantly Protestant societies such as Scotland and Northern Ireland would also have a tendency to adopt more punitive criminal justice responses.[28] As noted above, the Republic of Ireland, however, as a state profoundly shaped by Catholic morality and ideology has not pursued a punitive regulatory agenda on sex offending with the same rigour as the United Kingdom, and legislation enacting supervisory methods for sex offenders has often emerged some years later.

A third argument relates to the integrated nature of state-citizen relations in the United Kingdom. It has been argued in this context that late modernity is characterized by a public distrust of experts unless what they opine accords with its own worries and perceptions about risk (Best, 1990; Petrunik and Deutschmann, 2008). In other Western European jurisdictions, however, such as Germany (Zedner, 1995; Savelsberg, 1999) or the Scandinavian countries (Pratt, 2008a, 2008b), state apparatus are intensely bureaucratic and expert-driven and decision-makers are afforded a greater degree of trust by the public. Law and order is expressly the preserve of the state and there is no expectation that ordinary citizens should have an influence on or involvement in the policy process (Petrunik and Deutschmann, 2008). This insulation of the legal system from political influence has generally halted the spread of 'penal populism' across much of Europe (Tonry, 2001: 207). Similarly, in the Republic of Ireland, as noted above, reduced reliance on formal methods of social control has been attributed, inter alia, to high levels of confidence in the police and other justice agencies (O'Donnell, Baumer, and Hughes, 2008: 126). In the United Kingdom, on the other hand, risk is grounded in a 'wider politics of fear and insecurity' (Seddon, 2008: 312) concerning sex offenders where professional assessments are often subjected to emotive and sometimes misplaced populist assumptions about future risk.

[28] In the 2001 Census, for example, 42.4 per cent of people in Scotland stated that their religion was Church of Scotland, while in Northern Ireland, a similar percentage of 39.5 per cent of people gave their religion as Protestant (either Presbyterian, Church of Ireland, or Methodist), with the remaining figure in both countries being made up of Catholics, other religion/Christian, or no religion stated. See respectively Northern Ireland and Scotland Census 2001, <http://www.scotland.gov.uk/Publications/2005/02/20757/53570> and <http://www.nisranew.nisra.gov.uk/census/Census2001Output/UnivariateTables/uv_tables1.html#community%20background> (both accessed 10 May 2011).

A move from elitist to more populist penal policy-making, where governments consult the views of ordinary people prior to formulating new crime policies (Johnstone, 2000), has ultimately resulted in harsher, less tolerant policies towards sex offenders.

Key Developments in Sex Offender Risk Management

As outlined at the outset of this chapter, within 'postmodern penality' (Pratt, 2000a) sex offenders are singled out as an extraordinary class of offender (Garland, 2001) by virtue of the emotive nature of the crime and the special risk they are seen as presenting (Pratt, 2000b). This 'differential justice' (Weaver and McNeill, 2010: 274) for sex offenders has been reflected in a policy of 'punishment plus' which has in turn been manifested in two main ways—via extended 'public protection' sentences and enhanced post-release supervision in the community. As Kemshall and Wood have argued, '[e]ffective regulation is in effect secured by exclusion, either by selective incapacitation or by intensive and restrictive measures in the community' (2007: 211).

Reference has already been made to the higher number of life or indeterminate sentences in England and Wales and Scotland. Supervisory measures for managing sex offenders effectively extend the sphere of control from prison into the community (Kleinhans, 2002: 244–6). From the late-1990s onwards, there was a reactionary and sustained focus on the community surveillance of sex offenders within the broad political rhetoric of risk management and increased public protection (Parton et al, 1997; Kemshall and Maguire, 2001; Parton, 2006). The overt politicization of deviant sexual behaviour has resulted in 'hyper innovation' (Moran, 2003; Crawford, 2006) and a flurry of regulatory activity to preventively govern risk within a few short years. A range of proposals to control sex offenders in the community more effectively were formulated (Home Office, 1996) based on the twin aims of specific deterrence and community protection (Shute, 2004: 14; McAlinden, 2007a: 107–8). These eventually became embodied in a comprehensive range of legislation in England and Wales in particular as well as the United Kingdom as a whole. Two key areas, however, have been subject to significant legislative and policy focus—sex offender notification and pre-employment vetting. These broader regulatory developments are also indicative of the drive to tighten behavioural controls on sex offenders in the community and to pre-emptively manage the risk of sexual harm.

Notification was initially provided for by Part I of the Sex Offenders Act 1997 and later replaced by much enhanced arrangements under Part 2 of the Sexual Offences Act 2003 (Thomas 2003).[29] The scheme, which applies to the whole of the United Kingdom, requires certain categories of sex offender to notify the police in person of their name and address and any subsequent changes to these details. The conditions attached to notification and the degree of public disclosure vary depending on the assessed level of risk.[30] The scope of notification has also been widened through two further measures—notification orders[31] and foreign travel orders.[32] The former require offenders who have received convictions for sexual offences abroad to comply with the legislation. The latter specifically prevent those offenders with convictions involving children from travelling abroad and targeting children in other countries. Part 2 of the 2003 Act also introduced risk of sexual harm orders (RSHOs)[33] and sexual offences prevention orders (SOPOs)[34] (Shute, 2004). Additional provision has been made for SOPOs in Scotland[35] where RSHOs have also been legislated for separately, although on similar terms.[36] SOPOs can be used to prohibit the offender from frequenting places where there are children such as parks and school playgrounds. RSHOs seek to criminalize the preparatory acts involved in abuse and can be used whether or not the individual has a prior record of offending. Sex offenders can also be subjected to a wide range of conditions as part of a SOPO. This may include, for example, prohibitions or restrictions on accessing the internet (Walden and Wasik, 2011).

In the Republic of Ireland, the Sex Offenders Act 2001 provided for a major package of reforms designed to protect the public against

[29] For a comprehensive critique of notification and related orders, see McAlinden (2007a: ch 5 and 131–7). See also Cobley (2005: 361–75) and Thomas (2005: 153–67).

[30] The Supreme Court has ruled that a lifetime notification requirement, without periodic review, breaches privacy rights under art 8 of the ECHR (*R (on the application of F and Thompson) v Secretary of State for the Home Department* [2010] UKSC 17).

[31] Sexual Offences Act 2003, ss 97–103.

[32] Ibid, ss 114–22, as amended by The Policing and Crime Act 2009, ss 23–5.

[33] Ibid, ss 123–9.

[34] Ibid, ss 104–13.

[35] Protection of Children and the Prevention of Sexual Offences (Scotland) Act 2005, ss 2–8.

[36] Ibid, s 17.

sex offenders, including post-release supervision (McAlinden, 2000). This also included, inter alia, a comprehensive notification procedure or tracking system for all convicted sex offenders which is provided for by Part 2 of that Act. The notification provisions apply also to persons convicted outside the Irish state and to those intending to leave the state for a brief period, in much the same way as notification orders and foreign travel orders in the United Kingdom as outlined above. Similarly, sex offender orders within the Irish legislation apply in a similar way to SOPOs in the United Kingdom. However, there is no specific provision for RSHOs in the Republic of Ireland.

As noted above, the RSHO, as a civil preventive measure, can be used to try to capture acts which may feature as a prelude to abuse, including the grooming of children, where an individual has been identified as posing a risk to children. It may be made by a magistrates' court on application by the police where a person has, on at least two occasions, engaged in sexually explicit conduct or communication with a child, and where this is deemed necessary to protect the child from physical or psychological harm. The preemptory nature of this measure and the fact that it can be used whether or not the individual has a record of offending also makes it rather controversial (McAlinden, 2007a: 135). The provision is so widely drafted that some legitimate acts with a non-sexual motive might also be caught (Cleland, 2005). Moreover, in line with the broad theoretical framework outlined above, such measures share a common limitation in terms of protecting children from sexual harm—they are focused on known risks and not the hidden and, therefore, potentially most dangerous ones (McAlinden, 2006a).

The primary legislative responses to sexual grooming as a particular category of risk posed by sex offenders in the community, are in the form of pre-employment vetting and the offence of meeting a child following sexual grooming. With the former, there are a number of inherent problems with the recent expansion of the regulatory framework on sex offending as well as with the process of vetting in particular. With the latter, there are a range of potential evidential issues as well as inherent practical problems for law enforcement. It will be argued further that collectively such difficulties have negative implications for capturing and preventing grooming behaviour within a purely legal framework.

Multi-agency arrangements on public protection

In the United Kingdom, the legislative and policy framework on sex offender risk management has been enhanced by the development of a cohesive inter-agency infrastructure which emphasizes the exchange of relevant information about offenders who pose a serious risk to public safety (Kemshall and Maguire, 2001, 2002). Since at least the late 1990s, previously informal initiatives by various agencies (Sampson et al, 1988) have been reinforced by the adoption of 'joined up' working (Cowan, Pantazis, and Gilroy, 2001: 439) and 'the end to end management of the offender'.[37] In place of a model of professional 'expertise', is one that emphasizes inter-agency cooperation and the importance of diverse knowledgeable agencies (Crawford, 1997: 59). This is part of a broader trend in governmental approaches to crime control which prioritizes the related notions of 'active citizenship', 'partnership', and 'multi-agency working' (Crawford, 1997; Sullivan, 2002; Gilling, 2007) as the most modern, effective, and efficient means of policy formulation and service delivery (Crawford, 1997: 55–6; Stoker, 2003; Huxham and Vangen, 2005) in responding to crime and anti-social behaviour (Burnett and Appleton, 2004; Hough, Millie, and Jacobson, 2005; Squires, 2008; Harvie and Manzi, 2011).[38] Such developments have been particularly evident in relation to the twin areas of child protection (Wigfall and Moss, 2001) and sex offender management (see eg Kemshall and Maguire, 2001, 2002; Maguire and Kemshall, 2004). As Cowan, Pantazis, and Gilroy argue, the upshot of these recent developments in the area of risk 'has been the evolution of an organisational paradigm of "protection of the public" which crosses institutional boundaries' (2001: 440). It is proposed to briefly outline the multi-agency approach to sex offender

---

[37] In England and Wales, since 2004, the probation and prison services have been combined under the auspices of the National Offender Management Service (NOMS), <http://www.justice.gov.uk/publications/docs/noms-agency-framework.pdf> (accessed 10 May 2011).

[38] Although the terms 'multi-agency' and 'inter-agency' are used interchangeably in the literature (Liddle and Gelsthorpe, 1994), Crawford and Jones draw attention to the differences between various conceptions of 'partnership' work. They make the distinction between 'multi-agency' relations, which simply involve the coming together of a range of agencies in relation to a given problem, and 'inter-agency' relations which entail some degree of fusion of relations between agencies (1995: 30–1).

risk assessment and management in the United Kingdom and the Republic of Ireland as a prelude to the inclusion of the primary data from interviews with key criminal justice and other professionals which features in Parts II and III of the book.

Multi-agency arrangements in relation to the effective assessment and management of sex offenders were in part formalized as a result of Part I of the Sex Offenders Act 1997, which came into force on 1 September 1997,[39] and required certain categories of sex offenders to notify their name and address to the police. In accordance with the guidelines issued under the Act, agencies were required to cooperate more closely to identify, assess, monitor, and manage the risk presented by registered sex offenders in the interests of public protection and a better exchange of information (Home Office, 1997). These arrangements were further formalized with the introduction of Multi-Agency Public Protection Panels (MAPPPs), first in England and Wales, and later elsewhere, which are coordinated nationally by the Public Protection Unit within the National Offender Management Service (Kemshall and Maguire, 2001, 2002; Maguire et al, 2001; Bryan and Doyle, 2003; Lieb, 2003; Maguire and Kemshall, 2004).

In England and Wales, sections 67–68 of the Criminal Justice and Courts Services Act 2000 (Maguire and Kemshall, 2004) place a duty on the police and probation services as 'the responsible authority' to establish arrangements for assessing and managing the risks posed by sex offenders and other potentially dangerous offenders in the community. These arrangements were enhanced by the Criminal Justice Act 2003 which extended the responsible authority to include the prison service.[40] The Act also established a reciprocal 'duty to co-operate' between the responsible authority and a number of other agencies such as local education, housing, health, and social services authorities.[41] While the central role in risk management meetings is undertaken by the police, probation, and prison services, other agencies feed into this process. Important contributions are also made by other bodies such as social services, local housing authorities, mental health providers, as well as a range of voluntary agencies such as the National Association for the Care and Resettlement of Offenders

---

[39] These provisions have since been re-enacted by the Sexual Offences Act 2003. See also note 29 and accompanying text above.

[40] Criminal Justice Act 2003, s 325(1).

[41] Ibid, s 325(6).

(NACRO),[42] who provide training and employment initiatives, independent or private treatment providers, as well as those involved in victim counselling and support (Cowan, Pantazis, and Gilroy, 2001). The presence of a strong, vibrant voluntary sector throughout the United Kingdom as a whole, and within Northern Ireland in particular, has provided a professional, pragmatic, and considered approach to questions relating to sex offenders that has prevented the United Kingdom from adopting some of the more extreme measures of the United States and other jurisdictions (McAlinden, 2007a: 30).

The central task of Multi-Agency Public Protection Arrangements (MAPPA) is to facilitate the exchange of information between agencies and classify sex offenders into risk categories based on a high, medium, or low risk of re-offending in order to allocate resources appropriately and develop individual offender management plans (Kemshall and Maguire, 2001, 2002; Maguire et al, 2001).[43] The categories of offender to whom public protection arrangements apply are broadly consistent across the United Kingdom.[44] For example, while category three (high risk) offenders are managed on a multi-agency basis, category one (low risk) offenders are managed on a single agency basis, usually by the police or probation. The logic of this risk assessment is that it targets those offenders who pose the greatest risk to the public (Bryan and Doyle, 2003; Lieb, 2003), sometimes referred to as the 'critical few'. As noted above, these panels now have the power to disclose information about offenders to schools, voluntary agencies, and other groups in the community which is currently one of the most controversial areas within the recent developments relating to sex offender risk management (Power, 2003). More recently, members of the public are also being recruited to contribute to the strategic risk management of MAPPA (Home Office, 2002: 15).

In Northern Ireland, the Multi-Agency Sex Offender Risk Assessment and Management (MASRAM) arrangements were formally

---

[42] The Northern Irish and Scottish equivalents are NIACRO and SACRO.

[43] See MAPPA guidance for England and Wales: <http://www.lbhf.gov.uk/Images/MAPPA%20Guidance%20(2009)%20Version%203%200%20_tcm21–120559.pdf> (accessed 10 May 2011).

[44] Note that England and Wales has an additional 'very high risk' category in addition to high, medium, and low risk. See Stafford et al (2011) for a detailed critical discussion.

launched in May 2002. Following the enactment of Part 3 of the Criminal Justice (NI) Order 2008, the MASRAM arrangements were replaced with broader and enhanced statutory arrangements for protecting the public from the risk posed by sex offenders under the auspcies of the Public Protection Arrangements Northern Ireland (PPANI) (McAlinden, 2009: 37–9).[45] The framework has now been extended to non-sexual violent offenders and includes lay advisers who work on a voluntary basis, as happens in England and Wales. Similar Multi-Agency Public Protection Arrangements had a phased introduction in Scotland under sections 10–11 of the Management of Offenders etc (Scotland) Act 2005 from September 2006 (Weaver and McNeill, 2010).[46] There are, however, some notable differences between the schemes (Weaver and McNeil, 2010: 280).

Unlike MAPPA in England and Wales, in Scotland the 'responsible authorities' are the police, the prison service, and the local authority social work departments (criminal justice social work or probation) (Stafford et al, 2011). MAPPA in Scotland also generally exclude young sexual offenders, who are dealt with through the diversionary Children's Hearing system (Stafford and Vincent, 2008); only registered convicted offenders and those acquitted on the grounds of insanity are managed, and not those, for example, subject to a probation or supervisory order; at the time of writing, violent and other dangerous offenders are not included; and there is no provision for lay advisers. In addition, as noted above, the Risk Management Authority (RMA) in Scotland exists as a unique body to oversee and administer the assessment and management of risk and to manage the OLR process in particular.[47] On conviction, the 'lead authority'—the Scottish Prison Service in respect of an offender who has received a custodial sentence, or Criminal Justice Social Work, where the offender has received a community disposal—has a legal requirement to submit a Risk Management Plan to the RMA. Risk assessment, in this respect, may also be carried

---

[45] See arts 49–51 and *Public Protection Arrangements—Guidance to Agencies*, issued under art 50, <http://www.nio.gov.uk/public_protection_arrangements_-_guidance_to_agencies.pdf> (accessed 10 May 2011).

[46] See MAPPA guidance for Scotland: <http://www.scotland.gov.uk/Publications/2008/04/18144823/3> (accessed 10 May 2011).

[47] The RMA was set up under Part 1 of the Criminal Justice (Scotland) Act 2003.

out by accredited risk-assessors, usually forensic or clinical psychologists who are responsible for reporting their findings to the RMA and the High Court in relation to the making of an OLR (Darjee and Russell, 2011). The introduction of ViSOR (Violent and Sexual Offender Register) across the United Kingdom from August 2005 has facilitated cooperative working between core agencies, such as police, probation, and prisons, in the management of information about individuals who pose a risk of serious harm. This searchable computer database standardizes information and allows for instant information sharing.[48]

The UK paradigm has generally been endorsed as an exemplar of best practice (Bryan and Doyle, 2003; Lieb, 2003). While the Republic of Ireland has in some respects tried to enhance its recent penal policies on sex offender management following the UK model, there is no formal inter-agency structure at present. As noted above, a number of initiatives have been set up to facilitate the exchange of information between key agencies, such as the police, on both sides of the border in Northern Ireland and the Republic of Ireland. In this vein, further efforts to formalize inter-agency cooperation and the exchange of relevant information about offenders between criminal justice and other agencies within the Republic of Ireland are ongoing. Following responses to a Department of Justice and Law Reform (2009) Discussion Document on *The Management of Sex Offenders*, the Sex Offender Risk Assessment and Management Model is being piloted in five regions—Louth, Mayo, Tipperary, Dublin North, and Cork City—ahead of the drafting of a statutory framework. As also noted above, however, the complexity of inter-agency cooperation is enhanced when an offender subject to MAPPA arrangements moves between jurisdictions within the United Kingdom and Ireland.

Coordination is clearly the touchstone of inter-agency processes which are based around a federation rather than a unification of agencies with the same core goal of public protection (Parton et al, 1997; Kemshall and Maguire, 2001). However, differences in approach to the problem of offender management may result in fragmented working practices and in a breakdown of effective communication of information about offenders. As Young (1991) puts it, different

---

[48] The ViSoR scheme was heralded as a major step forward in crime prevention. See eg 'Offender Database to Cut Crime', *BBC News On-line*, 19 August 2005, <http://news.bbc.co.uk/1/hi/uk/4163764.stm> (accessed 19 April 2011).

criminal justice agencies may have a different 'purchase on a given crime problem' due to their particular expertise. The potentially problematic nature of inter-agency relations is well documented in the literature in terms of the competing organizational cultures, functions, priorities, philosophies, and working practices (eg Young, 1991; Crawford, 1997; Kemshall and Maguire, 2001).

Deep-seated power differentials which exist between agencies are said to underpin inter-organizational networks (Blagg et al, 1988; Sampson et al, 1988, 1991; Pearson et al, 1992; Crawford and Jones, 1995; Crawford, 1997: 127–31) and may have particular resonance for the issue of information sharing and privileged access to confidential information about offenders (Sampson et al, 1991: 132). Moreover, there may be institutional resistance to multi-agency discourses where 'partnerships' located high in the rank structure at senior managerial level are difficult to operationalize on the ground (Hope and Murphy, 1983; Crawford, 1997: 107–8). More recently, it has been argued in relation to domestic violence, for example, that the ascendancy, inter alia, of criminal justice and managerialist discourses has resulted in the dominance of the statutory sector and the consequent marginalization or alienation of the voluntary sector, including victims' advocate groups (Harvie and Manzi, 2001). Ironically, therefore, in seeking to manage risk across organizational boundaries, it is the pursuit of risk management itself which may undermine the ideology and practice of multi-agency partnerships. As noted in Chapter 1 (and Appendix 1), inter-agency cooperation, including that across jurisdictional boundaries, is a related subsidiary issue in this research. Differences in organizational experience and responses to grooming behaviours across the various agencies and jurisdictions will be highlighted in the second part of the book.

Conclusion

This chapter has outlined the legislative and policy frameworks on sex offender risk management within and across the United Kingdom and the Republic of Ireland which represent pre-emptive and preventive approaches to anticipated sexual harm. In this respect, as Newburn has written regarding comparative penality in general, there is evidence of 'diffusion, differentiation and resistance' (2010) in relation to regulatory policies on sex offending in general and on grooming specifically. Broadly speaking, exclusionary penal policies on sexual crime, based largely on incapacitation and targeted surveillance, have diffused themselves throughout the four jurisdictions of the United Kingdom and Ireland with plenty of examples of convergence but with 'some differences in the detail' (Stafford et al, 2011). In each of these four regions, sex offenders have been subjected to deliberate and sustained public, political, and organizational focus because of the special risk they are seen as presenting. As a result, a large body of legislation based on situational attempts (Wortley and Smallbone, 2006) to control the location and actions of sex offenders has been enacted within the last decade. The recent legal and policy innovations to combat sexual grooming and prevent harm to children even before it occurs represent the high point of this ascendant regulatory momentum.

There are, however, also points of divergence between these various countries and in relation to the Republic of Ireland in particular, more localized responses to combating sexual crime. It is interesting and quite telling, however, that while most but not all mechanisms for preventively controlling the risk posed by sex offenders against children translate across all nations, the offence of meeting a child following sexual grooming/certain preliminary contact/for the purpose of sexual exploitation features prominently in the recent regulatory frameworks of all four jurisdictions. This fact is indicative of a number of important points in relation to the social and political construction of sex offender risk which transcends differences in social and political economies—it provides further evidence of the differential treatment of sexual crime as a special category of offence meriting an extra-legal response, particularly where children are concerned; it is also broadly reflective of the current 'panic' that exists in the public sphere, and which has made its way in turn into official criminal justice policy, concerning the risks of grooming, particularly in on-line situations. Moreover, as will be discussed in the last part of the book, the current inflated levels of public and official unease and suspicion surrounding the risk posed by sex offenders towards children also have implications for advocating the integration of a broader social response to sex offending to work in tandem with the existing regulatory framework.

PART II

Grooming Processes and Preventive Policies and Procedures

4

The Grooming of Children, Families, and Communities

We do not wish to believe such callousness exists, but it does and always has. A sign of a robust syndrome is when it is found in vastly different time periods and cultures (Salter, 2003: 128).

Following on from the exposition of the broad typologies of grooming behaviour which were set out in the first part of the book, this chapter seeks to critically examine the multiple meanings of grooming within the context of offending processes as they take place with particular children, families, and communities. It will be demonstrated that the offender's sphere of control may extend beyond the direct grooming of the intended victim to the psychological grooming of their family and manipulation of the surrounding environment (Wolf, 1985; Leberg, 1997; Craven, Brown, and Gilchrist, 2006). Each of these forms of grooming creates the capacity or opportunity to abuse while reducing the possibility of discovery or disclosure.

To fully understand the nature of grooming and its significance in sexual abuse cases, it is necessary to first consider theories of sexual offending and the acknowledged role of grooming within the offending process. In critically discussing the intricacies and subtleties implicit in the processes of child grooming, familial and societal grooming, the chapter also draws out the important differences between intra-familial and extra-familial contexts as well as those between on-line and face-to-face settings. The chapter concludes with a detailed critical examination of the grooming process which has emerged from the primary research for this book—interviews with key stakeholders who work in the fields of child protection, victim support or sex offender assessment, treatment, and management.

Locating Grooming in the Cycle of Sexual Offending

A comprehensive discussion of the various theories of sex offending against children is beyond the scope of this work.[1] A key critique of the main etiological models is that most assume the heterogeneity of offenders, whereas in reality sex offenders are a very diverse group with a wide range of offending patterns (Hollin and Howells, 1991; Grubin, 1998; Prentky, 1999; Bickley and Beech, 2001). The current analysis does not intend to put forward its own typology or model of sexual offending behaviour, but is motivated by a desire to illuminate the broader patterns and processes which underlie the onset of sex offending against children and to examine the role of grooming within these processes.

Some theories preclude explicit consideration of the grooming variable and are focused instead, for example, on offender vulnerability[2] or psychological dysfunction[3] as essential precursors of the motivation to offend. For others, grooming may have an implicit role to play according to the typology of offender. One example is the dichotomy between 'preferential' offenders—who are sexually attracted to children by preference—and 'situational' offenders—who are sexually orientated towards children in particular circumstances (Cohen, Seghorn, and Calmas, 1969; Howells, 1981; Groth, Hobson, and Gary, 1982).[4] This dichotomy has also been used to differentiate between 'fixated pedophiles' who abuse outside the family and 'incest offenders' (Beech, 1998; Bickley and Beech, 2002).

With 'preferential offenders' or 'fixated paedophiles', grooming may have a greater role to play where the offender is pre-disposed to sexual offending against children and sets out from the outset to initiate sexual activity with a child previously unknown to them. Such a distinction, however, may be over-simplistic in that grooming

---

[1] For a critical overview see Ward and Hudson (1998a); Bickley and Beech (2001); and Sheldon and Howitt (2007: 48–69).

[2] See Marshall and Barbaree's (1990) 'Integrated Theory'. See also Hall and Hirschman's (1992) 'Quadripartite Model'.

[3] See Ward and Siegert's (2002) 'Pathways Model'. See also Chambers et al (2009).

[4] Note that other writers further differentiate offenders into three categories: situational (who offend in the course of routine interaction with children); opportunistic (who exploit opportunities when alone with children); and committed/predatory offenders (who seek out positions or relationships involving access to children) (Wortley and Smallbone, 2006: 13–18; Smallbone, Marshall, and Wortley, 2008: 160–2).

can and does occur within intra-familial contexts as well as in those situations where an opportunity to offend presents itself. Indeed, the picture painted of the grooming process in this chapter and the next, is unquestionably intricate. As Elliott, Browne, and Kilcoyne (1995: 109) concluded in their in-depth examination of the grooming strategies and offending patterns of 91 convicted sex offenders, 'There is no foolproof profile'.

A further example is provided by Ward and Hudson's (1998b) 'Self-regulation' or 'Pathways Model' which describes multiple routes into sexual offending based on how offenders self-regulate their actions. These four pathways are classified by the offender's orientation towards sexual offending—by approach or avoidant goals—and by the choice of strategies selected to achieve these goals—explicit/automatic and active/passive. The first two pathways incorporate grooming behaviour in the classic sense. The 'approach-explicit' pathway, for example, involves the offender having a clear desire to sexually offend and the use of careful and explicit planning to carry out the offending, while the 'approach automatic' pathway involves the offender engaging in over learnt scripts for offending with impulsive and often poorly planned behaviours. Indeed, these first two pathways may also relate to the 'preferential/situational' offender dichotomy outlined above. That is, while some offenders desire sexual interaction with children and take deliberate steps to achieve this end, for others, offending may happen in certain situations where the opportunity presents itself. As Sheldon and Howitt argue, however, (citing Sullivan and Beech, 2003), 'such systematic and planned preparation does not always occur' (2007: 59). In the latter situation, I would argue that while grooming may not have an explicit role to play in creating the opportunity to first abuse, it may be effective in facilitating subsequent abuse and in preventing the child's disclosure. This model has been very influential in recent discourses on sex offender assessment and treatment (Ward, Yates, and Long, 2006), generating an array of supporting empirical research (Bickley and Beech, 2002; Webster, 2005; Yates and Kingston, 2006).

Several commentators have located the term grooming within the overall framework of the cycle of abuse where grooming emerges as an integral part of the offence process in terms of what offenders 'think' and 'do' (Howitt, 1995: 73–102; Salter, 1995: 45–97). Three primary models explicitly acknowledge and incorporate the grooming factor, describing how sex offenders rarely abuse indiscriminately. Instead, they carefully plan their abuse, deliberately targeting and recruiting a potential victim and securing their compliance.

The first is Wolf's (1985) 'Addiction Cycle' with its emphasis on 'distorted thinking errors'. This model was influential in the development of early treatment programmes (see Erooga, Clark, and Bentley, 1990; Grubin and Thornton, 1994; Mann and Thornton, 1998; Beech and Fisher, 2004). His model begins with the offender's emotional or social difficulties, managed and compounded by social withdrawal and cognitive distortions. The 'planning stage' involves targeting the victim, setting up the situation, and abusive power relationships. The perspectives of offenders attest that for some sex offenders at least, covert and overt 'premeditation' (Hudson, 2005: 69) and planning may occur both before and after victim targeting (see also Marshall, Serran, and Cortini, 2000). Such foresight on the part of offenders involves invoking deviant sexual fantasies (Swaffer et al, 2000), often fuelled by the use of pornography, as well as the grooming of potential victims (Hudson, 2005: 69). Following the offending behaviour, denial may be replaced by guilt and low self-esteem. This is usually overcome by minimization of the wrongness of sexual contacts with children which allows them to continue abusing a child. The time taken to travel the cycle is shorter as the abuse becomes more ingrained. Grooming not only works to enable sexual offending to take place but, since the victim may have been silenced and the abusive activities normalized via a range of techniques, it may also serve to perpetuate and further entrench patterns of abusive sexual behaviour. Wolf's model presupposes that all sex offenders have poor self-image or other emotional or social shortcomings (see also Ward et al, 1995; Marshall, Anderson, and Champagne, 1997). As Brackenridge (2001: 109) notes, however, in the context of sexual exploitation within sport, offenders often have 'good social skills, high visibility, popularity and a high level of confidence and assertiveness' (Brackenridge, 2001: 109). This argument warns against the dangers of stereotyping and a 'one size fits all' approach to explaining and categorizing grooming behaviour. As will be highlighted further below, these dynamics have particular resonance within organizational and, to a lesser extent, familial contexts.

The second is Finkelhor's (1984) older but much cited 'Precondition model' which establishes four psychological preconditions to sexual abuse. First, is the motivation to offend or the predisposition towards sexual contact with children. This factor may consist of emotional congruence with or a sexual interest in children, as well as the unavailability or unsatisfactory nature of sexual relationships with adults. Secondly, is the ability to overcome internal inhibitions against abusing a child. Thirdly, is the ability to overcome external inhibitors which may reduce the opportunity to offend. These include legal and social norms that tend to mitigate sexually deviant behaviour as well as the protective reach of the child's family and others in the local community. Fourthly, is the need to overcome the victim's resistance to abuse. This may range from threats and coercion to more 'subtle' interactions with victims such as emotional manipulation and 'incentives' (Howitt, 1995: 78–9; see also Pryor, 1996). It is the last two factors—overcoming the victim's resistance, as well as displacing external exhibitors in order to provide the opportunity to offend—which bring grooming in its various guises into play. While Finkelhor's model has been criticized as over simplistic and lacking empirical foundation, it has been 'very positively regarded and extremely influential' (Sheldon and Howitt, 2007: 59; see also Colton and Vanstone, 1998; van Dam, 2001: 89–113; Ward, 2001).[5]

The third is Ward et al's (1995) 'Descriptive Model' which provides a detailed account of the various stages of the sexual offending process based on descriptions of thoughts and feelings provided by 26 incarcerated child sex offenders about their most recent or typical offence. This model identifies nine separate stages which denote the cognitive and behavioural elements which combine to form the offence chain: (1) the offender's background factors; (2) distal planning of access to potential victims, whether implicit, explicit, or by chance;[6] (3) contact with the victim; (4) cognitive restructuring, with either positive or negative outcomes; (5) proximal planning, which has either a self-focus, a victim-focus, or a mutual-focus; (6) the sexual offence itself; (7) further cognitive restructuring; (8) self-evaluation and reflection concerning desistance or continued offending; and (9) the impact of these resolutions on the offender's life. As Craven, Brown, and Gilchrist (2006: 291) note in their critique of this model, since sex offenders may come

---

[5] As Craven, Brown, and Gilchrist point out (2006: 290), while Finkelhor's theory does not expressly use the terminology of 'sexual grooming', later writers have critiqued his work using this term (see eg Morrison, Erooga, and Beckett, 1994; Sampson, 1994, cited in Craven, Brown, and Gilchrist, 2006; see also Ward and Hudson, 2001).

[6] See also Ward and Hudson (2000) for a conceptual overview of implicit planning in particular.

from dysfunctional family backgrounds which are often marked by violence and neglect (Craissati, McClurg, and Browne, 2002), they frequently have a particular need to belong which enhances their sensitivity to social cues (Pickett, Gardener, and Knowles, 2004) and allows them to identify potential vulnerabilities in others (Craven, Brown, and Gilchrist, 2006: 294). They also contend that the process of implicit planning, at the second stage above, may provide a plausible explanation as to why the majority of victims know their offender. While for some offenders, access to a child may occur by chance, the 'cues' which trigger the preparatory stages of abuse are heightened within a familial or quasi-familial context where children are more closely proximate to the offender (Craven, Brown, and Gilchrist, 2006: 293–4). Moreover, to return to the rubric of 'risk', outlined at length in the previous chapter, these various explanations of offending behaviour indicate that the risk posed by sex offenders is not static but rather fluid and that sex offenders may pose different risks at different times within the offending cycle (Ramm, 2011).

Other writers have also provided explanations of the overall place and prevalence of sexual grooming within the context of the interaction between sex offenders and their victims. Canter, Hughes, and Kirby (1998), for example, in their study of behavioural interactions of 96 incarcerated sex offenders against children identified three distinct repertoires—'acknowledged aggressive', which was marked by the use of violence, force, or threats; 'criminal-opportunist', which tended to be one-off random offences perpetrated on strangers; and 'intimate', which was characterized by the use of sexual grooming. This latter category accounted for 45 per cent of their sample. This figure, however, although sizeable, may not be fully representative of the actual extent of sexual grooming used by offenders against children. As a very high proportion of child sex abuse victims know their abuser, offenders have a vested interest in preventing victim disclosure where they would be likely to be readily identified as the perpetrator (Craven, Brown, and Gilchrist, 2006: 289).

Self-grooming

The offender's self-justification of their sexual interest in children is a neglected dimension in current discourses on grooming. To overcome internal inhibitions against engaging in sexual activity with children (Finkelhor, 1984), sex offenders employ 'cognitive distortions' (Ward et al, 1995; Hartley, 1998) or rationalizing discourses which 'redefine reality' (van Dam, 2001: 92). Consistent with Sykes and Matza's (1957) 'techniques of neutralisation', sex offenders adapt a range of excuses and justifications which are often 'maladaptive and supportive of sex with children' (Craven, Brown, and Gilchrist, 2006: 292; see also De Young, 1988). Ward and Keenan (1999) also suggest that such cognitive distortions manifest in the form of what they term 'implicit theories' (see also, Ward, 2000) which relate to how sex offenders see themselves, their victim, and the world around them, allowing their diminution of guilt, shame, and responsibility. Cognitive distortions also facilitate 'self-grooming' because they prevent offenders 'from negatively evaluating themselves' (Craven, Brown, and Gilchrist, 2006: 296).

There is also a degree of overlap between self-grooming and other forms of grooming. In the absence of overt symptoms of harm or the victim's failure to voice objection to the abuse, offenders may believe that the child seduced them or was a willing participant in their activities (Craven, Brown, and Gilchrist, 2006: 292). 'Success' in grooming the child or their family, these authors argue, may further entrench sexually harmful behaviours and motivations, while failure may lead offenders to either desist from sexual offending or further hone their grooming skills. In this respect, excerpts from some of the earliest interviews with convicted sex offenders conducted by Tony Parker in the 1960s demonstrate their tendency to fail to recognize the inappropriate nature of their relationships with children. One offender convicted on numerous occasions of sexual offences against young boys commented:

I must admit I did go so far as to forget myself, I laid hands on them. Nothing serious, please don't think that, I didn't attack them or anything of that kind. Only playing about, touching them, that was as far as it went. They didn't object, they didn't complain, it was a harmless bit of fun you might say. It never crossed my mind they hadn't liked it, they seemed willing enough (Soothill, 1999: 125–6).

Other offenders admitted their behaviour but blamed the victim (see also van Dam, 2001: 127): '... the boys had made things difficult for me ... Hardly left me in peace at all they didn't, Sunday after Sunday they'd be round' (Soothill, 1999: 130). Some sex offenders employed euphemisms to refer to their commission of sexual offences against children such as 'my usual trouble' or 'this other thing'

(Soothill, 1999: 145, 131).[7] During the course of treatment, some offenders also try to either justify or deny their abusive behaviour towards children (van Dam, 2001; Vanhoeck and van Daele, 2011). Justification and denial lie at the heart of cognitive distortions on the part of sex offenders which many modern treatment programmes are designed to address (Cowburn et al, 1992; Grubin and Thornton, 1994; Beech and Fisher, 2004; Marshall and Marshall, 2011). Self-grooming, therefore, may ultimately impact upon the effectiveness and outcomes of sex offender treatment programmes.

Child Grooming

The term 'grooming' was first highlighted by Anna Salter (1995) to describe the methods used by offenders through which children are 'selected, recruited and maintained' (Conte, Wolf, and Smith, 1989: 293) in a situation of sexual abuse. The expression is generally used to refer to the process by which a potential sex offender skilfully manipulates a child into a situation where he or she can be more readily sexually abused and is simultaneously less likely to disclose (Wyre, 2000; van Dam, 2001).

Trust plays a key role not only in the offender's interactions with the child but also with their family, and within the local community. As noted in Chapter 2, the abuse of trust underlying the grooming process has resonance in establishing intimate and social relationships in a variety of contexts, using a range of deception devices. As Hudson has argued, this might involve an element of inducement or coercion of the child 'or it may simply consist of ensuring that no-one is around' (2005: 155). The grooming process can occur over a short period but more commonly occurs over a longer period to allow the child to feel comfortable (Finkelhor, 1984; Howitt, 1995: 82–4; Davidson, 2004). While some offenders concentrate on a single child (Gillespie, 2008), the patience of the offender can also be partly explained by the fact that it is not uncommon for them to be targeting or grooming several children simultaneously. If the child feels uneasy and breaks off the relationship, other potential victims are readily available. Sex offenders may also undertake a 'dry run' to risk assess the process (Terry and Tallon, 2004: 21).

---

[7] For further examples of denial and minimization by offenders against children, see Silva (1990).

While the earlier literature has been written mainly from the perspective of grooming within face-to-face situations in the real world, a number of insights have more recently emerged into the process of on-line grooming. This chapter differentiates between both forms of grooming for the purposes of clarity and critical discussion. However, while not all sexually exploitative on-line contacts result in meetings off-line, research shows that there is correlation between use of the internet and contact sexual offences (eg Wilson and Jones, 2008) and between 'digital and traditional threat victimisation' (van Wilsem, 2011) more generally. The connection between internet and contact sexual offences is unlikely to be a 'unidirectional path' as many internet offenders also have a history of contact sexual offences (Mercado, Merdian, and Egg, 2011: 520). This blurring of the boundaries between real and virtual worlds (Talamo and Ligorio, 2001: 11) reinforces the potential breadth of abusive behaviour towards children.

Face-to-face contexts

As noted in the first part of the book, the meaning of grooming in legal and sociological contexts is uncertain, reflecting something of the phenomenon itself. Many sex offenders, however, adopt a range of well-developed 'subtle and non-aggressive techniques' (Sas and Cunningham, 1995: 24) for manipulating children and normalizing sexually harmful relationships. A primary consideration, largely absent from the existing literature, is to differentiate those situations where 'stranger' abusers tend to ingratiate themselves with a child or their parents or carers in order to become part of the family, from those where the abuser is part of the family or a trusted 'intimate' of the child. Grooming within face-to-face situations can be further subdivided into extra-familial and intra-familial contexts. The categories of extra-familial or intra-familial abuse are not mutually exclusive (Itzin, 2001; Studer et al, 2011). Indeed, Kelly and colleagues have argued that it is 'dangerous' to create such separate classifications (Kelly, Regan, and Burton, 2000: 14), based on a perceived level of risk. Within the 'continuum of child sexual abuse' (Kelly, 1988: 76; see also Itzin, 2001: 40–2; Studer et al, 2011: 499), for example, there may also be a number of overlapping features, including the fact that individuals can abuse their own as well as other people's children. Nonetheless, while there are shared elements within each type of grooming process there are also important distinctions.

Extra-familial abuse

In many cases the offender is previously unknown to the child or their family and the purpose of grooming behaviours in such a context is to create a situation where the child in particular feels comfortable with and trusts the offender. Every victim's experience will be different, particularly because offenders modify their behaviour based on the reaction and responses of the child during the grooming process. There are, however, several documented stages to this process (see generally, Budin and Johnston, 1989; Conte, Wolf, and Smith, 1989; Berliner and Conte, 1990, 1995; Christiansen and Blake, 1990; Hunter, Goodwin, and Wilson, 1992; Watkins and Bentovim, 1992; Elliott, Browne, and Kilcoyne, 1995; Smallbone and Wortley, 2000). Grooming, in this sense, has been termed a 'cyclical process' (Howitt, 1995: 82–4). While there may be a sequential sense of progression through the various stages, some of the earlier elements—including the offender's emphasis on the 'special' nature of their relationship with the child, and their use of sexual materials or conversations to invoke shame or guilt on the part of the victim—may reoccur to ensure that the child remains entrapped and is less likely to disclose.

First, grooming typically includes befriending a potential victim by becoming familiar with the child's interests and being helpful and confiding to gain their confidence and trust. Offenders who victimize children outside their immediate families employ various strategies to recruit victims including frequenting places where children are likely to go such as parks or schools (Lang and Frenzel, 1998), and 'taking the chance' if a child approaches them (Elliott, Browne, and Kilcoyne, 1995: 584). Many sex offenders select and identify vulnerable children and their families and then use that vulnerability to initiate a 'friendship' as an avenue to eventually sexually abuse a child (Elliott, Browne, and Kilcoyne, 1995: 584; Salter, 1995: 39, 62). In the study by Elliott and colleagues (1995: 584), for example, nearly half of offenders (49 per cent) based victim selection on children who seemed to lack confidence or had low self-esteem, and a third of offenders 'worked on becoming welcome in the child's home'. As Sas and Cunningham note, the issue of 'differential vulnerability to abuse' is highly complex and not easily studied (1995: 67). It includes, for example, children with special needs and learning disabilities (Gallagher, 1998: 807–11) or with a physical or mental disability or both (Powell, 2007: 34–5). It also includes children 'who have experienced a significant degree of emotional, social and economical disadvantage' (Sas and Cunningham, 1995: 78) who are facing a range of 'family problems' as well as 'personal challenges' (Sas and Cunningham, 1995: 67; see also Salter, 1995), such as those who 'lack confidence or…[have] low self-esteem' (Elliott, Browne, and Kilcoyne, 1995: 584). Offenders also target children who have already been victimized by others in the belief that they will be easier to re-victimize (Boney-McCoy and Finkelhor, 1995; Leberg, 1997).

Secondly, the offender will cultivate a 'special' friendship by bestowing a variety of inducements or rewards such as money, comics, or sweets or even unexpected treats such as trips to the cinema or fast-food restaurants. This stage also takes the form of the bestowing of extra privileges such as 'friendship, attention, security, [and] love' (Sas and Cunningham, 1995: 68) rather than tangible 'reward' and is the integral element of inherent coercion which lies at the heart of the grooming process (Conte, Wolf, and Smith, 1989: 293). The adoption of a 'pseudo-parental role' (Powell, 2007: 29–30) and the emphasis on the exclusivity of the relationship helps to 'distance' the child from their parents or others who represent a source of safety and prevent the abusive behaviour from being detected by others.[8] It also enables the offender to control the victim through the giving or withholding of rewards. In some cases, bribes or rewards escalate into threats or the use of force against either the child or their family to ensure the child's continued secrecy and compliance (Smallbone and Wortley, 2000).

Thirdly, the offender often uses 'forbidden fruit' type activities such as cursing, telling 'dirty jokes', or showing the child pornography in order to introduce sexual themes into their conversations and to make them more susceptible to abuse (Lanning, 1998).[9] Drugs or alcohol have also been used to make the victim more compliant (Kaufman et al, 1998). This stage includes talking about

[8] While the majority of writers consider isolation of the victim from others as part of the grooming process (eg Budin and Johnson, 1989; Conte, Wolf, and Smith, 1989; van Dam, 2001), others regard this as distinct from grooming (eg Warner, 2000; Leberg, 2007).

[9] The use of pornography as part of the grooming cycle is generally well established (Taylor and Quayle, 2003; Ost, 2009). A minority of writers, however, disagree with this position arguing that there is a lack of clear evidence in this regard (Williams, 2004: 251).

sexual and other topics, such as marital problems, that are not age appropriate. It also includes invading the child's privacy by, for example, walking in on him or her in the bathroom or while they are undressing, or exposing themselves while they are getting dressed together. This not only normalizes sexual behaviour but is used to entrap the child further. The use of pornography in particular encourages feelings of shame and guilt which the offender can exploit by persuading the child that they were complicit in these activities. These factors in turn reinforce the secrecy of the abusive activities, further isolate the child and make them less willing to tell others because they feel that no one would believe them. In particular, offenders may reinforce the child's fear about the reaction of their parents or carers if they found out what they had been doing. As one offender commented in Elliott, Browne, and Kilcoyne's study (1995: 590), 'secrecy and blame were my best weapons'.

Finally, the offender will exploit the child's natural naivety and trust by introducing increasingly intimate physical contact such as play acting, tickling, or wrestling and even hugging and kissing to gradually sexualize contact with the child. The use of touch is particularly important as this determines whether or not the child is receptive and begins the process of desensitization—gradually the abuser escalates boundary violations of the child's body in order to desensitize the victim to further abuse. As part of the desensitization stage, the offender may talk about other totally unrelated topics to deflect attention away from the act of sexually touching a child. The process eventually culminates in enticing the child to concede to engaging in sexual activity. The grooming process continues after the abuse as the offender needs to avoid detection and ensure the child's silence. Victims have also been groomed to introduce further victims to the process of grooming and abuse (McAlinden, 2006a: 347).

There are also differences in the grooming of younger and older children (Sanderson, 2004: 178–83). Younger children whose social skills are not yet developed are less able to identify 'relevant cues' (Choo, 2009: x) such as 'inappropriate remarks' (Lamb and Brown, 2006; Olson et al, 2007). Younger children may also see sexual abuse as normal and may not recognize it as abuse (Sanderson, 2004: 259) while older children may be 'recruited' without their parents also being groomed (Sanderson, 2004: 180). As noted, however, a minority of writers have argued that although grooming 'is not new behaviour', it does not always 'follow an identifiable pattern' (Gillespie, 2007b: 6). This particular issue, which also makes grooming difficult to address within legislative and policy contexts, will be returned to below in relation to the primary research.

Indeed, the innocuous nature of much of the relationship forming with a child as a prelude to abuse (Gillespie, 2005: 4; 2006: 240), as outlined in the brief overview of the literature above, makes it difficult to isolate and pinpoint any 'insidious and malignant' (Sas and Cunningham, 1995: 78) motivation on the part of the offender, particularly in the early stages of the process. The difficulties inherent in the early identification of sexual motivation towards children which goes beyond harmless and inoffensive behaviour makes grooming extremely problematic to regulate and police proactively, particularly within intra-familial situations in off-line or face-to-face encounters. It could be argued that these early stages of the 'grooming process'—for example the befriending or relationship-forming stage where offenders may offer a variety of inducements or treats—are usually only identifiable with the benefit of contextual hindsight—once a disclosure or discovery of child abuse has been established.

Others have contended that the grooming procedure is very effective, and that consequently, the vast majority of child sexual abuse remains hidden and undisclosed or is subject to significant delays in reporting or disclosure (see eg Sas and Cunningham, 1995) (see Chapter 2). In research by Conte, Wolf, and Smith (1989), for example, offenders' accounts demonstrated that the fear of disclosure affected the strategies they employed and specifically how and when they abused their victims. Feelings of 'affection, dependency, repugnance, and fear' (Sas and Cunningham, 1995: 68) towards the offender, together conspire to silence children and inhibit their disclosures of abuse. At the same time, however, a complex range of emotions on the part of the child such as embarrassment, guilt, and shame concerning their sexual victimization are the latent consequences of child sexual abuse. It is these emotions, together with the power imbalance between victims and offenders, which secure the child's silence alongside any conscious or deliberate actions on the part of the offender. There are notable gender differences in this respect as boys are statistically less likely to report than girls (Baker and Duncan, 1985; Hunter et al, 1992; Watkins and Bentovim, 1992; Smallbone and Wortley, 2000; Palmer, 2001; Walrath, Ybarra, and Holden, 2003; Tewksbury, 2007), particularly in relation to immediate disclosures of abuse (Finkelhor, 1984).[10]

Intra-familial abuse

As Itzin (2001: 35) has argued, within 'the dominant discourse currently of policing and policy...."paedophilia" and "child sex offending" have become synonymous, and incest abusers are invisible'. The principal corollary of such constructions of risk is that incest offenders are often 'dismissed as "just incest offenders"' (Studer et al, 2011: 501) with little or no risk of reoffending. In fact, 'incest offenders' may groom their victims and their families over a much longer period and consequently while such offenders usually have fewer victims in total than extra-familial offenders, they may commit a far greater number of offences (Eher and Ross, 2006). In this respect, one of the core tasks of this book is to highlight that contrary to contemporary public and official perceptions of sexual offending against children, as being located in the public sphere and largely committed by predatory strangers, grooming also occurs within intra-familial contexts where children are abused by parents or other relatives.

In common with the grooming of the child by someone previously unknown to them, the purpose of child grooming within an existing familial relationship is to develop and maintain an exclusive relationship with the child as a prelude to abuse, to normalize such abuse and ensure that it remains undiscovered (eg Phelan, 1995; Salter, 2003). There is, however, one significant difference. As Craven, Brown, and Gilchrist acknowledge (2006: 293), '[i]n the case of intrafamilial child sexual abuse, offenders are already in a position of trust and integrated in an environment where they can access potential victims'. Within such a context, I would argue that grooming may have less resonance at the onset of offending—it may work less towards enabling child abuse, because offenders are

---

[10] In relation to the gendered nature of sex offending against children, large-scale research by Elliott and colleagues demonstrated that offenders generally had a gender preference: 58 per cent targeted girls; 14 per cent targeted boys; while the remaining 28 per cent targeted both boys and girls (Elliott, Brown, and Kilcoyne, 1995: 583). Similarly, Grubin (1998) found that 60 per cent of child molesters target only girls, about 20 to 33 per cent boys, and about 10 per cent children of either sex. Baker and Duncan (1985), on the other hand, reported that 44 per cent of the males in their survey reported being a victim of extra-familial abuse compared to 30 per cent of the girls which may be indicative of under-reporting by boys.

already in a relationship with a child, but more towards preventing disclosure in the aftermath of abuse.

Indeed, consistent with the findings in a range of studies on child sexual abuse as outlined in the first chapter (eg, Grubin, 1998; Leggett, 2000), sexual activity with children may 'grow' out of 'already existing family interactions' (Phelan, 1995: 7). Phelan's research based on in-depth interviews with fathers/stepfathers and their daughters/stepdaughters establishes that incest often begins and extends from 'ordinary' and 'routine' behaviours that are 'already established and patterned within the family' and which are 'embedded in a milieu of nonverbal cues and messages' (Phelan, 1995: 10, 13). The fathers' first approaches were usually 'subtle', leaving the daughters unsure as to whether abuse had actually happened eventually progressing to more overt and unambiguous sexual activity (Phelan, 1995: 12). Such cases have underlined the 'compelling and addictive nature of the incestuous relationship' and 'control, power and anger' as well as 'sexual gratification' as the motivating factors (Phelan, 1995: 20–1). Further, there was also a 'belief that sexual activity with a child outside the home was much more serious than sexual activity with their "own" child' (Phelan, 1995: 20). This not only reinforces the range of rationalizing and neutralizing techniques employed by sex offenders as part of 'self grooming', as outlined above, but also the potential level of risk which children may face within intra-familial contexts.

As I will argue in the next chapter, certain elements of intra-familial abuse, including ready access to children, latent power, secrecy, and trust make abuse within intra-familial contexts closely akin to abuse within institutional environments. Indeed, often the abuser lives with the child at the onset of the abuse or has a care-providing role with respect to the child (Elliott, Browne, and Kilcoyne, 1995; Sas and Cunningham, 1995). In Sas and Cunningham's (1995: 22–3) large-scale study of disclosure in over 500 cases of child sexual abuse, for example, 84 per cent of children had an existing relationship with the abuser either through family or social connections. Grooming was most common in intra-familial cases, in particular where abusers were fathers or 'father-figures' in a care-taking role, being noted in two-thirds of those cases (Sas and Cunningham, 1995: 79). In relation to incestuous relationships between fathers and daughters in particular, several writers have made the analogy with traditional courtship rituals, where the father essentially adopts the role of male suitor towards their daughter (eg Herman, 1981; Christiansen and Blake, 1990; Howitt, 1995; Phelan, 1995). The offender tries to interact with the child on the child's wavelength (van Dam, 2001) and often the child's status is elevated to that of an adult (Wilson, 1999) and their role promoted to that of 'partner' or confidante, displacing that of the mother (Leberg, 1997).[11] As the pattern of sexual activity becomes more established, 'brooding, withdrawal and anxiety in these daughters [is] increased, spilling over and altering their relationships with their mother, siblings, and friends' (Phelan, 1995: 19). This increased isolation of the child also serves to prevent either detection by others or self-disclosure by the child.

The negative psychological and social consequences of incest for children and adolescents are well documented (Herman, 1981; Berliner and Conte, 1985; Browne and Finkelhor, 1986; Phelan, 1995). In particular, the sexual abuse of children by a family member augments the emotional confusion experienced by the child in the aftermath of abuse (Phelan, 1995: 18). It also makes them less likely to disclose, particularly in relation to the unquestioning trust placed in the abuser and the latent fear and sense of responsibility and guilt about undermining the family unit (Sas and Cunningham, 1995: 12). As such, children and young people face considerable problems when attempting to disclose (Berliner and Conte, 1995; Tucker, 2011). Other documented fears which inhibit early disclosure include 'fears about the reaction of others' (Berliner and Conte, 1995: 383), fear of harm to self or others; fear of 'bad consequences' such as disbelief or rejection by a parent (Sas and Cunningham, 1995: 27); fear of upsetting their mothers, or of 'getting into trouble' (Phelan, 1995: 19); as well as the guilt, embarrassment and stigma associated with the abuse. The patriarchal role of the father in particular can also inhibit disclosure. Earlier clinical research by Giaretto (1978) describes the acute sense of relief coupled with intense exhilaration felt by the child once the abuse is first exposed and the father's power is 'broken'. These arguments also lend further credence to the contention, contrary to the dominant public and policy fixation with grooming by strangers, that the emotional and psychological dynamics between the perpetrator and the victim

---

[11] A minority of writers, however, have found that the offender's tendency to interact at the child's level was more pronounced with boys compared to girls, where the primary concern is sexual gratification (see eg Wilson, 1999).

are significantly more powerful, potent, and complex when child sexual abuse takes place within families rather than outside them.

On-line grooming

The preponderance of recent research in the area of sexual grooming of children has centred on on-line forms of grooming. Durkin (1997: 14) has suggested there are four main purposes for which the internet may be misused by those with a sexual interest in children: trafficking of child pornography;[12] locating children to abuse; engaging in inappropriate sexualized communications with children; and communicating with other offenders. Each form of child sexual exploitation has resonance in the context of on-line grooming practices. While there is a significant degree of uniformity between face-to-face and on-line settings, the sex offender who grooms within the on-line environment has their own 'repertoire of offending behaviour' (Quayle and Taylor, 2001: 597). In this respect, in comparison with face-to-face contexts, the onset of sexualized contact with children appears to be a more tangible and unambiguous process within the on-line environment. Nonetheless, the issues concerning the early identification of on-line grooming, particularly because of the opportunities for anonymity and misrepresentation of identity, are no less complex within the virtual context. Indeed, sexual grooming and offending on the internet also 'challenge[s] traditional views of what constitutes child sexual abuse in the real world' (Davidson and Martellozzo, 2008b: 351).

The process of on-line grooming

On-line grooming, much like its off-line counterpart, would appear to be a 'staged' yet variable process (Martellozzo, 2011: 109) 'of socialisation during which an offender interacts with a child in order

---

[12] Use of the term 'child pornography' has been criticized by a number of writers as a passive term which does not reflect the realities of abuse (eg Davidson and Martellozzo, 2008b: 352, citing Edwards, 2002: 1–21). Such writers prefer the terms 'indecent images of children' or 'child abuse images'. The term 'child pornography', however, is retained throughout this book in keeping with its use within legislation where often both sets of terms are used interchangeably (see eg Sexual Offences Act 2003, ss 48–50; Protection of Children and Prevention of Sexual Offences (Scotland) Act 2005, ss 9–12; and the Child Trafficking and Pornography Act 1998).

to prepare...[them] for sexual abuse' (Davidson and Martellozzo, 2008b: 351; see also Davidson and Gottschalk, 2011: 79–103). O'Connell (2003: 6–13) has expounded a typology of what she calls 'cybersexploitation', of which on-line grooming practices form a part. The first stage in this process is the use of victim selection methods which typically involves the offender masquerading as a child of a particular age within chat rooms or social networking sites (such as Facebook and Twitter) in the hope of initiating contact with a child. Sexually harmful subcultures take place in a range of on-line settings including, inter alia, e-mail exchanges, blogs, and messaging via fixed or mobile environments, gaming sites, discussion forums, and photo and video-sharing sites (eg YouTube) (Malesky and Ennis, 2007; Kierkegaard, 2008: 41–3), many of which are brought together 'on a single service' through user interactive social networking sites (Warren, 2008: 165). Indeed, access to the internet is increasingly available through public Wi-Fi networks, as well as via the use of games consoles and mobile phones. '[A]s such services grow, so do the risks associated with them' (Warren, 2008: 165).

While some offenders wait for an individual child to respond with answers to preliminary 'test' questions, others observe conversations between a number of children and then introduce themselves to one particular child via private messaging. Although many offenders pose as a child or a teenager themselves in order 'to obtain a false sense of trust' (Hörnle, 2011: 4), it is important to note that not all adults who are interested sexually in children use the 'subterfuge' of posing as teenagers or children (Powell, 2007: 118). Indeed, many are truthful and open about their identity, including age (see also Wolak, Finkelhor, and Mitchell, 2004: 428; Webster et al, 2012: 8, 46–8). The distinction has also been made between the 'hyper confident groomer' and the 'hyper cautious groomer' (Davidson and Gottschalk, 2011: 107–9; Martellozzo, 2011: 107–9), where the latter, because they are more prone to lying and creating false identities, are harder to detect.

The second is the friendship-forming stage during which the offender requests a picture of the child. This has a two-fold purpose—to ensure that the person they are conversing with is actually a child, as well as one that matches their particular victim predilection. Typically, requests for pictures are initially confined to those of the child's face or those taken on family holidays which escalate to requests for sexually explicit images of the child. The provision of a recent photograph of the child also serves as a useful identifier if the on-line interaction later progresses to a meeting in the real world.

The third stage is relationship-forming where the offender endeavours to build a rapport with the child by discussing 'routine' topics such as home and school or television programmes or pop groups (see also Gallagher et al, 2006: 42). By giving the outward appearance of being an interested friend, the offender builds the child's trust. This stage is linked closely to, and may overlap with, the fourth stage—risk assessment—by asking the child about their family or home situation the offender is able to make an initial assessment of the likelihood of their activities being discovered. The purpose appears to be the selection of a child who is socially isolated from supportive relationships or who is vulnerable in some way (Palmer and Stacey, 2004: 26–7). Offers of modelling or acting contracts and other 'carrots' have also been used to entice children into an on-line relationship (Calder, 2004: 11).

The fifth stage establishes the exclusivity of the relationship where the child's confidence and trust in the offender are further augmented. The offender emphasizes the idea of the mutual importance and secrecy of the relationship and often introduces the issue of trust specifically at this point. The offender would 'in a very incremental, but also very purposeful manner, steer the interaction' so that it becomes 'increasingly personal, emotional and eventually, sexual' (Gallagher et al, 2006: 42). While the initial patterns of conversation vary slightly with young children, for example, in terms of providing fuller explanations of the meaning of sexual terminology, there is little to differentiate the offender's method of approach, the nature of sexual suggestion or the degree of coercion applied in terms of age (O'Connell, 2003: 13).

The process culminates in the sexual stage and eventually sexual activity with the child. This is perhaps the most intricate and involved part of the process where several different patterns and sub-stages emerge. In the case of offenders who wish to maintain a relationship with the child, progression through this stage is gradual. The sexual nature of the on-line conversation may be implicit at first, later progressing to explicit exchanges which focus on either potential sexual acts on the adult or the child. This pattern of conversation also typifies what Webster et al (2012: 14, 81–3) have referred to as 'intimacy seeking'—the on-line contact which later progresses to a face-to-face meeting which the anti-grooming legislation within the United Kingdom and Republic of Ireland is specifically designed to address (O'Connell, 2003: 10). Before meeting the child the offender usually undertakes a risk assessment which would involve persuading the child to destroy any records of their conversations (Carr, 2004: 2). Other research notes that while the majority of cases involved an offender and victim who were resident in the same country, most offenders were prepared to travel 'considerable distances' and 'a small, but notable, minority, involved an international component' (Gallagher et al, 2006: 37, 39–40, 43). For children who have previously been sexually abused, 'the adaptable offender' (Webster et al, 2012: 14, 83–5) modifies their behaviour in a way that advances the relationship towards sexualized contact more quickly, but which also reinforces the child's trust in the offender in stressing that the child can talk to the offender about anything.

Although not all offenders use pornography (Webster et al, 2012: 9–10, 54–5), the sexualized conversation often precedes the exchange and creation of child erotic and pornographic material. Typically, the offender forwards pornographic images to the child in order to 'desensitize' them and lower their inhibitions (Utting, 1997: 100–1; Itzin, 2001). An offender then 'moves' the interaction with the intended victim from a public to private chat room, or from public to one-to-one messaging within social networking sites, and on to the child or young person's mobile phone and, eventually, onto a web cam, which may have been posted directly to the young person's address by the offender (Gallagher et al, 2006: 43). Similar 'gifts' to the child or young person, which would also facilitate the offending process rather than simply function as an inducement or reward, also include mobile phones and digital cameras (Wolak, Finkelhor, and Mitchell, 2004: 428). Many offenders use images of children 'looking happy' (Sutton and Jones, 2004: 12). As O'Donnell and Milner (2007: 73–4) note, citing Utting (1997: 100–1), the effect on the victim differs depending on the age of the recipient: for younger children this could be used 'to "prove"…that what they were looking at was "fun"', while '[w]ith older children it could serve the purpose of sexual excitation, instruction and normalisation'. Moreover, the viewing of child pornography also helps sex offenders to overcome their own internal inhibitors (Sutton and Jones, 2004: 11).

Fantasy enactment, which is an important element of such on-line relationships (Quayle and Taylor, 2001: 603), and often happens in real time, includes 'overt coercion' (O'Connell, 2003: 11), where the offender can be threatening, controlling, bullying, and aggressive. It also encompasses emotional blackmail through which the offender will try to 'wear the victim down', invoking their sympathy and guilt or personal responsibility for the 'relationship' (Gallagher et al, 2006: 43). 'Emotional coercion' (Sutton and Jones, 2004: 14) in particular, and the persistent psychological manipulation of the child (Gallagher et al, 2006: 38) also helps to explain sexually aggressive behaviour by children towards other children for the purpose of producing child pornography for offenders (O'Connell, 2003: 11; see also Palmer and Stacey, 2004: 23). The process culminates with 'damage limitation' (O'Connell, 2003: 12) with the offender emphasizing the need to maintain the secrecy of the relationship and often an affirmation of their 'love' for the child in order to reduce the risk of disclosure. With some offenders, however, particularly those not interested in extending contact with the child, by either a further on-line exchange or a face-to-face meeting, there is rarely an interest in damage limitation.

For such offenders, which O'Connell refers to as being 'hit and run' (2003: 13), and Webster et al (2012: 14, 85–6) as 'hyper-sexualised', two important points emerge concerning policing and criminalization: First, there may be even lower chances of discovery because the seemingly one-off and random nature of the encounter may mean that a pattern of deviant sexual behaviour has not emerged which makes detection especially difficult. As Davidson and Martellozzo (2005: 3) have written in the context of child pornography more generally but which could also be applied to grooming specifically, 'law enforcement agencies are now employed in an increasingly difficult global race to track down the child victim and the perpetrators involved'. In the context of the high profile 'Wonderland' investigation,[13] for example, referred to in Chapter 1, only 16 of the 1,263 children who had been sexually abused by members of a criminal network have been identified (Sutton and Jones, 2004: 17). In such cases, detection depends on

---

[13] This international police operation resulted in simultaneous arrests in 12 different countries (including the United Kingdom, Belgium, Austria, France, Italy, Finland, Norway, Australia, and the United States) involving an estimated 145 male offenders: See 'Paedophiles Jailed for Porn Ring', *BBC News*, 13 February 2001, <http://news.bbc.co.uk/1/hi/uk/1168112.stm> (accessed 18 February 2011).

victim disclosure. As noted above, where the child has been involved in not only looking at but also in the making of indecent images of children, there may be an enhanced sense of guilt, shame, embarrassment, or fear which attaches to disclosure to parents in particular.[14]

Secondly, not all on-line sexual encounters between children and offenders culminate in a face-to-face meeting (Webster et al, 2012: 10, 59–60), which is a specific requirement for the offence under the anti-grooming legislation. It does not govern, for example, those situations in which a person grooms a child on-line for the purposes of the production of child pornography where the offender has no intention of actually meeting the child (Gillespie, 2007b: 5). It is recognized that in some cases the on-line contact does progress to serious contact abuse (Beckett, 2011: 55). As Sutton and Jones have noted, citing Taylor and Quayle (2003), and underlining an important but sometimes overlooked distinction: 'Those offenders who produce child pornography are by definition contact sexual abusers but not all Internet sex offenders who distribute and download abusive images of children will go on to sexually abuse children' (2004: 23). It is important to note that while some offenders want the sexualized on-line interaction to progress to an actual face-to-face meeting with the child, others appear 'just happy with the cyber sex' (Quayle and Taylor, 2001: 602). Döring (2000) contends, however, that 'cyber sex', while taking place in a virtual world, is much more than a conversation about sex, but is rather a form of sexual encounter and, therefore, constitutes child exploitation in itself. In the contemporary focus on on-line grooming as a prelude to off-line abuse within popular and official discourses, however, the fact that other forms of sexual exploitation and harm to children may also be occurring on-line, prior to or in the absence of face-to-face contacts, can be overlooked. Indeed, while the distribution or production of child pornography or getting children to agree to participate in sexual activities (see eg Gallagher et al, 2003; Taylor and Quayle, 2003; Akdeniz, 2008) may be captured by a range of possible sexual

---

[14] Moreover, as O'Connell (2003: 4, 11) notes, where the child has been involved in taking or recording a pornographic image or video of themselves and then sending this to the offender, technically they may be said to have become both the producer and distributer of child pornography. This also distorts the traditional boundaries between victims and offenders.

offences,[15] they do not specifically come within the anti-grooming legislation. Moreover, as Ost (2009: 135–47) has argued, the act of grooming in itself also constitutes harm and sexual exploitation of children.

A comparison with face-to-face contexts

In terms of victim and offender characteristics, in common with abuse in face-to-face encounters (Sas and Cunningham, 1995: 22, 68),[16] the overwhelming majority of on-line grooming cases involve male perpetrators and female victims (Wolak, Finkelhor, and Mitchell, 2004: 428; Gallagher et al, 2006: 42; Choo, 2009: xii). In the study by Wolak and colleagues, 99 per cent of victims were aged between 13 and 17, and 75 per cent were female (Wolak, Finkelhor, and Mitchell, 2004: 428). Compared to contact sexual offences, where the average age of victims is generally younger,[17] 'most on-line offenders are adults who target teens and seduce victims into sexual relationships' (Davidson and Gottschalk, 2010: 39; see also Choo, 2009: 32). Indeed, as noted in Chapter 2 and discussed further below, on-line forms of grooming are considerably more complex than media portrayals might suggest (Gallagher et al, 2003: 9).

While females are at a much higher risk of receiving sexual solicitations on-line (Mitchell, Finkelhor, and Wolak, 2001, 2007; Gallagher et al, 2006: 41–2), a minority of studies have found significantly higher proportions of male victims and female perpetrators of on-line grooming.[18] In one American study, for example, a quarter of victims were male (Wells and Mitchell, 2007). In addition, nearly half of the victims in Wolak, Finkelhor, and Mitchell's study were described as 'being in love with or feeling close bonds with the

---

[15] See eg the Sexual Offences Act 2003, ss 10–12, in the context of England and Wales, and the Sexual Offences (NI) Order 2008, Part 3, in Northern Ireland. For the broadly equivalent offences in Scotland: see eg the Protection of Children and Prevention of Sexual Offences (Scotland) Act 2005, ss 9–12; and for the Republic of Ireland: Child Trafficking and Pornography Act 1998, ss 4–5, the Criminal Law (Sexual Offences) (Amendment) Act 2007, s 2.

[16] In Sas and Cunningham's study of over 500 cases of disclosure, over 99 per cent of abusers were male (1995: 68).

[17] Sas and Cunningham (1995) also found that the average age of victims in the context of face-to-face grooming was 11.

[18] Finkelhor, Mitchell, and Wolak (2000: 7) found that while females were targeted at twice the rate of males, 34 per cent of victims were male, and as noted in Chapter 2, 19 per cent of offenders claimed to be women.

offenders' (2004: 428). As also highlighted in Chapter 2, such findings serve to highlight inaccurate stereotypes about on-line grooming, in particular those relating to the use of force or deception by male adult predatory paedophiles previously unknown to the child victim. '"Compliant" or "statutory" victims' (Wolak, Finkelhor, and Mitchell, 2004: 432) who may have developed strong emotional attachments to offenders, pose unique challenges for law enforcement (see Chapter 6) and for prevention efforts in particular. Considerably lower numbers of internet offenders are acquainted with their victims (Mercado, Merdian, and Egg, 2011: 511, citing Simon, 2003). In the study by Gallagher and colleagues, for example, with one exception, the offender was a 'stranger' to the young person.[19]

In relation to offender demographics, while earlier research has established that on-line offenders are usually considerably older than contact sexual offenders (Wolak and Finkelhor, 2004; Mitchell, Finkelhor, and Wolak, 2005), a growing number of on-line sex offenders are young people (Choo, 2009: xiii; Elliott et al, 2009). While the offender's age can range from 12 to late 70s (Sas and Cunningham, 1995: 22), most are between young adulthood and early middle-age (Wolak, Finkelhor, and Mitchell, 2004: 428;Gallagher et al, 2006: 42). The research to date also suggests that internet offenders are in general more likely to be employed and better educated than those who commit offences off-line (Burke et al, 2002; Mitchell, Finkelhor, and Wolak, 2005). In the study by Gallagher and colleagues (2006: 42), some on-line groomers were attracted to children either especially or exclusively while others also had relationships with women. While most offenders appear to work nationally on a lone basis (Gallagher et al, 2006: 37–40; Choo, 2009: xiii),[20] some recent high profile cases of internet grooming involving child pornography demonstrate that sex offenders may use 'virtual communities' (Taylor and Quayle, 2003:

---

[19] In one case, the offender was the non-cohabiting boyfriend of the victim's mother who had purchased a computer with internet access for the victim at her home and who then contacted her from his own home computer (Gallagher et al, 2006: 42), presenting as a 'stranger' but using his knowledge of the girl and her background to increase the effectiveness of grooming.

[20] The one exceptional case in this instance involved 'two international co-offenders'—a husband and wife who travelled from Canada to Wales to meet an eight-year-old girl whom the man had met on the internet (Gallagher et al, 2006: 37–40).

120–47), or 'the pedophile subculture online' (Holt, Blevins, and Burkert, 2010) for criminal networking and organized criminal activities (Durkin, 1997: 16–17; Adam, 2002: 13–14; Davidson and Martellozzo, 2005: 3).

There are also important differences between the onset of sexual abuse within on-line and off-line contexts, particularly regarding victimology and offending patterns (O'Connell, 2003: 2).[21] When sex offenders operate in the virtual rather than the real world, 'new offence pathways' (Davidson and Martellozzo, 2005: 2) are created which do not always map on to those in the real world.[22] In particular, the parameters and dynamics of sexual grooming are altered fundamentally with respect to three distinct but closely related variables: 'accessibility, opportunity and vulnerability' (O'Connell, 2003: 3; see also Quayle and Taylor, 2001: 598; Cooper, McLaughlin, and Campbell, 2000).

The internet makes potential victims more accessible to sex offenders, with 'twenty-four seven' access (Middleton et al, 2006). It affords would-be offenders an enhanced opportunity to begin an association with a child, often without any supervision or suspicion and without having to manipulate the child's family. Moreover, the on-line environment gives sex offenders the opportunity to have daily contact with a child which would not otherwise be possible unless the offender was a family member or care worker.[23] As Nair (2006: 180, 177) argues, the widespread use of and access to the internet by children and young people in both 'fixed' and 'mobile' environments, increases victim accessibility and offender opportunity for targeting, grooming, and sexually exploiting victims.

---

[21] For comparative research on the cognitive distortions of on-line and contact sexual offenders, offence pathways and motivations and the differential risk management and treatment approaches required therein, see generally Middleton, 2004; Howitt and Sheldon, 2007; Elliott et al, 2009; Davidson and Gottschalk, 2011: 153–85).

[22] It has been argued in this context that 'traditional' etiological theories do not effectively capture the different characteristics of on-line offending (see eg Calder, 2004; Middleton et al, 2006; Elliott et al, 2009), and that consequently, there is a need for further research in this area (Beech and Elliott, 2011; Mercado, Merdian, and Egg, 2011).

[23] See also Home Affairs Select Committee—Sexual Offences Bill, Briefing Paper by Childnet International: *The Need for a New Clause 17 Grooming Offence*, <http://www.childnet-int.org/downloads/SOBclause17.pdf> (accessed 6 April 2011).

In an age of domestic internet access, children are increasingly vulnerable to potential sex offenders within the on-line environment. Research with children and young people has demonstrated the extent of their computer literacy as well as their use of the internet (Livingstone, 2005; Livingstone and Bober, 2004, 2005; Davidson and Martellozzo, 2008a, 2008b). According to one UK study, most children surveyed, aged between ten and 14, had access to the internet outside school, either at home, at a friend's house or at an internet cafe, with 76 per cent spending long unsupervised periods of time on their computers (Davidson and Martellozzo, 2008a: 282). Webster et al (2012: 16–20, 101–18) found, through focus group research with young people aged 11 to 16 years in the United Kingdom, Italy, and Belgium, that time spent on-line ranged from five minutes to six hours, and that virtually all young people used Facebook, with 'friends' numbering from 50 to 1,000. In a study commissioned by the National Literacy Trust, 85.5 per cent of 17,000 school children surveyed in the United Kingdom, aged between seven and 16, had their own mobile phone.[24] Children's strong sense of ownership and privacy concerning mobile phones suggests there is even less parental supervision and controls of mobile devices compared to home computers (O'Connell, 2003: 3; Nair, 2006: 178).

In general terms, '[o]n the internet, the opportunity to commit crime is never more than three or four clicks away' (Demetriou and Silke, 2003: 220). As Gillespie points out specifically in relation to offending against children, the internet 'provides an opportunity for those minded to abuse children to do so in a way that exposes them to less risk, thus reducing the likelihood of detection and potentially leading to an increase in actual abuse' (2002a: 411). Moreover, 'cyberspace offers unparalleled opportunities for the deceit and secrecy on which child sexual abuse relies' (Harrison, 2006: 368). As outlined above, the internet enables sex offenders 'to entice multiple victims at once' (Kirkegaard, 2008: 42; see also Mercado, Merdian, and Egg, 2011: 511–12). Children are often unaware of the dangers posed by the on-line environment. They can 'feel at ease and more secure behind the computer screen than they would in the real world, and sex offenders are well aware of this' (Davidson and Martellozzo, 2005: 9) allowing strangers to become 'virtual friends'

---

[24] Reported in G. Paton, 'Children "More Likely to Own a Phone than a Book"', *The Telegraph*, 26 May 2010.

(Davidson and Martellozzo, 2005: 1). Children can engage in risk-taking behaviours in the on-line environment such as providing personal information including their address, and photographs or agreeing to meet someone off-line (Goodstein, 2007; Livingstone and Helsper, 2007; Kierkegaard, 2008; Somners, 2008; Webster et al, 2012: 14–15, 92–5). As Gallagher et al (2006: 42) state, the use of technology enables the offender to ensure that their interaction with the young person becomes 'increasingly private, intimate and controlled'. As noted earlier, there is evidence, however, that messages about on-line safety are getting through to a group of 'resilient young people' who are able to deflect unwanted contacts on-line (Webster et al, 2012: 16, 100–1).

Regarding, vulnerability, on one level, grooming in an on-line environment allows the offender to more easily expose the child to other forms of sexual exploitation such as child pornography. Multi-media messaging services mean that such material can be instantaneously sent to and from the child. This also makes it more difficult to decline the receipt of such material or to decline the request for a picture of themselves (O'Connell, 2003: 4). The 'troubled' personal and emotional circumstances of children and young people also makes them more vulnerable to on-line sexual exploitation as they seek to form on-line relationships 'to meet the compelling needs for intimacy, self-validation and companionship' (Wolak, Mitchell, and Finkelhor, 2003:116, citing Buhrmester, 1996). 'Loneliness and depression' or 'gay and questioning boys' who are exploring their sexual orientation may also be 'vulnerable populations' (Wolak, Finkelhor, and Mitchell, 2004: 432), as are teenagers who have poor relationships with parents (Wolak, Mitchell, and Finkelhor, 2003: 105). In common with face-to-face contexts, other vulnerabilities identified in victims of on-line grooming include low self-esteem, a history of self harm, family break-up, and ongoing sexual abuse by other men (Webster et al, 2012: 15, 90–2), rule-breaking behaviour (Wolak et al, 2008) or simple, adolescent curiosity about sex (Berliner, 2002; Olson et al, 2007). The range of vulnerabilities experienced by potential victims, means that such adolescents may lack the supportive and protective networks of not only their parents, but also other adolescents (Wolak, Mitchell, and Finkelhor, 2003: 116; Wolak, Finkelhor, and Mitchell, 2004: 432).

It is also important to emphasize that the 'vulnerability' of victims within the on-line environment does not always accord with traditional notions of victimhood as outlined above. In the small sample of cases of internet-initiated grooming in the study by Gallagher and colleagues, they found that what seemed to be '*conspicuous* about this group was the *absence* of risk factors' (emphasis in original) (Gallagher et al, 2006: 42). In one of their vignettes of 'internet-initiated grooming of children for sexual abuse' they found that the victim was not 'typical' or in 'any way vulnerable' (Gallagher et al, 2006: 40). Rather, '[s]he was an educated child, at a good school, she had a nice family and plenty of money... [and]... a good relationship with her mother and a good network of friends' (Gallagher et al, 2006: 40). The fact that children and young people exploited via on-line grooming do not always exhibit 'underlying vulnerable factors or the current risk indicators' (Montgomery-Devlin, 2008: 388), which may be common in grooming in off-line contexts, also has implications for policing and prevention at both the macro- and micro-levels. At a broader level, it becomes more difficult to predict which children and young people might be vulnerable to on-line forms of grooming (Montgomery-Devlin, 2008: 388). It may also cause parents or carers to lower their guard in the belief that their children are safe in their own homes where they know their whereabouts. In challenging traditional notions of vulnerability this finding also underlines the latent dangers to children which are enhanced by the potentially ambiguous and surreptitious nature of on-line interactions between would-be offenders and potential child victims. Offenders, therefore, seek out children who may be susceptible to grooming and abuse, not only due to their social isolation or lack of a stable family background, but simply by virtue of their being impervious of the potentially threatening and hazardous nature of the on-line environment and of the need to be mindful of internet safety.

Indeed, a further important difference between the two offending contexts, not explicitly identified by O'Connell (2003), but underlined by a number of other writers is 'the anonymous nature of cyberspace' (Durkin, 1997: 15; see also Quayle and Taylor, 2001; Davidson and Martellozzo, 2005: 3; Kirkegaard, 2008: 41; Hornle, 2011: 2). Such anonymity completely alters the nature of victim-offender interaction and may be more facilitative of sexually harmful behaviour. In the absence of visual (Short, Williams, and Christie, 1976; Wells and Mitchell, 2007) or social cues (Kiesler, Siegal, and McGuire, 1984; Sproull and Kiesler, 1986), the conduit of the internet becomes in itself 'a tool of seduction' (O'Donnell and Milner, 2007: 73) where 'trust' must be built solely through communication (Whitty and Joinson, 2009: 97–108) and is ultimately less dependent on effective interpersonal skills. In particular, without 'social context cues...to regulate social interaction...people's behaviour will also become uninhibited [and] anti-normative' (Whitty and Joinson, 2009: 22; see also Danet, 1998; Quayle and Taylor, 2001).[25] As noted above, the on-line environment can disinhibit offenders as well as young people (Lamb, 1998; Webster et al, 2012). As Davidson and Martellozzo (2005: 10) state, underlining the nature and significance of the on-line world as an alternative social space, 'the Internet is more than just a medium of communication, it constitutes a new virtual reality, or a cyberworld with its own rules and its own language'. This is conveyed particularly through the style and speed of writing and responses, including the use of punctuation, abbreviations, and emoticons (Mantovani, 2001; Quayle and Taylor, 2001: 599; Choo, 2009: x). The anonymous nature of on-line interactions with children and the seeming disengagement with the real world may also be used by sex offenders to formulate accounts of their behaviour which justify their actions, minimize or deny potential harms to children and condemn those who would sanction their behaviour (Durkin and Bryant, 1999).

The 'face less' nature of the internet, has been likened to the effect of wearing a mask (Danet, 1998), enabling offender 'metamorphosis' (Taylor and Quayle, 2003: 97–119). Although not every offender lies about their age, the internet allows would be offenders to misrepresent themselves and to assume a different persona or identity (Durkin, 1997: 15; Quayle and Taylor, 2001; Whitty, 2002; Whitty and Joinson, 2009: 19–32)—an 'electronic double' (Davidson and Gottschalk, 2010: 4)—perhaps self-representing as a like-minded child or young person (Quayle and Taylor, 2001; Davidson and Martellozzo, 2008a: 282).[26] As Mercado, Merdian, and Egg (2011: 516) argue, '[m]ispresentation of oneself may also be a

[25] This also links to the psychological theory of 'deindividuation' whereby self-control and internal inhibitions are removed when people are not regarded or seen as individuals. See especially Demetriou and Silk (2003: 214–15) in the context of the internet.

[26] For a detailed critical discussion of the issue of identity in cyberspace and the related notion of the truth-lies dichotomy, see especially Whitty and Johnson (2009). See also Talamo and Ligiorio (2001).

grooming technique'. In terms of the twin goals of the grooming process outlined at the outset of this chapter, such on-line anonymity 'reduces the odds of being caught and increases his chances of snaring a victim' (O'Donnell and Milner, 2007: 60). It masks not only the offender's adult status, at least for a time, and their potential danger to children in terms of their harmful sexual intentions, but it may also serve to help children 'lower their guard', especially if their on-line interaction with the offender does not fit their impression of 'stranger danger'.

As will be discussed further in relation to legislative and policy responses to grooming and in particular the implications for the policing of such behaviour, anonymity works both to the benefit and detriment of the offender. While the operation of grooming in the on-line world increases the victim's accessibility and vulnerability and the offender's opportunity to offend, the tangible record of evidence of sexualized conversations between the victim and the offender creates what O'Connell (2003: 3) has termed, a 'virtual crime scene'. Where grooming has occurred over a period of time, this trail of computer-based and documentary evidence should, in theory at least, make on-line forms of grooming easier to pinpoint, police, and prosecute and constitutes a further key difference from off-line forms of victim-offender interaction.

Furthermore, the combination of these variables, particularly the easier methods of accessing victims, and the greater vulnerability of children in the on-line environment, combines to expedite the process. It is established that grooming within an on-line environment generally takes place over a significantly shorter period (see Gillespie, 2004b: 10, 2005: 4, 2007b: 3; Kirkegaard, 2008: 43; CEOP, 2010: 14). Not all offenders, however, progress through the various stages of on-line grooming sequentially. On-line grooming, like its off-line counterpart, is not a linear but rather a cyclical process which involves a pattern of 'adoption, maintenance, relapse and readoption' as part of offence maintenance and risk management (Webster et al, 2012: 6; 61–79). Some remain in one stage for longer periods than others and some skip one or more stages, depending on their precise motivation and the malleability of the victim to sexualized contact (O'Connell, 2003: 8). A final point of comparison relates to the overlap with familial forms of grooming. Some offenders target and groom single mothers first via the internet as a means of getting access to their children (Gallagher et al, 2006: 43). This device has also been used in off-line forms of grooming.

Street grooming

As noted in Chapter 2, most of what is known about this form of grooming derives from media coverage of a number of recent high profile cases. What little research there is, locates this form of grooming within the continuum of sexually exploitative behaviour towards children (Scott and Skidmore, 2006; Montgomery-Devlin, 2008). Scott and Skidmore (2006: 1), for example, acknowledge that:

...sexual exploitation incorporates a spectrum of experience ranging from what is generally referred to as 'child sexual abuse' at one end, to 'formal prostitution' at the other. Many young people are first drawn into 'informal exploitation' where sex is exchanged for drugs or somewhere to stay. Many young women become engaged in a coercive relationship with an adult man who sometimes grooms them for more formal prostitution.

The grooming context may be different but the purpose is the same—'to normalise the activity and desensitise the child to sexual activities that may become increasingly abusive' (Montgomery-Devlin, 2008: 383).

Montgomery-Devlin (2008: 383) cites Chase and Satham (2005) in noting that prostitution, trafficking, and on-line sexual exploitation involving children are 'inextricably linked'. Indeed, the patterns of street grooming share some of the features of other forms of child grooming as previously outlined. In terms of victim identification or selection, often 'the most vulnerable children in our society' are targeted, including those with 'unmet emotional, social or physical needs' which leave them open to manipulation, control, and exploitation by adults (Montgomery-Devlin, 2008: 383). Factors such as poverty, emotional difficulties such as low self-esteem, difficulties at school, disrupted family life, negative experiences in the care system, going missing, and previous emotional, physical, or sexual abuse 'are not predictors of being abused, but do increase the risk' (Montgomery-Devlin, 2008: 389–90; see also Barnardo's, 2009). In particular, there are tangible links between going missing and grooming and sexual exploitation with 'looked-after' young people in residential care being at a significant risk (Beckett, 2011). Although most of the high profile cases involve female victims and young women who are much more likely to be victimized (Scott and Skidmore, 2006: 4), boys and younger men can also be targeted (Barnardo's, 2011: 7). The methods employed include 'befriending, exchange of favours, control, and exploitation' (Kosaraju, 2008: 14).

Kosaraju (2008) explains how offenders target children and young people outside the home, some as young as nine, at shopping centres, cinemas, entertainment arcades, bus and train stations, driving by in cars, or alternatively through the use of mobile phones. Initially the (usually older) perpetrator buys the young person presents and is attentive towards them. An 'inappropriate relationship' then develops where the perpetrator obtains power and control over a young person, whether it be physical, emotional, or financial (Barnardo's, 2011: 6). For those offenders who operate in groups, as was the case with all of the high profile instances of street grooming outlined in Chapter 2, the girl will usually be targeted by a boy or younger man. The younger man may not actually take part in the abuse but introduces the girl to other men where the sexual exploitation becomes part of 'gang culture',[27] and where 'gang grooming can lead to gang rape'.[28] This is sometimes referred to as 'the boyfriend model' of sexual exploitation and grooming (Montgomery-Devlin, 2008: 392; Barnardo's, 2011: 6), due to the girl's initial perception of the relationship as that of 'boyfriend' and 'girlfriend' and as one that they have freely entered into. This particular model also helps to normalize exploitative behaviour and serves to entrap and control victims and further perpetuate abuse (Montgomery-Devlin, 2008: 392).

Following the bestowing of gifts, the girl is enticed into using alcohol and drugs and taken to hotels, flats, or 'party houses',[29] where over a period of time involvement in sexual acts are eventually sought as 'an exchange of favours' (Kosaraju, 2008: 15) and as a means of paying back the investment of time and money spent on her.[30] Gradually, the young girl may distance herself from her family and friends, truant from school or go missing where they are either held in flats owned by the perpetrator (or perpetrators) or, at worst, trafficked to other areas. Thus, 'organised/networked sexual exploitation or trafficking' is the most serious, complex and sophisticated form of child sexual exploitation (Barnardo's, 2011: 6) which relates to the process of 'street grooming'. The girl complies with this process out of fear for their own or their family's safety. Alienation from

---

[27] A. Topping, 'Case Studies Reveal Horror of Child Abuse', *The Guardian*, 17 January 2011, <http://www.guardian.co.uk/society/2011/jan/17/childprotection-children> (accessed 1 July 2011).

[28] 'Britain's Sex Gangs', *Dispatches*, Channel 4, 7 November 2011.

[29] Ibid.   [30] Ibid.

family and other support networks means that even if the girl should manage to escape, 'reversion to the exploitative situation is not uncommon' (Kosaraju, 2008: 15). Young people are also used to 'recruit' other children and young people into exploitative situations as they are likely to be more trusting of a child of the same age rather than an adult (Montgomery-Devlin, 2008: 393). A further inhibiting factor for the young person preventing them from exiting the situation is that 'they are told implicitly and explicitly that they are as guilty as the adults' (Montgomery-Devlin, 2008: 393). A report by CEOP on 'localised grooming' in the United Kingdom, cited in Chapter 2, confirms the vulnerability of victims and their experiences of this type of grooming. This form of grooming, for a range of reasons, however, is one of the hardest to target via legislative and policy responses and 'extremely difficult to police while the legal emphasis is still on the child to make a complaint' (Barnardo's 2009: 10) (see Chapter 6). The difficulties which victims face in extricating themselves from an exploitative situation and seeking help are substantial.

As also noted in Chapter 2, in the sustained media coverage of recent high profile cases in England and Wales (namely Derby, Rochdale, and Telford respectively) much was made of the strong racial or ethnic minority element of the abuse—essentially Asian men working in groups to target and victimize young white girls. In particular, commentators have pointed to perpetrator perceptions of victim vulnerability, and the stark differences in the portrayal of and attitudes to women and young girls within mainstream white popular culture and Asian communities respectively.[31] It has also been argued that the racial element to this type of grooming has inhibited public discourse as well as official recognition of the problem, for fear of inciting racial tension.[32] This also feeds into and reinforces the predatory stranger danger myth, or the 'othering' (Garland, 2001) of sex offending which has been highlighted at the outset of this chapter and will be further addressed in the second and third parts of the book.

Indeed, while these cases may have been influenced or shaped by racial stereotypes, there is a dearth of research into child sexual abuse in ethnic minority communities. It is generally acknowl-

---

[31] Ibid; 'Muslim Minister Says Race *Was* Factor in Grooming Case', *Daily Mail*, 19 May 2012.
[32] Ibid.

edged that sexual abuse occurs across all groups in society (Cawson et al, 2000), although defining and recognizing it as such can present considerable challenges for some communities. Owen and Statham (2009) argue that there is a 'Disproportionality in Child Welfare' in that while children from black and ethnic minority backgrounds are overrepresented among 'looked after children' or children in care, Asian children tend to be underrepresented. While little is known about why this might be the case, this statistical deficit might be attributed to restraint in reporting rather than the absence of abuse. Gilligan and Akhtar (2006), for example, contend that in some ethnic minority communities, in common with some white communities, there are cultural barriers to disclosure, including reluctance to discuss the issue as a 'taboo' or 'hidden' subject, lack of appropriate vocabulary, and relatively high levels of denial in relation to elements of child sexual abuse. As discussed in the last part of the book, this also points towards the need to engage all sections of society in a coordinated public health approach.

There is also, however, a discernible opportunistic/situational component to these offences. In several instances, for example, the offenders in the Rochdale case were taxi drivers arguably affording them easy access to victims. Moreover, as discussed further below, many of the victims of 'street grooming' are vulnerable 'looked after' children from residential children's homes (Barnardo's, 2009; Beckett, 2011). Grooming and sexual exploitation in such cases would appear, therefore, to be as much about victim vulnerability as offender opportunity.

Peer-to-peer grooming

Research into abuse by adolescent sexual offenders has found that the strategies used to begin offending against children, whether within their own families or in an outside context, are influenced strongly by situational factors and the location of the abuse in particular (Leclerc, Beauregard, and Proulx, 2008; see also Wortley and Smallbone, 2006). The offender's home, when no one else is present, is the most likely place for offenders to adopt manipulative or grooming strategies. There are also differences between intra-familial and extra-familial adolescent sex offenders. The former are more likely to give gifts to obtain the victim's trust (Kaufman, Hilliker, and Daleiden, 1996), and the latter, in common with adult extra-familial offenders, more frequently use drugs or alcohol to gain the victim's cooperation (Kaufman et al, 1998). Adolescent offenders who abused both boys and girls adopt a wider array of grooming strategies than those who abused only boys or girls (Kaufman, Hilliker, and Daleiden, 1996). This research suggests that young or peer abusers also 'adopt specific sets of strategies and commit their crimes once they assess the costs and benefits involved' (Leclerc, Beauregard, and Proulx, 2008: 58).

To date, beyond mention of children being used to 'groom' other children for offenders into becoming part of sexually exploitative behaviours or activities as outlined above (see eg O'Connell, 2003: 11; Palmer and Stacey, 2004: 23), there is little existing literature on peer-to-peer grooming specifically. A report by Barnardo's, however, showed that a quarter of their services across the United Kingdom identified peer-based exploitation within age-appropriate relationships as becoming more prevalent (Barnardo's, 2011: 1, 3). Both forms of grooming are examined further, relying on data gathered from the primary research.

Familial and Societal Grooming

In tandem with the broad distinction adopted above, in relation to the two very different offending contexts of extra-familial and intra-familial abuse, the same subtle but crucial distinction also needs to be made within the process of grooming the child's family in particular.

Extra-familial grooming

Contrary to the media-inspired popular belief, sex offenders are not instantly recognizable. Part of their skill is to ingratiate themselves with children, infiltrating into unsuspecting families, communities, and organizations. To be successful, they present as being nice men who simply like children[33]—to invoke the much-used phrase 'monsters do not get children, nice men do' (Long and

---

[33] Approximately 5 per cent of sex offences against children are known to have been committed by women (see Grubin, 1998; Vandiver and Walker, 2002; NCIS, 2003), although other research places this figure as considerably higher (eg Fergusson and Mullen, 1999). See generally Ashfield et al, 2010; Gannon and Cortoni, 2010.

McLachlan, 2002: 6). Sex offenders, to avoid suspicion, find ways in which they can legitimately have contact with children and acquire power over them (Salter, 1995: 55). Sex offenders not only groom children but also their families and local communities perhaps as the means of beginning an association with a child. Ambiguities surrounding the grooming process in both legal and sociological terms are not clearer when extended into familial and institutional contexts. However, indicators of the sex offender's behaviour in the preparatory stages of abuse have been established within the literature.

Skilful offenders also gain access by establishing a friendship with the child's parent or adult caretaker rather than, or in addition to, that with the child (Salter, 1995: 54–5). Adults are primed and controlled for victimization in similar ways to children. Based on in-depth interviews with convicted sex offenders, Salter (2003) explains how sex offenders, who often have good social skills, act with careful premeditation and use sophisticated deception techniques to avoid suspicion, sometimes playing double roles in the community. The grooming of the child's family also has a dual purpose: securing the confidence and trust and thus the cooperation of their carers in gaining access to the child; and reducing the likelihood of discovery by creating an atmosphere of normality or acceptance.

As previously noted, one of the first stages in the grooming process is victim identification or selection. Aside from choosing a victim that has general appeal, ease of access and vulnerability are pivotal variables (van Dam, 2001). Sex offenders sometimes plan their assaults around a category of child 'experiencing a significant degree of family disorganization and dysfunction' (Sas and Cunningham, 1995: 66) whom they believe they can safely victimize (Salter, 1995: 39, 62; Gallagher, 2000: 807–11). Research also suggests that sex offenders are highly skilled in singling out and targeting children and families with obvious vulnerabilities (Conte, Wolf, and Smith, 1989; Elliott, Browne, and Kilcoyne, 1995). They will select a dysfunctional family where the parents are having marital problems (Gruber and Jones, 1983; Finkelhor, 1984), where the mother is ill (Herman, 1981; Finkelhor, 1984), or where the child has a generally poor relationship with their parents or friends (Berliner and Conte, 1990) or is being emotionally neglected in some way (Finkelhor, 1984; Bagley and Ramsey, 1986). Further, 'parental alcoholism' and 'residential instability' are two interdependent variables also statistically associated with increased risk of victimization (Sas and Cunningham, 1995: 67). The research by Elliott et al (1995), referred to above, reported that sex offenders most often chose children who had family problems, were alone, lacked confidence, and were indiscriminate in their trust of others. In other words, offenders will find and fill a void in the child's life.

Often the target will be single parent families where usually the woman herself is vulnerable either economically or emotionally (Herman, 1981; Bagley and Ramsey, 1986; Elliott, Brown, and Kilcoyne, 1995; Gallagher, 1998). These include women who seek a 'father-figure' for their children or those who are drug-addicted who will trade their children for drugs (Salter, 1995: 39). One of the easiest ways to make contact with a child is to live with one. Offenders seek out single mothers by placing or responding to advertisements in 'lonely hearts' columns in the eventual hope of forming a family relationship—either moving in with or marrying that person in order to gain access to their children (Salter, 1995: 55; NCIS, 2003). In Sas and Cunningham's study (1995: 22), for example, while 30 per cent of the children had been abused by someone their mothers had never met, in 30 per cent of cases the offender and victim had lived together, and in half of all cases, the mothers were good friends of, or related to, the abusers (Sas and Cunningham, 1995: 74). Offenders also aspire to find a partner with whom they can have children which provide ready access to victims to abuse (McAlinden, 2006a: 349).

Additionally, the absence of either or both parents is also a risk factor (Bagley and Ramsey, 1986). Several studies have identified separation from the father as a risk factor (Finkelhor, 1984; Russell, 1986). Other studies have found that the absence of the biological mother from the child's life has a strong impact on the likelihood of becoming a victim of sexual abuse (See Herman, 1981; Finkelhor, 1984). Children with absent parents have less protection than those within a traditional family unit, since it may be potentially easier to create opportunities to be alone and unsupervised with the child (Craven, Brown, and Gilchrist, 2006: 293).

Familial grooming is intended to make the victim's guardians feel comfortable with the offender, affording them easy and recurring access to their children. Some offenders have been successful in persuading the child's parents to consent to their child having unaccompanied outings or overnight stays with the offender, providing the abuser with an opportunity to offend with impunity (Salter, 2003: 5; Powell, 2007: 38). In addition, a trusting relationship with the child's family ensures that parents or carers will be less likely to believe any potential accusations or disclosures made by children.

Intra-familial grooming

Intra-familial and quasi-intra-familial abusers also isolate the child victim from potential sources of protection such as the other non-abusing parent, siblings, or friends (Craven, Brown, and Gilchrist, 2006: 293). Leberg (1997) outlines a range of strategies employed by the offender to this end. These include encouraging the other parent, mothers usually, to develop social activities and hobbies outside the home in order to create opportunities to be alone with their victims; isolating the other parent from friends or other family members to prevent them confiding any concerns they may have in someone outside the home; and encouraging alcohol dependency to reduce the awareness of the other parent about the ongoing abuse or their wider credibility in the event of disclosure. Indeed, following Sykes and Matza's (1957) neutralization theory, the child's family or even the wider community may also be groomed by employing rationalizing mechanisms. This 'cognitive dissonance' on the part of parents and carers may work to assist offenders' efforts at grooming (Craven, Brown, and Gilchrist, 2006: 293). If a parent has instinctive concerns about the trustworthiness of the offender after a period of time once their acquaintance and acceptance of the offender has become well established, their thoughts and reasoning can be changed to become consistent with the offender's and their own behaviour (van Dam, 2001: 100).[34] This also allows the offender to gain useful clues about the practices and dynamics of a particular family, or 'insider status' (van Dam, 2001: 156–7, 182–5) long before any abuse actually takes place. This reinforces the potential longevity of grooming behaviour (Sanford, 1982) and the assiduous planning which may lie behind it.

---

[34] This accords with what psychologists and sociologists refer to as self-perception theory that individuals infer their attitudes from their own behaviour (see van Dam, 2001: 100, citing Brehm and Kassin, 1993).

Grooming the community

Aside from the child's family, the community can also be primed and controlled through the grooming process as further gatekeepers of access to a particular child or multiple children. Many offenders tend to adopt a pattern of socially responsible and caring behaviour in public as a means of integrating themselves within the local community. They endeavour to build a good reputation and to create a strong social perception of themselves as being a trustworthy and dependable member of the local church or community, a charming or nice man exceptionally kind to children or helpful to adults (Salter, 2003: 34). In this vein, offenders can pretend to be parents themselves to gain the social acceptance and trust of other parents and carers (Powell, 2007: 27–8). Offenders also make themselves indispensable to the local community by undertaking jobs that other people are reluctant to do (Leberg, 1997; Powell, 2007: 26–7).

In helping out in the local community, offenders 'are considering how their efforts will be rewarded later when they can then abuse the children in that community' (Craven, Brown, and Gilchrist, 2006: 293). As Hare and Hart (1993) argue, offenders are able to 'read' the community and assess what they need from their surrounding environment in order to abuse and then take the necessary steps to fulfil those needs. Numerous excerpts from Anna Salter's book, based on interviews with convicted sexual offenders, reinforce the proposition that sex offenders employ a range of techniques aimed at social deception which are often tailored to the dynamics of the particular social situation. A particularly telling statement comes from a violent rapist of both adults and children: 'I lived the life of a chameleon or a salamander, changed colors with the wind. I didn't just lead a double life. I lived multiple lives. Whatever life the situation called for, I lived it...I could feed back to people what I thought they wanted to see and what I thought they wanted to hear (2003: 34–5). This underscores the highly skilled nature of some sex offenders and also the potentially far-reaching and multi-layered nature of grooming behaviour.

Further, in a similar way as occurs with the child's family, the community is often also groomed so that if the victim makes a disclosure, the community will support the perpetrator rather than the victim, because the social perception of the offender is that they are considered more believable than the child (Craven, Brown, and Gilchrist, 2007: 293). An examination of a high profile case of sex offending against children in Northern Ireland—the McDermott brothers' case—provides a clear example of the key variables of grooming as they operate with both victims and within the local community. This case involved four brothers who faced 60 charges of child abuse in the small community of Donagh in County Fermanagh spanning five decades. One of the brothers was sentenced to nine years in 2010 and two were deemed mentally unfit to stand trial and were released back into the community.[35] The principal reasons why the local community remained ignorant of the abuses for years was attributed to the fact that the brothers 'operated below the radar'; had 'carefully chosen victims', who were 'criminalised' in that they may have committed minor vandalism so that they would tend not to be believed; used 'threats or treats' with victims; and had 'the trust of the local community' (Mowen, 2011).

Primary Research: The Grooming Process

The critical review of the literature above indicates that grooming is a highly complex and prevalent sexual behaviour, permeating the offender's inter-personal and social interactions with victims, significant others, and the immediate environment. Grooming has emerged as an intricate and integral part of the offending process in terms of how offenders may overcome internal and external barriers to offending. The term encompasses a broad range of preparatory behaviours which precede abuse and prevent its discovery or disclosure. Offenders use these techniques with children (in both on-line and face-to-face settings), and with their families, and the wider community in both extra-familial and intra-familial settings. In particular, however, the dominant construction of grooming within the research-based literature to date is that of a conscious process undertaken by a sexually motivated offender which is axiomatic to the onset of extra-familial sexual offending against children. What follows draws out the major themes that emerged from the primary research highlighting original and significant insights into conceptualizations of 'grooming', the dominant paradigms, and its role in sexual abuse cases.

---

[35] The case led to a Criminal Justice Inspection of the handling of sexual offences cases by the justice agencies in Northern Ireland (Criminal Justice Inspection Northern Ireland, 2010).

Conceptualizing the grooming process

Professional conceptualizations of grooming were largely congruent with the theoretical literature with some notable variations. In the course of the 51 interviews, a number of recurring phrases were used by interviewees to denote their understanding of 'grooming'. These included, 'the setting up of a situation' or 'the creation of an environment', and 'the establishing of a relationship' and, in particular, 'trust'. Professionals made reference to a variety of synonyms to describe the grooming process such as 'enticing', 'ensnaring', 'persuading', 'entrapping', 'enabling', 'befriending', 'preparing' or 'making ready', 'manipulating', 'ingratiating', 'initiating', and 'targeting'. For many, grooming was explained by explicit reference to the psychological literature and specifically Finkelhor's (1984) internal and external exhibitors. One senior statutory sector practitioner involved in work with offenders gave what emerged as a typical definition: 'a psychological process used by a perpetrator to befriend and engage with a victim for the purposes of exploitation'.[36]

A key theme to emerge from the primary data is the complexity and multi-faceted nature of grooming. Interviewees were cognisant of the intricacies and subtleties of grooming on a number of levels. First, there was disagreement as to whether grooming was a subtle or a more overtly coercive process (Howitt, 1995: 78–9; Pryor, 1996). Most interviewees took care to emphasize the absence of coercive or forceful aspects in this type of behaviour. One senior statutory sector professional involved in sex offender treatment or management described it as: 'the process that a person goes through…to surreptitiously achieve his end of sexual offending'.[37] These dual and conflicting aspects of the process, however, were also expressed by a handful of interviewees within the same sentence where the inherent coercion of 'bribes and offering nice things'[38] (Conte, Wolf, and Smith, 1989: 293) were seen as going hand in hand with 'intimidation or scaring tactics'.[39] These malevolent and benign aspects of the process are also reflected in the range of verbs used by interviewees outlined above which range from 'befriending' and 'persuading' at the lower non-offensive end of the scale to 'ensnaring', 'manipulating', and 'entrapping' at the other.

---

[36] RI 8 (23 June 2011).   [37] RI 5 (14 June 2011).
[38] RI 1 (11 May 2011).   [39] Ibid.

For one practitioner involved in sex offender risk assessment, the 'spectrum of ways in which individuals get control of a victim',[40] means that it is difficult to produce a one-size-fits-all definition (Elliott, Browne, and Kilcoyne, 1995: 109). As they acknowledged, such behaviour encompasses a breadth of individual offender motivation and offending pathways:

… from people who don't use any psychological manipulation…and then you have those who just use physical violence or threats…through to cases who use much more sophisticated…power dynamics or interpersonal skills…to set up situations that allow them to develop that relationship with a potential victim, and…take that further in a more graded way…I think it is quite difficult to then say there is a dividing line between these different ways of controlling victims.[41]

This analysis also tends to confirm, that in tandem with public discourses (Gillespie, 2004a: 586; McAlinden, 2006a: 341–2), within professional circles, as one senior voluntary sector practitioner conceded, grooming 'is a very woolly term that gets thrown around and used in all sorts of ways'.[42]

Stereotypical views also appear to permeate professional as well as public discourses on sexual offending. Many interviewees described grooming as part and parcel of the 'manipulative' or 'devious', 'sophisticated' skill set possessed by sex offenders. Grooming, however, was also pinpointed by a small but significant minority of interviewees as a regular technique characterizing routine human interaction with others where we are 'lured into a false sense of something'[43] or engaged in 'impression management'.[44] As one police officer succinctly put it, 'grooming is inherent, I think, in people's psyche generally'.[45] Another professional involved in offender management elaborated further:

I suppose it is important to look at in terms of…how do we actually interact with each other. Now if you take the sexual bit out of it,…I think it's part of a continuum of what is normal people behaviour, in terms of how we interact with each other, how as children we learn to get what we want, how as parents we get children to do what we want, how genders interact, how relationships form, how we manage our managers, how we manage our staff…As people, we are constantly working with other people for

---

[40] SC 9 (24 August 2011).   [41] Ibid.
[42] EW 1 (1 September 2011).   [43] RI 3 (16 May 2011).
[44] EW 8 (14 September 2011).   [45] NI 8 (6 July 2011).

whatever ends…Quite often we are working to get something out of a situation ourselves. And the sexual grooming is no different in a way…[46]

As a result, as one treatment professional stated, the important distinction for offenders in particular is that 'It is not the behaviours that are wrong. It is the fact that it is an inappropriate target, that's the difference'[47] (see also Fernandez, 2006: 191). The particular difficulties attached to separating grooming type behaviours which were more usual and innocuous from those that had an ulterior harmful motive were also related to the 'sexual motivation' or 'intentionality' of the offender (Finkelhor, 1986; Norrie, 2005). For some professionals, there were identifiable patterns of behaviour tending to separate out those who had potentially harmful intentions towards children. This was described by one interviewee involved in victim support as: 'you're looking at things like repetition and over identification with kids'.[48] That grooming often constitutes 'everyday behaviour',[49] however, also highlights the particular difficulties in targeting and criminalizing such behaviour within current legal and policy frameworks, particularly in the early part of the grooming process and before actual abuse occurs (see Chapter 6).

The purpose and process of grooming

Most interviewees categorized grooming in terms of gaining access, securing victim compliance, or reducing their resistance to abuse. There was also broad affirmation, as this book has contended, of the variety and intricacy of the process. One independent practitioner made reference to the 'whole continuum [of grooming]…from very sophisticated to more simplistic methods of just using rewards…giving attention to children, making them think they're important'.[50] As they noted, this often goes against the stereotypical view of the grooming process with some very important consequences. One independent interviewee involved in work with both victims and offenders asserted:

The most basic thing is around this whole idea of giving them sweets or that sort of stuff, whereas in actual fact an awful lot of the time it's not…a lot of the cases I've worked with where the victim will say…they stood up for me, maybe when mummy came in and got cross or mummy wouldn't

---

[46] NI 9 (14 July 2011).   [47] SC 11 (7 September 2011).
[48] RI 1 (11 May 2011).   [49] NI 13 (27 July 2011).
[50] NI 4 (1 June 2011).

allow me to do…daddy would have always said, sure let her go. So really what they experienced was my daddy was really good, my daddy let me do things that my mummy wouldn't…and that's that splitting of the…protective parent/child relationship.[51]

Only four professionals, who had worked with both victims and offenders, however, commented that grooming also has a secondary purpose beyond facilitating the commission of the offence (Salter, 1995, 2003). One interviewee phrased it rhetorically: 'How do you compromise the wellbeing and the safety and the voice of the child, both in the process of becoming a victim, but also in not revealing that afterwards?'[52] This noteworthy omission within professional discourses about the dual purpose of grooming also stems from the literature as outlined in Chapter 2.

Within this broader context, for a handful of assessment and treatment professionals, grooming had most resonance in normalizing sexually harmful behaviour (Ost, 2004: 148) to the extent that the victim did not even perceive themselves as having being abused. As one interviewee commented acknowledging the fact that grooming can stem from ordinary and routine patterns of behaviour within the family (Phelan, 1995: 10, 13): 'a lot of the abuse if the children are young can take place around the normal routines of a household…the bathing, the bedtime, and children, if they're very young will…normalize it to a degree because they won't have known anything different'.[53] For another interviewee this lack of firm sexual or personal boundaries was also clearly related to a process of 'unaware' or 'subconscious grooming'.[54] According to this view, while there is 'usually some degree of planning…it is about how conscious to the man that is, and…very often, that's not a conscious thing'.[55] These important viewpoints go against the grain of the literature by acknowledging that preparatory behaviours which normalize abuse can be as much about intuitive and innate actions on the part of offenders as opposed to more deliberate or conscious processes. As another practitioner involved in work with offenders stated succinctly, 'that's the big thing about grooming, isn't it. It is so powerful it doesn't need to be said'.[56]

Indeed, such views reinforce the powerful and potent role which grooming plays within intra-familial abuse in particular, whether of

---

[51] NI 2 (23 May 2011).   [52] EW 13 (22 September 2011).
[53] NI 4 (1 June 2011).   [54] RI 11 (5 July 2011).
[55] EW 4 (12 September 2011).   [56] SC 5 (22 August 2011).

the child or the family environment (Phelan, 1995; Sas and Cunningham, 1995; McAlinden, 2006a). As I have argued above, the shame and guilt which lie at the heart of the abusive process when combined with the power dynamics between adults and children within intra-familial relationships also help to ensure the child's silence whether or not the offender has specifically warned the child not to disclose. As one professional who has worked with both perpetrators and survivors stated: 'you get perpetrators using the *we* word...it's not what I'm doing to you, it's what *we're* doing. So they...induce guilt in the kid that I'm doing something shameful or bad...But...a lot of survivors didn't need to be told, don't tell. The power relationship actually guaranteed that they wouldn't tell...because it's daddy doing this'.[57] These twin dynamics—the normalization of abuse and the power imbalance in such abusive relationships—mean that in its most extreme form, grooming can also work at an 'inter-generational level'[58] within an 'incestuous family'[59] to facilitate sexual offending, to ensure that 'these things become quite entrenched and engrained',[60] particularly with younger abusers, and ultimately inhibit effective professional intervention.

The consequences for victims

The majority of existing work has focused on the effects of the abuse itself on victims rather than the effects of the pre-abuse grooming process (Berliner and Conte, 1985; Browne and Finkelhor, 1986; Phelan, 1995; Sas and Cunningham, 1995; Lewis and Mullis, 1999). As a result of the processes of normalization, however, it is not only the consequences of abuse which can be extremely damaging for victims but the legacy of being groomed in particular can often be very difficult for survivors to manage. For several interviewees, the primary focus on the actual offence means that often grooming emerges as the 'forgotten' aspect of sexual abuse. A probation professional commented:

Suddenly their whole life is turned upside down. Can they trust people again? Their whole belief system in themselves is completely eroded. They don't know who they are any more. They don't know what the world means any more. And that actually is often ignored, or not seen in terms of how to deal with victims and how they understand what has happened to themselves.[61]

---

[57] RI 7 (20 June 2011).   [58] NI 14 (3 August 2011).
[59] NI 11 (18 July 2011).   [60] Ibid.   [61] NI 9 (14 July 2011).

In the words of one social services professional 'for the victim…it's often the methods of grooming that are used, that nearly cause the most emotional damage in the long term…even sometimes more than the sexual abuse itself'.[62] This is because, in the words of a treatment professional, 'they [victims] understand the subtleties of what was happening when they were ten, eleven, twelve, that they didn't understand at the time…and the betrayal of trust can be much more traumatic for somebody, than the actual sexual abuse piece'.[63] Grooming also causes long-term effects for victims where particular triggers may invoke past memories of abuse (Commission of Investigation, 2011: para 27.10). As one interviewee explained: 'that's what they remember…that's where they used to take me, or that was the perfume…or that was the clothes they bought me, or that's how they smelt when they were close by me or whenever we went to…In the same way for any of us, but we use familiarization with a positive memory'.[64] Once more, as argued throughout, such consequences are even more devastating within the context of intra-familial abuse, largely because of the complex psychological processes that happens when children are groomed by an adult who is caring for them (Giaretto, 1978; Phelan, 1995; Sas and Cunningham, 1995). As a senior statutory sector professional explained:

When they disclosed against their abuser and that abuse was stopped, they lost the one person in their life who was their emotional support…And I think in terms of the recovery process for them, that was really affected by the fact that they didn't get the emotional support from the family, because the person who was their emotional support was also the abuser, and that contact had to cease.[65]

The impact of grooming on work with victims will be addressed further in Chapter 6.

Dominant modes of grooming

While some interviewees had encountered a mix of cases, there was broad acknowledgement of the various typologies of grooming outlined earlier. The most common forms of grooming encountered by professionals were intra-familial grooming both in terms of adult-child relationships and, to a lesser extent, within sibling

---

[62] RI 4 (13 June 2011).   [63] RI 10 (5 July 2011).
[64] NI 2 (23 May 2011).   [65] RI 5 (14 June 2011).

relationships. Interview responses reflected the words of a treatment professional, while 'a lot of it is about grandfather on granddaughter and father on daughter abuse',[66] cases of intra-familial abuse could also involve close neighbours or friends or members of the extended family (Sas and Cunningham, 1995; Davis et al, 1999). Across the jurisdictions and the professional spheres, a growing number of internet-related cases were noted (see also Martellozzo, 2012). As another practitioner stated: 'on our sex offender programme at least a third of the sex offenders we work with have engaged in some form of internet abuse, be it ranging from downloading images of children being abused to actually actively seeking out children through the internet'.[67] This was also commonly recognized across all four jurisdictions as a growth area for the future, which would be likely to involve increasing numbers of young people.

The befriending and targeting of the family in particular surfaced as a significant dimension of grooming and, as part and parcel of gaining access to the child, often took precedence over the grooming of the child themselves (McAlinden, 2006a: 348–9). A senior statutory sector interviewee involved in the provision of sex offender treatment commented: 'the most common way in which people get access' was 'getting to know the family, babysitting, offering to help, being very well liked by the family, trusted by the family'.[68] Similarly, the seeking out of families or adults with obvious vulnerabilities, including single mothers, victims of domestic violence, or those with learning difficulties, was commonly regarded as a key feature of the offending process (Elliott, Brown, and Kilcoyne, 1995; Gallagher, 1998). This was described by the same interviewee:

Adults very often would groom other adults but they may have vulnerabilities...quite a lot of grooming goes on with a more vulnerable person, sometimes, to gain access to her and sometimes her children. And therefore she doesn't have the protective factors that are needed in order to protect her children or in order to protect herself.[69]

While both parents and the child may be groomed, the motivation for the offender is quite different. As a professional involved in child protection pointed out: 'the motivation for the victim is about sexual abuse, but the motivation in terms of grooming the adult is

---

[66] SC 7 (23 August 2011).   [67] RI 2 (11 May 2011).
[68] NI 1 (23 May 2011).   [69] Ibid.

about control'.[70] This emphasis on family vulnerability, however, was not to minimize the role of individual victim identification and selection. Another interviewee involved in child protection stated: 'we often have families where there's only one particular child...that has been abused, even though there might be other children that fit the type in terms of age and gender. So I think a big question for me is always, what is it about that particular child...that allowed that to happen within that family.'[71] In this context, victim selection may be as much about congruence with the child in terms of their emotional vulnerability (Finkelhor, 1984) as well as physical characteristics (van Dam, 2001). Further significant issues were raised regarding new and emerging forms of grooming.

On-street grooming

Despite growing evidence of its existence within the literature (Barnardo's, 2009; Beckett, 2011) and in a range of high profile cases discussed in Chapter 2, many interviewees had never heard of the term 'street'/'on street' or 'localized grooming'. Of those who had, they commonly described a case they had encountered, usually within the context of 'gang culture', which fitted this typology though they did not explicitly use these terms. One interviewee stated:

We're very much aware of a situation in X where that's happened. You're looking at twelve and thirteen year olds...it's just the way the gangs of kids developed, and it got to a situation where nobody could distinguish who was doing what to who. There was the sense that there was a couple of girls and a couple of boys and they were interchanging sexually where there was supposed to be relationships, but there is that sense that peer pressure/ grooming is happening...And again you're looking at the kids that just don't have the capacity or understanding to think any differently.[72]

Interviewees conceded that as professionals they had limited capacity to intervene in such situations. This same interviewee continued: 'but we've got no evidence for it, the [police] couldn't do anything about it because it wasn't clear where the consent lay and where the problem lay'.[73] Those involved in front-line services with children were more familiar with this process. 'Street grooming' at an organized level for the purposes of child sexual exploitation,

---

[70] NI 13 (27 July 2011).   [71] RI 4 (13 June 2011).
[72] RI (11 May 2011).   [73] Ibid.

has emerged as a significant and growing phenomenon in both Northern Ireland and England and Wales, where children living in residential care appear to be especially vulnerable (Barnardo's, 2009; Beckett, 2011). In Birmingham, in common with some of the cases outlined in Chapter 2, 'that usually takes the form of Asian males in the city grooming young white females',[74] and where 'individuals sit in cars outside our children's homes'[75] (see also CEOP, 2011a). A practitioner in Northern Ireland noted that much remains unknown about this particular aspect of grooming and agencies 'haven't got to grips with it 100 per cent in terms of how it operates'.[76]

A number of features, however, stood out. The use of mobile phones features heavily in this process indicating a potential cross-over with on-line forms of grooming: 'they would text saying, you're loved, you're wanted...there's a party going on do you fancy a good time...and if so, text back...we don't know how that person got the young person's number. But certainly the mobile phone is a big, big problem'.[77] There was also a cross-over with peer forms of grooming and, as previously discussed, a blurring of the lines between victim and perpetrator within the continuum of offending (Montgomery-Devlin, 2008). As a senior police officer explained: 'if you think of your sexual exploitation cases in residential units, where a young girl is maybe encouraging other young girls into getting involved, so they are actually turning into an offender themselves'.[78] As will be argued further in the final part of the book, given the newness and complexity of this dimension of sexual exploitation and grooming more needs to be done, therefore, to raise awareness of these and other possible sources of harm to children, not just among the public but also at a professional level.

Peer-to-peer grooming

Another developing theme was the multiple constructs of the concept of 'peer-to-peer' grooming, a concept which has not been explicitly recognized in the generally small literature on adolescent abuse (Kaufman, Hilliker, and Daleiden, 1996; Kaufman et al, 1998; Leclerc, Beauregard, and Proulx, 2008) as well as the further

---

[74] EW 5 (13 September 2011). See Gilligan and Akhtar (2006) for a discussion of cultural issues surrounding child sexual abuse (Chapter 2).
[75] Ibid.   [76] NI 3 (26 May 2011).   [77] Ibid.
[78] NI 7 (30 June 2011).

novel aspect of older adult offenders grooming younger offenders. Police officers in Northern Ireland and Scotland recounted case examples of 'sexting'[79] among the 13 to 17 age group—where a young male would perhaps send naked photographs of a girl around a peer group via a mobile phone with other young males then threatening the girl with telling her parents or a teacher if she did not comply in sending them more images. This was commonly regarded, in the words of one police officer, as 'the fastest growing area of indecent images of children, essentially them with their mobile phones taking photos of themselves, where some of that will be down to grooming'.[80] Another police officer commented: 'the peer to peer grooming is so rife...and peer to peer cyber bullying as well. You know the whole grooming/bullying thing really just meshes together. It's hard to determine where one ends and the other begins'.[81] This also broadly accords with the literature which suggests that the issue of 'cyber bullying' (Koefed and Ringrose, 2011) and 'sexting' are fairly prevalent[82] and highly complex. They involve threatening and coercive behaviour by peers, gendered risks (girls are most adversely effected as well as ever younger children), reveal wider culturally specific sexual pressures, and are amplified by technology (Livingstone and Helsper, 2009; Ringrose and Erikson Barajas, 2011; Ringrose et al, 2012).

Several interviewees also made reference to offenders grooming other offenders, an issue not previously highlighted by the literature. This typically occurred within the context of group treatment programmes, usually where there is an age differential between offenders. One interviewee recounted a specific case, describing how they had become aware that two members of the group were meeting outside the programme:

There was an older guy in the group and his orientation was young males...I was really taken aback. This [young] guy, he suffers from

---

[79] 'Sexting' has been defined as 'the creation and transmission of sexual images by minors' (Lounsbury, Mitchell, and Finkelhor, 2011) or 'creating, sharing and forwarding sexually suggestive nude or nearly nude images through mobile phones and the internet' (Lenhart, 2009).

[80] SC 2 (22 August 2011).

[81] NI 8 (6 July 2011).

[82] In an overview of the research-based evidence, Ringrose et al (2012: 6) found that quantitative research on sexting has established rates of between 15 to 40 per cent among young people, depending on age and the way sexting is defined and measured.

Asperger's,…and the other man was a teacher. And one day the young guy had a book and I said, that's a very interesting book and he said, yeah, the other guy gave it to me…he asked me for my number a couple of weeks ago and phoned me, and said he had it, so once I had read it we'd meet for coffee and chat about it. So I could see it, you know, in exactly the same format he used to get young guys into his house…So it was like it was happening actually in front of us.[83]

However, despite the differences in context, for this professional, it was 'just the same modus operandi, just setting it up'.[84] This novel extension of the grooming concept also has implications for the content and effectiveness of sex offender treatment and management programmes, as discussed in the last part of the book.

Young sexual abusers

Following on from the previous section, a further significant theme to stem from the primary data was the variation in the nature of grooming according to the age or gender of the offender. In relation to younger offenders, although several practitioners recalled examples of cases of young sexual offenders involving the internet, particularly indecent images of children, there were mixed findings in relation to grooming and its role in face-to-face contexts. In relation to sibling abuse, for example, although many of the dynamics were considered similar in terms of the 'the relationship, [and] the secrecy',[85] preparatory strategies as a prelude to offending, as might be expected, also emerged as being more experimental and less well developed and sophisticated than with adult perpetrators. One treatment professional summed up the differences in the processes of initiation and continuation of such abuse:

It's adolescent abuse rather than adult abuse, when there's a lot of confusion for the adolescent around their own sexual identity and what's happening for them in the world…It would be more…inappropriate behaviour towards family members…I'm talking maybe a couple of years difference,…maybe a fifteen year old and a twelve year old, I'm not talking about a seventeen year old and a five year old.[86]

For other interviewees, however, 'adolescent cases…were less subtle in a way and very often more coercive'[87] as often there is 'a power differentiation, [where] there's an older sibling with a younger

---

[83] RI 3 (16 May 2011).   [84] Ibid.   [85] SC 9 (24 August 2011).
[86] RI 6 (14 June 2011).   [87] EW 1 (1 September 2011).

child',[88] and the process can be more about 'intimidation and threatening behaviour, basically bullying somebody who was a bit more inadequate into doing what they didn't want to do'.[89] As an interviewee involved in therapeutic work with young sexual abusers explained: 'sexual offences committed by adults and children are the same and tend to follow the same patterns, but they do it for different reasons. So the motivation behind it might be different, but the actual act probably isn't...they still have to get round those external factors to be able to commit the offences they commit'[90] (see also Finkelhor, 1984).

These findings go against the grain of the literature which has generally established that intra-familial adolescent sex offenders are more prone to using less overtly coercive strategies to obtain the victim's trust such as the giving of gifts (Kaufman, Hilliker, and Daleiden, 1996). Sexual crime committed by young offenders, however, can also be conceptualized as a transitory phase rather than evidence of the onset of a criminal career (Lussier and Davies, 2011). As a senior police officer cautioned: 'we should be digging a bit deeper and finding out...is it experimentation or is there something deviant starting to go on'.[91]

Gender differences

The differential impact of grooming on male and female victims has been noted above and below. Institutional studies of child sexual abuse (Barter, 1999; Gallagher, 1998) and those based on interviews with abuse victims (Hunter et al, 1992; Watkins and Bentovim, 1992) make it clear that boys and girls may be equally susceptible to 'grooming behaviour'. However, on one level, the process might be said to be more effective with boys who have demonstrated lower levels of victim disclosure (Hunter et al, 1992; Watkins and Bentovim, 1992). In comparison to the vast literature on male sex offending, female sexual offending has only recently emerged as a distinct realm of study, rather than as an adjunct of the dominant male paradigm.

The number of female offenders remains low, typically fewer than 5 per cent (Grubin, 1998; Vandiver and Walker, 2002; Cortoni and Hanson, 2005), although anecdotal evidence from this and

---

[88] RI 1 (11 May 2011).   [89] SC 8 (23 August 2011).
[90] NI 11 (18 July 2011).   [91] NI 7 (30 June 2011).

other studies would place this figure as slightly higher (Fergusson and Mullen, 1999; Finkelhor, Mitchell, and Wolak, 2000; Ashfield et al, 2010).[92] Existing work in the area has tended to concentrate on the differential assessment and treatment needs of female sex offenders (Ashfield et al, 2010; Gannon and Cortoni, 2010) and to a lesser extent offending pathways (Matthews, Matthews, and Speltz, 1989; Gannon, Rose, and Ward, 2008; Harris, 2010). There is little work, to date, however, which has specifically examined 'grooming' as a distinct variable in the pro-offending process. The current study, however, suggests important gender differences in terms of how the grooming process or the preparatory stages of abuse may operate.

Grooming and abuse by female offenders was commonly regarded, in the words of one interviewee involved in sex offender assessment, as being 'more subtle … more relational, and … less overt'.[93] This finding tends to contradict the literature which suggests that males are more likely to engage in grooming behaviours than women (Kaufman et al, 1995), who in turn are more likely to use force or violence (Moulden, Firestone, and Wexler, 2007: 399). While the highest risk female offenders shared many of the offence patterns of their male counterparts in terms of increased use of violence or force, this same interviewee acknowledged that on the whole, 'a lot of it was more about emotional affirmation than it was about sexual need'.[94] The available data on female abusers in this and other studies remains scant thus undermining concrete and reliable conclusions. The differential offending patterns of young sexual abusers and female abusers which precede actual abuse, however, are noteworthy issues which are absent from the existing literature and merit further detailed research.

In making these assertions, care must also be taken to guard against the socially and culturally conditioned perceptions of female sexuality and offending more generally which may negate concerns about risk. In this respect, women are typically regarded as passive in the sexual sphere and more likely to be regarded as victims than offenders, even within some professional discourses

---

[92] Cortoni and Hanson's (2005) analysis of prevalence studies of female sex offenders in the United States, the United Kingdom, Canada, Australia, and New Zealand, found an unweighted average of 3.8 per cent across the five countries.

[93] RI 11 (5 July 2011).

[94] Ibid.

(Denov, 2004; Bunting, 2005, 2007; Frey, 2010). Public perceptions of female sex offenders are firmly linked to high profile cases involving very serious sexual abuse or murder of children, including most recently Vanessa George and the Little Ted's Nursery case (see Chapter 5). One professional involved in work with female sex offenders commented: 'if you mention female sex offenders, immediately people think of Myra Hindley, Rose West and probably now, Vanessa George. So we have no frame of reference for anybody other than that'.[95] This discrepancy may stem, at least in part, from the unsettling thought that either women or children, who are traditionally thought to be vulnerable to abuse, are capable of grooming or abuse (Hetherton, 1999; Kemshall, 2004). In particular, such high profile cases suggest a number of typologies of female sex offending (Matthews, Matthews, and Speltz, 1989): teacher/ lover (where the woman has abused a position of trust); predisposed/intergenerational (where there is a history of family violence or abuse); and male coerced/co-offender (where the offending takes place in conjunction with a male).[96]

Such perceptions of the potential risk posed by sexual offenders, however, can be highly problematic. This same professional underlined the complexity of grooming as related to female sexual offenders and the knock-on effects of such cultural and gender bias in terms of both offender access and victim disclosure:

It is impossible to think about any notion of grooming without looking at the cultural niche in which women tend to live and demonstrate their behaviours…as far as women are concerned, there don't appear to be any external inhibitors…it is very easy for women to have unlimited access to children per se, simply because people don't question their motivations…[and] we can find different motivations attached to individual children…we also know…from what victims tell us, [that] it is so much more difficult to disclose abuse by a female and the likelihood of you being believed is much less. [97]

Moreover, gender differences in conceptualizations of 'grooming' and how the process may operate also have important consequences for how we may respond to it. In particular, underlying public

---

[95]   EW 14 (30 September 2011).
[96]   These broad typologies were based on a small number of female sexual offenders (16), although later studies have supported their validity (Matthews, 1998; Nathan and Ward, 2002; Vandiver and Kercher, 2004).
[97]   EW 14 (30 September 2011).

misconceptions about sex offenders being adult male predatory strangers belies the fact that sex offenders against children can also be female and, in some cases, children and young people. As discussed in Chapter 7, it becomes important then to address these misconceptions concerning the gendered and age-related aspects of grooming and abuse in developing protective and preventive education strategies aimed at reducing opportunities for abuse.

The role of grooming in gendered and sexualized violence

Grooming within intra-familial sexual abuse emerged as being embedded within gendered and sexual violence, including domestic and 'family violence' (Gelles, 1986), which causes significant trauma for victims (Herman, 1997). In this respect, one senior treatment professional explained how the dynamic may work with both child as well as adult victims, including those within same sex relationships: 'for offending against children the pathway may be different to offending against adults, but there's a huge power, control, violence dimension to the whole abuse system...the two are inextricably linked'.[98] In relation to the role of grooming within sexual abuse in particular, however, there were mixed responses in terms of both its usefulness as a theoretical concept as well as in clinical practice.

Deconstructing the terminology

While the overwhelming majority of interviewees emphasized the importance of the term 'grooming' within discourses on child sexual abuse, a few critical voices pointed out the dangers inherent in the injudicious use of what they regarded as a pejorative term (McAlinden, 2007a) (see Chapter 1). As a treatment professional explained:

The press take it up and they interpret it as...oh this is what they all do. And then before we know where we are...the next generation of therapists and psychologists...start to look for how they groomed. So, we're actually creating something by starting to put this into a discourse, as though it exists. And I think there are other ways of thinking about how men go about abusing...that's based...on rational choice and on intentionality and whatever, we've got to be really, really careful. And I don't think there's nearly enough work done on interrogating the

---

[98] NI 1 (23 May 2011).

perpetrators...ways of understanding and all that, without them also being influenced by the discourses...by the therapeutic discourses or the social discourses in which they're embedded...it's like a form of othering, I think.[99]

In this view, the term 'grooming' was ultimately unhelpful as 'language doesn't describe things...language creates'.[100] The notion of grooming, therefore, may be inherently problematic not only by reason of its likely negative impact on media and public opinion but also importantly its effect on the cognitive processes of offenders themselves (Fernandez, 2006: 191) as well as the knock-on effects in shaping future treatment and management discourses.

Several interviewees also pointed out that although preparatory behaviours which preceded offending were examined within the course of sex offender programmes, in the context of 'decisions', 'planning', and 'choices' the offender has made, the term 'grooming' was not used specifically. This was a term that offenders are often very resistant to, at least at first, primarily because of the implied deliberate motivation or intention to harm for which they seek to abdicate personal responsibility (Hudson, 2005: 70). For many offenders, there is a perception that they had a loving relationship with the child. As a senior treatment professional explained, 'from the offender's perspective it's not always grooming...it can be what they perceive to be love gone wrong...even in the current group I can think of guys who would completely retaliate at the idea of grooming, because grooming means planning and I didn't plan anything'.[101] Such avoidance on the part of offenders may also be related to the negative and unmitigated use of the term grooming within popular discourses and by the media in particular which tends to dehumanize sex offenders (Simon, 1998; Wykes, 2002; Hudson, 2005: 54).

While such views were most prominent in relation to an overemphasis on the term grooming, for a voluntary sector interviewee involved in reintegration work with offenders, the danger lay in its use as a euphemism in masking what they regarded as a very 'risky' process (see also Howitt, 1995: 176; Gallagher, 1998, 2000):

I think grooming is a very weak word for what I see as a very dangerous process. For somebody to have the confidence and the ability to go out and target a victim, and have the patience to wait, should it be a year, should it

---

[99] RI 7 (20 June 2011).   [100] Ibid.   [101] RI 5 (14 June 2011).

be six weeks. But...if they have that sexual urge...to have the ability to wait that long on it actually happening, to me, they're a very dangerous person.[102]

Ultimately, however, while the term was not one favoured by practitioners or commonly used in their work with offenders, most conceded that the type of preparatory behaviours which might be labelled as 'grooming' were a prominent feature of the majority of sexual abuse cases if not as a prelude to first offending, then at least subsequently.

Preferential v situational offending

Regarding the actual role of grooming in the child sexual abuse cases encountered by professionals, the division in views was generally congruent with the 'preferential'/'situational' dichotomy outlined earlier in this chapter (Cohen, Seghorn, and Calmas, 1969; Howells, 1981; Groth, Hobson, and Gary, 1982; Wortley and Smallbone, 2006: 13–18; Smallbone, Marshall, and Wortley, 2008: 160–2). That is, while some offenders are sexually attracted to children by preference, others are sexually orientated towards children in particular circumstances. The typical view of most interviewees, in the words of a senior police officer, was that 'if you set aside sexual offences where the victim is a stranger, there is normally an element of grooming involved in preparation for the crime'.[103] This also accords with Canter, Hughes, and Kirby's (1998) analysis of offending repertoires outlined above which distinguished between 'criminal-opportunist', which tended to be one-off random offences perpetrated on strangers; and 'intimate', which were characterized by the use of sexual grooming.

In the context of the current study, emphasis was placed in particular by professionals on the sequential nature of grooming, and the often meticulously planned, deliberate, and pre-determined course of conduct. One interviewee commented, for instance: 'I also find that...there's a lot of thinking and planning in it, so it's not opportunist...they've targeted their victim...It's not just about committing the offence. They seem to get pleasure out of the build up to commit the offence'.[104] Similarly, another professional stated: 'the preparation is often immaculate...people can plan for years,

---

[102] NI 5 (22 June 2011).   [103] SC 1 (22 August 2011).
[104] NI 5 (22 June 2011).

or work for years to create a situation to allow offending to take place'.[105]

A small but significant minority, however, downplayed the role of grooming in the onset of sexual abuse. For these professionals who worked across a range of spheres, 'there will be sex offences committed against children where there is not any preplanning or premeditation',[106] and where it is more about 'just taking advantage of opportunities that are there anyway',[107] in a 'situation where they have access to a child that they probably didn't plan it very well, to be that way'.[108] As an assessment professional who had consulted on over 170 cases explained: 'in terms of the classic stereotype of grooming, it is far less common an MO of sex offenders than people think it is...and the classic picture of the manipulative, predatory groomer is not what I come across in most serious sex offenders'.[109] The fact that most cases of child sexual abuse are not committed by predatory strangers as indicated in the existing literature (Grubin, 1998; McGee et al, 2002), but appear to emerge from uninhibited or emotionally close relationships with children also has implications for prevention and protection, as discussed in the last part of the book.

First time and subsequent offending

In describing the onset of sexual abuse, other interviewees who worked in offender treatment made the crucial distinction between first time and subsequent offending. This important aspect of the research, which has not previously emerged from existing work, highlights that grooming becomes a much more 'conscious' process at the 'point where it switches from that sort of opportunistic discovery, to actually becoming something that he wants to perpetuate and see through'.[110] One interviewee explained further:

Sometimes the first offence is intentional. And often the first offence is not intentional. It emerges in a kind of a context of a whole range of things happening. The second offence is always intentional. Having done that, having crossed that divide once, next time people know what they're doing...So...in many cases there may not have been grooming, before the first offence. In my clinical experience I have met a lot of men where the first time it happened, you could almost say, by accident. Rough and tumble games on the

---

[105] SC 1 (22 August 2011).   [106] SC 3 (22 August 2011).
[107] NI 4 (1 June 2011).   [108] EW 3 (12 September 2011).
[109] SC 9 (24 August 2011).   [110] EW 8 (14 September 2011).

floor, never having seen the child in a sexual light, but liked the kid, but issues going on in his own life…hits the child's breast, suddenly has a sexual thought…then it becomes locked in…and taken from there. And I think that it's wrong for survivors and wrong for the men to assume that there's always been a grooming process in the beginning.[111]

Similarly, another interviewee involved in victim support reflected:

I think a lot of them had relationships that turned sexual with children…and once that happened, I think grooming was crucial, but I think the initial crossing of the line wasn't necessarily a deliberate act for the majority of people that I met…but once they did it, and they wanted to do it again, then we're into grooming mode…they were setting up situations. So it plays a big role once they've crossed the line the first time.[112]

There was also some acknowledgement that the 'internet may well be very different…where men deliberately falsify their identity to make contact with children'[113] (see also Durkin, 1997: 15; Quayle and Taylor, 2001; Whitty, 2002; Whitty and Joinson, 2009: 19–32). Opportunity or accessibility, however, as outlined above, also play a huge role in on-line forms of sexual offending against children for those who have a propensity to offend (Cooper, McLaughlin, and Campbell, 2000; Quayle and Taylor, 2001: 598; O'Connell, 2003: 3). In this respect as another treatment professional told me, 'with internet offenders, we call it the pre-discovery group, where there isn't a conscious acknowledgement of child related sexual interest until the accessibility that the internet provides allows them to view images…with some individuals that predisposition will remain in abeyance forever…until the trigger situation occurs'.[114]

Thus, a more nuanced account of grooming emerges from the primary research which challenges the claim that 'grooming is a ubiquitous feature of the sexual abuse of children' (Thornton, 2003: 144). The findings from the current research reveal this proposition to be somewhat of an overstatement in the sense that grooming does not operate as a *preamble* to sexual offending against children in all cases. This analysis has also afforded a more sophisticated and insightful analysis of grooming and its role in cases of child sexual abuse, particularly within intra-familial contexts.

---

[111] RI 7 (20 June 2011).   [112] RI 1 (22 May 2011).
[113] RI 7 (20 June 2011).   [114] NI 12 (26 July 2011).

While grooming may have less resonance at the onset of sexual offending in cases where offenders are already in a close relationship with a child, in many cases, it nonetheless emerges as a core aspect in the aftermath of such abuse as part of the process of 'deception and control'[115] (Salter, 1995, 2003). It may work to reduce the 'chances of (a) being caught, somebody walking in on them, (b) the child telling, and (c) other people picking it up',[116] as well as in facilitating subsequent offending. As argued above, grooming would appear to fit neatly within the 'approach/automatic' and 'approach/explicit' pathways to offending (Ward and Hudson, 1998b) where, in the words of one interviewee, 'constant choices are being made...about how to abuse',[117] either as part of a conscious or unconscious process.

It is also important to acknowledge that in other cases, however, the offender may not deliberately set out to sexually offend against a child, but may simply take advantage of a precise set of circumstances, rather than engineer them (Wortley and Smallbone, 2006: 13–18; Smallbone, Marshall, and Wortley, 2008: 160–2). For first-time offending in particular, the opportunity to offend often arises through a confluence of factors—the offender had at least a partial motivation to offend and was presented with access to a potential victim. This route into sexual offending against a child is also consistent with Ward and Hudson's (1998b) two other offending pathways—avoidant/active—where the offender attempts to control pro-offending thoughts or behaviour but the strategies are ineffective or counterproductive, and avoidant passive—where the offender wishes to avoid abusive behaviour but lacks the coping skills to prevent it from happening. Even within these offending contexts, however, for those offenders who commit second and subsequent offences, grooming must have a role to play in maintaining the child in a situation of abuse. These arguments are also reinforced by the fact that after the known commission of a sexual offence, offenders are subject to a host of regulatory mechanisms and unlikely to be allowed contact with potential victims. The fact that the opportunity to commit further offending is also limited or taken away also goes some way towards explaining the generally

---

[115] EW 12 (19 September 2011).   [116] NI 2 (23 May 2011).
[117] NI 12 (26 July 2011).

low recidivism rate for sexual offenders, particularly those who
have only committed one offence.[118]

Conclusion

This chapter has attempted to counter the prevailing misconceptions surrounding grooming and, in particular, to deconstruct the
term and provide a more critical and nuanced account of the multiple understandings and manifestations of this process and its role
in child sexual abuse cases. In this respect, the term 'grooming' has
emerged as a 'useful shorthand...[which] then requires some
unpacking'.[119] The dominant public and policy paradigms of
grooming are fixated primarily on on-line risks to children as well
as those within organizational environments. The primary research
has established, however, that grooming behaviour becomes no less
threatening when extended into intra-familial and other social settings. Predominantly, this research belies the traditional use of the
term within the existing literature as a *preparatory* behaviour which
is *systemic* to child sexual abuse (Howitt (1995: 176; Gillespie,
2002a: 411; Thornton, 2003: 144; Kierkegaard, 2008: 42) (see
Chapter 2) and demonstrates that the onset of sexual offending
against children is considerably more complex than has previously
been suggested.

Within this broader context, I have shown that although grooming does not occur before the first offence in all cases, it nonetheless
emerges as a highly significant or, in the words of one interviewee
in this study, 'an implicit part of the process of sexual abuse'.[120] It
may work to normalize sexualized contact with children and breakdown interpersonal and social barriers to offending, as well as to
secure the child's compliance and facilitate subsequent offending in
the aftermath of the initial abuse. Further, it is this process of normalization and the ensuing betrayal of trust which ensures that, for
victims, grooming and associated behaviours which precede abuse
are as harmful as the sexual abuse itself.

---

[118] Whilst some studies suggest higher rates of recidivism for sex offenders (eg
Falshaw, Friendship, and Bates, 2003), Harris and Hanson's (2004) meta-analysis
of over 4,500 sexual offenders found a long-term re-offending rate of 24 per cent
over 15 years and that first-time offenders are significantly less likely to sexually
re-offend than those with previous convictions for sexual offences.

[119] EW 13 (22 September 2011).   [120] Ibid.

Fuller conceptual and practical understanding of the onset of the offending process with children, including the role of grooming, can enhance child protection and sex offender risk management and treatment discourses. As will be discussed further in the last part of the book, enhanced knowledge of the range of strategies employed by offenders to abuse children and ensure that it remains hidden has clear policy implications at the micro-level of social control for assessing and managing the risk posed by *known* sex offenders who have already come to notice. Moreover, these multiple understandings and realities of pro-offending behaviour also have policy implications for the prevention of child sexual abuse at a broader macro-level (Conte, Wolf, and Smith, 1989)—for developing effective public education and social protection programmes (Budin and Johnson, 1989) which address the diverse forms of sexualized contact with children and, in turn, for identifying potential or *unknown* risks before sexually harmful behaviour occurs.

5

'Institutional Grooming' and Abuse

> Entrapping them [children] involves deceiving and disarming
> adults also. Abusers may be good at their jobs, winning respect,
> affection, or fear from their colleagues and admiration from
> the parents whose children they corrupt. They are adept at
> avoiding detection and disciplinary or criminal charges—in
> which they are inadvertently assisted by the assumptions and
> values of our social institutions (Utting Report, 1997: 5).

Research has shown that many extra-familial sex offenders will
seek to make contact with children through employment settings
or through involvement in voluntary organizations (Morrison,
Erooga, and Beckett, 1994; Sullivan and Beech, 2002; Erooga,
2009a, 2009b). Despite the psychological literature which exists
on grooming and the legislative and policy framework which exists
to prevent unsuitable people from working with children, however,
the two have never been properly integrated (see McAlinden,
2006a, for an isolated example). There has been very little research
to date on the underlying institutional issues which allow such
abuse to arise (Colton, 2002: 34). Instead, most of what is known
about institutional abuse derives from case studies and official
reports.

This chapter critically examines current understandings of the
abuse of trust and authority within an institutional context as 'an
alternative method of gaining control' (Gillespie, 2002a: 240) over
a child and the immediate environment. Sex offenders are also
skilled in the process of targeting and grooming entire organizations, as much as individual children and those who work within
them. In this respect, I have previously coined the phrase 'institutional grooming' to describe the process in which offenders make
use of the unique features of an organizational environment—such
as power, authority, opportunity, anonymity, secrecy, and trust—
to abuse children, often over a period of time, with sometimes

complete impunity (McAlinden, 2006a). Moreover, sex offenders also appear to have an astute understanding of 'how institutions think' (Douglas, 1986) and are able to circumvent protective procedures or exploit system weaknesses to facilitate abuse and avoid exposure.

The range of public inquiries and official reviews into institutional child abuse in England and Wales, Scotland, Northern Ireland, and the Republic of Ireland have highlighted the prevalence of grooming behaviours with other staff, parents or carers, and children within an organizational environment (McAlinden, 2006a). Others have pinpointed the grooming process as it occurs within youth serving organizations, such as those related to sport (eg Brackenridge, 2001; Brackenridge and Fasting, 2005). I argue that the phenomenon of institutional child abuse within the context of care homes and residential schools run by Catholic religious orders provides additional insights into the processes of institutional grooming. In particular, some of the peculiar features of institutional grooming, including secrecy, autonomy, lack of supervision, and accountability, are especially heightened in relation to the organizational subculture which exists within an omnipotent institution such as the Catholic Church. Further, this analysis extends the notion of 'institutional grooming' beyond the current confines of institutional abuse to the processes of interaction between offenders and professionals who are responsible for their assessment, treatment, and management.

Public Inquiries and Official Reviews

The issue of what Sullivan and Beech (2002) have termed 'professional perpetrators'—sex offenders who use their employment as a 'cover' to target and sexually abuse children—has received worldwide attention. In Australia (Forde, 1999), Canada (Law Commission of Canada, 2000), and the United States (John Jay College, 2004, 2011), for example, there have been a number of high profile cases of institutional physical and sexual abuse of children. Such cases have occurred in both religious and secular settings, culminating in a range of public inquiries and reviews.[1] Within the United Kingdom and the Republic of Ireland, a number of tragic cases

---

[1] For an overview see in particular Llewellyn (2002) and Brennan (2007).

of institutional abuse have demonstrated the vulnerability of children in environments usually considered safe such as homes, clubs, and schools (McAlinden, 2006a: 350–2). Indeed, while the issue has resonated in each of the jurisdictions within the United Kingdom and Ireland, it has assumed a different focus and momentum within localized contexts. Within each of these four jurisdictions, the issue of institutional and institutionalized child abuse has also been subjected to sustained media and public outcry, providing the impetus for legislative and organizational change.

England and Wales

In England and Wales, a number of public inquiry reports or official reviews have resulted from the disclosure of institutional physical and sexual abuse in children's care homes (see Reder, Duncan, and Gray, 1993; Corby, Doig, and Roberts, 2001). The inquiries have included the Pindown Inquiry into allegations of excessively punitive regimes in Staffordshire children's homes (Levy and Kahan, 1991); the Ty Mawr Inquiry following allegations of misconduct in Gwent children's homes (Williams and McCreadie, 1992); the Leicestershire Inquiry into allegations of sexual abuse by management and staff in children's homes (Kirkwood, 1993); and the Waterhouse Report (2000) into the abuse of children in care homes in North Wales. The reviews have included the Warner Report (1992) on the selection, development, and management of staff in children's homes; the Utting Report (1997) on the safeguards for children living away from home; and the Nolan Committee Report (2001) on child protection policies in the Catholic Church in England and Wales. In contrast to the Republic of Ireland, with the exception of the Nolan Report, all of the major inquiries and reviews have involved state-run, secular institutions. These have highlighted systematic failures to respond to suspicions, reports, or allegations of abuse and have concluded that the extent of institutional child abuse and the implications for the management of the problem are extensive.[2]

---

[2] Following an investigation into abuses at Haut de la Garenne former children's home in Jersey, a number of individuals were found guilty of sexual assaults against children and young people: see eg I. Cobain, 'Jersey: Haut de la Garenne Children's Home Abuse Scandal Ends with One Last Conviction', *The Guardian*, 7 January 2011.

As noted in Chapter 1, these reports made similar recommendations to protect children, which have not been followed through (Parton, 2004; McAlinden, 2006a: 351–2). Several inquiries raised doubts about the accuracy of vetting and the consistency with which agencies use such systems. The Warner Inquiry (1992) found that 10 per cent of the heads of care homes and a third of employees were able to commence work before any formal references were received. The Utting Report (1997), some six years later, also expressed serious concerns about the handling of police checks and highlighted that insufficient consideration was given to references. The Waterhouse Report (2000) listed an index of inadequate procedures and breaches of policy from recruiting staff informally without obtaining references to failure to check foster families or employees before they commence work. Indeed, the report of the Bichard Inquiry arising from the 'Soham murders',[3] also highlighted 'systemic and corporate failures' in the local police management of their intelligence systems (2004: para 8). As Sullivan and Beech (2002) argue, such repeated failures raise questions not only about the speed and process of organizational change but also, more worryingly, whether any lessons have actually been learned.

Other recommendations resulted in a range of legislative developments within a short few years. These measures have generally attempted to improve child care practice and prevent offenders from making contact with children through organizations (Gallagher, 2000). In particular, the Safeguarding Vulnerable Groups Act 2006 in England and Wales, enacted in the aftermath of the Bichard Inquiry (Bichard, 2004), and its equivalent in Scotland[4] and Northern Ireland,[5] sought to streamline vetting and barring initiatives for those who wish to work with children and vulnerable adults. The potentially wide ranging remit of this legislation, in that it applied to all who would seek to work with such groups on a paid or voluntary basis, has been scaled back.[6] Nonetheless, the initial

---

[3] School caretaker, Ian Huntley, was convicted of the murders of Holly Wells and Jessica Chapman in Soham in 2002. The subsequent Bichard Inquiry examined vetting procedures in two police constabularies in England and Wales and the effectiveness of information sharing.

[4] The Protecting Vulnerable Groups (Scotland) Act 2006.

[5] The Safeguarding Vulnerable Groups (NI) Order 2007.

[6] See the Protection of Freedoms Act 2012, Part 5.

enactment of this regulatory framework is indicative of the contemporary panic and fear which exists within both popular and state discourses concerning sex offenders accessing children and grooming them for abuse through organizations.

Scotland

In Scotland, there have been fewer public inquiries into specific cases of institutional child abuse. Instead, there have been a greater number of historic reviews into the provision of residential care for children more broadly (eg Clyde Committee, 1946; Kilbrandon Committee, 1964; Skinner, 1992; Kendrick, 1995; Kent, 1997). In common with the Republic of Ireland, the predominant early concerns were focused on delinquency and neglect, as well as extreme corporal punishment, rather than sexual abuse (Magnusson, 1984; Hendrick, 2003). As noted in Chapter 3, the gradual emergence of child sexual abuse as a serious social problem in the United States (Kempe, 1978; Finkelhor, 1979; Parton, 1985) did not occur in Europe until some years later. It was only with the advent of the Cleveland Inquiry in England (Butler-Sloss Report, 1988), and the Orkney scandal in Scotland (Clyde Report, 1992) in the late 1980s to early 1990s, that there was a greater professional, social, and political awareness of child sexual abuse in Britain as a whole (Bagley and King, 1990: 25–37; La Fontaine, 1990), including the experiences of those who had been living in residential care (Shaw, 2007: 28; see also Colton et al, 2002; Hendrick, 2003).

The Shaw Report (2007) undertook a systemic review into historical institutional abuse in residential schools and children's homes in Scotland covering the period 1950–95. The review examined, inter alia, the regulatory framework which governed the running of such institutions, including the systems for monitoring and inspection, and compliance with these, as well as former residents' experiences of abuse. The report highlights a number of points relating to the circumstances surrounding the abuse: internal management of complaints about mistreatment or abuse was the preferred option (Davis, 1980) to 'avoid bad publicity and minimise disruption' (Shaw, 2007: 28); the response of staff upon learning of allegations of abuse was often to move the offender (Holman, 1996; Kahan, 2000); and the abuse of children and young people in care by other residents occurred in approximately 50 per cent of cases (Shaw, 2007: 31–2, citing Westcott and Clement, 1992; MacLeod, 1992).[7]

There have been three major independent inquiries into abuse in residential care in Scotland, along with two key official reviews. In relation to the inquiries, the Edinburgh inquiry was set up following the conviction of two men for the sexual abuse of children in care homes in Edinburgh and Lothian between 1973 and 1987 (Marshall, Jamieson, and Findlayson, 1999). Similarly, the Fife inquiry was set up following the conviction of a child care employee on 30 counts of child sexual abuse during the period 1959–83 in various child care settings (Black and Williams, 2002). Both inquiries recommended additional safeguards regarding staff recruitment and training, adequate record-keeping, and the prioritization of young people's concerns and 'whistle blowing'. The 2009 inquiry into the circumstances surrounding emotional, physical, and sexual abuse within Kerelaw residential school and secure unit identified a 'complex mix of cultural factors' (Frizell, 2009: para 1.40) which allowed abuse to happen and go unchallenged:

There were cliques and factionalism and inappropriate relationships which inhibited challenge and attempts at change, for which there was limited capacity . . . There was no robust system for performance management and supervision of staff was inadequate. The complaints system was inconsistent and poorly monitored and there was little follow-through from fact-finding investigations of young people's allegations (Frizell, 2009: para 1.40).

These factors also speak directly to the existence of an institutional subculture of 'control' which draws in and entraps other non-abusing staff, and facilitates abusive and harmful behaviour towards children and young people—an issue to which I shall return below.

As regards the reviews, the Skinner review of residential child care (Skinner, 1992) recommended independent investigation of allegations of abuse including the need to inform police of suspected abuse. The Kent review (Kent, 1997), a parallel of the Utting Report (1997), also examined the safeguards to protect children living away from home. It made a number of recommendations regarding improving complaints procedures and the vetting of staff, as well as internal and external monitoring. Other allegations

---

[7] Such forms of peer violence can include physical, emotional, and verbal abuse as well as 'unwelcome sexual behaviour' including flashing, inappropriate touching, and rape (Barter, 2007: 141).

of historic abuse in residential care in Scotland have included those relating to the Sisters of Nazareth which first emerged through newspaper coverage in the late 1990s.[8] In late 2009 the government launched plans to develop an 'Acknowledgement and Accountability Forum' as a form of truth commission and a national strategy for survivors of historic child abuse. A pilot forum, modelled on the Confidential Committee of the Commission to Inquire into Child Abuse (2009) (the 'Ryan Commission') in the Republic of Ireland, was established for survivors from Quarriers children's homes in Scotland. Following a report from the pilot forum (Shaw, 2011) and its recommendations, the Scottish government is to develop a national confidential forum.

Northern Ireland

In Northern Ireland, some of the most high profile cases have centred on the wrongdoing of individuals rather than institutions. A series of public inquiries, reports, and guidelines underlined the importance of developing effective procedures to prevent unsuitable people from working with children. In the early 1980s, for example, the Kincora scandal involved the systematic abuse of boys through vice rings and prostitution in Kincora hostel in East Belfast. An inquiry highlighted a history of offences dating back at least two decades as well as failures to investigate allegations of abuse (DHSS, 1982; HMSO, 1985; see also Kelly and Pinkerton, 1996; Moore, 1996). Care worker Martin Huston was convicted in 1992 on 25 counts of sexual offences against children. He had been on probation for two years between 1987 and 1989 for committing sexual offences, yet was able to find employment with a voluntary agency involving work with children (SSI, 1993). The Huston Inquiry recommended that agencies which provide services to children should foster a culture of openness and trust that encourages colleagues and children to report and share any concerns they may have about the behaviour of staff. Similarly, headmaster Lindsay Brown, the then vice principal of a Bangor Grammar School, was convicted in 1999 of abusing nine boys over three decades (DENI, 1999). In the 'Barnardo's case' in 2004, two individuals were found

---

[8] See eg *The Independent*, 'Nuns "abused hundreds of children"', 16 August 1998, <http://www.independent.co.uk/news/nuns-abused-hundreds-of-children-1171988.html> (accessed 8 August 2012).

guilty of a total of 70 sexual offences against eight children which took place at a Barnardo's home between 1977 and 1981,[9] but were later acquitted on appeal.

The survivors of institutional abuse in care homes in Northern Ireland have campaigned for a public inquiry into historical institutional abuse. This campaign was given impetus by the publication of the 'Cloyne Report' (Commission of Investigation, 2011),[10] the fourth in a series of such reports in the Republic of Ireland. The Northern Ireland Executive formally announced the inquiry into allegations of abuse in children's homes and other care institutions dating back to 1945 on 29 September 2011,[11] which, at the time of writing, is expected to take two years to complete. Moreover, the issue is an ongoing one which also crosses jurisdictional boundaries. In May 2012, a BBC television documentary revealed that in 1975, a 14-year-old boy who had been sexually abused by Fr Brendan Smyth gave the then Fr Sean Brady the names and addresses of other children who had been abused, details of which were not passed to the police or parents.[12] The Justice Committee of the Northern Ireland Assembly agreed to write to the Chief Constable to ask what action the police were taking in the light of accusations about Cardinal Sean Brady, currently the Catholic Primate in Ireland.[13]

The Republic of Ireland

In the Republic of Ireland, early state inquiries into the care of children took place against a backdrop of instititional care within industrial and reformatory schools. The reports of the Cussen (1936) and Kennedy (1970) Commissions were highly critical of the system of institutionalized care of children in Ireland and the excessive use of corporal punishment (Raftery and O'Sullivan,

---

[9] *BBC News On-line*, 'Pair Jailed for Child Sex Crimes', 21 September 2004, <http://news.bbc.co.uk/1/hi/northern_ireland/3676714.stm> (accessed 19 July 2011).

[10] *UTV News*, 'Call for Cloyne-Style Inquiry', 14 July 2011, <http://www.u.tv/News/McGuinness-calls-for-Cloyne-style-inquiry/a5086c67-4047-4178-ba6e-e43f62b66174> (accessed 19 July 2011).

[11] *Belfast Telegraph*, 'Ministers Decide on "Full" Abuse Inquiry', 29 September 2011. See also Inquiry into Historical Institutional Abuse Bill 2012.

[12] *BBC Northern Ireland*, 'This World', 1 May 2012.

[13] See <http://news.bbc.co.uk/democracylive/hi/northern_ireland/newsid_9718000/9718170.stm> (accessed 7 May 2012).

1999; Arnold, 2009) . In the 1990s, there were a number of inquiries into abuse within intra-familial settings. The Kilkenny Incest
inquiry (McGuinness, 1993) and the McColgan case (North Western Health Board, 1998) documented failures in information sharing between statutory agencies and their general unwillingness to
intervene due to an emphasis on preserving the sanctity of the family unit and a lack of professional awareness about child sexual
abuse (McAlinden, 2012b).

The primary contemporary focus, however, of media, public,
and political attention in the Republic of Ireland has been institutional child abuse committed by members of Catholic religious
orders (Ferguson, 1995; Jenkins, 1996; Keenan, 2011). The issue
first came to public attention in Ireland with the highly publicized
Fr Brendan Smyth case (Ferguson, 1995; Moore, 1995) referred
to above.[14] Smyth was sentenced to 12 years in prison after plead-
ing guilty to the sexual abuse of 20 young people over a period of
36 years. He previously served four years in a Northern Ireland
prison for similar offences. There have also been cases involving
the sexual exploitation and abuse of children within sport, and
swimming specifically, the dynamics of which will be addressed
further below (Murphy, 1998; McCarthy, 2010). The range of
official inquiries and historic reviews into institutional child
abuse in Ireland, predominantly within the context of child care
institutions run by the Catholic Church on behalf of the Irish
state, have included the 'Ferns Report' (Murphy, Buckley, and
Joyce, 2005), the 'Ryan Report' (Commission to Inquire into
Child Abuse, 2009), the 'Murphy Report' (Commission of Investigation, 2009), and the 'Cloyne Report' (Commission of Investigation, 2011).

The Ferns inquiry investigated the handling of over 100 allegations of child sexual abuse against 21 priests in the diocese of
Ferns between 1966 and 2002. It highlighted the failure of the
Church to respond to complaints of abuse, chiefly by non-remov-
al of priests from active ministry and the non-reporting of complaints to the civil authorities. It also highlighted the subsequent
failures of state agencies to investigate effectively and prevent
the further abuse of victims. The five-volume report produced by the

[14] *The Irish News*, 'Priest Abuses 10 Children', 14 December 1996; *The Irish
Times*, 'Priest Given 12 Years for Sex Assaults', 7 April 2000.

Ryan Commission[15] in May 2009 revealed a litany of abuse (physical, sexual, emotional, and neglect) of thousands of children involving more than 800 religious and lay perpetrators in over 26 institutions which were tolerated by both Church and state. The report was highly significant because it highlighted the fact that the abuse of children, and the failure of Church and state authorities to adequately respond to the problem, was *systemic* in Irish child care institutions.

The report of the Murphy Commission of Investigation into the Catholic Archdiocese of Dublin examined the handling of complaints and suspicions of child sexual abuse by Church and state authorities. The report concluded that clerical child sexual abuse was 'covered-up' during this period. A common Church response upon learning of allegations of abuse was to transfer the suspected perpetrator to another parish or diocese where they continued to have access to minors and the opportunity to abuse again. The Commission's report into the Diocese of Cloyne examined the handling of allegations and concerns in respect of 19 priests during the period 1 January 1996 to 1 February 2009. The historical remit of the report is significant because, as the report itself acknowledges, 1996 is the year in which the Catholic Church in Ireland first put in place procedures to deal with allegations of sexual abuse and is also two years after the Smyth case first began to emerge. The report concluded that the response of the Church was 'inadequate and inappropriate' (Commission of Investigation, 2009: para 1.71) and catalogued a number of failures including, inter alia, failure to carry out proper canonical investigations; and to report all complaints to the Gardai or the health authorities.

The Ferns Inquiry and the Ryan Commission made a number of recommendations principally in relation to improving institutional policies and the provision of services for children in care. In contrast to the United Kingdom, and England and Wales in particular, the Republic of Ireland, however, has not pursued a neo-liberal regulatory agenda with the same vigour (see Chapter 3). Indeed, as will be discussed further below, it is only in the aftermath of the publication of the Cloyne Report that seismic change, in terms of

---

[15] The Commission was set up under the Commission to Inquire into Child Abuse Act 2000. See also the Commission to Inquire into Child Abuse (Amendment) Act 2005. The Residential Institutions Redress Board was also set up as a compensation scheme for victims of institutional abuse under the Residential Institutions Redress Act 2002.

new legislation to prevent unsuitable individuals from working with children and to make provision for the sharing of 'soft' information on offenders, seems likely to come to fruition.

Key themes arising from the inquiries and reviews

An examination of these cases suggests a number of common themes:

- the abuse normally took place over a number of years and its extent went unrecognized for some time (McAlinden, 2006a: 350);
- usually more than one victim was involved, and often more than one offender (Finkelhor, Williams, and Burns, 1988; White and Hart, 1995; Gallagher, 1999; Waterhouse, 2000; Shaw, 2007);
- there was often a culture of acceptance or disbelief where other staff were afraid to challenge inappropriate behaviour or act on initial suspicions (Frizell, 2009; Plymouth Safeguarding Children Board, 2010);
- many complaints were not formally reported, and victims were afraid to disclose the abuse (McAlinden, 2006a: 350);
- or when they did no action was taken, either because there was a conspiracy to keep allegations quiet or a ready acceptance of the denial by the alleged perpetrator (Sullivan and Beech, 2002: 161);
- there were poor internal management and external governance frameworks in place including the absence of an effective system for complaints (Berridge and Brodie, 1996; Colton, 2002).

The latter criticisms have been made in particular within the context of sexual abuse within churches or faith communities (Berry, 1992; Francis and Turner, 1995; Nolan, 2001). These factors are confirmed by the general literature on child sexual abuse which suggests primarily that the complaints appear to be of a sexual nature, involving both boys and girls, and that the majority have not been reported (Gallagher, 1998; Barter, 1999). Many of these themes, including delays in disclosure; a culture of silence; and denial and minimization of allegations relate directly to the process of institutional grooming and will be returned to below.

These themes serve to underscore not only the existence of grooming in both facilitating institutional abuse and preventing its disclosure, but also the overlap between various forms of grooming (such as peer-to-peer grooming and institutional grooming), and the complexity of the victim-offender continuum within an organizational context. The gamut of offending behaviour may variously involve child and adult, victims and perpetrators, as 'insiders' or parties to the abusive process, as well as the duplicity and compliance, unwitting or otherwise, of outsiders in failing to acknowledge or act on suspicions of abuse. This argument also has resonance in relation to the wider processes of social denial (Cohen, 2001) concerning institutional child abuse by the clergy in Ireland and will be revisited below.

Given the body of legislation which exists and the number of public inquiries which have taken place, it has long been recognized that individuals may use their employment in order to access children. The danger is that these developments have largely been reactive responses to the problem. Moreover, they have also been focused on developing external controls to prevent known sex offenders from making contact with children. What is needed, however, is greater understanding of the internal process of institutional grooming in order to develop proactive responses to problems before they occur.

The Utting Report (1997), as one of the major inquiries into institutional child abuse in the United Kingdom, proposed a 'protective strategy' comprised of four main elements: (1) a threshold of entry to paid and voluntary work with children which is high enough to deter committed abusers; (2) management which pursues overall excellence and is vigilant in protecting children and exposing abuse; (3) disciplinary and criminal procedures which deal effectively with offenders; and (4) an approved system of communicating information about known abusers between agencies with a need to know.

This strategy, however, fails to acknowledge fully the characteristics of the offender and the nature of his or her behaviour within institutions on a number of important levels (McAlinden, 2006a: 352). The focus on an entry threshold misses the point that sex offenders may use grooming techniques in order to cross any threshold in their quest to access children. The emphasis on vigilant management and swift disciplinary measures does not take account of the fact that sex offenders may actually constitute the management within an institution which may allow the subsequent onset of abuse to go undetected or unpunished. Finally, the value placed on information sharing is based on the known, identifiable, and preventable risk and not the unknown, hidden, and therefore the most dangerous one.

Indeed, the institutional gaze of official and public discourses has been too narrow in focus and has tended to impede a meaningful and effective review of policy and procedures (McAlinden, 2010a: 30).[16] In short, the rather linear focus on accountability and apportioning blame for individual acts or omissions within the context of a particular crisis or scandal impedes an examination of the systemic problems of child care institutions and the wider policy issues concerning the identification and management of sex offenders within institutionalized contexts.

Sexual Offending in the Institutional Context

As happens with the grooming process more generally, the unique features of the institutional environment facilitate abuse and prevent discovery or disclosure. In common with the internet, which has been used as a ruse to groom children for abuse, certain forms of employment allow an abuser to access children in a way that would not otherwise be possible. These occupations relate to a wide variety of settings (Stanley, 1999), including not just religious work but also secular work within voluntary organizations (Smith, 1993), private and public schools (La Fontaine and Morris, 1991; Brannan et al, 1993), residential homes (Corby et al, 2001), and a range of community-based child care settings, such as nursery schools (Finkelhor, Williams, and Burns, 1988; Hunt, 1994; Plymouth Safeguarding Children Board, 2010), schools (DENI, 1999; Bichard, 2004) and foster care placements (Browne and Lynch, 1999; Waterhouse, 2000).

Children in residential care are more susceptible to abuse than those within the community (Dawson, 1983; Siskind, 1986). The imbalance of power between adult perpetrators and child victims is exaggerated by the offender's 'caring role and the children's traumatic or abusive histories' (Erooga, Allnock, and Telford, 2012: 62). The specific context of a local authority secure or residential facility where some children may have emotional or learning difficulties, behavioural or psychiatric problems, or drug or alcohol

---

[16] Academic discourses have inclined towards a cynical view of the inquiry process arguing that official discourses may be socially and politically constructed. See eg Scraton, 2004; Rolston and Scraton, 2005.

addiction can provide a captive vulnerable population for abusers (Utting, 1997: 5; Powell, 2007: 39). Vulnerable or challenging children may also be regarded as having little or no credibility and tend not to be believed if allegations of abuse or inappropriate behaviour are made (Powell, 2007: 39).

There may also be a high degree of cross-over in the broad offending context. In the context of the 'Irish swimming scandals', for example, several priests used swimming pools as places to access children (Murphy, 1998; McCarthy, 2010: 65). Professional perpetrators also abuse within the voluntary or charity sectors as well as within their own profession (Sullivan and Beech, 2004: 49). Similarly, organizational offenders have also used technology to groom victims and perpetuate abuse (Erooga, Allnock, and Telford, 2012: 10, 59–60). These findings not only denote the intersection between different modes of abusive activities towards children and young people but also the difficulties of neatly classifying grooming behaviours into precise categories. While institutional abuse is a sub-category of extra-familial abuse, there are also clear elements of institutional grooming and abuse which closely resemble the dynamics of intra-familial abuse. In particular, the proximate and ongoing relationships between adults and children within an organizational environment, where adults may have sole responsibility for the welfare of children, 'often place them *in loco parentis*' (Sullivan et al, 2011: 58). Within such contexts, pre-abuse grooming may also relate to significant others and the surrounding environment since the offender is already proximate to the child.

The range of professions demonstrates that perpetrators will adapt to gain access to children in other settings as the opportunities to abuse within some institutions become restricted (Sullivan and Beech, 2002: 159). The worst offending adults will simply find ways around legal and policy frameworks which have been designed to pre-emptively capture grooming and stop abuse before it occurs. The picture depicted by most of the inquiries and reviews is that the problem of institutional abuse is confined mainly to residential contexts. The reality is, however, that probably every profession or organization that has contact with children in terms of their care, education, or social or leisure activities is vulnerable to infiltration by those minded to abuse (Beyer, Higgins, and Bromfield, 2005; McAlinden, 2006a: 353). Having provided the broad context within which institutional abuse may occur, the remainder of this section will examine three key themes which are integral to an understanding of institutional grooming.

Categorizing the institutional offender

Sex offenders may become affiliated with youth groups or children's clubs or a range of other professions which allow one-to-one unsupervised contact with children (Powell, 2007: 22–3, 37–9). Some sex offenders have taken on paid or voluntary work as coaches or assistants in sports clubs or play groups in particular which allows close contact with children (Brackenridge, 2001: 106). Alternatively, however, offenders may be installed in a position of trust with children prior to any clear intention to sexually offend (Finkelhor, Williams, and Burn, 1988). For these offenders, 'the motivation is less tangible and possibly situationally as well as personally derived' (Erooga, Allnock, and Telford, 2012: 52). This dichotomy also echoes the categorization of offenders as 'preferential' or 'situational' (Cohen, Seghorn, and Calmas, 1969; Howells, 1981; Groth, Hobson, and Gary, 1982; Wortley and Smallbone, 2006: 13–18; Smallbone, Marshall, and Wortley, 2008:160–2), outlined in the previous chapter. That is, while some offenders may deliberately choose a career which provides contact with children, for others, the institutional environment may provide the opportunity to offend once they have become installed in their position (John Jay College, 2011). The opportunistic nature of sexual offending against children means that for many 'professional offenders', 'the key factor is not the particular sexual attraction but rather the availability and vulnerability of the children' (Erooga, 2009b: 65). As noted above, identifying vulnerable children is a particularly salient factor for organizational abusers, where such vulnerabilities are often easier to perceive when the abuser has more than casual contact with children (Erooga, Allnock, and Telford, 2012).

The literature suggests that the former category of 'professional' sex offenders—those who deliberately choose careers which provide contact with children—accounts for a sizeable proportion, although not the majority, of those who abuse within organizational contexts (Colton and Vanstone, 1996; Ritchie, 2001; Sullivan and Beech, 2004). Smallbone and Wortley (2000) found that 20 per cent of extra-familial offenders reported having accessed children though a child or youth organization, with 8 per cent having joined primarily to commit a sexual offence. Sullivan and Beech's (2004) study of 41 'professional perpetrators', however, reports higher percentages. While only 15 per cent were motivated to exclusively obtain employment which would provide them with access to children, for a further 41.5 per cent, abusing children was a partial if not primary motivation for working with children. Other research has shown, however, that it is difficult to disentangle motivations for taking positions within organizations to abuse children from legitimate motivations (Erooga, Allnock, and Telford, 2012: 10, 30). Nonetheless, as will be discussed further in the last part of the book, these broad findings also underline the importance of having effective supervision and controls on institutional culture and individual working practices in settings which involve 'close and contact interaction' with children (Erooga, 2009b: 65).

As with grooming more generally, however, the difficulties in early detection of potential risks to children stem from the fact that emotional congruence with children may at once be indicative of a potential risk to children as well as a desirable characteristic of those most effective in working with children (Sullivan et al, 2011: 70). Indeed, as outlined previously, there is no 'typical' (Erooga, 2009a: 4) or 'full-proof' profile (Elliott, Browne, and Kilcoyne, 1995: 109) in that abusers may 'share many relevant characteristics with the "general population"' (Erooga, 2009a: 4), the difference being one of the underlying motivation to sexually offend. Such inherent difficulties in identifying and predicting likely sources of harm mean that 'it will be difficult if not impossible to detect potential abusers' (Erooga, 2009a: 4), within organizational or other contexts, on any kind of proactive and accurate basis.

A further interesting dimension of the existing literature is whether 'professional perpetrators' have different characteristics to those who abuse children outside a professional setting (Sullivan and Beech, 2004; Sullivan et al, 2010). While research in general shows that such offenders do not differ significantly from other sex offenders against children (Haywood et al, 1996; Langevin, Cunroe, and Bain, 2000), there are a number of notable differences. There is a clear gendered dimension to institutional child abuse, with 'a negative, male-dominated culture in residential settings' (Erooga, 2009b: 43). As with child sexual abuse more generally, the vast majority of offences are committed by men (Pringle, 1993; Colton, 2002), with higher rates of male victimization in particular (Commission to Inquire into Child Abuse, 2009; Parkinson, Oats, and Jayakody, 2009), and with victims also being in the older age range of adolescents rather than young children (Loftus and Camargo, 1993; Elliott, Brown, and Kilcoyne, 1995; Haywood et al, 1996; Grubin, 1998; Sullivan and Beech, 2004, Sullivan et al, 2011). This of course is subject to the caveat, as highlighted above, of general non-disclosure and under-reporting by boys (see eg Baker and Duncan, 1985; Hunter et al, 1992; Watkins and Bentovim, 1992; Grubin, 1998).

Professional perpetrators would also appear to use a mixture of physically forceful means (Langevin, Cunroe, and Bain, 2000) as well as more persuasive or 'emotionally coercive' grooming techniques (Sullivan and Beech, 2004: 47; McCarthy, 2010: 64). Equally, befriending and socialization with the family is common (Terry and Tallon, 2004). Professional perpetrators, however, may 'tak[e] children away from the normal work environment' by either arranging to meet children outside work or an overnight stay to facilitate sexual abuse (Sullivan and Beech, 2004: 47–8; see also Powell, 2007: 38; McCarthy, 2010: 18). This factor, however, may not be strictly attributable to higher 'levels of sophistication or intricacy' among professional offenders as Sullivan and Beech (2004: 50) claim, but more a case of simple and enhanced opportunity. Indeed, while those who sexually assault children in a professional context may not be that different from those who abuse outside such contexts, they may 'constitute a particular public health danger, given the power entrusted to these individuals and their ready access to children' (Mercado, Terry, and Perillo, 2011: 526, citing Abel et al,1994).

Using the features of the organizational environment

Research by Sullivan and Quayle (2012) has documented the intricate 'manipulation styles' of abusers who work with children, which they use against both adults and children within the organizational environment, in order to commit sexual abuse. Grooming operated in the conventional way: 'manipulating perception' of the child or other 'potentially protective' adults; 'creating opportunities' to be sexual with children; and 'preventing suspicion, discovery or disclosure' of the abuse. There were, however, a range of manipulation styles employed by offenders based on their 'inherent strengths and abilities'. These included, inter alia, 'Integrity Manipulation'—the most common, the person presents themselves as a 'person of integrity' who is 'beyond suspicion' and which also supports them in the denial of inappropriate behaviour; 'Liberal Manipulation'—the person presents as being broad-minded and liberal in their attitudes to sex in particular; and 'Blocking Manipulation'—the offender 'obstructs' interactions which may impede their actions, or 'jests' with others to encourage a view of them as fun and risqué while at the same time normalizing their inappropriate behaviour, or 'confounds' by using ambiguous actions or words to deflect from their behaviour. This diverse range of behaviours helps to explain why it is so difficult to pinpoint potential risks to children within an organizational environment (Sullivan and Quayle, 2012). While sex offenders are a highly heterogeneous population with diverse motivations and manipulation styles, there are, I would argue, a number of particular features of the organizational setting which allows the range of grooming and other pro-offending behaviours to flourish. It is these unique facets of 'vulnerable organisations' (Erooga, 2009b: 38), or what Hall terms 'the institutional syndrome' (Hall, 2000, cited in Erooga, 2009b: 38), which enable offenders to manipulate perceptions, create opportunities, and prevent suspicion.

The particular dynamics of the institutional environment which sex offenders may use to facilitate abuse and prevent disclosure by children and other professionals include features such as trust, opportunity, anonymity, secrecy, and power. The gaining of trust, or 'emotional seduction' (Salter, 1995: 74), plays a pivotal role in the grooming process with respect to children, their families and the wider community. Within the institutional setting, the intimate and social relationships created with the child and other adult carers who might protect them are also based on the creation of loyalty and trust. As noted in Chapter 2, scholars define trust as a behaviour or attitude which permits risk-taking behaviour (Johnson-George and Swap, 1982; Luhmann, 1988; Coleman, 1990). Organizational positions of trust facilitate the grooming process (Leclerc, Proulx, and McGibben, 2005). The modus operandi of organizational offenders is based on their position of trust in that they are perceived as non-threatening and so can easily build a relationship with a child by presenting variously as peer, father figure, or rescuer (Colton and Vanstone, 1996; Leclerc, Proulx, and McGibben, 2005).

Three key themes from the work of Ben-Yehuda (2001) on trust have particular resonance for institutional grooming and abuse within organizational contexts. First, trust involves establishing the perception of reliability, genuineness, and loyalty (Ben-Yehuda, 2001: 11–13) in order to create a sense of belonging or shared community (Ben-Yehuda, 2001: 27–8). The offender, often by the very nature of their job, will be regarded by others within the institution and by society as a whole as a *bona fide* individual who is unusually dedicated to their job and gets a particular enjoyment from working with children. Secondly, a breach of trust typically involves a range of deception techniques that mask reality and make betrayal possible (Ben-Yehuda, 2001: 6–7). With institutional grooming in particular, it is the offender's job and related status which provide a ready vehicle for this deception. Offenders may use their position in the community and are able to either generate or make 'use of existing environments of pervasive secrecy' (Sullivan and Beech, 2004: 39; see also Sullivan and Beech, 2002). Thirdly, trust is a moral and social construct the violation of which may amount to infringement of deeply ingrained moral codes within society (Ben-Yehuda, 2001: 6–7). When sex offenders offend against children within an organizational setting they have abused their position of trust and defaulted on their moral obligation and commitment to ensure the safety and well being of children in their care. This argument also helps to account for public indignation when allegations of institutional abuse come to light.

Institutions can create multiple opportunities for the manipulation and abuse of children and can allow the offender to take on a different persona and remain anonymous in terms of their deviant sexual tendencies. The organizational culture itself may be conducive to abuse of power, the 'corruption of care' (Erooga, 2009b: 39–40) and erosion of the primary functions of care and protection. Child care institutions appear to be 'especially self-protective, secretive and closed by nature' (McAlinden, 2010a: 30), where an emphasis is placed 'on apparently effective functioning with a minimum of disruption' (Erooga, 2009b: 44). As such, they discourage the drawing of attention to any deficiencies in policies and procedures and the signs of abuse, out of fear of damaging the reputation or credibility of the institution (Westcott, 1991: 15–17; Brannan et al, 1993: 273; Sullivan and Beech, 2002: 162; Shaw, 2007: 32–3). Several studies and inquiries have established that staff either ignored signs of abuse or failed to act upon disclosures by children as an attempt to preserve the reputation of the institution or disguise the lack of proper procedures in place (Dawson, 1983;

Waterhouse, 2000; Commission to Inquire into Child Abuse, 2009: vol IV, para 29). Furthermore, if these organizations are held in high esteem by local agencies or parents, children may experience added difficulties in both resisting and disclosing the abuse (Gallagher, 2000: 810).

Moreover, the particular role which these offenders play within certain institutions may also make the environment more facilitative of abuse. The offender may be in a primary management position with free reign over the institution, with little checks and balances on their behaviour and no clear lines of accountability. It is this status or authority that may give them the necessary control over the organizational culture, or 'the power to betray' (Ben-Yehuda, 2001: 28)—it may provide an opportunity for those minded to abuse children to do so in a way that exposes them to less risk, thus reducing the likelihood of detection and potentially leading to an increase in abuse. Power disparities in particular, are a component of the offender's ability to maintain abuse over time (Erooga, Allnock, and Telford, 2012: 10, 61–2). The isolated position of the offender, either in emotional or geographical terms, as a characteristic of their organizational role, is also a factor in some cases (Erooga, Allnock, and Telford, 2012: 10, 57–9).

Institutions as individuals

Colleagues may be either unaware of the abuse or partially aware but fail to act on that information (Erooga, Allnock, and Telford, 2012: 74–7). The popularity of an individual member of staff may disempower other staff and make them reluctant or less willing to challenge suspicious or inappropriate behaviour for fear of undermining their own position within the organization. The serious case review into child abuse within Little Ted's Nursery in England and Wales in 2010,[17] for example, concluded that 'K's power base within the setting and her capacity to draw other members of the staff team into her world... effectively silenc[ed] them' (Plymouth Safeguarding Children Board, 2010: para 5.73). In such a context, 'the development of an inward-looking, defensive ethos in which

---

[17] Nursery worker Vanessa George had been abusing children in her care and sharing images of the abuse with Colin Blanchard whom she had met via the internet. The case is also significant as it represents a high profile case of female sex offending and involved a network or 'ring' of offenders against children (see also Chapter 4 for a discussion of the gender differences in grooming).

loyalty to one's colleagues, or at least to those perceived as being on one's side, takes precedence over other obligations' (Frizell, 2009: para 9.4), including the welfare of children.

Moreover, the notion of child care organizations as 'imagined communities' (Anderson, 1983) may be invoked by offenders to foster a climate of fear and suppress dissent in relation to abuses of power. The sociologist Mary Douglas argues that 'institutions are particularly prone to developing and re-producing their own rationality, their own reason for being', where 'sameness [is] shaped by the shared thoughts, values, and information within the institutions' (1986: 53). It is these facets of status and power which underpin the institutional setting (Sullivan and Beech, 2002: 164), combined with the sense of belonging and the notion of the organization as a tightly knit unit, which also make the behaviour of the professional offender closely akin to that of the intra-familial offender. In effect, as noted above, sex offenders also appear to have a nuanced understanding of 'how institutions think' (Douglas, 1986) and are able to negotiate their way around protective individuals or organizational procedures, exploiting personal relationships or system weaknesses to facilitate abuse and avoid exposure.

The failure of professionals to challenge pro-offending behaviour exhibited by offenders at the first signs of suspicious behaviour is especially important in preventing patterns of grooming and abuse from becoming more sophisticated and entrenched. Further, it is fundamental to confronting the offender's self-grooming, principally in terms of challenging offender denial or minimization about the inappropriateness of their behaviour. As the Plymouth serious case review also noted, for instance, 'By drawing others partially into her activities, K made challenge even less likely and may have interpreted the behaviour as implicit support' (Plymouth Safeguarding Board, 2010: para 5.4). As will be discussed in Part III of the book, the prevention of institutional child abuse involves, at a minimum, the provision of effective internal as well as external controls over the organizational environment to inhibit opportunities for abuse.

A system of pre-employment vetting has been introduced as an external control on grooming by screening those suitable to work with children and young people. At best, it can only ever be effective, however, where there is a clear record of offending and where the identity of the person being vetted is known and assured. At worst, it will not capture those offenders who have never come to notice which may in fact account for a sizeable proportion of the overall incidence of sexual offending against children.[18] Current policies and procedures, therefore, can do little to stop offenders when they are at their most dangerous—when their deviant sexual behaviour remains hidden and when they have managed to persuade those responsible for children, through grooming, that they are genuine, respectable, and worthy of belief. These arguments underscore the importance of developing a range of carefully coordinated social responses to complement legal and policy frameworks. It will be argued that such approaches, based on the twin aims of protection and prevention, offer the potential to manage the full range of potential harms to children on a proactive and anticipatory basis rather than as a somewhat linear, and often less effective, reactionary response after particular cases have occurred.

Institutional Grooming and Child Sexual Exploitation within Sport

Since at least the mid-1990s, the issue of sexual grooming and abuse in sport has emerged in a range of countries encompassing various sporting fields from local sporting clubs to national and even international competition level. A number of high profile cases of sexual exploitation and abuse within sport have emerged, for example, within the context of swimming in Britain[19] and Ireland (Murphy, 1998; McCarthy, 2010), ice hockey in Canada (Robinson, 1998), and, most recently, Penn State University football.[20] Such cases share many of the key themes arising from the public inquiries and reviews into abuse within predominantly residential child care institutions identified above. This includes the fact that the abuse normally took place over a number of years and its extent went unrecognized for some time; usually multiple victims were involved; and there were poor internal management and external

---

[18] Research shows that fewer than 5 per cent of sex offenders are apprehended (Salter, 2003) and only 12 per cent of rapes involving children (Hanson et al, 1999; Smith et al, 2000) are ever reported to the police.

[19] L Donegan, 'Olympic Coach Jailed for Rapes', *The Guardian*, 28 September 1995.

[20] 'Penn Sex Abuse Scandal', *The Guardian* website <http://www.guardian.co.uk/world/penn-state-sexual-abuse-scandal> (accessed 2 April 2012).

governance systems as evidenced by 'a culture of silence' and the lack of an effective complaints procedure.

The seminal work of academics such as Celia Brackenridge and others on sexual exploitation and abuse within sport (eg Brackenridge, 1997, 2001; Brackenridge and Kirby, 1997; Brackenridge and Fasting, 2005) has been instrumental in raising the public profile of the issue. Empirical studies of sexual harassment and exploitation with athletes have been conducted in Canada (Kirby and Greaves, 1996), the United States (Volkwein et al, 1997), Denmark (Toftegaard, 1998), Norway (Fasting, Brackenridge, and Walseth, 2002; Sundgot-Borgen et al, 2003), Australia (Leahy, Pretty, and Tenenbaum, 2002), the Netherlands (Cense, 1997), and Britain (Yorganci, 1993; Brackenridge, 1997). Quantitative studies on the nature and extent of child abuse within sport have shown high rates of prevalence. Kirby and Greaves' (1996) Canadian study, for example, showed that 21.8 per cent of the athletes surveyed had had sexual intercourse with 'authority figures'.[21] Similarly, Toftegaard's (1998) Danish study found that 25 per cent of sport college students either knew of or had experienced sexual harassment by a coach. Moreover, as a study undertaken jointly by the NSPCC and the Amateur Swimming Association (Myers and Barrett, 2002) concluded, where serious abuse has occurred, there has usually been a significant process of grooming which preceded the abuse. In this respect, the grooming process is said to mirror the classic stages, namely: 'confidence, seduction and abuse' (Toftegaard, 1998, cited in Brackenridge, 2001: 125).

The broad similarities with grooming more generally include selecting vulnerable victims (Brackenridge, 2001: 113), including athletes with physical or learning disabilities (Russell, 1996; Kerr, 1999); giving or withholding of intangible rewards such as promoting the victim's self-esteem and confidence as well as tangible rewards in the form of 'team selection' (Brackenridge, 2001: 95); increasing emotional dependence on the coach and their isolation from other sources of support such as parents or friends (Brackenridge, 2001: 121, 35–6). In particular, as Brackenridge (2001: 36) contends, 'The power afforded to the coach in his position of

---

[21] This broad term reflects the wide range of those who might hold power over an athlete including medical staff, administrative staff as well as senior peer athletes. It is predominantly, however, associated with coaching staff (see Brackenridge, 2001: 26) for a discussion of the term.

authority offers an effective alibi or camouflage for grooming and abuse'. Sexual exploitation and abuse within sport is often equated as 'virtual incest' (Brackenridge, 2001: 95), since the coach-athlete relationship mirrors that of the traditional patriarchal family, where such power imbalances may facilitate secrecy, shame, and emotional blackmail as the hallmarks of intra-familial abuse.

There are also a number of distinct features, however, which may make the sporting context especially facilitative of abuse. These relate to the predominantly masculine culture of sport (Messner and Sabo, 1990; Messner, 1992; Robinson, 1998: 181–202) and the traditionally high tolerance of sexually exploitative practices and conversations (Curry, 1991), within the private space of the locker room (Kirby and Greaves, 1996). Much like domestic violence and intra-familial child abuse, abusive practices and behaviours in such private contexts tend to challenge traditional notions of what constitutes abuse (Saraga, 2001), and are instead normalized as being 'all part of the game' (Brackenridge, 2001: 19). 'The physicality of sport' (Brackenridge and Fasting, 2005: 37) where direct physical contact with children is often the norm (Powell, 2007: 22, 38), in a range of 'uniquely intimate' settings (McCarthy, 2010: 262) such as changing rooms or showers is also conducive to the gradual erosion of 'ambiguous' interpersonal and sexual boundaries (Garlick, 1994). Intrusions into the athlete's personal life, such as the sharing of intimate details about menstrual cycles (McCarthy, 2010: 17), and contraceptive habits, 'are justified on the grounds of performance enhancement' (Brackenridge, 2001: 95). It can be particularly difficult, therefore, to accurately distinguish between innocuous behaviours and potentially more sinister ones (Brackenridge and Fasting, 2005: 48). As will be discussed further in the next chapter, however, despite the enhanced opportunities for abuse to occur, the sporting context lies outside the dominant organizational settings such as schools and residential homes to which regulatory legislative and policy frameworks were intended to apply.

Institutional Grooming within the Catholic Church

Child sexual abuse occurs in faith communities other than the Catholic Church[22] and, as noted above, in organizational contexts

---

[22] See eg Parkinson, Oats, and Jayakody (2009) in relation to reported sexual abuse in the Anglican Church.

other than religious ones. Nonetheless, revelations about institutional child abuse in Ireland committed by priests present a further interesting dimension to institutional grooming, not previously highlighted by the literature. Although the issue of institutional child abuse by the clergy, in particular members of Catholic religious orders, has resonated recently in a range of jurisdictions including the United States (Rosetti, 1990; Berry, 1992; Plante, 2004; John Jay College, 2004, 2011),[23] the historic, enmeshed nature of the Church-state relationship in Ireland makes the Irish situation particularly noteworthy and fairly unique.

As I have argued elsewhere, there are two principal factors which may help to explain failures to uncover the full 'truth' when allegations of institutional child abuse eventually come to light as well as why such abuse was allowed to remain hidden in the first instance. These relate to denial and minimization by both Church and state in the wake of allegations of abuse and the failure of these entities to accept a malevolent version of their 'imagined selves' (McAlinden, 2012b). In the context of the present study, a third explanation which may be posited, however, is the existence and prevalence of institutional grooming. Opportunities for institutional grooming and abuse, in both making abuse possible and masking its disclosure, I would argue, are heightened within an organization such as the Catholic Church chiefly by the abuse of trust, and the power, authority, and status of an hierarchical, 'closed', and largely unaccountable institution (Keenan, 2011: esp chs 2 and 8).

For decades, arguably until the emergence of the abuse scandals beginning in the 1990s, the Catholic Church had a 'moral monopoly' in Ireland (Inglis, 2008). Catholic morality, epitomized by the Victorian obsession with purity (Harrison, 1997) and the associated feelings of shame, embarrassment, and guilt that came to be linked with sex, was used by the Church as part of a wider process of patriarchal social control (Inglis, 2005). There was a prevailing culture of secrecy, denial, and shame concerning discourses on sex and sexuality which were never talked about openly in any public context. As Frawley-O'Dea (2007) contends, as a result sex and sexuality came to be harnessed to the shadowy subtexts of silence,

---

[23] See eg *The New York Times*, 'Catholic Order Reaches $166 Million Settlement with Sexual Abuse Victims', 25 March 2011 <http://www.nytimes.com/2011/03/26/us/26jesuits.html> (accessed 29 March 2011).

denial, and secrecy which set the stage for the abuse and its subsequent cover-up.

Afforded cultural and political deference within Irish society, the Catholic Church had immense power and authority in a range of areas of social and political life including education, health, and censorship (Ferriter, 2005: ch 5; McAlinden, 2012b).[24] As happened in many of the high profile cases of institutional abuse such as those within sport, referred to above, if an organization is held in high regard by professionals, parents, and wider society, children may have additional difficulties in deflecting and uncovering the abuse (Gallagher, 2000). As O'Toole argues in relation to the Catholic Church, '[t]he perpetrators abused children because they could. They drew that power from the immense stature of the church, its ability to command deference and to intimidate dissenters...'.[25] This point reflects the defensiveness one may feel when challenged about one's religious beliefs in general as well as the particular historic reverence towards Catholicism in Ireland. As one complainant stated in the Cloyne Report, 'It was 1990. There was no such thing out at that time about abuse cases or priests abusing or anything like that, who was going to believe me' (Commission of Investigation, 2011: para 27.5).

The organizational culture of the Church itself helps to create an environment which both facilitates abuse and obfuscates its existence. In short, child sexual abuse may be perceived as 'an individual problem enabled by the organization' (White and Terry, 2008: 674). A multiplicity of systemic factors means that the nature and extent of institutional child abuse goes well beyond the 'rotten apple' theory (White and Terry, 2008: 659). The structural factors which are inherent to an organization such as the Catholic Church and which are conducive to the onset of grooming and abuse have been summarized by the John Jay College research team (2011: 92–3) as 'the authority of the priests, the public perception of them, the isolation of their positions, and the high level of discretion and lack of supervision in their positions'. There is, therefore, a clear 'situational component' to clerical sexual abuse (Terry and

---

[24] Note, however, the complex constitutional picture as regards Church and state in Ireland (McAlinden, 2012b) where the reference to the 'special position' of the Catholic Church in the 1937 Constitution had no particular legal significance and was in fact removed via the Fifth Amendment in 1972. See also Hogan (2005) and Keogh and McCarthy (2007).

[25] F. O'Toole, 'Law of Anarchy, Cruelty of Care', *The Irish Times*, 23 May 2009.

Ackerman, 2008: 643) which relates to the 'contextual factors...and opportunity structures' as well as 'the trust inherent in the position' which heighten opportunities for offending and the likelihood of abuse in such contexts (Mercado, Terry, and Perillo, 2011: 531, 534; see also Keenan, 2011: 171–4).

Clerical offenders were able to make use in particular of the pervasive 'subculture of secrecy concerning sexual abuse' within the Church (White and Terry, 2008: 672). There is an enduring reluctance on the part of the Vatican in particular to admit the full extent of its historical knowledge of child abuse by clergy.[26] The Church has maintained a policy of secrecy throughout and has striven to frame the problem as an aberrational rather than a systemic one in order to protect its privacy and its closed and highly privileged world (Formicola, 2004: 480; Doyle, Swipe, and Wall, 2006; Keenan, 2006: 6). The inadequate response of Church authorities in responding to allegations or suspicions of abuse has been highlighted at the outset of this chapter. Both the Ryan and the Murphy reports concluded that the protection of children was, in many cases, subordinate to the 'desire to protect the reputation of the Congregation and institution' (Commission to Inquire into Child Abuse, 2009: Vol IV, para 6.20) and 'the obsessive concern with secrecy and the avoidance of scandal' (Commission of Investigation, 2009: para 1.32).[27]

It has been demonstrated that trust has resonance not only at the micro-level within interpersonal relationships—such as those between offenders and children—but also at the macro-level in terms of the relationships between the offender and the wider community as well as the institution in which they work (McAlinden, 2006a: 344). The inquiries confirm that abusive practices were deeply embedded and maintained within institutions run by the Church through a conspiracy of silence, fear, and coercion. The Ryan

---

[26] It has emerged that the Vatican warned Irish bishops not to report all suspected child abuse cases to the police but sanctioned the internal handling of such cases within the confines of Canon law. See S Pogatchnik, 'Vatican Letter Cited As Cover-up', *The Associated Press*, 19 January 2011.

[27] See also the *Guardian* investigation into the sexual abuse of young offenders by prison officer Neville Husband which also highlighted institutional failures to deal adequately with complaints about sexual abuse: 'Prison Service Admits Failings in Service over Sexual Abuse', *The Guardian*, 13 April 2012 <http://www.guardian.co.uk/society/2012/apr/13/prisons-chief-failings-sexual-abuse?-INTCMP=SRCH> (accessed 11 June 2012).

report also describes a 'culture of silence' (Commission to Inquire into Child Abuse, 2009: vol IV, para 29) and the fact that 'complaints were ignored, witnesses were punished, or pressure was brought to bear on the child and family to deny the complaint and/ or to remain silent' (Commission to Inquire into Child Abuse, 2009: Executive Summary, see also vol III). Some victims remember nuns and brothers who showed them kindness (Raftery and O'Sullivan, 1999: 33; Commission of Investigation, 2009: vol III, ch 10) but who never dared speak out against their more violent colleagues, so that the system was reinforced by the group dynamic and allowed to continue.[28] The Ryan report also documents how children were abused by lay workers as well as other residents within institutions and not just members of religious orders (Commission to Inquire into Child Abuse, 2009: vol 3, para 9.57). This also underlines the rippling effect which may occur when abuse takes places within institutions where ultimately the organizational culture ensures a complete blurring of the boundaries between appropriate and inappropriate behaviour and indeed between victims and perpetrators via the perpetuation of a culture of abuse.

Furthermore, it is not only children themselves who may be 'groomed' within an organizational context, but also wider society. Over the lengthy period when institutional and institutionalized abuse was taking place in Ireland, civil society failed to appreciate the possible risks to children, simply by virtue of a 'culture of disbelief' concerning clergy sexual abuse (O'Malley, 2009: 100). In this respect, the power and status of the Catholic Church and the traditionally high degree of trust and respect placed by Irish society in its clergy also contributed to a wider process of cultural and social denial about the existence of institutional child abuse in Ireland (McAlinden, 2012b). As the Murphy report acknowledges, 'it may be that the very prominent role which the Church has played in Irish life is the very reason why abuses…were allowed to go unchecked' (Commission of Investigation, 2009: para 1.90). As noted above, 'the inherent betrayal and exploitation by someone in a position of trust' (Mercado, Terry, and Perillo, 2011: 526, citing Moulden, Firestone, and Wexler, 2007), which is enhanced in a religious context, also helps to explain the opprobrious public reaction and the 'deep hurt' (Kline, Mackin, and Lezotte, 2008) and spiritual

---

[28] 'Law of Anarchy, Cruelty of Care', see note 25 above.

damage (Rosetti, 1995) expressed by Catholics the world over in response to perceived betrayal by the institutional Church.

While clerics who commit sexual offences generally exhibit the same characteristics as other offenders (Loftus and Camargo, 1993; Haywood et al, 1996; Langevin, Cunroe, and Bain, 2000; Mercado, Tallon, and Terry, 2008; Tallon and Terry, 2008), there are some differences in the patterns of grooming behaviours. Tallon and Terry (2008), for example, have noted that priests who were more versatile in terms of victim age and gender had more victims over a longer period, an earlier onset of abusive acts and displayed more grooming behaviour. Although there were no significant differences between 'specialists' and 'generalists' in terms of types of enticements used, generalists were more likely to socialize with the families of their victims. This may suggest that those sex offenders with no fixed victim preference, that is who offend against both boys and girls, may tend to exhibit a greater range of grooming behaviours. This is highly significant for as these authors note: 'extensive grooming behaviour would likely lead to a delay in reporting of the abuse, which would in turn allow for a longer criminal career' (Tallon and Terry, 2008: 626), and a lower likelihood of early detection.

Primary Research: Institutional Grooming and Abuse

The preceding section has highlighted that sexual offending against children may take place in a range of professional settings; that abuse may have particular resonance in an institutional context where sex offenders are able to make use of the special features of an organizational environment in order to both facilitate abuse and avoid detection; that there are similarities between how abuse occurs within institutional and intra-familial settings; as well as the dynamics of the grooming process with particular reference to the two case studies of sexual exploitation within sport and historic institutional child abuse within the Catholic Church. In particular, institutional abuse appears to be a combination of individual facilitating factors—such as the use of grooming approaches, identifying vulnerable children and power disparities—and institutional factors, relating to organizational messages, organizational culture, and recruitment practices (Erooga, Allnock, and Telford, 2012). This section of the chapter seeks to draw out the key themes arising from the analysis of the primary data with reference to notable variations or departures from this established literature. The two broad areas stemming from the empirical research relate to the onset of offending within child care organizations, including the role of 'institutional grooming', and the grooming of professionals as an extension of this concept.

Grooming within child care organizations

A number of sub-themes emerged from the primary research in relation to institutional grooming and abuse. The picture which materializes is in some respects congruent with the theoretical literature and in others is much more complex than existing work would tend to suggest.

Preferential v situational offending: the organizational context

The interviews reinforced the fact that not all offenders actively seek opportunities to abuse (Erooga, Allnock, and Telford, 2012). There was a clear split in the views of interviewees as to whether offenders deliberately take jobs or volunteer in order to access children or whether harmful sexual tendencies are more prone to develop once an individual is ensconced within an organizational environment through, for example, positions of power, authority, and trust. This tension, which reflects the 'preferential'/'situational' offender dichotomy outlined above (eg Howells, 1981; Groth, Hobson, and Gary, 1982; Smallbone and Wortley, 2000; Sullivan and Beech, 2004; Wortley and Smallbone, 2006: 13–18; Smallbone, Marshall, and Wortley, 2008: 160–2), was consistent across all four jurisdictions and a wide range of professional spheres.

In relation to the former view, a treatment professional affirmed the archetypal view of institutional grooming and abuse: 'you've got...people in authority. We had a guy here, a head teacher in a school for children with learning difficulties...got himself in there, ingratiated himself and then abused them. So he used that, he groomed them up to that'.[29] Another treatment professional recalled: 'all of the offenders, bar none, that I've worked with have all got themselves into situations that definitely are a back door, or a side door...into having access to children'.[30] This pattern of offending was related to an 'approach explicit' pathway (Ward and

---

[29] RI 6 (14 June 2011).   [30] RI 3 (16 May 2011).

Hudson, 1998b) and more ingrained and deliberate forms of offending. One independent interviewee who had worked with victims and offenders stated: 'it is more likely that what we would call the entrenched child sex offender, i.e. somebody whose needs, so emotionally, socially, sexually, are only met by children is more likely...to be involved in institutional abuse, just simply because they will seek an environment where there is the ability to access victims'.[31]

For other interviewees, however, institutional abuse is 'very situation specific'[32] as offenders may be installed in a position of trust with children prior to the crystallization of any motivation to sexually offend. One senior voluntary sector interviewee explained how the sexual preference for children may not always be a conscious process on the part of the offender but may stem from emotional resonance with children in combination with personal stresses within the offender's life:

Now certainly with some of them I would suggest...there was no predisposition that they knew about or that anybody else could know about, to sexually abuse. And out of that emotional intimacy and other circumstances, they then went on to abuse...if they had intended to do that at the beginning, the behaviour would have looked the same...So the issue really becomes, at what point were they aware of it?...there are some for whom they will abuse if they get the opportunity, but equally their perception of potential risk is such that it may extinguish the possibility that they will. They might have a level of desire to do that, but won't do it if they think the risks are too high. For others, I don't think they had any predisposition to abuse. I think it was a function of what was happening in their lives, what was happening in the emotional relationship with the child that they sexualized.[33]

Similarly, institutional abuse was strongly correlated to organizational issues or situational risk factors. An independent interviewee explained:

When people work in institutions, if they're closed institutions or relatively closed, then they can actually become influenced by the culture there...in terms of the secrecy...I don't really think there's that many people who join a profession in order to abuse...but sometimes the circumstances of the roles that they play...give them a sense of power. Or they may have personal difficulties of their own...I think it's more about

---

[31] EW 12 (19 September 2011).   [32] EW 13 (22 September 2011).
[33] EW 1 (1 September 2011).

being in a position where you can...have a lot of power implicit and explicit and there is an element of that that can corrupt people and they can start to behave in ways...We always talk about offenders and their psychological makeup, as being the main cause of abuse. But situational risks have to be very high also...institutions are a situational risk.[34]

While the pattern of grooming appears to broadly map onto what is outlined in the literature cited above in terms of identifying children who are isolated or emotionally vulnerable (Utting, 1997: 5; Powell, 2007: 39; Erooga, Allnock, and Telford, 2012: 10, 66), this is enhanced by the offender's access to resources and their status within the organization. Interviewees outlined a range of specific factors which 'contribute to a climate where those with some level of control and power will exploit those with less so'.[35] These included 'a pressured environment...the element of solo working...[and] the lack of physical boundaries'[36] between children and the staff responsible for their care. It is this blurring of roles and boundaries in particular which may serve to normalize the onset of physical and later sexualized contact with children. As a senior treatment professional explained highlighting the potentially volatile synthesis between an organizational environment and a proclivity to offend: 'If you're thinking about a background to mixed-up thinking or entitlement, you've got a perfect breeding ground there.'[37]

Taken as a whole, therefore, the primary research has demonstrated the tension between the nature-nurture dualism regarding the onset of sexual offending against children within an institutional environment. The fact that some offenders actively seek situations which will bring them into close proximity with children underscores the fundamental role of external controls such as vetting and barring systems in preventing unsuitable individuals from gaining access to children via employment or work-based activities. As will be discussed in the last part of the book, however, the fact that other sex offenders, in the words of one interviewee 'appear to go bad in a specific situation',[38] also endorses the additional importance of effective internal supervisory and support systems within organizational contexts.

---

[34] NI 4 (1 June 2011).   [35] EW 13 (22 September 2011).
[36] SC 6 (22 August 2011).   [37] RI 5 (14 June 2011).
[38] EW 13 (22 September 2011).

Comparing institutional and intra-familial contexts

A further prominent theme was the similarities between grooming within intra-familial and institutional contexts as highlighted in the previous chapter. These commonalities were related to two principal factors. The first is the fact that offending can often emerge from within routine interactions with children. As a senior voluntary sector interviewee reflected, 'it was striking the way that almost having the position seemed to negate the notion that there might potentially be risk'.[39] This viewpoint also highlights the dominant and dangerous social perception of risk to children as being linked to 'stranger danger' and located in the public sphere with conversely those closest to children being regarded as safe simply because they are well known to the child or their family. The other is the imbalance of power entrenched within abusive relationships which both facilitates access to children and inhibits disclosure (Sullivan and Beech, 2002: 164; McAlinden, 2006a: 353). Another professional involved in support services explained the difficulties for victims in such circumstances:

It's almost equally difficult for a child to disclose that their uncle has been grooming...and has abused them, than it is for them to say that the parish priest has done the same. The dynamics might be different, but it is all about a high status individual who is held in the esteem of other adults, abusing that position.[40]

A key point of difference between intra-familial and institutional contexts to emerge, however, not previously highlighted by other work in the field, relates to the potential role of grooming within clerical abuse cases. In offending outside of a physical institutional setting, the formulaic grooming of the child as well as their family and the wider community was often discernible when reviewing historical cases, particularly within the Republic of Ireland. An interviewee involved in victim support told me:

Very typically the priest would befriend a family, very often a family where there's already a vulnerability like where there's been a death of a parent or something like that, or where there's been an illness. Typically in the past families would be quite chuffed that the priest would single them out for special attention or special friendship and then within that the child would be groomed and would be placed in an impossible position where they

---

[39] EW 1 (1 September 2011).   [40] RI 2 (11 May 2011).

know that the priest is held in very high esteem by their parents and yet they know what's going on and often have found either they couldn't tell or if they did tell, weren't believed.[41]

As a minority of interviewees noted, in such cases there was often no need to groom in the conventional sense, since their position served to both facilitate access to children as well as minimize perceptions about risk. In the words of one interviewee who had worked with both victims and offenders:

They didn't have to wait for a funeral or somebody to die, they just had access because the position of the Catholic Church in Ireland certainly, and in the US within Catholic families... I think that's where the celibacy comes into it, that celibacy equalled safe—that because he's celibate he's a good man, a holy man, unlikely to hurt anyone, ever. So I think it's power and... celibacy. But I mean these guys had unlimited access to children by definition. They... were there at all junctures in people's lives. Because of the sacramental embeddedness of Catholicism... they didn't need to work to gain access... What they had to do then though was to try and pretend that they were safe.[42]

The literature outlined above indicates that clerical sex abusers generally exhibit the same characteristics as other abusers (Loftus and Camargo, 1993; Haywood et al, 1996; Langevin, Cunroe, and Bain, 2000; Mercado, Tallon, and Terry, 2008) with some notable differences in grooming patterns (Terry and Tallon, 2008). This particular finding—that mistaken assumptions about risk were linked to societal views concerning celibacy—becomes highly significant, therefore, in augmenting the established literature and in distinguishing clerical abusers from perpetrators who offend in other institutional or organizational contexts.

As regards grooming and the onset of clerical sexual abuse within an institutional setting, however, the process would appear to be considerably more involved than previous work tends to suggest. A small minority of interviewees conveyed examples of the grooming process which tended to follow the conventional view of grooming as outlined in the previous chapter—the selection of a vulnerable child, the bestowing of gifts or favours or special attention either as a prelude to abuse or in its aftermath to prevent disclosure (Conte, Wolf, and Smith, 1989; Elliott,

---

[41] Ibid.   [42] RI 7 (20 June 2011).

Browne, and Kilcoyne, 1995; Sas and Cunningham, 1995; Salter, 1995; Powell, 2007). An interviewee involved in victim support stated:

Many people...we've met, will have talked about the fact that one particular brother or nun may have been kind to them, and may have picked them out particularly, given them a little treat, an apple or something, even something as simple as telling them that, you know, they were talented at sport or music or whatever, and that certainly played a significant part in...the institutional grooming.[43]

For the majority of interviewees, however, in the context in which abuse unfolded, in the words of a social worker: 'there was more physical force used than maybe emotional or psychological grooming'.[44] Many interviewees described how institutional clerical abuse was often perpetuated through extreme forms of power and control alongside physical violence where 'the grooming was fairly minimal because they just had such absolute power anyway'.[45] Another independent interviewee who had worked with both victims and offenders in a range of settings explained the significance of this and the consequences for victims:

That's a big one, the grooming in itself was also abuse, whereas often we would think of the grooming being a pleasant thing where the child would be made to feel special...But in actual fact for a lot of the institutional ones, alongside that was serious physical abuse, so that in itself wasn't pleasant, so that at no level were you made to feel...well balanced against that for the few minutes he does to me, at least I've got this nice bit of him.[46]

Further, for some of these interviewees, there were clear differences in this regard between contemporary cases of institutional abuse involving the clergy in Ireland and those related to historical institutional abuse where the abuse would have happened many years ago. The same interviewee explained:

So there was a level there that they didn't even have to groom, because nobody was going to believe that Brother So and So, or Father So and So, has done this, because at that stage in rural Ireland, nobody believed... Whereas I think cases I'm involved in currently, some of the priests, there is maybe...what has become the norm in grooming, where there's the treats and the special interest...that special grooming we all know of, but

---

[43] RI 2 (11 May 2011).   [44] RI 4 (13 June 2011).
[45] RI 5 (24 June 2011).   [46] NI 2 (23 May 2011).

the institutional one was completely different because it would often have been alongside physical abuse.[47]

These contextual differences in the grooming patterns of Catholic clergy in particular are also directly attributable to the historic cultural and political deference to the Catholic Church in Ireland (McAlinden, 2012b) and in particular to the social and cultural disbelief concerning clergy sexual abuse (O'Malley, 2009: 100). This analysis confirms my earlier contention that the dynamics of institutional grooming are arguably more intricate and acute within the context of a hierarchical organization such as the Catholic Church.

Peer-to-peer abuse and 'staff seductions'

Two further constructs of the paradigm of institutional grooming surfaced from the analysis of the primary material—that of children being abused by other children within institutions; as well as the grooming or manipulation of colleagues and others within the institutional environment. In relation to 'peer-to-peer abuse', a victims' group interviewee explained this important but often hidden dimension of institutional grooming and abuse and the critical consequences of this for the provision of victim support:

Children who were brought up in the various institutions...would have been abused not only by their carers as in the Christian Brothers or the nuns, but by other children in the institutions...That is very typical and really hasn't emerged at all in a lot of the inquiries or indeed in the literature. But if you attend any function where there are a lot of survivors, you will see a lot of tension where individuals are identified as somebody who abused other children, who was also a victim themselves. And there are a lot of consequences, I think, for the person who abused as a child, because they're in a sense being excluded from the support groups. So that is very common and you can anticipate that would have been so with the high level of abuse that was going on.[48]

This important finding undermines traditional constructions of institutional abuse as relating to adult perpetrators and child victims which characterize the existing literature. Furthermore, it also lends further support to the notion of 'peer-to-peer' grooming and abuse within an institutional environment as highlighted by a minority of studies cited above (see Shaw, 2007: 31–2, quoting

---

[47] Ibid.   [48] RI 2 (11 May 2011).

Westcott and Clement, 1992; MacLeod, 1992). As I have argued above, within the institutional environment, therefore, where abusive practices have become normalized, the ripple effect surrounding abuse may mean that there are augmented difficulties in separating out victim and offenders within the continuum of offending behaviour. This point also highlights the fact that within this particular historical institutional context, clerical abuse operated at a more systemic, prolific if not organized level than abuse in other organizational contexts committed by individuals acting alone.

In relation to the second element, the grooming of colleagues within an institutional environment may completely replace the grooming of the child. Several interviewees explained that the purpose of such grooming would be to avert the suspicion or attention of those who would provide a source of safety or support for the child. One interviewee stated:

I've had cases where there was a residential social worker and it was more the grooming of the colleagues as opposed to the grooming of the child... so sometimes the grooming can be around creating with others, who should be calling into question what are you doing, that the grooming is ensuring... that's who I need to work on and not necessarily any grooming of the victim as such, particularly if it's a very painful abuse and the victim from the very start does not want to do it, is crying, is screaming. It's more, why did nobody else come and that's the grooming of others.[49]

Other interviewees pointed out these individuals were often the most popular with the staff and the children (Bithell, 1991; Erooga, Allnock, and Telford, 2012: 10, 27). As one senior practitioner stated, reflecting on previous cases:

They were seen as just very positive... two of them were actually the child protection officers, so they took on the mantle of protecting children and were seen in that light, and therefore in a way become inviolable... if they are doing something it must be ok... because they have the responsibility and they are so caring.[50]

The notion of 'institutions as individuals' (Douglas, 1986), whereby offenders seek to navigate or exploit system weaknesses or personal relationships in order to abuse, has been outlined above (see also Plymouth Safeguarding Children Board, 2010: para 5.73).

[49] NI 2 (23 May 2011).   [50] EW 13 (22 September 2011).

As will be discussed further below, what Salter terms 'staff seductions' (2003: 139–56), and Robben 'emotional allurement' (1995: 83), may be 'particularly acute in prisons…residential homes, and half-way houses where offenders and staff/volunteers may spend long periods of time together' (Salter, 2003: 140). The insidious nature of grooming within this context, however, as one of these interviewees also explained, is often extremely difficult to detect ahead of the discovery of actual harm or abuse. One interviewee used the phrase 'system grooming'[51] to explain this process: 'he's grooming the staff, he's grooming the environment, he's grooming for example the rota system. He's doing all of that, but you wouldn't have spotted it because…he didn't show any specific interest in the victim, so teaching about that wouldn't have rang any bells with anybody because his grooming efforts were through a different system'.[52] As highlighted above and discussed in the last part of the book, the significance of inherent collusion by others within organizational contexts reinforces the importance of developing effective internal child protection procedures and, in particular, staff training around issues specific to offender behaviour.

The grooming of assessment, treatment, and management professionals

The notion of 'institutional grooming' may also be extended further by applying the label to interactions between sex offenders and professionals and by examining, in turn, how this may affect the outcomes and effectiveness of assessment, treatment, and management processes.

When asked whether modes of institutional grooming ever occur with professionals, nearly all interviewees were prepared to concede that what many termed 'professional grooming' was 'an occupational hazard of working in the field',[53] or at the very least that 'it's something you always have to be aware of'.[54] The offenders interviewed in Anna Salter's (2003: ch 8) study outlined the social strategies and personal techniques they used in relationship building with staff including, inter alia, obtaining information about staff; selecting a target perceived as 'vulnerable' based on

---

[51] NI 2 (23 May 2011).   [52] Ibid.   [53] NI 4 (1 June 2011).
[54] NI 2 (23 May 2011).

this information; using 'reciprocity' as a key 'tactic of seduction', where in giving information, advice, or a favour, the staff member will feel obliged to reciprocate with a similar gesture; and finally a 'demand' for something back by which time the staff member will have crossed the boundaries of appropriate interaction and become 'entrapped'.

Several authors have previously noted the processes of 'cognitive dissonance'[55] or 'emotional congruence' along the continuum of interactions between prison staff and prisoners more generally (Bates-Gaston, 2003: 244–5), between 'treatment' professionals and those who display sexually harmful behaviour including children and young people (Ashurst, 2011), and within the context of police interviews with suspected sex offenders (Benneworth, 2009; Lippert et al, 2010).

Prisoners and prison staff

Bates-Gaston (2003: 255), within the context of terrorism and imprisonment at the height of the political conflict in Northern Ireland, describes how 'terrorist' prisoners within the Maze Prison would often exploit the process of cognitive dissonance. Through the 'development, manipulation and maintenance' of 'familiarity and social affiliation' between prisoners and prison staff, the officer would become amenable to manipulation (Bates-Gaston, 2003: 255). The significance of 'the various kinds of manipulation and conditioning', much like the process of institutional grooming of professionals who may assess, treat, and manage sex offenders, is that 'these approaches were subtle and invidious and staff found such behaviour confusing and difficult to counter because these tactics exploited and manipulated familiar and conventional social norms and relationships' (Bates-Gaston, 2003: 254, 245). This process whereby 'there are constant little tests',[56] in the words of a senior prison service interviewee, was also explained more fully by a treatment professional in terms of offenders trying to find a common interest with professionals:

---

[55] Festinger's (1957) psychological theory of 'cognitive dissonance' suggests that this process arises when an individual finds him or herself compromised by another person or situation and, as a result, feels uncomfortable or put at a significant disadvantage by their own actions.

[56] SC 7 (23 August 2011).

You will see some male sex offenders try to collude with male officers and kind of get them onside. So that's part of a grooming process. It is about... 'You'd think about that too, John, you know what I mean John'... Little things like that, that kind of bring the officer over to their side. And of course that officer can get more drawn into that collusion so we have to be very aware of that, and that collusion is kind of grooming as well.[57]

The relevance of this form of institutional grooming was also explained as a 'means to an end' within the prison environment and by reference to 'the more subtle approach of getting people onside and getting them to do things for them'.[58] In relation to sex offenders specifically, several interviewees took care to emphasize that this would relate more to 'those who are more socially skilled... more sophisticated in terms of how they manipulate and groom people',[59] rather than those who are 'the very vulnerable and almost childlike themselves in their social skills'.[60] Such inflated levels of suspicion and mistrust of not only sex offenders but prisoners in general on the part of some professionals, which appears to be historically embedded within the Northern Ireland establishment in particular, are ultimately unhelpful, however, in enhancing our understanding of offending behaviour. They can potentially contribute to the 'othering' of sexual offending (Garland, 2001; Ashenden, 2002; Silverman and Wilson, 2002; McAlinden, 2005: 378–80, 2007a: 130–1) by further perpetuating the notion of a sex offender as a particularly deviant and manipulative individual who behaves markedly differently from the rest of us.

The 'therapeutic alliance'

The literature emphasizes the importance of establishing and maintaining a successful 'therapeutic alliance' (Tamatea, Webb, and Boer, 2011: 317) within the context of sex offender assessment and treatment. An effective 'rapport' between professionals and offenders is considered necessary to build a collaborative relationship, and maximize the quality of interaction and the effectiveness of interventions with particular client groups in clinical settings (Suchman et al, 1997; Halpern, 2003), such as sex offenders in general

---

[57] NI 1 (23 May 2011).   [58] Ibid.
[59] SC 4 (22 August 2011).   [60] NI 1 (23 May 2011).

(Bordin, 1994; Fenske, 2007; Ross, Polaschek, and Ward, 2008; Frost, 2011: 439–40; Tamatea, Webb, and Boer, 2011: 317–18), female sex offenders (Ashfield et al, 2010) and young people who display sexually harmful behaviour (Bovard-Johns, 2009; Ashurst, 2011). While 'emotional intelligence' or 'congruence' (Ashurst, 2011) on the part of professionals is clearly important as the foundation of effective interpersonal interaction and professional intervention with sex offenders, care needs to be taken that such affiliation and engagement with offenders does not spill over into what may be regarded as a further dimension of 'institutional grooming'. A treatment professional recounted:

I'm working with a supervisee at the minute who…worked really, really well with this very difficult client, and so much so that he did divulge very devious sexual behaviour. She found it very difficult to separate out his offending behaviour, from him…she is a very, very astute therapist, it's almost like she was taken over as well. I actually felt, 'God you really have to mind that boundary', of almost having something like a strategy, the minute this is heard, I have to put on another hat to deal with this right now…I do feel, all the time we get groomed.[61]

Another treatment professional, whilst acknowledging that 'some of that might be very positive and a whole social thing to do', admitted that 'sometimes…there was another flavour to it' in terms of 'the subtle building of alliances':[62] 'They would be very subtle in terms of working out what people's interests were, where they were from…and there would be other conversations about it that in some ways, I think, fudged the boundaries.'[63] Many interviewees, however, were also keen to point out that there were supervisory systems in place to maintain clinical objectivity and to guard against the risks of institutional grooming. Such checks and balances included joint facilitation of treatment sessions, often using the combination of male and female facilitators, staff awareness training, and supervision of treatment processes by treatment managers in terms of screening video tapes of each session, providing feedback to facilitators, and agreeing final risks and needs assessment reports. As a victim support interviewee acknowledged:

That's part of the reason…we had two facilitators. It's very hard to manipulate everybody and I think certainly in one to one it can happen

---

[61] RI 3 (16 May 2011).   [62] RI 10 (5 July 2011).   [63] Ibid.

much easier because you develop a relationship…Whereas if you're in a group, there's a different facility with a different type of personality and different sets of questions…there's more people looking at him, there's seven or eight other individuals in the group who could ask questions and know where he's coming from, I think that's a harder place to manipulate. But on a one-to-one basis I think it can easily happen.[64]

A particularly noteworthy finding is that several interviewees reported a greater occurrence of such behaviour on the part of those offenders who had already gone through treatment. A police officer stated: 'I tend to find that I am groomed more by those people who have been through the programmes than those who haven't, because they have learned the language of change'.[65] A voluntary sector worker explained further: 'they would be very conscious of what responses they need to give…So I think any institutionalized delivery of programmes, they are going to know how to tick the box'.[66] As highlighted above, such efforts on the part of offenders were also regarded as part of an ongoing process of what professionals termed 'impression management'[67] or 'transference'[68] in terms of presenting a more positive image of themselves as 'being very friendly and very compliant'.[69] There was also broad recognition that 'an attempt…to ingratiate and manipulate, but very cleverly'[70] might in turn influence risk assessment, ongoing risk management plans or even the outcome of treatment programmes. These viewpoints highlight a very real difficulty, therefore, for those administering offender treatment programmes and assessing the suitability for release of higher risk sex offenders in particular. Part of the ethos of treatment is to help the offender on the path towards an offence-free life, or as the literature on desistance and reintegration terms it, to develop pro-social concepts of self (Burnett and Maruna, 2006), or a redemptive self-narrative (Maruna, 2001). On the other hand, the iatrogenic effects of treatment interventions with sex offenders are worth highlighting at this juncture and might also merit further exploration in future research. That is, while the 'language of change' adopted by offenders is a desirable characteristic in potentially indicating that such pro-social or redemptive processes are well underway, there

---

[64] RI 1 (11 May 2011).   [65] NI 8 (6 July 2011).
[66] NI 5 (22 June 2011).   [67] EW 8 (14 September 2011).
[68] RI 10 (5 July 2011).   [69] EW 9 (14 September 2011).
[70] EW 12 (19 September 2011).

is also an underlying difficulty for professionals in ascertaining that any perceived metamorphosis is genuine rather than false and manipulative.

The police and other professionals and 'suspect' offenders

The literature also establishes that within the context of police interviews with suspect offenders (Durkin and Bryant, 1999; Benneworth, 2009; Lippert et al, 2010), there may be 'interactional difficulties' in 'negotiat[ing] an account of what actually happened' (Benneworth, 2009: 555–6). This facet of routine interaction between professionals and perpetrators, however, may go well beyond the police and extend to others who work closely with offenders such as probation officers, psychologists and psychiatrists, and prison staff. As Robben (1995) argues within the context of any ethnographic encounter, there are considerable problems in ascertaining the truth devoid of emotion and personal involvement and in simultaneously understanding through empathy and detachment. In the view of a senior police officer, this was very much an ongoing process but, at the same time, currently a neglected dimension of discourses around sex offender behaviour:

> We've certainly had some big operations, very, very skilful grooming undertaken by a group of paedophiles around the UK and it's ongoing now they're in prison and they're setting up networks in there. They try to groom the prison staff. They have definitely attempted to manipulate the police during inquiries and during management and I think if there is one area we need...it's not that we let it slip, I just don't think there's enough focus on the fact that that takes place and that when you go out and do a home visit, you are equally as capable of being groomed as anyone else...it's manipulating situations to suit themselves and avoid management, or avoid ongoing management, which makes it easier to conceal their true activities.[71]

As Sullivan and Quayle (2012) have noted, offenders will 'typically attempt to influence how people interpret their behaviour, generating potentially self-serving testimonies'. There may also be difficulties in obtaining a full or partial confession from suspected sex offenders in the absence of other corroborative evidence including child disclosure (Lippert et al, 2010). As outlined above, offenders may adapt ' "suffering" manipulation styles' where they self-represent as a martyr or victim in need of sympathy and support (Sullivan

---

[71] SC 1 (22 August 2011).

and Quayle, 2012). Some sex offenders, however, may need enhanced support, particularly young sexual abusers. Indeed, such difficulties in striking the appropriate balance between emotional engagement with offenders in order to illicit an accurate account of events, and obtaining objectivity may be enhanced where 'clients' appear to be caught up in a cycle of abuse in which they appear variously in the dual roles of both victim and perpetrator (Ashurst, 2011: 102).

In this respect, several interviewees acknowledged, in the words of a senior social services professional, that the offender will often 'try to present as the victim; they will use alcohol or drugs or adult mental health or their other experiences as an excuse for their abuse'.[72] This may impact directly upon professional interaction with offenders as, in the view of a treatment professional: 'the men themselves are very clever in holding on to the identity of somebody who is vulnerable, suicidal, or whatever, and then won't be pushed or pressed or encouraged to do work with it'.[73] The offender's self-presentation as victim appears to occur within a wide range of treatment, assessment, or management settings, but particularly within the course of interviews by social workers in suspected cases of child sexual abuse or of suspected sex offenders by police. A social worker recalled an example where: 'he comes in and he's very slight... and he'd be huddled up and "I don't know what I did"... so always really like the poor little victim... you'd nearly forget what he's after doing'.[74] Similarly, a police officer reflected: 'well they'll have different masks. A lot of them, and again it's quite classic, is the "poor me" mask... the old, "I'm the victim" and "I'm misunderstood" and "look at the life I've had", so they will nearly groom you into feeling sorry for them'.[75]

An alternative presentation by the offender in this context was that of a 'joker' or a 'clown'. Another police officer explained how one older offender: 'did just essentially through the interview play the... "I've been a silly old buffoon"... And clearly what he had been saying, backwards and forwards on-line, was not the thinking of a silly old man, but... an attempt to portray himself in one way to everybody else'.[76] This also accords with what Sullivan and Quayle (2012) have identified as a 'blocking manipulation' style—

---

[72] NI 14 (3 August 2011).   [73] RI 10 (5 July 2011).
[74] RI 4 (13 June 2011).   [75] NI 8 (6 July 2011).
[76] SC 2 (22 August 2011).

where the offender 'jests' with others in order to promote a view of themselves as fun and risqué while also normalizing their inappropriate behaviour. Others, however, are fully cooperative with the police. Two investigating officers explained: 'they want to come across to us as, "yes, I'm getting this all off my chest" and "I've been sitting here waiting for this day". We hear this quite a lot... "I'm glad you've caught me"... I would say the majority of the ones that we get are fully cooperative'[77] [and] 'some of them are very arrogant and think they're doing nothing wrong, but others put their hands up'.[78] In essence, therefore, there are a range of behaviours displayed by offenders when confronted with their offending behaviour in the course of interactions with professionals.

This analysis, however, also highlights a very important but largely unarticulated tension between the human and emotional side of work with sex offenders who, in many cases, will have committed horrific offences, and the customary and habitual component of regular and ongoing contact with such offenders. A particularly telling statement, in this regard, is one made by a treatment professional: 'I think I'm pretty hard line about things, but you do see the men as individuals and where offending is part of that and it's horrible and it has a horrible impact on you as well as other people, but they have also got strengths about them. So I think there definitely could be conflict there at times'.[79] If assessment, management, and treatment professionals are vulnerable to 'institutional grooming', therefore, this is by virtue of their routine interactions with this challenging group of offenders which may distort their perceptions of offenders or offending behaviour over time.

As part of this process, many interviewees also explained how offenders can play professionals off against each other which can result in 'the watering down of the evidence'[80] or in professionals 'los[ing] sight of the risk that someone poses'.[81] For female sex offenders in particular, as one interviewee explained, this behaviour can be enhanced yet vary according to the gender of the professional subject:

I guess men do it as well, but I think it has sometimes an added edge with women... So almost developing like a girls together dynamic... And then

---

[77] Ibid.   [78] SC 3 (22 August 2011).
[79] SC 4 (22 August 2011).   [80] NI 13 (27 July 2011).
[81] SC 9 (24 August 2011).

at the point where other professionals are saying 'This woman, she's of risk', then I will struggle with that, because the dynamic I've developed with you is one which feels quite friendly...the other route that women will use...will be sexually very provocative, particularly with male workers, and that can be hugely intimidating.[82]

The occurrence of this form of institutional grooming may have increased with the advent of 'joined up' thinking (Cowan, Pantazis, and Gilroy, 2001: 439) and the blurring of organizational roles and boundaries which underpins multi-agency work on sex offender risk management (Kemshall and Maguire, 2001, 2002; Maguire et al, 2001; Bryan and Doyle, 2003; Lieb, 2003; Maguire and Kemshall, 2004). In the view of one senior police officer, 'the introduction of MAPPA has greyed boundaries and that has given offenders an opportunity to play on doubts...And they will manipulate information that they are getting from social work, from the prison staff...in order to try and influence parole board decisions or prerelease case conferences and influence their management in the community'.[83]

While the literature cited above tends to highlight the processes of conditioning or grooming of prison, treatment, or police professionals, the current study also generated some examples of this occurring with other professional groups such as social workers and voluntary sector organizations. As one senior social worker explained, highlighting the dangers for professionals in engaging with offenders at an inter-personal level:

I do see people getting very close to the person they are working with. And they are trying to get them housing and they are trying to get them work...they go, I feel sorry for him...I know he's horrific but he has had a horrific background himself...I'll bring him in a coat. But the minute you would bring him in that coat, he has got to you on a level, because he knows you are willing at some stage to pass over that boundary. And then it is very difficult for you to get yourself out of that situation...and it can make it very, very murky...So you know it is very hard to disassociate sometimes, you have to pull yourself back...it is very easy to forget...you have to remind yourself, 'let's go back to the offence'.[84]

The challenge for professionals, therefore, was presented by several interviewees as not only remaining objective, but as also having a

---

[82] EW 14 (30 September 2011).   [83] SC 1 (22 August 2011).
[84] SC 10 (24 August 2011).

balanced view of the offence and the surrounding circumstances. In the words of one risk assessment professional: 'one of the most difficult things in forensic work is trying to stay in the middle all the time...not over identifying with victims; not over identifying with offenders. It is not being drawn into...completely seeing the side that the offender wants you to see, but also seeing the other side'.[85] The importance of having a balanced view within discourses on sex offending which encompasses both child protection/victim and offender management issues will be discussed further in the last part of the book.

Self-grooming or self-preservation?

Such outward presentation on the part of the offender may also be a manifestation of inward cognitive distortions as part of the process of self-grooming which prevents offenders from negatively evaluating themselves (Craven, Brown, and Gilchrist, 2006: 296). Several treatment professionals stated that self-grooming was particularly pertinent with clerical offenders who displayed 'that sort of denial around what they were doing and the absolute inability to look at the darker side of themselves'.[86] One police officer explained in relation to sex offenders in general: 'I don't necessarily see it across the interview table as lying. I think they have convinced themselves so what they are telling you is a twisted truth, as opposed to a lie'.[87]

This, however, may not be very different for other classes of offender or indeed for people more generally as 'when we are under pressure...we will use whatever our standard survival mechanisms happens to be'.[88] In the words of a probation professional: 'none of us want to be told we've done something wrong and in that sense any offender going into the police, the instinct is to defend, to lie, to excuse, to rationalize, to blame the victim...In that way I don't think sex offenders are probably any different to that'.[89] For a minority of interviewees, the use of the term 'grooming' in this context 'takes on a much more Machiavellian terminology'[90] and 'gets overlaboured and used' because 'it is not grooming unless it is something more conscious'.[91] Such comments also

---

[85] SC 9 (24 August 2011).   [86] RI 5 (14 June 2011).
[87] NI 8 (6 July 2011).   [88] EW 14 (30 September 2011).
[89] NI 9 (14 July 2011).   [90] NI 12 (26 July 2011).
[91] EW 1 (1 September 2011).

serve as a warning against over extending the term so that its use-fulness as a concept becomes diluted. Indeed, as argued in the previous chapter, the use of the term to describe a pre-meditated, planned, preparatory course of conduct on the part of the offend-er does not accurately reflect the onset of child sexual abuse in all cases, particularly those which occur within intra-familial contexts.

There was broad acknowledgement, nonetheless, of what one assessment and treatment professional pinpointed, as a sense of 'being tested...[or] being pulled into some sort of relationship dynamic that really shouldn't be going on'.[92] Sex offenders, how-ever, may have an enhanced motivation to engage in this manipula-tion style. Another senior treatment professional noted: 'it so happens that domestic violence and sexual offending are shameful so...it might be easier to admit to a violent burglary because they needed the money, but you can't say I needed sex from a child'.[93] A probation officer attributed this to self-preservation stemming from the consequences of the 'sex offender' label, particularly for more serious offenders:

And at the end of the day, particularly for the guys we are dealing with who are the category threes, they don't want to be category threes. So it's in their interests to tell us what we want...what they think we want to know...to come across as...'I've no issues', 'I'm cured', 'I've learned my lesson', 'I'm doing everything that's asked of me'...'I don't need to be cat three.' Because that label alone means they are really...they are moni-tored, they are managed, they are seeing every aspect of their life scruti-nized to a much more intense level. So they want to get rid of that label as quickly as possible.[94]

Moreover, in the words of one treatment professional: 'and unfor-tunately the media and all of that sort of public thing is...evil monster...It only increases people's desire not to be one of those people...who wants to be a monster?[95] These latter viewpoints in particular represent a more balanced view of offender behaviour and highlight the reality for many offenders when charged with a sexual offence. Sex offenders are not demons with superhuman powers, but rather are human beings who find themselves in a superhuman situation of having committed a crime deemed

---

[92] SC 11 (7 September 2011).   [93] NI 1 (23 May 2011).
[94] NI 9 (14 July 2011).   [95] NI 4 (1 June 2011).

unthinkable and unpalatable by society. The instinctive reaction, therefore, may be to justify or rationalize this behaviour in order to protect themselves or look for a lifeline or a way out of their situation.

Conclusion

This chapter has highlighted the multifarious process of institutional grooming including how it may relate to children themselves, other staff, their parents or carers, professionals, and wider society. The analysis of the primary research has in some respects accorded with the established literature. It has, for example, highlighted the potential overlap with other forms of grooming (Erooga, Allnock, and Telford, 2012: 10, 27–8) such as intra-familial, peer grooming and self-grooming as well as the difficulties of extricating victim and offender behaviour (Ashurst, 2011: 102). It has also demonstrated that not all 'professional perpetrators' (Sullivan and Beech, 2002) will deliberately choose a career which affords access to children.

A number of new insights into institutional grooming and abuse, however, have also emerged from analysis of the primary data in this study. First, for some offenders, the onset of offending may emerge as a convergence of situational risk factors—including power, authority, secrecy, isolation, inadequate supervision of staff and the absence of clear and appropriate physical boundaries between children and those responsible for their care—and dynamic risk factors such as emotional resonance with children. In short, much like intra-familial abuse, the occurrence of institutional abuse has been presented as the intersection of three factors—a motivated offender, a suitable victim, and the lack of an appropriate and capable guardian.[96]

Secondly, it has also provided a more nuanced understanding of the onset of clergy sexual abuse, including the potential role of grooming. For those who offend outside of a physical institutional context, celibacy rather than grooming emerges as a key factor in deflecting any concerns about potential risk. For those who offend within an actual institutional environment, in historical cases the onset of sexual offending against children appears to be

---

[96] See also routine activities theory (Cohen and Felson, 1979). See also Smallbone, Marshall, and Wortley (2008: 39).

related more to the use of physical violence, with more contemporary cases following grooming patterns in the conventional sense.

Thirdly, in relation to peer-to-peer forms of grooming and the grooming of other staff within institutions, this research has suggested that these forms of grooming may be considerably more prominent than has previously been highlighted. In relation to the former, in cases of historical institutional child abuse, children may have been groomed and abused by other children within the institutions. In relation to the latter, the grooming of other staff may in some cases completely replace the grooming of the child.

The chapter has also further conceptualized the notion of institutional grooming as applied to interactions between offenders and professionals, including prison staff, treatment providers, social workers, and police, which may in turn impact upon risk assessment, treatment, and management. In particular, stereotypical assumptions about the innate yet identifiable qualities of sex offenders also appear to pervade professional discourses on sex offending. At the same time, however, there are also clear difficulties which may be encountered by treatment and assessment professionals in establishing genuine rather than manipulative motivations on the part of offenders. Moreover, professionals are also faced with considerable challenges in dealing with sex offenders devoid of human sentiment and emotion and in maintaining a balanced outlook which encompasses both victim and offender viewpoints. Finally, while the grooming of professionals may be interpreted as a further manifestation of 'self-grooming' (Craven, Brown, and Gilchrist, 2006: 296) or cognitive distortions, it also emerges as part and parcel of the pursuit of self-preservation on the part of sex offenders largely because of the shame, and the social and legal consequences associated with the sex offender label.

The picture which emerges from this study, therefore, further accentuates the complexity of the grooming issue, the difficulties of making generalizations about the behaviour of sex offenders or the causes of institutional abuse, and of developing appropriate, proactive responses to child sexual abuse. As will be argued in the next chapter, the respective legal and policy frameworks on vetting and the offence of meeting a child following sexual grooming, are replete with practical difficulties in terms of pre-emptively responding to the range of abusive and grooming behaviours which may operate upon not only children, but also their surrounding environment and those closest to them. Indeed, the task of devising appropriate and more effective strategies to combat abuse may be considerably more complex in institutional settings, since such abusers will have managed to displace child protection messages within the workplace (Sullivan and Quayle, 2012).

6

Legislative and Policy Responses to Grooming

> Quite often it's only once an offence has taken place that the law...that anybody has actually power...In terms of the legislation, there's not a lot...that specifically looks at grooming because...how do you define it unless you have identified that this person does pose a significant risk?[1]

Public and political concerns about 'grooming' and the dangers posed to children by potential sex offenders within the dual contexts of child care institutions and the internet have been reflected in broad legislative and policy trends designed specifically to capture such 'risks'. This chapter will critically examine the regulatory frameworks on pre-employment vetting and barring as well as the offence of 'meeting a child following grooming/certain preliminary contact/for the purpose of sexual exploitation' which have been designed to pre-emptively manage grooming in each of the four jurisdictions in the United Kingdom and Ireland. While the former is designed to address 'institutional grooming' and to prevent offenders from making contact with children or the vulnerable through organizations, the latter targets 'on-line grooming'. Although the respective provisions are broadly similar in scope and content, there are some significant variations between jurisdictions which may also have implications for policing grooming behaviour.

The chapter will argue that there are a range of practical difficulties intrinsic to responding to grooming behaviour if viewed solely through a legalistic lens. In relation to vetting, such measures are only effective where the person has already come to notice as a sex offender and where their identity is known and assured. Regarding the offence of meeting a child following sexual grooming, although communications between the offender and the child can take place either on-line or off-line, the inherent problems surrounding the

---

[1] Senior probation officer (NI 9, 14 July 2011).

criminalization and policing of grooming behaviour mean that in reality it may be very difficult to apply the offence to grooming which occurs in face-to-face situations. The chapter includes a brief examination of the various transnational mechanisms and protocols which have been implemented within the European Union in particular to combat on-line grooming. It concludes with an analysis of the major themes emerging from the primary research in relation to legislative and policy responses to grooming.

Pre-employment Vetting and Barring Schemes in the United Kingdom and the Republic of Ireland

Over the last few decades in England and Wales, Scotland, Northern Ireland, and the Republic of Ireland, a series of public inquiry reports and official reviews into high profile cases of 'institutional abuse' have highlighted the link between institutions and the sexual abuse of children in particular (Corby, Doig, and Roberts, 2001; McAlinden, 2006a) (see Chapter 5). As noted in Chapter 1, many of the inquiries made similar recommendations which were not fully enacted (Parton, 2004), while other recommendations resulted in a series of legislative provisions devised to strengthen pre-employment vetting and barring schemes. These developments have perhaps been most prolific in England and Wales (McAlinden, 2010a: 30–1). For example, section 3 of the Sexual Offences (Amendment) Act 2000 made it an offence for an adult to engage in sexual activity with a child if they are in a position of trust[2] and Part V of the Police Act 1997 established the Criminal Records Bureau (CRB), set up in 2002, to coordinate criminal record checks.[3]

---

[2] The initial offence applied in Northern Ireland and Scotland, and has since been extended in England and Wales (see the Sexual Offences Act 2003, ss 16–24) and amended and re-enacted in Northern Ireland (see the Sexual Offences (NI) Order 2008, arts 23–31) and Scotland (see the Sexual Offences (Scotland) Act 2009, ss 42–45). There is no equivalent offence in the Republic of Ireland, although with sexual offences against those older than 15 but younger than 17, a higher penalty is attached if the offender is in a 'position of authority' (see the Criminal Law (Sexual Offences) Act 2006, s 3(3)(b)).

[3] Broadly speaking, disclosure may be either basic/standard—which provides details of convictions and cautions; or enhanced—which also includes any relevant information held on local police files, for those regularly involved in working with children. Although Part V of the 1997 Act applies throughout the United Kingdom, Northern Ireland and Scotland have their own government agencies—Access NI and Disclosure Scotland, to perform this function.

The Safeguarding Vulnerable Groups Act (SVGA) 2006[4] was enacted in England and Wales with reciprocal arrangements in Scotland and Northern Ireland to avoid cross-border loopholes.[5] The SVGA introduced a new statutory framework which gave legislative effect to many of the recommendations of the Bichard Inquiry (Gillespie, 2007a).[6] It recommended, inter alia, the introduction of a national registration system for all those deemed suitable to work with children and the vulnerable and improved information sharing between agencies (Bichard, 2004: 13–17). In England and Wales and Northern Ireland, the legislation established a centralized on-line register of every person who works with or volunteers with children or vulnerable adults both directly (referred to as 'regulated activities') as well as indirectly through ancillary work such as administrative settings ('controlled activities'). In short, it was designed to apply to all those who would work directly with children or vulnerable adults as well as those, for example, who have access to sensitive information about them. It was intended to address the deficiencies of previous regulatory schemes and streamline vetting procedures by combining previously separate disqualification lists;[7] removing ministerial decision-making and placing decisions about suitability to work with children in the hands of an independent statutory body (the Independent Safeguarding Authority (ISA)) on a case-by-case basis; and making provision for inclusion on one or both lists where evidence suggests risk of harm to children or vulnerable adults, as well as following an actual caution or conviction for related offences (McAlinden, 2010a: 31–3).

The Scottish legislation operates in a similar way, except that the relevant 'lists' are subdivided into the 'children list' and the '(vulnerable) adults list', rather than by the type of activity undertaken.

---

[4] As amended by the Policing and Crime Act 2009, Part 8, Ch 1. Sections 90–2 of the 2009 Act also make corresponding amendments for Northern Ireland.

[5] See respectively the Protection of Vulnerable Groups (Scotland) Act 2007, and the Safeguarding Vulnerable Groups (Northern Ireland) Order 2007.

[6] The Bichard Inquiry was set up following the conviction of school caretaker, Ian Huntley, for the murders of Holly Wells and Jessica Chapman in Soham in 2002. It examined vetting procedures in two police constabularies in England and Wales (Humberside Police and Cambridgeshire Constabulary) and, in particular, the effectiveness of information sharing.

[7] See eg 'List 99' (maintained by the Department of Education and Employment), the Protection of Children Act 1999 list, and the scheme relating to the Protection of Vulnerable Adults. For an overview see McAlinden (2010a: 31–2).

Since the proposed changes to the statutory frameworks in Northern Ireland and England and Wales were postponed pending further review, at the time of writing, Scotland has a quite different vetting and barring scheme to the rest of the United Kingdom (Stafford et al, 2011). The expansive remit of the SVGA has been scaled back significantly in England and Wales in particular as part of the Protection of Freedoms Act 2012 to a much softer approach.[8] In the main, the proposed registration scheme for individuals working with children is to be eradicated, 'controlled activities' are to be abolished, 'regulated activities' are to be restricted, inter alia, to relevant personal care, health care, and physical assistance, and the functions of the ISA and the CRB are to be transferred to a single agency—the Disclosure and Barring Service.[9]

In the Republic of Ireland, section 26 of the Sex Offenders Act 2001 makes it an offence to apply for work or to perform a service which involves having unsupervised contact with children and vulnerable adults without informing their prospective employer of their sexual offending history. Currently, however, vetting operates on an ad hoc and non-statutory basis. There are a range of statutory regulations which apply to the vetting of childcare workers in certain employment settings such as residential care, pre-school services, and foster care.[10] The Garda Central Vetting Unit (GCVU) provides pre-employment vetting for organizations which employ individuals to work with children or vulnerable adults. The standard vetting form, which is completed by the vetting subject, includes details of all prosecutions, pending or completed, and any convictions recorded in the state or elsewhere. Checks may also be performed on the PULSE system which includes intelligence relating to alleged abuse of children where no prosecution has been initiated. However, such 'soft information' is only disclosed to the Health

---

[8] See Part 5. The original proposals were scaled back in part because of public opposition to the expansion of vetting. See eg the campaign led by Philip Pullman which focused on categories of individuals to be excluded from such checks such as authors visiting schools.

[9] This amendment will also extend to Northern Ireland (see Part 5, ch 3). At the time of writing, the criminal records regime in Northern Ireland is also subject to a review by the Department of Justice (Mason, 2011, 2012).

[10] See eg the Child Care (Special Care) Regulations 2004; the Child Care (Pre-School Services) (No 2) Regulations 2006; the Child Care (Pre-School Services) (No 2) (Amendment) Regulations 2006; and the Child Care (Placement of Children in Foster Care) Regulations 1995.

and Safety Executive where there is a child protection issue, and is not provided as part of vetting disclosure.

In the aftermath of the publication of the Cloyne Report (Commission of Investigation, 2011), new legislation was announced. The National Vetting Bureau Bill 2011 establishes a new National Vetting Bureau, and allows for exchange of 'soft information' on abusers. The proposed framework, which is intended to expand vetting to all organizations which recruit people with substantial and unsupervised access to children and vulnerable adults, is similar in some respects to the schemes in the United Kingdom with some key differences. It will also remove responsibility for vetting from the police to a centralized government agency. On the other hand, it has a rather narrower remit by expressly excluding persons minding a child or vulnerable adult in the family home at the request of a parent or guardian and those assisting or volunteering in sports, community or other organizations on an ad hoc basis, where there is no 'regular or ongoing unsupervised contact with children or vulnerable adults'.[11] Such exclusions and omissions are significant in terms of the effective management of risk both within and between jurisdictions, as discussed further below.

This chain of policy and legislative enactments common to all four jurisdictions has resulted in the 'institutionalisation of vetting' (Furedi and Bristow, 2008: xii) which has further entrenched the rhetoric of precaution (McAlinden, 2010a: 27). Pre-emptive measures are heavily premised on the assumption that it is possible to effectively pre-determine who poses a potential risk to children (McAlinden, 2010a: 27, citing Zedner, 2009: 35). The upshot of ever-expanding forms of precautionary regulation of sexual offending against children, however, has produced 'a myriad of uncertainties in the form of raised public expectations, unintended and ambiguous policy consequences and, in due course the undermining of their core aim of effective risk management' (McAlinden, 2010a: 33).

Public and official discourses on 'risk'

The realities of potential harm to children via grooming are clouded by misapprehensions about perceived risk within official and public discourses. Reactionary forms of policy-making, often in the

---

[11]   National Vetting Bureau Bill 2011, s 6.

aftermath of high profile cases, create fear about the perceived omnipresence of sex offenders in society and conflate levels and types of risk in the public imagination. Sex offending against children tends to be equated with sex offending as a whole and all sex offenders are deemed to pose the same degree of very high risk. Punitive political rhetoric about specific risks posed by sex offenders, in particular the threats posed by predatory strangers on-line and within child care institutions, fuels public fears about such risks and creates more demand for such sanctions in the form of ever expanding regulatory frameworks (McCold, 1996). In seeking to govern under conditions of extreme uncertainty—that is in trying to criminalize 'grooming' as behaviour which preludes actual abuse and capture potential sexual risks to children before harm occurs— the state has, however, created what Brownlee has termed a 'punishment deficit' (1998: 313). The state unrealistically raises public expectations about its ability to control sexual crime and respond effectively to the threat posed by grooming through the expansion of retributive, regulatory frameworks.

In introducing ever more stringent penal policies in direct response to public anxieties concerning the presence of predatory sex offenders, the state has fuelled 'the politics and culture of fear' (Furedi, 2006a, 2006b) surrounding sex offenders against children in particular. The state's overreliance on vetting in order to increase society's feelings of safety about perceived risks about grooming and address the dangers to children within an organizational environment, may actually be counter-productive. In common with the offence of 'meeting a child following sexual grooming', generalized forms of precautionary risk regulation such as vetting have created indiscriminate 'risk' strategies which 'treat all as potential suspects' (Zedner, 2009: 47) or 'cast the net of suspicion on all' (Ericson, 2007: 259). As a result, such pre-emptive approaches to grooming may have the undesirable effect of propagating embedded levels of societal suspicion and unease concerning potential sex offenders (Furedi and Bristow, 2008), to the detriment of interpersonal relationships within civil society. At the same time, the resulting feelings of insecurity and mistrust which attach to all who come into contact with children undermine our ability to make discerning judgments about the likelihood of harm. This may ultimately help to further mask 'unknown risks' until they manifest themselves in the form of actual harm to children or the vulnerable. As Hebenton and Seddon (2009: 12) note quoting Sunstein (2002), this is symptomatic of the 'risk-risk' problem of the precautionary approach where over emphasis on managing or reducing one set of risks can create enhanced risks elsewhere.

Public concerns about the risk posed by sex offenders often outweigh actual levels of danger. A body of work by Soothill and colleagues has identified three typologies of sex offender risk: 'known and high risk'; 'known, but low risk'; and 'unknown risk' (Kirby et al, 2005; Soothill et al, 2005a, 2005b). This categorization of offenders has important implications for quantifying 'unknown risks' and for evaluating the likely success of vetting measures. Their research estimates that of sexual recidivists known to the police, under one third will come from convicted offenders in the high risk category. Approximately another third will come from convicted offenders in low/medium-risk categories with 'unknown offenders' also accounting for the final third. It is this latter category of offender which presents most problems.

Societal stereotypes about 'institutional grooming' have also become ingrained within recent legislative frameworks on vetting resulting in potential problems of scope which may reduce their effectiveness in addressing grooming. The offence of abuse of a position of trust was enacted primarily to apply to particular organizational contexts such as schools and residential homes, and is not easily applied to other institutional settings such as sport (Brackenridge and Fasting, 2005) or faith-based organizations (NIACRO, 2008: para 3.2) which lie outside of educational settings (Northern Ireland Assembly Research and Library Service, 2010b: 2). As noted in Chapter 2, stereotypes about risk to children within residential or educational institutions have tended to dominate public and policy discourses on 'grooming' for the past few decades. Such an omission is significant, however, since the community and voluntary sectors may also provide extensive access to children and young people where 'by virtue of their role', they may 'exercise a measure of authority...and are therefore afforded a level of trust' (NIACRO, 2008: para 3.2). Some estimates place the sports sector as second only to education in terms of the level of contact between adults and children (NSPCC, 2010: para 12),[12]

---

[12] For example, the 2010 Young People's Behaviour and Attitudes Survey (YPBAS) of 11 to 16-year-olds in Northern Ireland showed that 75 per cent of children and young people aged between eight and 18 played sport outside school while 59 per cent belonged to a sports club or team (cited in NSPCC, 2010: para 12).

and consequently there are potentially many opportunities for abuse to occur. Similarly, the draft legislation in the Republic of Ireland expressly excludes from the proposed framework on vetting, volunteering in sports, community, or other organizations on an occasional basis. These arguments also underline the tendency to adopt the ethos of situational crime prevention (Wortley and Smallbone, 2006) in efforts to combat grooming, irrespective of wider concerns about harms which would normally lie outside the dominant paradigms or 'sites of danger' (Saraga, 2001).

Official information about 'risk'

The success of vetting as a preventive measure in managing risk and pre-emptively targeting grooming is based on the concept that simply having a list of known 'risky' individuals will make children or the vulnerable safe. This notion, however, is erroneous on three important fronts. First, vetting relies almost entirely on the use of accurate information. The tensions which underpin inter-agency processes mean that power differentials between core agencies (see eg Blagg et al, 1988; Sampson et al, 1988; Crawford, 1997: 127–31) may especially influence other forms of inter-agency conflict such as struggles over confidentiality and access to privileged information (Sampson et al, 1991: 132). Differences in approach to the problem of the risks posed by sex offenders may result in fragmented working practices and in a breakdown of effective communication of important information about offenders (see Chapter 3).

In relation to the Ian Huntley case, for example, inadequate information recording and sharing led to 'systemic and corporate failures' in police handling of intelligence and ultimately to Huntley being cleared to work in Soham primary school (Bichard, 2004: 2, para 8). It later emerged that Huntley was known to two police forces for a series of previous allegations of sexual offending where no action was eventually taken. Huntley's date of birth and a number of aliases were not properly recorded or checked on police files. This led to this information being missed during the background check. Police forces failed to pass on details about his offending past largely because relevant information had been deleted. The effectiveness of vetting and barring schemes as a frontline response to institutional grooming, therefore, ultimately depends on the actions of the police in keeping information and intelligence timely, accurate, and up to date.

Secondly, and following on from the previous argument, particular difficulties are attached to the use of 'soft' intelligence on suspect offenders where significant concerns exist about future risk of harm. Those offenders 'strongly suspected of serious sex crime and future danger' (Kirby et al, 2005) are what Zedner calls 'known unknowns' (2009: 47)—those sex offenders 'we know, we don't know about'. This would cover those individuals such as Ian Huntley, thought to be offenders by the police but who have not actually been apprehended or formally adjudicated upon. As Kirby et al note (2005: 226), '[t]here are considerable operational and ethical concerns to confront' in dealing with suspected offenders. Improving traditional mechanisms for securing convictions for this group, such as increased intelligence, investigation, and surveillance would further increase pre-emptive regulatory activity by the state with further resource implications. At the same time, this would also arguably be without offering a concomitant realistic prospect of addressing effectively the risks underpinning grooming behaviour which typically do not manifest themselves prior to actual harm.

Thirdly, vetting only takes account of past actions based on a known record of offending and cannot predict how someone with no record will behave in the future (Furedi and Bristow, 2008: 7). Checking for previous convictions, therefore, is an important element of the recruitment process, but insufficient in itself to prevent potential offenders entering organizational environments where there are children (Erooga, Allnock, and Telford, 2012: ch 1). Vetting and barring frameworks may also encourage a culture of complacency and a false sense of security within organizations. In this context, there are obvious, yet on the whole unacknowledged, limitations of official knowledge about risks posed by what Zedner (2009: 47) has termed 'unknown unknowns'—those offenders 'we don't know we don't know about'. The majority of abuse and prospective risks to children remain hidden and undisclosed (Smith et al, 2000; Salter, 2003; Gilbert et al, 2009), particularly that from within intra-familial contexts. Vetting in particular creates a false sense of security that it is possible to prevent an individual from ever harming children in their care (Furedi and Bristow, 2008: 6–7). It is axiomatic, however, that regulatory frameworks, which are dependent on the effective use of information, can only hope to deal effectively with 'known' risks, that is, those sex offenders who have already come to notice. As such, the reality is, therefore, that legal mechanisms such as vetting can only ever have a limited impact in tackling grooming behaviour and in managing the overall risk presented by sex offenders.

Institutional implementation of policies on 'risk'

The differential implementation of policies on risk within multi-agency frameworks has been highlighted in Chapter 3. In particular, there may be organizational resistance to multi-agency discourses where managerial 'partnerships' are difficult to operationalize on the ground (Hope and Murphy, 1983; Crawford, 1997: 107–8). Uneven and incongruous implementation of policies on risk, and on vetting in particular, may also work on two further levels: one is how policies may operate within a given organization; and the other, how policies may work on a transnational level among national authorities (McAlinden, 2010a: 38–9).

In relation to the first level, what Garland and Sparks (2000: 201) have termed 'institutional epistemology' acknowledges the cognitive processes and internal relational dynamics of institutions. As outlined in the previous chapter, institutions are apt to develop and re-organize their own rationale as the basis for collective action which is shaped by a 'sameness' of shared thoughts, values, and information (Douglas, 1986: 53). This argument has resonance at both the formal and informal level. Organizational culture is imbued with wider forms of social interaction which produces 'informal norms' such as those between members of staff working within a given institution. It is also marked by more formal organizational rules, such as vetting procedures, and monitors compliance with them. The ultimate success of vetting measures in preventing entry to institutions by would-be abusers and in thwarting grooming behaviour may also depend, therefore, on how rules and regulations are received and negotiated within institutions at an individualized localized level. This differential implementation of formal rules may also help to explain the slow progress of organizational change in failing to implement the same key recommendations from a series of inquiry reports and reviews which would improve policy, practices, and procedures on vetting and prevent institutional grooming.

In relation to the second level, the difficulties of policy implementation within inter-organizational contexts are likely to be compounded when it comes to multi-agency working across juris-dictional boundaries. In particular, criminal records information may be very difficult and time consuming to obtain from some states which may be reluctant to release information (Magee, 2008). Information is currently exchanged within the European Union via, for example, the Schengen Information System (SIS) and Interpol (Fitch, Spencer Chapman, and Hilton, 2007: 19–21). Enhancing police and judicial cooperation and enforcement within and across the European Union is an issue of ongoing concern (Ramage, 2007; Constantin, 2008; Jacobs and Blitsa, 2008). As noted in Chapter 3, however, effective cross-border cooperation between the two police forces in the Republic of Ireland and Northern Ireland, for example, has tended to be based on good working relationships rather than formal mandates (Walsh, 2011).

There are also potential disparities in vetting and barring frameworks across the United Kingdom and Ireland which may have implications for the effective management of risk (Ritchie, 2001; Fitch, Spencer Chapman, and Hilton, 2007). There are varying systems across the European Union as a whole in terms of standardized criminal record information and arrangements to track sex offenders and prevent unsuitable people from working with children which present significant challenges to inter-country cooperation and exchange of relevant information about offenders (Fitch, Spencer Chapman, and Hilton, 2007). While the United Kingdom has recently extended vetting to all posts involving access to children or the vulnerable, in Sweden health sector workers are not vetted, and in Poland most can work in children's homes without pre-employment checks (Fitch, Spencer Chapman, and Hilton, 2007). There are also particular concerns about the use of 'soft information' for pre-employment vetting which varies between countries (Fitch, Spencer Chapman, and Hilton, 2007: 27). In addition, the United Kingdom does not record conviction data of overseas workers unless copies of fingerprints are also supplied (Amroliwala, 2007). These differences are significant because they inevitably mean not only that vital information about perceived risk may be lost, but also that individuals may exploit differences between countries and seek employment in other jurisdictions where vetting and barring systems are not as stringent (Thomas, Katz, and Wattam, 2000).[13] Such concerns are becom-

---

[13] Similar concerns were also raised in the latter stages of the parliamentary debates on the SGVG Act 2006. See eg Baroness Walmsley, *Hansard*, HL Debs, cols 370–1 (1 November 2008); Baroness Morris of Bolton, *Hansard*, HL Debs, cols 357–8 (6 November 2008).

ing increasingly pertinent given the significant cross-border movement of individuals within the European Union (Fitch, Spencer Chapman, and Hilton, 2007: 47–8) and between the United Kingdom and the Republic of Ireland in particular (see Chapter 3).

Meeting a Child Following Sexual Grooming etc/Certain Preliminary Contact/for the Purpose of Sexual Exploitation

As noted above, specific legislation has been enacted in all four jurisdictions of the United Kingdom and Ireland in response to the perceived risk of sexual victimization posed by the internet and the dangers of 'on-line grooming'. The offence of 'meeting a child following sexual grooming etc' was first introduced in England and Wales and Northern Ireland under section 15 of the Sexual Offences Act 2003. The offence was extended in England and Wales under the Criminal Justice and Immigration Act 2008[14] and subsequently re-enacted in Northern Ireland in revised form under article 22 of the Sexual Offences (NI) Order 2008. The offence covers the behaviour of an offender who meets, or seeks to meet, a child with the intention of committing a sexual assault, if he has met or communicated with that child on at least two occasions. There is no requirement that the communications be sexual in nature. In fact, as Ormerod argues, 'they may well be deliberately non-sexual in nature in order to build a relationship of trust with the child by discussing innocuous topics' (2011: 342).[15]

Further, the offence is not restricted to on-line behaviour. It requires face-to-face meetings to either occur or be arranged in order for the offence to be triggered. It is the communication surrounding this meeting which can take place either on-line or off-line. This means that no actual abuse need take place before this offence is invoked. The purpose of section 15 is not to act against those who have sexually abused children but to criminalize the preliminary acts involved in abuse and allow intervention well before the occurrence of actual sexual harm (Hornle, 2011: 3).[16] As

---

[14] See s 73 and Sch 15, para 1.

[15] See also *R v G* [2010] EWCA Crim 1693.

[16] Prior to the introduction of the 2003 Act, child grooming was governed by a range of more generic legislation such as the criminal law on 'attempts' or child abduction. There were, however, anomalies and loopholes particularly if applied to on-line grooming. For a critical overview see Gillespie, 2002a; Ost, 2004; Bohlander, 2005).

Gillespie puts it, summarizing the mischief behind the offence, it 'seek[s] to prevent the sexual contact occurring by criminalizing the small space between the grooming and the substantive sexual offence' (2006: 235). In this sense, section 15 and its equivalent have been described as 'a "post-grooming" offence' (Cleland, 2005: 201). With this in mind, the phrase 'grooming offence' is nonetheless used throughout this chapter as a short-hand reference.

The original offence under section 15 of the 2003 Act required proof that the offender (A), a person aged 18 or over, met or travelled to meet the victim (B) with the relevant sexual intent. The revised offence, however, in England and Wales and Northern Ireland is comparatively broader. The offence may now also be triggered if A arranges to meet B or, importantly, if B travels with the intention of meeting A in any part of the world. These additions are significant because they would capture (a) an arrangement to meet which stops short of an actual meeting, and therefore potentially allows earlier legal intervention, prioritizing the child's safety; and (b) a situation where the victim is enticed to travel to meet the offender, which also closes the previous loophole which may have allowed offenders to evade liability by claiming that they had not actually travelled anywhere themselves. In the case of 'arranging to meet', as Ormerod argues, 'the risk of sexual harm is even less proximate' (2011: 342) and it becomes even more important to prove sexual intent, as discussed further below.

Scotland and the Republic of Ireland have followed this lead and enacted reciprocal provisions. In Scotland, section 1 of the Protection of Children and Prevention of Sexual Offences (Scotland) Act 2005 also makes it an offence to 'meet a child following certain preliminary contact'. This offence, although broadly similar to its legislative counterpart in England and Wales, contains 'some important adaptations which are arguably beneficial to the effectiveness of the provision' (Gillespie, 2006: 239). One such modification is that the age of the offender (A) is not specified which would presumably mean that the offence could also apply with 'peer-to-peer' forms of grooming where there is little age difference between A and B (eg a 15-year-old male and a 13-year-old female).[17] Secondly, the offence may be triggered if A has met or communicated with B on at least *one* occasion. This reduction from two occasions to one, may be

---

[17] Although, as Gillespie argues, in Scotland where the offender is under 16, it is more likely that they will be referred to a children's hearing (2006: 233).

problematic in terms of establishing 'the course of conduct' which would appear to be required to demonstrate clearly A's intention to engage in unlawful sexual activity with B. As argued below, the pattern of behaviour from which sexual motivation towards a child may be inferred might be more difficult to establish in face-to-face contacts. It is more easily identifiable, however, within the context of on-line grooming where there is usually a written and unassailable record of the nature and content of the communications (O'Connell, 2003: 3) which should help to demonstrate intention to engage in unlawful sexual activity with a child (Cleland, 2005: 202) (see Chapter 4). In any case, as McLaughlin argues, 'the need to establish a pattern of behaviour is somewhat superfluous given the inherent nature of grooming itself' (2009: 5) where typically trust is built up over time and a series of meetings or communications (Gillespie, 2006: 234).

In the Republic of Ireland, the history of legislative provision with regard to grooming has been described as a 'veritable hotchpotch' (McLaughlin, 2009: 4). Section 6 of the Criminal Law (Sexual Offences) (Amendment) Act 2007[18] introduces the offence of 'meeting a child for the purpose of sexual exploitation'. The Irish provision, like the Scottish legislation, does not specifically use the word grooming, but rather criminalizes sexual exploitation arising from grooming. It is similar in many respects to the original section 15 offence in England and Wales and Northern Ireland and applies where a person intentionally meets, or travels with the intention of meeting a child, having met or communicated with that child on two or more previous occasions. The Irish offence, therefore, is slightly narrower in that it does not include 'an arrangement to meet' within the terms of the offence and does not contemplate the child travelling rather than the adult. The Irish government, however, have expressly made separate provision for the commission of the offence within the state as well as where an Irish citizen commits the offence outside the state.[19] This contrasts sharply with provisions across the United Kingdom where although the previous meetings or communications with the child can have taken place in any part of the world, there must be some connection with the governing jurisdiction in that the travelling to the meeting must at least

---

[18] This section amends and inserts provisions into the Child Trafficking and Pornography Act 1998, s 3.

[19] Section 3(2B) of the Child Trafficking and Pornography Act 1998.

partly take place there (Gillespie, 2007b: 3; Choo, 2009: 55). The penalties on conviction are also higher—a maximum of 14 years' imprisonment, in comparison with a maximum of ten years in the other three jurisdictions.

As noted in Chapter 3, a further complementary measure may be invoked to address grooming. Sections 123–9 of the Sexual Offences Act 2003[20] introduce the 'risk of sexual harm order' (RSHO)—a civil preventive order which can be used to prohibit specified behaviours, including the 'grooming' of children.[21] It may be made by a magistrates' court on application by the police where a person has on at least two occasions engaged in sexually explicit conduct or communication with a child and where this is deemed necessary to protect the child from physical or psychological harm. It is possible for such an order to be made irrespective of whether such a person has previously been convicted of a sexual offence. This order criminalizes acts which may be carried out for the purposes of sexual grooming, but only after an individual has been identified as posing a risk to children (Ost, 2009: 81). As a civil order, the standard of proof is the balance of probabilities which lowers the evidential threshold required for pre-emptive measures against an adult who is thought to pose a risk to children (Norrie, 2005: 21). While there is a broadly equivalent provision in Scotland,[22] the Republic of Ireland has a narrower measure in the form of 'sex offender orders' which can be used on conviction to prohibit the offender from doing anything specified in the order following their release from custody.[23]

Consistent with broader concerns about risk management (Parton et al, 1997; Kemshall and Maguire, 2003) and preventive governance (Ashenden, 2004), the general aim of these provisions is to prevent or deter contact between children and would-be abusers and, if it does occur, to make it more liable to detection and reporting. Since they empower the police to identify and apprehend abusers before they are able to abuse a child, they have generally been welcomed as a positive advancement in child protection and as a

---

[20] These provisions apply in England and Wales and extend also to Northern Ireland.

[21] RSHOs in England and Wales replace and combine two previous measures—sex offender orders and restraining orders.

[22] See the Protection of Children and Prevention of Sexual Offences (Scotland) Act 2005, ss 2–8.

[23] See the Sex Offenders Act 2001, Part 3.

'step in the right direction' (Ost, 2004: 147).[24] However, they have also been criticized from a practical standpoint, particularly in relation to on-line forms of grooming. Indeed, while most of the critiques are drawn out and applied in relation to on-line settings, there are also enhanced evidential and practical issues in capturing face-to-face forms of grooming including those which occur within families, within institutions, and between peers.

Evidential difficulties

Critics point in particular to the potential difficulties of gaining sufficient evidence and of proving the requisite *mens rea* of 'harmful ulterior intent' (Ost, 2004: 347; see also Gillespie, 2002a; Khan, 2004; Spencer, 2004). This can include cases where a 'relationship' exists or develops between the victim and the offender, where the victim trusts their abuser (Gillespie, 2002a: 411). The timing of legal intervention is important since, as noted above, grooming can include activities that are legal in and of themselves especially in the early stages of the process but which ultimately escalate in terms of inappropriate behaviour towards children culminating in sexual harm.

In relation to the first line of critique, there are a range of potential evidential issues at the operational policing level of 'on-line grooming', as well as in terms of legal admissibility in court. Sommer (2002: 180) describes how police can monitor use of the internet in two main ways: 'passive scrutiny', where they simply observe activity and gather evidence but do not intervene, and 'active scrutiny' which involves interaction with suspected sex offenders as part of an investigation. It is the latter of the two methods of surveillance which provides most difficulties. In the course of covert 'cyber-sting' operations (Gillespie, 2008), police officers may pose as a child or young person in chat room settings in order to obtain evidence for the purposes of an investigation (Krone, 2005; Mitchell, Wolak, and Finkelhor, 2005; Newman, 2007).[25] As discussed in Chapter 4, the anonymity of the internet is something of a double-edged sword. On

[24] These assumptions about the supposed benefits of the legislation also appear to have underpinned the legislative debates on the Sexual Offences Act 2003. See eg Sir Paul Beresford, *Hansard*, HC Debs, cols 699–700 (12 June 2000); Lord Falconer, *Hansard*, HL Debs, col 1257 (1 April 2003).
[25] The media have also operated 'cybersting' operations (Gillespie, 2008) which are more difficult to justify in the absence of training and supervision (Levy, 2002).

one level, it enables abusers to be more clandestine in their prepara-tory abusive activities. At the same time, such facelessness also lends itself to proactive police operations and ensures that the offender does not know for certain whether they are talking to a child or undercover police officer (Gillespie, 2004c: 252). There are eviden-tial and civil liberties issues, however, pertaining to possible entrap-ment, which arise in the course of undercover operations to detect and arrest would-be sex offenders who engage in grooming behav-iour (Gillespie, 2002b). In order to avoid defence applications for the exclusion of evidence on the grounds of entrapment or a stay of proceedings for abuse of process, the police must use such opera-tions to 'detect' rather than 'entice' or 'create' crime (Roberts, 2000; Khan, 2004; Gillespie, 2008).[26]

In the United States and Canada, the defence of entrapment can be raised but this is not usually successful in cases of on-line child exploitation (Smith, Grabosky, and Urbas, 2004; Moore, Lee, and Hunt, 2007).[27] In some jurisdictions such as the United Kingdom,[28] Australia, and the Republic of Ireland,[29] there is no defence of entrapment per se and it is instead up to the trial judge to rule on the admissibility of evidence which may have been obtained through 'improper' investigative techniques (Choo, 2009: 30). A minority of writers have argued that 'cybercopping' (Kierkegaard, 2008: 54)

---

[26] See the House of Lords' decision in *R v Loosely, Attorney-General's Reference (No 3 of 2000)* [2001] 4 All ER 897 which endorsed the comments of Lord Bing-ham in *Nottingham CC v Amin* [2000] 1 Cr App R 426, at 431, and made the dis-tinction between giving someone 'an unexceptional opportunity' to commit a crime and pressurizing them into committing the crime. Where that proper distinction is drawn, proactive police operations can be legally justifiable. See Ashworth (2002) and Gillespie (2002a) for a detailed analysis of the impact of this case. The leading case in Scotland is *Brown v HMA* 2002 SCCR 684 where the Appeal Court considered the nature of entrapment as occurring when the state pressurized some-one into committing a crime which they would not otherwise have committed and referred with approval to the decision in *Loosely*.

[27] Moore, Lee, and Hunt (2007) in their analysis of US case law on 'on-line sting operations' have noted that the entrapment defence has tended to be based on a number of factors including the length of the relationship between the undercover police officer and the victim, the party responsible for initiating the first contact, and the degree of reluctance expressed by the offender.

[28] See also *R v Smurthwaite, R v Gill* [1994] 1 All ER 898.

[29] The Irish law on unconstitutionally obtained evidence is underdeveloped and the precise scope of the law in this area has yet to be defined. The case of *Syon v Hewitt and McTiernan* [2006] IEHC 376, however, appears to disregard a distinct defence of entrapment.

or proactive policing techniques (Gillespie, 2002a, 2002b) are an effective and appropriate way to apprehend on-line sex offenders. Others have argued, rightly in my view, that undercover or covert operations are replete with not only ethical but also practical difficulties (eg Khan, 2004; Smith, Grabosky, and Urbas, 2004; Gillespie, 2008) and are largely ineffective in preventing serious child exploitation. Fulda, for example, argues that empirical evidence shows that the persons caught in 'internet stings' are not genuinely dangerous and that genuinely 'dangerous pedophiles' are not generally susceptible to being caught by such stings (2007: 64).

According to the jurisprudence of the European Court of Human Rights (ECtHR), the offender must take the first step towards the commission of the offence themselves by volunteering 'spontaneous and unprompted statements' which are not 'induced by... persistent questioning'.[30] This may be a tricky balancing act to perform in practice where investigating officers are trying to establish a pattern of communication between the offender and the pseudo 'child'. In short, there is a 'proximity nexus' required for criminal liability in such circumstances (Gillespie, 2002b). The ECtHR, in this respect, has laid emphasis on whether the individual was 'predisposed' to offending in the sense of a prior record of such offending.[31] Although subsequent decisions by the higher courts in the United Kingdom have placed less weight on this requirement,[32] in any event, it may be difficult to use the legislation in practice where the individual has no prior convictions for sexual offences from which sexual motivation may be inferred (Craven, Brown, and Gilchrist, 2007: 65). As Choo helpfully summarizes in relation to the potential difficulties police and prosecutors may face in investigating cases of on-line grooming: 'Over time, as the jurisprudence develops globally, prosecutions may become less difficult,

[30] See *Allan v UK* [2003] 36 EHRR 12, at 143. See also Hofmeyr (2006); Squires (2006).

[31] In *Teixeira de Castro v Portugal* (1998) 28 EHRR 101, the applicant, who had no prior record of drug dealing, complied with the request of an undercover police officer to obtain drugs. The ECtHR regarded this as a breach of the right to a fair trial under art 6 of the Convention, drawing a distinction between a case like the present, where the applicant was not 'pre-disposed' to this type of offending, and a case where such predisposition existed. See, however, the decision in *Loosely* (note 26 above) where the House of Lords held that the primary issue in such cases is the conduct of the law enforcement agency and that factors such as predisposition towards crime are less important.

[32] See previous note.

but for the moment they remain somewhat burdensome, with their outcome often uncertain' (2009: 31).

There are also a number of challenges to bringing a successful prosecution for child sexual exploitation beyond the evidential issues of entrapment. As Kosaraju (2008) argues, the organized nature of such cases makes investigation and prosecution difficult. Offenders may be prone to using pseudonyms, false addresses or multiple mobile phones in order to avoid detection. These difficulties make investigating cases of sexual grooming considerably more complex and as a result of insufficient evidence, few cases result in charges being laid and even fewer being tried in court or resulting in a conviction (Kosaraju, 2008: 16). Furthermore, as argued throughout this book, the problems of identifying and verifying grooming in off-line contexts are compounded as '[i]n reality, it is extremely difficult to police and evidence grooming behaviour in "the real world"' (Davidson and Martellozzo, 2008b: 339). Not surprisingly, therefore, few cases of 'meeting a child following grooming' or its equivalent have been brought to court. [33] Although CEOP figures for 2009/10 show that there were well over 100 public reports involving on-line arrangements to meet a child off-line in the United Kingdom (CEOP, 2010: 13–14), there are much lower numbers of prosecutions.[34] Following on from the discussion of official statistics on grooming in Chapter 2, the 'sanction detection rate' for the offence of sexual grooming for England and Wales—that is the proportion of prosecutions compared to offences recorded—stood at approximately 40 per cent for 2009/10 and 2010/11 (Taylor and Chaplin, 2011: 16). Reports on the effectiveness of similar legislation in Sweden and Norway also show that the legislation has not been used effectively and that there were a limited number of convictions (Kool, 2011; ECPAT, 2012). The number of offenders convicted, however, 'is likely to be just the small tip of a very big

---

[33] The Scottish Parliament also notes that it was never envisaged that the 'grooming offence' would be commonly used: see *Justice 1 Committee Report, SP Paper 307*, vol 1, para 30.

[34] There were eight such cases of 'grooming' in Northern Ireland for the period May 2010 to May 2011, an increase from five for the same period in the previous year (Internal Police Service of Northern Ireland (PSNI) Statistics, supplied to the author on 1 July 2011). Similarly in Scotland, while there were 31 offences of meeting a child following certain preliminary contact recorded by the police in 2009/10, only five people were found guilty of the offence (Internal Scottish Government Statistics, supplied to the author on 22 November 2011).

iceberg' (Barnardo's, 2011: 17). Aside from non-reporting by victims, there are a range of factors associated with non-prosecution.

The main reasons for the low numbers of prosecutions for 'the grooming offence' are that grooming does not per se constitute an offence, and that in the majority of cases grooming has actually led to a substantive offence, although some offenders have been apprehended before a contact sexual offence could take place (Gillespie, 2002a: 2; Ost, 2009: 77–8). Certainly in some of the recent high profile cases of 'street grooming' as outlined in Chapter 2, the offenders were found guilty of a range of sexual offences and not just that related to grooming. As Craven, Brown, and Gilchrist contend, '[t]hus, the legislation has failed to be preventative, as was intended, and has merely provided an additional charge for those who would most likely have been convicted of a contact offence anyway' (2007: 68).

Ost argues, '[a] successful prosecution also depends on a cooperative victim' (2009: 77). Many cases are dropped because of a lack of evidence or because prosecutors have assessed the young person as an unreliable witness (Barnardo's, 2011: 17). As noted earlier in relation to street grooming, 'victims are unlikely to disclose exploitation voluntarily, as a result of fear of exploiters, loyalty to perpetrators, a failure to recognise that they have been exploited and a negative perception or fear of authorities' (CEOP, 2011a: 11). Getting victims to go to court when they have an emotional attachment to their abuser or because they do not perceive themselves as victims is often one of the biggest challenges for law enforcement (Beckett, 2011: 5; CEOP, 2011a: 14).[35] Even when cases are brought, often they are not reflective of the true scale of abuse or exploitation suffered by the victim, particularly in cases of intra-familial abuse where 'sample counts' may be used to represent many months or years of abuse.

A particular problem is that prosecutors often place overreliance on the child or young person's testimony in court. The grooming process, however, means that victims may be fearful for their safety and consequently unable to give testimony well enough to sustain a guilty verdict (Kosaraju, 2008: 16). Furthermore, as Barnardo's have argued, 'the jury's lack of understanding of the issues, including the level of influence grooming can have... mean that the young

---

[35] 'Britain's Sex Gangs', *Dispatches*, Channel 4, 7 November 2011.

person is viewed as consenting to the abuse' (Barnardo's, 2011: 17). Other possible sources of evidence such as statements by parents or carers, forensic evidence, or corroborating evidence of other victims, where the defendant has abused two or more victims, are often not explored by the prosecution in such cases (Kosaraju, 2008: 16).

In relation to the second line of critique, the offence of meeting a child following sexual grooming could be said to fall within what has become known as 'thought crime' (Liberty, 2003: 10; Gillespie, 2004c: 248–9). In George Orwell's, *Nineteen Eighty Four* (1949) 'thought crime'—the act of thinking about committing a crime—is an even more serious offence than actually committing the crime. This concept is particularly evident in recent legislation and public policy on sexual assaults against children where the distinction has been increasingly towards making the thoughts criminal as well. In the United States, allegations of on-line communication with children as a prelude to sexual activity have been successfully deflected by suspected offenders using the 'fantasy defence' (Smith, Grabosky, and Urbas, 2004; Choo, 2009: 30). The central element of this common law defence is that the accused's actions were merely an expression of fantasy and were not indicative of real intentions or plans for future conduct. The associated difficulties of making a clear distinction between potentially harmful and innocuous behaviour by adults towards children, could lead to innocent conversations and actions being criminalized, which are outside the ambit of the danger it was intended to address (Gillespie, 2002a: 419).[36] As Cleland argues in relation to the scope of the Scottish offence but which has general applicability, 'the section is so widely drawn that some activities that might be regarded as legitimate are also caught' (2005: 203). In essence, however, the relevant *mens rea* for the offence is that at the time of meeting the child or the travel with the intention of meeting the child or making arrangements to meet the child, the offender had the intention to commit a relevant sexual offence. It is this intention to 'pursue a course of criminal

---

[36] These potential difficulties were also recognized when the legislation was being considered by the Westminster Parliament. See eg Mr Oliver Letwin, *Hansard*, HC Debs, col 508 (19 November 2002); Baroness Noakes, *Hansard*, HL Debs, cols 777–8 (13 February 2003); Baroness Gould, *Hansard*, HL Debs, col 786 (13 February 2003).

conduct' (Gillespie, 2004a: 249), however difficult it is to prove, which takes the offence out of the realms of 'thought crime'.

The concept of intention within criminal law has been the subject of much contention (eg Lacey, 1987; Simester and Chan, 1997) and is historically one of the more difficult species of *mens rea* to prove (Gillespie, 2004b: 11). With regard to grooming behaviour in particular, Craven and colleagues have highlighted the 'seemingly impossible task of proving beyond reasonable doubt that the ambiguous behaviour is sexually motivated' (Craven, Brown, and Gilchrist, 2006: 297). As noted above, the task of proving 'intention' to meet a child following sexual grooming will inevitably be easier where the offender has used the internet, mobile phones, or other communications-based technologies to groom a child (McLaughlin, 2009: 12). Many sex offenders can now be tracked, to some degree at least, by examining the internet and computer usage of those who may have been reported. In this respect, the actual content of conversations will play a crucial role in establishing the sexual intent behind the communications with the child (O'Connell, 2003: 14–15). Conversations between victims and offenders may be saved in a number of ways ranging from the victim's hard drive on the client side to the Chat or IM Service Provider's server. O'Connell also argues, however, that conversations sent via SMS,[37] MMS,[38] video messaging, and voice mail on 3G mobile phone devices have a much more limited capacity to store copies of such communications. New and more advanced forms of technology, therefore, may continue to throw up legal and evidential difficulties as offenders find ever more inventive ways of evading law enforcement. In particular, 'the use of cryptography, steganography[39] and anonymising protocols make the task of tracking communications difficult for police and regulators alike' (Choo, 2007: xi).

With the process of face-to-face grooming, however, there is much less likely to be tangible evidence in the absence of witnesses who are able to recognize the behaviour as such (Craven, Brown, and Gilchrist, 2007: 64). The evidential difficulties of proving an

---

[37] Simple Messaging System, or plain text messaging.

[38] Media Messaging System, or photo messaging.

[39] Steganography is the art of writing hidden messages, typically within an image, so that no one but the sender and the intended recipient suspects the existence of the message.

ulterior intention are likely to be increased by the absence of a 'digital footprint' (McLaughlin, 2009: 12) in the form of a written record of communications between the offender and the child. As Khan (2004) has argued, presumably would-be offenders would have to take significant steps towards the actual commission of a sexual offence before a clear intention can be discerned. Gillespie (2005a: 6) argues that the *actus reus* of travelling to meet the child creates the necessary proximity for the offence (together with the requisite *mens rea*) and also ensures that the police do not have to risk the safety of a child by observing an actual meeting. The relevant intention can also be inferred from circumstantial evidence (Ost, 2009: 78). Emails to other sex offenders providing 'updates' on the grooming process (Quayle and Taylor, 2001: 601), communications between the victim and the offender (such as emails, transcripts of chatroom, or Instant Messenger conversations or records or telephone calls) (Gillespie, 2006: 237–8), as well as physical evidence found in the offender's possession at the time of arrest (eg diaries, comics, toys, condoms, lubricant jelly, alcoholic drinks, or receipt confirmation of a hotel room reservation, or a PDA (personal data assistant) device containing child pornography websites or details of other children the offender had contacted) may also be used by the prosecution to persuade the jury as to the likely intent of the offender (Gillespie, 2004b: 11, 2005a: 6; Ost, 2009: 73–8).[40] Norrie (2005: 21) argues that it will be difficult in practice to secure a conviction merely through the possession of articles associated with sexual activity because there will always be a reasonable doubt that they were intended for use with another adult and not with a child. While one of these items of evidence on its own may be unlikely to convince a jury of criminal intent, arguably the cumulative effect of such information, that is incriminating articles plus details of the sexualized communications which preceded the meeting, may be enough to help the tribunal of fact infer intent.

In order to gather enough evidence to show an intention to commit a relevant sexual offence, I would argue, however, that it is necessary to at least identify that an offender has targeted a

---

[40] See also the briefing paper produced by Childnet International for the Home Affairs Select Committee prior to the implementation of the Sexual Offences Bill which details the types of cases that arose within the UK: *The Need for a New Clause 17 Grooming Offence*, <http://www.childnet-int.org/downloads/SOBclause17.pdf> (accessed 6 April 2011).

particular child and begun to groom them prior to sexual abuse. Indeed, without written or other supporting evidence from which it may be possible to infer such an intention, the offender may have to be allowed to go as far as meeting with the child, which potentially raises ethical concerns regarding the child's safety (Nair, 2006: 183). In cases of intra-familial and institutional child abuse, in particular, therefore, it is highly unlikely that the police will be able to detect all instances of grooming which occur prior to the contact abuse (Gillespie, 2002a, 2004a; Ost, 2004).

Practical problems for law enforcement

The need for the government to be seen as 'doing something' and 'getting serious about crime' (Bohlander, 2005: 712) has led to the expansion and reach of the criminal law (Hornle, 2011: 3) without due regard for the practicalities of law enforcement. There are a range of arguments pertaining to the difficulties for law enforcement in terms of both the limited scope of the legislation within the United Kingdom or the Republic of Ireland as well as key differences in the legislative provision between jurisdictions.

First, in relation to the scope of the legislation, a potential problem in applying the legislation concerns the age of the offender. In England and Wales and Northern Ireland, within the terms of section 15 of the Sexual Offences Act 2003 and art 22 of the Sexual Offences (NI) Order 2008 respectively, the offence of meeting a child following sexual grooming specifically applies where the offender is a person aged 18 or over. Section 13 of the 2003 Act makes express provision for 'child sex offences committed by children or young persons' and makes it an offence for a person aged under 18 to do anything that would be an offence under sections 9 to 12 if he were aged 18 or over. Therefore, where a 16-year-old or 17-year-old grooms a 12-year-old, section 15 would not apply (McLaughlin, 2009: 14). This is a significant omission since a growing number of sexual assaults against children are committed by other children (Grubin, 1998). Research suggests that approximately one-third of all reported cases are committed by those under 18 (Richardson et al, 1997; Grubin, 1998; Masson, 2004). In this vein, the notion of 'peer-to-peer grooming'—children who groom other children for the purposes of sexual abuse or exploitation—which has more recently emerged, would appear to lie outside the scope of the legislation in England and Wales and Northern Ireland. As noted above, in the other two jurisdictions—namely Scotland and the Republic of Ireland—the legislation does not suffer from this deficit being broader in scope and applying to 'A/Any person', with no specific mention of the age of the offender. The non-applicability to peer-to-peer forms of grooming may be particularly pertinent within the on-line environment. As outlined in Chapter 4, contrary to public perception, internet perpetrators are often younger and the faceless nature of on-line interaction facilitates the concealment of an individual's true identity, including their age.

Secondly, a further key difference between the respective legal frameworks on grooming concerns the age of potential victims. In all of the jurisdictions with the exception of the Republic of Ireland, the legislation specifies that 'B' is a person 'aged under 16'.[41] As was noted in the public consultation exercise on the then Draft Sexual Offences (NI) Order 2007, 'in some instances this strict determination on age may fail to recognise the vulnerability of some 16 + 17 year olds who are also at risk of being victim to activities such as grooming' (NIACRO, 2008: para 3.2). Indeed, as discussed in the previous two chapters, patterns of grooming behaviour often do not conform to the dominant stereotype of sexual offending which is comprised of an adult male offender and a much younger, usually female, victim. Within the continuum of grooming and abuse, within families and institutions as well as within the on-line environment, children may be both victims and perpetrators of abuse and there may not always be a clear age differential between the parties.

In addition, McLaughlin (2009: 11–12) has argued that the differing ages of consent within and across European states as well as internationally may constitute a serious obstacle to the establishment of a coordinated pan-European approach to policing grooming behaviour. Such difficulties are compounded particularly where aspects of the process take place in different jurisdictions. As Gillespie has stated, 'legislating for extraterritoriality is fraught with difficulties' (2004c: 251) and in particular it raises 'constitutional issues about whether it is permissible for one country to ad hoc regulate another country's society' (2004c: 252). Moreover, as

---

[41] See, respectively, the Sexual Offences Act 2003, s 15(1)(c); the Protection of Children and Prevention of Sexual Offences (Scotland) Act 2005, s 1(1)(c); and the Sexual Offences (NI) Order 2008, art 22(1)(c).

Shannon contends in relation to the Republic of Ireland, the potential ambiguity concerning whether both the communication and
subsequent meeting with the child must take place within the same
jurisdiction may pose 'a particularly acute problem having regard
to the border with Northern Ireland, and also in an age where internet communications are prevalent' (2007: 48). Within the United
Kingdom, the age of consent is currently 16 years whereas it is
17 years in the Republic of Ireland. Gillespie (2007b: 3) uses the
example of an Irish citizen, or person ordinarily resident in Ireland,
living in the United Kingdom who meets a 16-year-old girl on the
internet and arranges to meet with the intention of having sex with
her. In this instance, while the individual has committed no offence
under UK law, they will have committed a criminal offence under
Irish law. As Bohlander has argued, commenting on the scope of the
Sexual Offences Act 2003 in particular but which could be applied
collectively to the respective legal frameworks on 'grooming', 'there
is no clearly defined group of protected persons and . . . there is no
coherent policy behind the Act's classification as to who can be an
offender and who can be a victim' (2005: 701).

Thirdly, as argued throughout, the various formulations of the
offence of meeting a child following sexual grooming within the
legal frameworks of the United Kingdom and Ireland do not translate easily from the on-line environment for which they were conceived to also fully capture off-line risks (Craven, Brown, and
Gilchrist, 2007: 65). In particular, given the legislative requirement
that the offender 'travels with the intention of meeting the child', it
is doubtful whether the offence would cover situations where the
offender is already known and physically proximate to the child in
the capacity, for example, of neighbour, family friend, babysitter,
parent, or other relative. Certainly, on this reading of the legislation, the primary policy focus appears, once more, to have been the
'stranger danger' concept, or 'when the child being groomed is outside the groomer's normal circle or communication and/or contact'
(Craven, Brown, and Gilchrist, 2007: 65).

Transnational Mechanisms and Protocols

The range of cooperative and information-sharing initiatives on
sex offender risk management and child protection which have
been implemented within and between the various jurisdictions of
the United Kingdom and Ireland have been outlined in Chapter 3.

In addition, there are a number of transnational policies and initiatives which have been formulated to combat the sexual exploitation of children, particularly in relation to the on-line environment. Others have written extensively on the provision of such measures in relation to child pornography (eg O'Donnell and Milner, 2007; Akdeniz, 2008). It is not proposed, therefore, to discuss these supranational and international measures at length but rather to critically examine those which may be relevant to the formulation of legal and policy responses to sexual grooming, adding a further layer to the policing of grooming beyond local or national levels.

The Child Exploitation and Online Prevention Centre (CEOP) was established in April 2006 comprising representatives from the police and other criminal justice agencies, funded by government and the communications industry. CEOP works across the United Kingdom and aims to raise awareness of the dangers of using the internet among children and parents and to build up intelligence about sex offenders.[42] The organization also uses proactive forms of police surveillance within chat rooms, as outlined above. It complements the National Hi-Tech Crime Unit and the local specialist units which operate throughout the United Kingdom, investigating on-line sexual exploitation and offences against children. These include those operated by the London Metropolitan Police ('The Paedophile Unit'), Lothian and Borders Police in Scotland ('Child Protection Internet Investigation Unit'), and the West Midlands Police ('Child Online Safeguarding Team'). Similarly, the Internet Watch Foundation is a government watchdog body based in the United Kingdom but part of the European Union's Safer Internet Plus Programme (Davidson and Martellozzo, 2008b:348). It operates an internet hotline for the public and IT professionals to report potentially illegal and harmful content (Warren, 2008) and is aimed, inter alia, at raising awareness of the dangers of the internet and promoting a safer on-line environment (Robbins and Darlington, 2003).

The Virtual Global Taskforce (VGT) is made up of several internal law enforcement bodies from within the United Kingdom (including CEOP), Canada, Australia, the United States, as well as Interpol. It aims to provide advice and support to children about on-line safety and has set up a bogus website to attract 'on-line sex offenders' (Davidson and Martellozzo, 2008b:348). There have

---

[42] <http://ceop.police.uk/> (accessed 28 November 2011).

also been cooperative initiatives at the international level and within the European Union (Fitch, Spencer Chapman, and Hilton, 2007: 25–7; Kierkegaard, 2008: 45–52; Davidson and Gottschalk, 2011: 56–8). The Convention on the Protection of Children against Sexual Exploitation and Sexual Abuse (CETS No 21), which has been signed by 43 countries and ratified by 15, was the first international instrument to tackle all forms of violence and exploitation against children, including on-line grooming (Alexander, Meuwese, and Wolthuis, 2000).[43] Aside from the United Kingdom and the Republic of Ireland, however, only a handful of other Western European countries have specific laws on sexual grooming (see Chapter 1).[44] Indeed, the wide ranging discrepancies between EU countries in terms of child protection arrangements, offender management systems, highlighted above, as well as social attitudes pose considerable problems for agreeing measures on implementation (Fitch, Spencer Chapman, and Hilton, 2007: 28).

There are two clear lines of critique, which underlie the formulation and execution of international crime control policies on sexual crime. These relate to 'the twin problems of jurisdiction and cross-border enforcement' (Hornle, 2011: 2; see also Durkin, 1997: 16; Fitch, Spencer Chapman, and Hilton, 2007: 28). The general difficulties of inter-agency working at the national or international level have been outlined above. In this respect, although the precautionary 'risk' principle also has resonance in the context of policy formation at a transnational level (see eg Fisher, 2002), differences in penal cultures, as outlined in Chapter 3, may mean that its effects are diluted to varying degrees in practice (Sparks, 2001). Fundamental differences across jurisdictions, in terms of legal systems, cultures, and frameworks include categories of sexual offences, criminal records information, or the age of consent. In addition, organizational priorities and working practices (Mercado, Merdian, and Egg, 2011: 512), may inevitably result in fragmented approaches to the policing of grooming behaviour where cases involve an intranational or international component. While police forces across the

---

[43] See art 23.

[44] In November 2011, there were two further signed agreements—one between the Council of Europe and the VGT, and the other, the legislative global engagement strategy presented at the INTERPOL General Assembly—which were formulated in order to further strengthen laws on child sexual exploitation and abuse and make the internet safer.

United Kingdom and Ireland currently share intelligence on sex offenders who move between these jurisdictions with broadly similar sex offender management systems, such inter-country cooperation may be more difficult where countries have very different approaches to sex offender management or child protection (Fitch, Spencer Chapman, and Hilton, 2007: 31).

The difficulties of policing the internet become more pertinent for international efforts to combat global child pornography operations involving organized criminal activities between 'rings' of sex offenders in a range of different countries (see eg Burke et al, 2002; Wells et al, 2007).[45] Others have argued that 'there are enormous practical difficulties policing, prosecuting and punishing' such crime (O'Donnell and Milner, 2007: 22; see also Davidson and Martellozzo, 2005: 11; Harrison, 2006). As Warren (2008: 165) puts it, '[j]ust as it is difficult to quantify the sector, it is virtually impossible to police it effectively'. There are a number of challenges for traditional policing within the on-line world more generally, many of which have been highlighted above. These include 'the quantity, nature and integrity of evidence' (O'Donnell and Milner, 2007: 165, 168), the absence of 'tangibility in time and space' (Akdeniz, 2001: 249), as well as 'the complexity of the technology which makes the investigation and prosecution of crimes resource and expertise intensive' (Hornle, 2011: 2; see also Mercado, Merdian, and Egg, 2011: 513). As Cleland argues, '[t]o have a chance of success, these preventive measures require one crucial element: effective monitoring' (2005: 205). As a result of such difficulties, however, very few victims are identified and given access to justice and support services (Sutton and Jones, 2004: 7).

Such concerns I would argue are also significant in relation to on-line grooming cases which cross jurisdictional boundaries, particularly where the offender resides in one jurisdiction and the victim in another. As outlined in Chapter 2, the study by Gallagher and colleagues of 'International and Internet Child Sexual Abuse and Exploitation' demonstrated that most offenders appear to work nationally on a lone basis (Gallagher et al, 2006: 37–40). The one exceptional case involved 'two international co-offenders'—a husband and wife who travelled from Canada to Wales to meet an

---

[45] See eg Operation Wonderland and Operation Ore discussed elsewhere in this book. For a critical overview see in particular O'Donnell and Milner (2007). See also Choo (2009: 24) and Sutton and Jones (2004: 17).

eight-year-old girl whom the man had befriended on the internet (Gallagher et al, 2006: 37–40). In such a context, the borderless medium of cyberspace (Akdeniz, 2008: 2; Davidson and Martellozzo, 2008b: 351), the disparity in legislation and 'the lack of direct governance by an international body' (Kirkegaard, 2008: 41) may pose considerable problems for law enforcement (Mercado, Merdian, and Egg, 2011: 520) in combating on-line forms of grooming.

Sites such as CEOP and VGT have led to a number of arrests[46] and a small number of convictions of sex offenders through, for example, victim reporting of on-line grooming (see VGT, 2006 cited in Davidson and Martellozzo, 2008b: 348). For the most part, however, such initiatives have failed to make significant inroads into the overall problem of child grooming. As Davidson and Martellozzo suggest, '[t]here is evidence to support the assertion that the number of children that are groomed, manipulated and eventually victimised every day online is increasing' (2008b: 352). Moreover, such initiatives cannot tackle off-line forms of grooming and abuse which are likely to be more prevalent, yet beyond the traditional reach of law enforcement. This also reinforces the importance of raising awareness of the dangers of grooming in multiple contexts—off-line as well as on-line and chiefly in intra-familial and not just extra-familial settings, as discussed in the final part of the book.

Primary Research: Legislative and Policy Responses to Grooming

The critical review of the literature has demonstrated that, due to a myriad of factors, sexual grooming is not easily captured by the criminal law which, as a result, will be rather limited in its response to this form of sexually harmful behaviour. These factors relate to the difficulties of separating innocent from more sinister behaviour towards children in the early stages of the offending process, the lack of tangible evidence, and a clearly identifiable point of intervention in relation to offending which takes place off-line, where

---

[46] For example, there were 513 arrests made by another agency following the dissemination of intelligence by CEOP and/or supported by CEOP resources in 2010–11, which represented an increase from a figure of 417 in 2009–10 (CEOP, 2011b: 8).

sexual motivation can only usually be inferred from a previous history of sexual offending. Moreover, the chief inherent limitation of such legislative responses, in common with vetting and barring schemes, is that they will not stop people grooming or abuse as a whole given the fact that the preponderance of abuse is committed by someone known to the child within an intra-familial setting, where it often remains hidden and undisclosed. This part of the chapter examines the core themes arising from the primary research in light of this literature: the difficulties of preventing, targeting, and criminalizing grooming; the impact of grooming on work with victims, responses to grooming across inter-agency or cross-jurisdictional contexts; and problems unique to the individual jurisdictions which are the subject of this study.

Preventing, targeting and criminalizing grooming

The limitations of pre-emptive policies on risk

In the interviews conducted for this book, there was generally a firm acknowledgement of the shortcomings of pre-emptive approaches to risk management (McAlinden, 2010a), as outlined in Part I. In the words of a social services professional: 'you don't get to see the grooming as it's happening. You might get to see it retrospectively in terms of gathering information about how this got to this position...Unfortunately the risk factors very often come when abuse has occurred'.[47] Several interviewees also conceded that the 'grooming offence' was limited, as the literature also suggests, to on-line grooming (McAlinden, 2006a; Craven, Brown, and Gilchrist, 2007: 65) and that legal interventions are powerless with intra-familial and other forms of grooming where risk has yet to manifest itself (Craven, Brown, and Gilchrist, 2007: 65; Gillespie, 2002a, 2004a; Ost, 2004). A senior police officer commented:

In terms of on line offending...that's about as far as it goes. If you're talking about institutional grooming, familial grooming...it's not an offence to ingratiate yourself with a family. We may know what the intention is, but for someone who doesn't have a previous conviction, or we have pre-intelligence about, we are fairly limited in what we can do and unless the potential victims are involved with social services already, or with health, and health recognize the risks, you're not going to get the intelligence. So

---

[47] NI 13 (27 July 2011).

it tends to be the offence is your first knowledge of the grooming and I do not know what the answer is to that.[48]

Others were cognizant of the limitations of regulatory frameworks specifically in terms of vetting (McAlinden, 2010a). An interviewee who has worked with both victims and offenders stated: 'vetting and barring schemes don't pick up grooming...all of these only kick into place when somebody has come forward and said it has happened'.[49] There were also difficulties of controlling access to children and the vulnerable outside of mainstream educational and residential contexts, as argued above (NIACRO, 2008: para 3.2; NSPCC, 2010: para 12), such as work undertaken in a personal capacity as 'private tuition'[50] or as 'magicians or clowns'.[51] A senior social services professional explained: 'I have seen people use recreational type jobs...as a way of selecting victims. I do recall a particular case that was a big challenge in terms of someone who was using his job in that way, to target children, and limited controls. He was advertising on the internet. Nobody was vetting or checking.'[52] These responses reinforce one of the central arguments of this book, that because grooming is rather nebulous, it is often only identifiable with the benefit of contextual hindsight—that is after an offence has taken place. As such, the prevention, targeting and criminalization of preparatory behaviours which precede actual abuse, including grooming, continues to pose significant challenges for criminal law.

A significant proportion of interviewees, however, gave a more nuanced account of the usefulness of regulatory frameworks in responding to grooming proactively, making clear the important distinction between adjudicated offenders where 'risk' has already been identified and those who have never come to notice (Kirby et al, 2005; Soothill et al, 2005a, 2005b). In the words of one independent interviewee who had worked with both victims and offenders:

Once we do get them, if somebody is convicted and we really do get a good sense of assessment and their way of working, then we can spot...he's grooming again. So it works for those who have already been convicted...

---

[48] SC 1 (22 August 2011).   [49] NI 2 (23 May 2011).
[50] SC 8 (23 August 2011).   [51] NI 13 (27 July 2011).   [52] Ibid.

that's where we could maybe pull them up for breach of a sexual offences prevention order, we could do that because we have evidence of their grooming. So you need to separate it out from those who get convicted...we can work on that, we can spot it, we can make assessments and treatment. The difficulty is for the individual who's never come to our attention.[53]

There are also residual difficulties, however, not addressed in the existing literature, in regulating preparatory behaviours even for offenders who have been adjudicated. As a senior probation interviewee commented, 'the problem is that with any restrictions, they always come to an end. Even if they are effective...they are going to finish at some point. Whereas if you can change a person's thinking, and if you can change a person's desire to commit offences, that is something that can last long after restrictions have ended.'[54] This important viewpoint also underscores the importance of ongoing reintegration work with families of offenders to complement formal regulatory mechanisms, as will be discussed in the next chapter.

While a minority of interviewees were critical of the government retraction on vetting towards a softer approach, particularly in England and Wales, many regarded this as a positive development acknowledging the consequences of vetting procedures for society as a whole. A senior statutory sector interviewee commented: 'I think you've got to get a balance really, between stopping people who really shouldn't be allowed access to children from working with them...and just the importance of adults getting involved with children in general, and not making people feel like criminals just because they want to work with kids.'[55] As I have argued above, inflated levels of societal fear, suspicion, and mistrust concerning potential sex offenders, particularly those who work with children (Furedi and Bristow, 2008), are a direct consequence of regulatory and expansive frameworks on risk management, often put into place in the aftermath of high profile cases of abuse (McAlinden, 2010a). Moreover, at the same time, regulatory frameworks may also generate a false sense of security among both the public and professionals that children are being adequately safeguarded. One senior voluntary sector interviewee commented:

---

[53] NI 2 (23 May 2011).   [54] EW 3 (12 September 2011).   [55] Ibid.

Whilst pre employment vetting and barring is absolutely essential, to do those and breathe out and say well 'that's fine', is a real mistake...It is necessary but not sufficient...It is a starting point for protecting children in an organisational setting, not all that we need to do.[56]

In terms of the prevention of sexual offending at a broader macro level, many interviewees underlined the general shortcomings of regulatory frameworks in preventing grooming or abuse. A victim support professional stated: 'I'd have a certain cynicism about the ability of any law or any conviction rate to prevent sexual violence unless it's associated with treatment and some form of community support, and I think we've a very long way to go on that'.[57] This issue of devising a coordinated social and community response to grooming to complement existing legal and policy frameworks will be discussed in the last part of the book.

The practical difficulties of vetting and barring procedures appear to be augmented within the Republic of Ireland where such schemes are in their infancy or, as several interviewees conceded, 'way behind'.[58] Many interviewees acknowledged, in the words of a social services professional, that 'there are still a lot of people working with a lot of direct contact with children who've never been Garda vetted and I think it's very risky'.[59] One victim support professional explained further in relation to the work of the Garda Vetting Unit and the knock-on effects of delays for employers:

But the problem we have now...they will do a vetting from today's date backwards all the way through the history of the individual staff member. But I could be hiring that person from a school where they've been working for ten years and...they're already vetted and cleared...So you're starting from scratch every time and the person that comes to me can't bring that vetting form with them, they don't own it...There's actually staff members who can't be hired because the vetting won't be coming through in time and it might be only a six month contract and they're stating at the moment it could take up to nine, ten months. So I think it's the right idea but it just needs to be done better.[60]

The reduction in bureaucracy, in terms of having on-line criminal record monitoring of every person who is employed or volunteers

---

[56] EW 1 (1 September 2011).   [57] RI 2 (11 May 2011).
[58] RI 4 (13 June 2011).   [59] Ibid.   [60] RI 1 (11 May 2011).

to work with children or the vulnerable, was one of the key impetus behind the introduction of the Safeguarding Vulnerable Groups (SVG) legislation in the United Kingdom (McAlinden, 2010a: 31–3). There is an often unarticulated tension, however, underlying the advocacy of expansive regulatory frameworks. This relates to the critical dichotomy between the aspiration to extend the scope and reach of child protection or offender management systems and the unfathomable pool of resources necessary to achieve such aims. Indeed, as acknowledged at the outset of the book, resource implications were, inter alia, one of the reasons for the government retraction from the initial SVG legislative framework.

Challenges for law enforcement

Many interviewees across a range of jurisdictions and professional spheres underscored the difficulty of proving intent which in turn limits the ability of the legislation on grooming to be used as a proactive tool in addressing the risk of sexual harm. As argued above, the difficulties of proving intent mean that in most cases grooming can only be positively identified after abuse has occurred in which case an offender is more likely to be charged with a substantive sexual offence (Gillespie, 2004b: 11; Ost, 2004: 152–3). One independent interviewee commented on the evidential difficulties for law enforcement:

I've no sense of the law being that subtle at all, really. I think from my experience of it, it's very much when there's hard facts, and that's the whole difficulty around...what might happen...It's very hard in terms of criminalising grooming behaviour because the person could mount a very good defence of...I was innocently doing that...how do you prove it?[61]

This frustration regarding what has been termed 'the fantasy defence' (Smith, Grabosky, and Urbas, 2004; Choo, 2009: 30) was also shared by the police. A specialist IT officer noted: 'the difficulties are...if they haven't actually met the child...and if I haven't actually said "I want to meet you to commit a sexual act" and all of that...it's very, very difficult to actually prove. So you end up going for lesser offences or looking for other...offences within the computer'.[62] Another police interviewee noted that the requirement to have two previous communications prior to meeting or travelling

---

[61] RI 10 (5 July 2011).   [62] EW 6 (13 September 2011).

to meet the child, as contained within the legislation in Northern Ireland, England and Wales, and the Republic of Ireland, limits the ability of legal frameworks to prevent harm:

> I'm not sure why there's this notion of two attempts to make the contact…I think, especially with chat room logs and things such as they are…any attempt to engage a child in a sexual way should be construed as just grooming…stand alone grooming, without this tag on of trying to meet, because a lot of harm can be done…I mean we are dealing with a wee girl out in X now at the minute, and she was sixteen at the time…having sent him images of herself masturbating and all manner of things. To me I don't really think he needs to meet her now, for her to have suffered significant harm, emotionally. Now ok, physically he hasn't had a contact offence on her, but you know a lot of these guys…are getting their sexual needs met by what they are getting on the internet. I think if there was a standalone grooming offence, we would probably get a lot more convictions, rather than this tag on of necessarily having to have a meeting.[63]

As argued in Chapter 4, on-line contact does not have to result in a face-to-face meeting for harm to occur (Döring, 2000). A 'standalone grooming offence', however, which this law enforcement professional proposes, would be extremely difficult to capture within a legal framework, particularly in off-line contexts. In face-to-face situations there would be augmented evidential difficulties in establishing the requisite intention to engage in unlawful sexual activity with a child at the early stages of the abusive process. Moreover, to proceed further in this vein would have a number of undesirable effects for wider society, particularly in terms of increasing societal suspicion and mistrust concerning potential sex offenders, thereby thwarting routine human interaction between adults and children.

There was a discernible tension in the responses of interviewees concerning the policing and criminalization of on-line grooming. Grooming via the internet was perceived broadly as being more amenable to being captured and targeted within the criminal law than grooming within face-to-face contexts. This was essentially attributed to the 'virtual crime scene' (O'Connell, 2003: 3), or 'digital footprint' (McLaughlin, 2009: 12) which is created in the on-line environment. Several interviewees stated that: 'the on line grooming can sometimes be a bit more obvious',[64] 'I think there

---

[63] NI 8 (6 July 2011).   [64] RI 4 (13 June 2011).

they have the evidence, they have it on the computer usually, so that's easier',[65] because the police 'are not so reliant on the victims to come forward and give evidence'.[66] One police officer explained the differences between the two offending contexts:

We have I suppose, tools that do it for us. Whereas in real life you have got to rely on someone being switched on enough to notice what is going on, to then actually make the next jump of thinking, well I had better tell a parent or the police about it, for then us to actually act on it. And from that point of view as well, depending on how good a job has been done from the point of view of the groomer, we could go and interview the child and they could be... 'oh no, you've got it all wrong... it's a guy I go to the football with and we're just pally'. Whereas when we get it through the internet, you actually tend to have literally chat logs, which obviously prove where it is going, rather than relying on the young person disclosing... when you're on line, at least we've got access to the real story.[67]

At the same time, however, a minority of interviewees acknowledged that the lack of an identifiable victim in many cases can make on-line offenders harder to both identify and apprehend than those who commit contact sexual offences. One voluntary sector interviewee commented: 'somebody who has committed harm physically against a person... the chances of catching them are higher because there is a victim... Whereas somebody who's committing an offence on the internet, sometimes victims don't know they're victims... So it's technology you're trying to catch them with. So to me they're a slippier character.'[68] Similarly, a senior social services professional stated: 'I think the on line grooming is getting stronger and stronger and stronger, with very, very loose compliance mechanisms'.[69] This broad tension in the views of professionals is indicative of the fact, as argued above, that while on-line grooming may, in one sense, be easier to prove than off-line grooming because of the digital chain of evidence (O'Connell, 2003: 3), it nonetheless continues to pose considerable and evolving challenges for law enforcement.

In this respect, several police officers acknowledged a range of practical difficulties relating to the policing of on-line forms of

---

[65] NI 3 (26 May 2011).   [66] EW 6 (13 September 2011).
[67] SC 2 (22 August 2011).   [68] NI 5 (22 June 2011).
[69] RI 9 (28 June 2011).

offending against children, not previously examined by the literature. These related principally to the timeliness of investigations and the difficulties of preserving forensic evidence. One senior police officer stated:

Quite often the intelligence which comes out from CEOP is months old by the time you get it, so the Sheriff's question is validity. You get a warrant, seize the equipment, forensic examination takes months...in the meantime the person is still out there, still able to access a computer elsewhere so the grooming hasn't necessarily stopped.[70]

Similarly, an investigating officer acknowledged:

The difficulty with the chat logs, unless it is set to save them, they are gone...Facebook it does not set to save them. So if an offender gets identified on Facebook, and if the family...contacts Facebook to express this concern about this user, Facebook delete the profile...everything's gone. So that could happen before the police are contacted, so all of your evidence is potentially lost before you get anywhere.[71]

Moreover, in the contemporary 'multi-media world' (Martellozzo, 2012), there are considerable challenges for policing and child protection in adapting existing legal frameworks to counter burgeoning advances in technology. Another investigating officer explained:

The law can be a bit inflexible, and maybe doesn't move as quickly as it needs to now. New offences using computers are appearing every day, and basically by the time the police have realized what is going on, and then sat down and written out guidelines on...it is probably obsolete and they have moved on to something else...And that is an issue...keeping up with technology...Mobile phones are a huge issue because it's not a mobile phone anymore; it is a computer in your pocket and how easy are they to get information from? Not as easy as a computer...and it is very difficult, just the constant technology advancements...It's just something that we'll have to play by ear because we don't know what's coming next.[72]

These difficulties related to policing the internet, in the words of one officer, mean that while 'there are covert operations going on across the world...you are only scratching the surface of it'.[73]

---

[70] SC 1 (22 August 2011).   [71] SC 3 (22 August 2011).
[72] SC 2 (22 August 2011).   [73] EW 6 (13 September 2011).

As I have argued throughout, however, with face-to-face grooming, particularly in situations where there is already a pre-existing relationship with the child, the legality of proving active grooming and ongoing risks to children are often more difficult to pinpoint and enforce. A social services professional underlined the enormous difficulties for families in interpreting behaviour and in recognizing potentially harmful intentions towards children:

The adults around a child that keep a child safe...how do they detect unusual behaviour within their own family setting? How is your average mum going to consider behaviours by her husband and the father of her children to be suspect or suspicious? How are we expecting people to monitor this?...In terms of identifying it before the abuse takes place, how could you tell that the older cousin or the uncle isn't just showing an interest or taking the younger kids to football...how do you know that's not genuine?[74]

Indeed, because grooming is, in the words of one interviewee, about 'seemingly insignificant decisions',[75] there are tremendous difficulties in preventing and targeting grooming within intra-familial contexts in particular where potentially harmful and inappropriate behaviour has been normalized. Therefore, I would argue, against the grain of the literature examined above, that it is not that on-line grooming is easier to prove than grooming within face-to-face contexts. Rather, each generates its own set of challenges for legal and policy frameworks and for the professionals tasked with applying them.

The impact of grooming on work with victims

While the dynamics of grooming in work with offenders emerged in the previous chapter as a further dimension of 'institutional grooming', several interviewees underlined the impact of grooming in undertaking work with victims. A social services interviewee explained: 'a huge part of the therapeutic recovery for a child involves looking at the grooming behaviours that were used to establish the circumstances in which they were abused...And understanding how they were groomed...can be really, really helpful in helping that child to recover.'[76] The long-term impact of

---

[74] RI 4 (13 June 2011).   [75] RI 11 (5 July 2011).
[76] RI 4 (13 June 2011).

shame and guilt, intrinsic to abuse (Berliner and Conte, 1990; Hunter, Goodwin, and Wilson, 1992; McAlinden, 2006a: 346–8) and accentuated by grooming (Christiansen and Blake, 1990; Conte, Wolf, and Smith, 1989; Elliott, Browne, and Kilcoyne, 1995; Sas and Cunningham, 1995; Pryor, 1996), and which inhibits immediate disclosure (Lewis and Mullis, 1999) can be very difficult to address in therapy. A victim support professional explained:

It's an issue that comes up a lot from the teenagers. Obviously the younger kids probably don't state things the same way, but teenagers need help understanding that it wasn't their fault and I think grooming is huge, when seen from the victim's point of view, it puts them in the position of feeling they've done it themselves, they've consented... So we have to work very hard to unpick that and to listen... you know... you said yes because he'd been putting you in that position for five years, or you were afraid... just giving them... a proper way to look at it. And I think if we don't address it, then it can leave big question marks for the child throughout their adult relationships.[77]

For professionals in Northern Ireland and England and Wales, such difficulties, however, are even more acute when working with 'non-statutory' or 'compliant' victims (Wolak, Finkelhor, and Mitchell, 2004: 432), particularly within the context of 'street grooming' (Barnardo's, 2009: 9; Beckett, 2011: 46–8). A social services interviewee explained: 'when you are working with those young people, they find it incredibly difficult to acknowledge that it isn't a relationship. They never see it as grooming or exploitation in any shape or form. They say, that is my boyfriend/partner/friend or whatever.'[78] A voluntary sector professional in Northern Ireland outlined the difficulties for professionals in trying to extricate the young person from an abusive situation:

They've really bought into this and believe these guys love them and that this is a relationship, even if you're talking about say a thirteen, fourteen year old girl and a man in his twenties or thirties, or even forties in some cases. There's that belief... that they're in love with this guy, so the power of that grooming is sometimes very great and quite frightening. And that makes it even more difficult for any of the agencies, and particularly us, working with that young person and trying to convince them otherwise... and even when there's violence with that, and even where the girls might sometimes allege rape against that person, often then they will with-

---

[77] RI 1 (11 May 2011).
[78] EW 5 (13 September 2011).

draw that…because it's almost like a pull-push scenario…all the time. They want to be with this person…but yet they don't like the violence or a lot of the sex that's going on…all they want is that affection and maybe the parties or whatever, that go on with it.[79]

This complex set of dynamics underlying the victim-offender relationship, in particular the victim's emotional dependence on their abuser and the imbalance of power (Montgomery-Devlin, 2008: 383; Barnardo's, 2011: 6), also makes this form of child abuse and exploitation closely akin to intimate abuse. In this vein, as will be argued further in the next chapter, an effective approach to combating grooming and exploitation, involves targeting both victims as well as perpetrators.

The literature establishes that the stigma, fear or embarrassment attached to being a victim of 'street grooming' and abuse may inhibit disclosure or that victims may have been groomed not to recognize themselves as victims (Barnardo's, 2009: 9; Beckett, 2011: 46–8; CEOP, 2011a: 11). An additional range of factors were outlined by interviewees as impeding victim disclosure as well as the investigation and prosecution of such crime. A senior police officer in Northern Ireland commented: 'some of them…don't like authority…So sometimes for those children to actually engage with police…they won't do that.'[80] Others outlined the specific importance of victim cooperation (Ost, 2009: 77) or witness credibility (Barnardo's, 2011: 17) for sustaining a successful prosecution and the detrimental impact of grooming on this variable. A senior social services professional explained: 'one of the biggest keys is, is the victim able to be interviewed, and give evidence and are they reliable? And when you look at the targeting of the victims, it's vulnerable people, and then that's more difficulties, and the reliability doesn't be as great. So it's harder to get convictions, it's harder to put them on the stand'.[81] Irrespective of victim cooperation or credibility there are also system controls which limit the number of prosecutions. A number of professionals involved in child protection or children's services shared the view of one children's services professional:

One of the biggest issues because of all the cut backs in the legal side is that there are fewer cases that are going to court. So Crown Prosecution Service is making decisions not to take things that to us look like they've got plenty

---

[79] NI 3 (26 May 2011).　　[80] NI 7 (30 June 2011).
[81] NI 13 (27 July 2011).

of evidence and very good witnesses, and they are just not going anywhere. So for us then, we are having to counsel very angry children because justice hasn't been served. So I think that is another complicating factor; when children do tell, and we know how hard that is, and they are believed, but then still nothing happens.[82]

Such systemic problems also sends out the wrong message in terms of social intolerance of the sexual abuse and exploitation of children which may ultimately inhibit further victim disclosures in the longer term. This point also highlights the need for training of legal professionals around issues relating to sexual exploitation and abuse as discussed further in the next chapter.

The inherent limitations of legal and policy frameworks in capturing grooming and protecting victims has meant that the police in Northern Ireland and England and Wales have used the offence of child abduction[83] as an alternative response:

Police would be using that and using it effectively to disrupt children going to the houses of adults...harbouring them...there's not a lot of evidence and these kids aren't going to come forward and say 'I've been sexually exploited' so we need to find other means of disrupting this and that seemed to be a really effective way of doing it.[84]

A senior police officer explained: 'we issue a Harbourer's notice which shows a photograph of the child saying, the parents or carers don't want their child to go with you...and then if that person doesn't take heed, they can be arrested'.[85] However, as another officer admitted: 'very few Harbourer's warning notice really lead to a prosecution...It's frustrating for a police officer because a lot of the time the legislation doesn't allow for an arrest'.[86] The fact that the police are utilizing other legislative frameworks not specifically designed to regulate grooming as a fallback position, however, is also illustrative of the inherent weaknesses of current regulatory frameworks on grooming in protecting children in the short term.

Even within professional discourses, the lack of understanding about the vulnerability of children and young people, particularly

---

[82] EW 7 (13 September 2011).
[83] See eg art 68 of the Children (NI) Order 1995 makes it an offence to take, keep, induce, assist, or incite a child away from a responsible person.
[84] NI 3 (26 May 2011).
[85] NI 7 (30 June 2011).   [86] NI 8 (6 July 2011).

those living in residential care, can be highly problematic. An interviewee involved in support services for young people explained how these perceptions can detract attention from the need for professional intervention:

There's the belief within some agencies that what they see happening, isn't sexual exploitation. These children, these young people are choosing to do this or they are going willingly. So it's an ongoing education of people about...this is a 13, 14 year old child we are talking about...they are on a full care order, they are going to be sexually exploited. They are not choosing to, they can't choose to...they are under the age of consent... sometimes there's quite a bit of blame goes on as well in terms of the child...and certainly not blaming any one agency, but there are problems. I suppose rightly so, there are a lot of police resources going into looking for these kids, bringing them back and they're running out again, and it's like a revolving door. So the focus is often on them going missing rather than the focus being on...right, who's grooming them? Who's taking them? Who are they going to and how can we disrupt that?[87]

A senior officer explained the difficulties and priorities facing the police, 'It's about protecting children and...we should be rethinking that as police officers...we're here to protect children, not necessarily to get somebody convicted. That's a second priority...and for the police officer on the ground, recognising what sexual exploitation is, it's very difficult for them'.[88] At the same time, however, an increased focus on public sites of grooming and exploitation can detract attention from other less visible, but likely more prevalent, sources of harm to children which exist in the private sphere such as those within intra-familial contexts. As will be discussed further in the next chapter, there is a need to work collaboratively to better identify children at risk outside the care or child protection systems and coordinate public and professional responses around those children.

Inter-agency and cross-jurisdictional contexts

Inter-agency risk assessment and management

For the vast majority of professionals interviewed within the United Kingdom, the introduction of inter-agency working and formalized structures such as MAPPA or PPANI was viewed as a

---

[87] NI 3 (26 May 2011).   [88] NI 7 (30 June 2011).

very productive policy development in the area of risk management (Bryan and Doyle, 2003; Lieb, 2003). One interviewee told
me: 'I think there's been a big shift in a positive way in the last few
years in terms of the statutory agencies being willing to share very
detailed information, even about individuals, with ourselves as the
voluntary sector. So I think we've come a long way'.[89] The multiple
viewpoints and personalities which underpin inter-agency working were also regarded as beneficial. One independent interviewee
who had worked with offenders framed these in terms of 'strengthening your risk assessments',[90] and finding someone 'who has the
rapport with the offender ... that [they] will work better with than
others'.[91]

In tandem with the literature outlined in Chapter 3, however,
many interviewees were prepared to acknowledge existing
weaknesses within multi-agency frameworks including those
relating to information sharing about risk (Sampson et al, 1991;
Crawford, 1997). Several interviewees conceded that sometimes
there is a lack of two-way communication about particular risks
and 'not enough involvement of the statutory agencies with
community and voluntary groups',[92] which often results in the
exclusion of the voluntary sector in particular (Harvie and
Manzi, 2001) who are 'only working with half the story'.[93] The
importance of bringing voluntary and community groups, as
well as wider society, more fully into risk management processes
in order to challenge the complex range of sexually harmful
behaviours towards children, will be returned to in Part III. In
particular, a minority of interviewees noted the 'lack of a common language between agencies',[94] particularly between those
agencies involved in the child protection end of the spectrum,
such as social services, and those tasked principally with offender
management such as probation or police. This raises the important issue of broadening professional, as well as public, discourses
around child protection to encompass offender management
issues, and vice versa, and will also be addressed further in the
next chapter.

---

[89] NI 3 (26 May 2011).   [90] NI 4 (1 June 2011).   [91] Ibid.
[92] NI 5 (22 June 2011).   [93] RI 10 (5 July 2011).
[94] EW 2 (12 September 2011).

The absence of a formal inter-agency structure within the Republic of Ireland, at the time of writing, which would facilitate information exchange and cooperative working, was regarded as a significant limitation of existing legislative and policy frameworks. In particular, the absence of cohesive policies and structures were framed in terms of competitive organizational cultures (Blagg et al, 1988; Sampson et al, 1988, 1991; Pearson et al, 1992; Crawford and Jones, 1995; Crawford, 1997: 127–31) which ultimately lose sight of 'risk' within child protection contexts:

We're well behind…So, I think that's a big problem in the South. I hope we are moving towards a bit more standardisation…The key to it [is] that everybody ha[s] to come out of their professional silos…to let go of all that professional baggage and I think that's a problem here for the Guards, it's a problem for the HSE[95] and it's a problem for the judiciary. They're all trying to do it their way and the children are getting crushed, lost, completely abandoned through the system…the system isn't focused around the children…We need to get things on a statutory basis, a formalized corporation where everybody benefits, and specifically the child.[96]

Several interviewees voiced concerns around the difficulties of sharing soft information (Fitch, Spencer Chapman, and Hilton, 2007: 27; McAlinden, 2010a: 37). As a social services interviewee explained: 'the enhanced stuff is the most important because very often the bit that will assist us is not what they have been convicted of in the past, but the bit that "we found this bloke around the corner talking to a child and the child was in their car…we're not sure what's going on"'.[97] In the Republic of Ireland, however, the difficulties surrounding the use and retention of 'soft' information on unadjudicated offenders, was exacerbated by the absence of a formal inter-agency framework. Many interviewees while acknowledging the utility of such information in formulating assessments about risk, faced a dilemma, as a senior treatment professional explained, in terms of 'what do I do with this stuff…where do I even record it, or can I record it?'.[98] The National Vetting Bureau Bill 2011 will facilitate the exchange of 'soft information' on abusers. A residual issue for the Republic of Ireland, however, will be the use of soft information within multi-agency contexts in the absence

---

[95] Health and Safety Executive.   [96] RI 1 (11 May 2011).
[97] EW 5 (13 September 2011).   [98] RI 5 (14 June 2011).

of a statutory framework. In this respect, it is interesting that such concerns were not, for the most part, specifically raised by interviewees in any of the other jurisdictions in the study which all have formalized multi-agency public protection arrangements (see Chapter 3). Broadly speaking, therefore, this would also tend to endorse inter-agency working as an effective means of service delivery (Bryan and Doyle, 2003; Lieb, 2003) in protecting the public from the risk posed by sex offenders in the community.

The cross-jurisdictional context

None of the interviewees in the study, including police officers, had encountered any cases concerning grooming with an inter-jurisdictional aspect—that is, where the offender resides in one jurisdiction but the meeting with the victim takes place in another. This also reinforces the above analysis, that the legislation which makes it an offence to meet a child following grooming, or its equivalent, is not likely to be used often in practice. Many interviewees, however, in the words of one senior police officer acknowledged that 'cross jurisdictional communication is a big issue',[99] as also highlighted by the literature (Magee, 2008; McAlinden, 2010a: 36–9), for both national and international police operations. In relation to the latter, several police officers voiced concerns about the timeliness of sharing and collating intelligence for offence prevention: 'offenders...they potentially could be anywhere in the world. And trying to find out who they are...you're just not going to get the information back, particularly within the timescales to try and prevent an offence taking place...is the hard part. You potentially will miss offenders just because you can't turn around the information quick enough'.[100]

In relation to national contexts, several interviewees in Northern Ireland and the Republic of Ireland had encountered difficulties in obtaining information about case histories from their counterparts in Great Britain. A social services professional recounted:

So much a part of my job is actually piecing together a picture of this family's history and how they operate and to look at what's going on now. And that can sometimes involve going back quite a while into their history to work out what the children's experience had been, where their protective factors are...Getting information from England where there's been court

[99] SC 1 (22 August 2011).   [100] SC 3 (22 August 2011).

cases has been so difficult because anything, even in the children's file that has been used for court, you can't get access to. It's really, really difficult to get good quality information.[101]

This interviewee who had worked previously in Scotland also recalled an example of a case where 'somebody was prosecuted as a minor in England for a sex offence and then moved to Scotland and again that information was very difficult to get a hold of. And that's even within the same country but across borders'.[102]

Interviewees on both sides of the border which separates the North and South of Ireland, however, commented favourably on cooperative initiatives between the police in particular:

The Garda...initially the police in the south were not connected but they're much more connected now, so if somebody is going to leave the jurisdiction...there are restrictions on his movement depending on what level of risk etc, but also then they would share information now much better than they did in the past. Presumably the police in the south will start to set up their own public protection arrangements as well, around children.[103]

Even within the United Kingdom, however, as one senior police officer admitted, 'I don't think offender management is consistently delivered across the country'.[104] In particular, the format in which information is held is not standardized. A Northern Ireland police officer explained, highlighting the difficulties potentially for all four jurisdictions in the United Kingdom and Ireland:

You're sitting with a fit for purpose risk management database VISOR, which is UK wide, but then you have different people manage them in different ways...you're not singing off the same hymn sheet across the UK borders, and certainly in the South of Ireland, they're probably about twenty years behind us...So that makes it very difficult, given the fact that we've a shared border there, there's a lot of guys just head south and disappear into the ether. And that makes it very difficult.[105]

This also reinforces the literature which suggests that the effectiveness of cooperative inter-jurisdictional arrangements may have more to do with informal working relationships than formal

---

[101] RI 4 (13 June 2011).   [102] Ibid.   [103] NI 1 (23 May 2011).
[104] SC 1 (22 August 2011).   [105] NI 8 (6 July 2011).

mandates (Hope and Murphy, 1983; Crawford, 1997: 107–8; Walsh, 2011: 327). In this vein, a senior statutory sector interviewee cautioned against the effect of 'a very top down approach...that actually goes against the whole process of safeguarding':[106] 'I think the focus on risk management has become so much an over arching ogre, that everything pales into insignificance in relation to that...I think there's a split going on between what's actually happening at a local level and what's happening at that sort of more corporate level.'[107] This viewpoint also highlights the 'something must be done' philosophy underpinning the widespread imposition of pre-emptive risk averse policies concerning sexual harm, which are perpetually implemented and enforced irrespective of their actual efficacy in terms of public protection. The need to re-evaluate current risk-based policy on sex offending will be revisited in the final chapter.

Problems unique to individual jurisdictions

While there were no unique problems singled out by professionals within Scotland and England and Wales in terms of discourses concerning the risk posed by sexual offenders, professionals in both Northern Ireland and the Republic of Ireland highlighted particular difficulties for these jurisdictions.

The Republic of Ireland

A minority of interviewees sought to explain the absence of strong regulatory frameworks on sex offending as being attributable to the written Constitution: 'constitutionally it's much harder to introduce some of the child protection measures that would just be absolutely taken for granted in any of the UK jurisdictions'.[108] Despite the existence of a written constitution, however, other countries such as the United States have harsh penal policies on sexual offending (Chapter 3). The primary issue which emerged was the legacy of a patriarchal, predominantly Catholic, society which would also impede public discourses concerning sexual offending (Inglis, 1998, 2005; McAlinden, 2012b), and 'an openness of discussions around sexuality, what is normal, what is appropriate,

---

[106] RI 5 (14 June 2011).   [107] Ibid.   [108] RI 2 (11 May 2011).

and where anything that becomes sort of under the radar has the opportunity then to be exploited'.[109] One children's services interviewee stated:

> The strong patriarchal society...certainly probably up until about ten years ago that was a huge influence on people not saying anything. The fact that the kids were often offended against by their father or grandfather or uncle; the huge role that a man had in the life of all the family so even if some of the other people did know, they wouldn't go against them...if you add to that the role of the church, in another sort of patriarchal context as well. It was this whole sense that you had to bow down and believe everything...your father was always your father, you don't disagree with him or disobey him. Likewise the same, there was no coincidence that you called the priest a Father...I think that's going away now and I think the kids that we see now probably aren't as affected by it, but that was a huge societal shift for the society of Ireland to take on board and I think that has opened us up and allowed us to protect the children better now...I think that's...maybe not specific to Ireland but maybe specific to the Catholic countries...there are different types of influences but we were so closed, it was Catholic and it was male and I think that really was a huge drawback for everybody.[110]

For other interviewees, however, such cultural influences and cognitive processes have not completely dissipated from Irish society. In the view of one senior probation professional: 'I think even culturally Ireland, we have not been particularly up front about our sexuality as a society...and that, at an individual level and a societal level, has caused us difficulties and continues to'.[111] Another victim support professional acknowledged these difficulties within the context of combating intra-familial abuse and in particular the anticipated referendum on Children's rights:

> It's a huge difficulty, again perhaps because of the Catholic tradition, in identifying the family as a place that needs to be addressed in terms of child abuse...I can see that it is going to be a bitter, divisive referendum campaign in that it will draw out every extreme right wing group, who see any attempt to allow the state to intrude into the family as a complete attack on the family...at the end of the day that it really is down to the Catholic culture where the family is sacrosanct, and the state has very, very little right to intervene.[112]

---

[109] R1 10 (5 July 2011).   [110] RI 1 (11 May 2011).
[111] RI 8 (23 June 2011).   [112] RI 2 (11 May 2011).

The significance of this confluence of a highly patriarchal and a staunchly Catholic society was articulated by the same interviewee: 'the threshold at which welfare cases become child protection cases is far too high in Ireland compared to [the] experience in the UK'.[113] As highlighted in the previous chapter, in some of the most high profile intra-familial child abuse cases, such as the McColgan case (North Western Health Board, 1998), there was a level of professional unwillingness to intervene due, inter alia, to an emphasis on preserving the sanctity of the family unit. Such cultural and societal influences would also have impacted on the child's ability to make a disclosure as well as their believability in the event that they did disclose the abuse (McAlinden, 2012b).

An interesting finding is that this inhibiting of disclosure was also related by one interviewee to a culture against 'whistle blowing' and the societal repugnance at the notion of 'informers':

You're looking at a macro version of it. How could I possibly rat on my friend?...I think there's something about informers in Ireland...In America it's very much seen as a positive and they're heroes. Here there's something about a whistle blower being a very bad thing...You shouldn't tell tales out of school and I think it goes back to the old teaching...if you were slapped in school and you came home and said it you were slapped again. Because you did something wrong...the teacher knows best...So again the message is always out there—just keep denying it, it will go away.[114]

In one sense, it is surprising that the issue of 'informers' was not raised specifically by any of the Northern Irish interviewees given the centrality of informers to the transitional context of Northern Ireland (Dudai, 2012). Nonetheless, other legacies of the conflict surfaced as unique problems relating to the jurisdiction in terms of the policing of sexual offending.

Northern Ireland

Several interviewees pinpointed the continued presence of paramilitary groups and the impact of this on public discourses around sexual offending, as highlighted in an older literature which predates devolution and the transitional justice processes (Leggett, 2000; Knox, 2002: 174). A police officer commented: 'we have that sort of paramilitary type activity still, whether we like to accept it

---

[113] Ibid.   [114] RI 1 (11 May 2011).

or not...there might be a hue and cry and he might be ousted from his community in England...But he's more likely to suffer significant harm at the hands of a paramilitary attack...that's still quite unique to us in Northern Ireland'.[115] One interviewee involved in therapeutic work with victims also explained the 'culture specific' dynamics of street grooming as well as the consequences for perpetrators in making a disclosure around sex offending:

Here in Northern Ireland...we have a different dimension as well because we have paramilitary involvement in things like that and clearly that has been a big part of grooming...because that would have a big indication of who is exploiting who and how that happens and for which side...quite a lot of the girls that I have spoken to or dealt with will say, when we were at such and such house...they are getting involved with paramilitaries. And clearly in that there's the power...and the collusion and coerciveness... young females, either they'll do it because they think they have to do it because of the consequences, or in another sense they do it because it gives them a lot of power to be attached to groups like this...and a lot of what they would deem as protection...I think the closest thing you might get in England is gang culture...but not for the same reasons...I've dealt with at least four [cases] where they've actually been moved out of their houses because the threat has been so high and the whole community then, and the paramilitaries, have gone and stood in a group outside...while the young person was marched out and they were all shouting, sex offender, get out...And the trauma of being responsible for your whole family being taken out is absolutely huge.[116]

For others, however, particularly those of 'outsiders looking in', the transitional justice context of Northern Ireland was regarded as a positive in terms of facilitating public discourse around the prevention of sexual offending. A voluntary sector interviewee stated: 'Northern Ireland, I mean it's a perfect size, it's small, so it's possible to do things relatively quickly. And again, perhaps because of the history in the North, that there is more of an openness or acceptance that change needs to happen'.[117] Similarly, another senior voluntary interviewee reflected: 'there seemed to be the ability to have a conversation about it that wouldn't happen in England in the same way'.[118] As will be discussed in the next chapter, these distinctive structural features pertaining to Southern Irish and Northern

---

[115] NI 8 (6 July 2011).   [116] NI 11 (18 July 2011).
[117] RI 2 (11 May 2011).   [118] EW 1 (1 September 2011).

Irish society respectively become especially significant in framing public discourses and formulating future societal responses to grooming which are culturally and politically sensitive and tailored to localized contexts.

Conclusion

This chapter has demonstrated that grooming behaviour and the associated risks posed to children as a prelude to abuse are not easily encapsulated within legal or policy frameworks. Both vetting and barring schemes and the offence of meeting a child following sexual grooming as the primary legislative responses to grooming are limited to 'known risk'—those situations where there is a clear record of prior sexual offending or at the very least where significant concerns exists about potential harm (Gillespie, 2002a, 2004a; Ost, 2004). Aside from their inherent limitations in protecting children and policing grooming within institutional and on-line contexts, '[t]hese offences will not stop people from grooming children, not least because the vast majority of abuse takes place by someone known to the child, usually within a family setting' (Gillespie, 2006: 239). As O'Donnell and Milner have argued in the context of child pornography legislation but which could be applied equally to regulatory frameworks on grooming: 'This is symbolic politics par excellence, which is not to say that it is not valuable, merely to be realistic about its impact' (2007: 222). While soft information emerges on the one hand as a useful tool in probing unknown risk, or non-adjudicated offenders, there are also inherent difficulties attached to the use of such information, including instances of false allegations of child sexual exploitation (Thompson and Williams, 2004).

Consistent with the literature, the primary research has reinforced the inherent limitations of pre-emptive policies on risk (McAlinden, 2010a) and the challenges for law enforcement in policing and evidencing both on-line (Khan, 2004; Smith, Grabosky, and Urbas, 2004; Gillespie, 2008; Kosaraju, 2008; Martellozzo, 2012) and face-to-face forms of grooming (Gillespie, 2006; McAlinden, 2006a; Craven, Brown, and Gilchrist, 2007; Davidson and Martellozzo, 2008b). It has also underlined the problems of managing risk across inter-agency and cross-jurisdictional boundaries within the United Kingdom and Ireland, particularly regarding information sharing (Sampson et al, 1991; Crawford, 1997). At the same time, however, the empirical data has also generated a number of significant new insights into the regulation of grooming behaviour not previously highlighted by the literature.

While the literature tends to suggest that on-line grooming may be more amenable to policing and criminalization than its off-line counterpart (O'Connell, 2003: 3; McLaughlin, 2009: 12), this study has established that there are a number of distinct challenges for law enforcement posed by both on-line and off-line forms of child sexual exploitation and grooming. The primary research has also highlighted the impact of grooming on work with survivors and the importance of addressing grooming within the context of therapeutic work with victims, reintegrative work with families as well as in the course of preventive measures aimed at offenders. Finally, there are also a number of emerging and interesting insights into the unique features of public and official discourses around sexual offending against children within individual jurisdictions. In particular, the legacy of the conflict in Northern Ireland, in terms of ongoing paramilitary activity and the patriarchal, Catholic ethos of the Republic of Ireland may hinder wider public dialogue concerning the prevention of harm to children. The latter jurisdiction also emerges in some significant respects as lagging behind the United Kingdom in terms of the efficacy of legislative and policy frameworks on sex offender risk assessment and management. At the time of writing, there are particular concerns about the use of soft information and the absence of a strong inter-agency mandate, pending the implementation of statutory frameworks (see Chapter 3).

In sum, there are twin challenges which must be addressed head on in terms of the formulation of future regulatory responses to sex offending against children. These relate to the targeting of potential risk that has yet to manifest itself in terms of actual harm to children or the vulnerable, as well as the difficulties of imparting accurate information to the public about the risks of sexual victimization in a considered and socially responsive manner, without inflating current levels of suspicion and concern. As will be discussed in Part III of the book, these arguments also underscore the necessity of broadening public and official discourses and responses to grooming beyond the current confines of institutional and internet abuse. Such discourses must encompass the wider and potentially more significant sources of latent harm to children, including new and emerging forms of grooming such as 'peer-to-peer grooming' and 'on street grooming', but particularly the onset of harm which arises from within intra-familial settings.

PART III

Future Policy Responses to Child Sexual Abuse

7

The Way Ahead: Prevention and Protection

> Until we have an effective child protection statutory system plus an effective public education awareness programme, things won't change.[1]

This chapter seeks to chart the direction of future regulatory responses to child sexual abuse which address the failings of current legal, policy, and public discourses on grooming. The first two parts of the book have demonstrated that there is a stark dichotomy between the widespread confusion surrounding the term grooming and the associated weaknesses of legal and policy responses on the one hand, and the complexities of the onset of sexual offending against children on the other. This tension points to the pressing need to broaden current discourses on the prevention of sexual offending against children beyond a narrow focus on 'grooming' and think more constructively about devising a wider, more effective social response to combating child sexual abuse as a whole.

The chapter advocates the development of a public health approach to child sexual abuse, to complement existing legal and policy frameworks. I argue that the widespread adoption of such an approach as an integral part of government and organizational approaches to risk management offers an effective and more realistic prospect of preventing and targeting child sexual abuse on a proactive basis by focusing on early intervention and reducing opportunities for abuse. The chapter begins with a brief examination of the theoretical literature on public health and preventive approaches before setting out a detailed programme of practical suggestions for informing future regulatory agendas on child

[1] Senior voluntary sector interviewee: RI 2 (11 May 2011).

protection and sex offender management drawn from the primary research.

Public Health Approaches: Addressing Sex Offender Risk

There are two main approaches to public protection: the 'community protection model' (Connelly and Williamson, 2000) and the 'public health model' (Laws, 1996, 2000, 2008) (see generally, Kemshall and Wood, 2007). In relation to the former, throughout the United Kingdom in particular, public protection, risk management, and preventive governance have become the key watchwords and structuring principles of legal, policy, and organizational responses to sex offender risk assessment and management (Kemshall, 2001; Kemshall and Maguire, 2001; McAlinden, 2012a) (Chapter 3). This approach is epitomized by regulatory mechanisms for controlling the activities and whereabouts of sex offenders in the community such as notification, vetting and barring schemes, and measures to criminalize the on-line 'grooming' of children before harm occurs (Chapter 6).

Within this genre, as Kemshall and Wood (2007: 203) point out, the task of public protection 'has been the preserve of professionals and vested with a few key agencies such as police and probation'. Public concerns around sex offending against children have become embedded within pre-emptive approaches to sex offender risk management via a policy of 'populist punitiveness' (Bottoms, 1995) or 'penal populism' (Johnston, 2000). At the same time, however, the elitist nature and professionalization of discourses on risk (Ericson and Haggerty, 1997), has meant that the public are officially excluded from such debates and are instead characterized as 'irrational' and a potential threat to expert-led risk management strategies (Kemshall and Wood, 2007: 207, 209–10). Indeed, one of the fundamental challenges presented by the advocacy of more participatory social approaches to preventing child sexual abuse is how can we demythologize sex offending against children and engage the public in the current 'politics and culture of fear' (Furedi, 2006a, 2006b) which exists around such offending without further exacerbating the problem?

Implicit within this challenge is the need to address a further notion which underlines the community protection model—the 'construction and demonization of the "predatory paedophile"'

(Kemshall and Wood (2007: 210–11). As I have argued throughout this book, the popular effigy of a 'child sex offender' as an omni-present yet unknown 'monster' (Simon, 1998) has underpinned contemporary popular and official discourses on sexual offending against children and grooming in particular. This 'demonizing dis-course' (Kemshall and Wood, 2007: 216) and the social, cultural, and political construction of the sex offender as 'outsider' (Becker, 1963) or 'other' (Garland, 2001) also belies the fact that the major-ity of child sexual abuse is intra-familial in nature and takes place within the private rather than the public domain (Grubin, 1988). As noted above and discussed in the next chapter, persuading the public, however, that children are more at risk of grooming and abuse from intimates than those previously unknown to them may be inherently problematic as it 'reverse[s] the order of danger' (Jackson and Scott, 1999: 92–3) in the popular imagination.

In contrast, advocates of alternative public health approaches to sexual offending usually premise these on the failures of traditional retributive and reactive responses to sexual crime (Mercy, 1999; Laws, 1996, 2000, 2008; McMahon and Puett, 1999; McMahon, 2000). Laws (2000: 30), for example, argues that criminal justice responses have been ineffective in reducing the overall incidence of sexual offending and have simultaneously tended to inflate public fear and stigmatization concerning sexual offenders. The concen-trated legislative enactment of a plethora of regulatory measures on sex offending, including grooming, within a relatively short period has failed to prevent sexual abuse, particularly within off-line, intra-familial contexts. At the same time, it has impaired and inflated public perceptions about the risks to children being tar-geted within on-line and organizational environments. These fears have in turn sustained 'a vicious policy cycle' (McAlinden, 2007a: 27) by providing the underlying rationale for the increased demand for regulatory measures.

Mainstream regulatory frameworks often combine consequen-tialist and non-consequentalist justifications of 'punishment' (Duff and Garland, 1994: 6–8)—that is punitive and backward looking censure for past offences is also used to predicate the need for pre-cautionary measures which mitigate the risk of future harm. The public health model, however, is instead exemplified by preventive, forward looking approaches where the language of risk, surveil-lance, and management is displaced by that of prevention and harm reduction (Kemshall and Wood, 2007: 211). Sexual offending is regarded as something which can be proactively addressed rather than something which has to be managed and responded to with stigma or exclusion (Kemshall and Wood, 2007: 213). Whereas regulatory legal and policy responses to managing sex offenders in the community focus on managing the behaviour and whereabouts of known 'risky' *individuals*, such social responses would be based on the identification and management of 'risky' *behaviour, methods, or situations* (O'Malley, 2004: 318–9), which could also encompass previously unknown offenders (McAlinden, 2006a: 355). Moreover, such approaches extend the responsibility for risk management and public protection well beyond the state to civil society, local communities, the general public, and the offender themselves. Key components are the premises that inappropriate behaviour is challenged; that there is an emphasis on self-risk management by sex offenders; and that the public as a whole has a vested role and interest in protecting children (Kemshall and Wood, 2007: 212).

What is significant about the public health approach is that it offers the opportunity to address grooming and abuse on a proactive basis by de-emphasizing disclosure and reporting by children as the triggers for intervention (Kemshall and Wood, 2007: 212). Instead, '[t]he public is seen as a source of…vigilance, disclosure and the custodian of offending opportunities…Literally, "spotting" and acting on grooming activities and actively manipulating risk avoidance strategies on behalf of their children' (Kemshall and Wood, 2007: 217–18). By directly addressing and challenging the popular myths concerning sexual offending, it neutralizes discourses on sexual crime. This in turn gives the public the language and tools to explore a range of appropriate responses to differing types of sexually harmful behaviour and discuss what can be a highly emotive and culturally sensitive topic (Kemshall and Wood, 2007: 212, 214, 218). It also helps to reduce the culture of fear and insecurity which surrounds sex offending against children (McAlinden, 2006a: 354–6).

The community protection and public health models are not mutually exclusive but can 'coexist as reasonably comfortable bedfellows often with the same agencies and personnel functioning in both spheres without experiencing any apparent contradiction' (Kemshall and Wood, 2007: 216; see also Kemshall, Mackenzie, and Wood, 2004). By opening up risk management processes to the wider community, however, the public are made consumers of knowledge about sex offender risk (Reiss, 1989) and become in and of themselves part of the risk management process (McAlinden, 2007a: 191–4). This 'opening up' of knowledge and awareness on the part of the community is especially important when one considers the grooming process. Criminal justice interventions can do little to prevent this unless the offender has already come to their attention. Families and communities can, however, by arranging networks of support and control where necessary (McAlinden, 2005: 388). Braithwaite (1999) uses the example of 'Uncle Harry', as a 'significant other' of the offender and says that 'Uncle Harrys' have a much more plural range of incapacitative keys that they can turn than a prison guard who can turn just one key. While others have argued for the application of a public health approach to combating on-line grooming specifically (Webster et al, 2012: 20, 119–25), I would argue for the wider extension of this approach to off-line, face-to-face contexts to encompass all forms of sexually harmful behaviour towards children.

Primary and Secondary Levels of Prevention

Public health approaches, as applied to sexually harmful behaviour, identify three levels of prevention: primary, secondary, and tertiary (Laws, 2000: 31, 2008: 612). The primary level of prevention is 'the classic public health approach' where the goal is to prevent sexually harmful behaviour before it occurs. This is exemplified by public education and awareness programmes which inform society about the facts surrounding sexual abuse, including how it occurs and how in turn it may be identified, challenged, and prevented. The secondary level of prevention is 'an intervention approach' where the aim is early identification and intervention and to engage with first time offenders to prevent them from progressing to more ingrained or generalized patterns of offending. This is aimed at adolescent and adult offenders including 'situational' or 'opportunistic' offenders who only offend in certain circumstances, such as those within families or organizations or where the opportunity presents itself (Wortley and Smallbone, 2006: 13–18; Smallbone, Marshall, and Wortley, 2008: 160–2). The tertiary level is 'the criminal justice approach', which also underpins 'the community protection model', and involves work with persistent and serious offenders where the objective is to stop or minimize sexually harmful behaviour through relapse prevention and effective treatment programmes.

Other scholars have written extensively on proposed reforms at the tertiary level of prevention in combating grooming and abuse, particularly within the context of harmonizing legislative and non-legislative responses at the international level to tackle on-line sexual exploitation of children (Gallagher et al, 2006: ch 12; Choo, 2007; Akdeniz, 2008; Davidson and Martellozzo, 2008a, 2008b; Davidson and Gottschalk, 2011: ch 3). Comparatively little attention has been afforded to prevention strategies aimed at the primary level of prevention which target sexual abuse before it occurs (NSPCC, 2011). Fewer individuals, however, are involved at the tertiary level which serves the smallest number of offenders displaying the most serious and entrenched problems (Laws, 2008: 613). Indeed, the paradox is that within current policy discourses on sex offender risk management, '[m]ost of our efforts are applied at the secondary or tertiary level where [they are] least likely to succeed' (Laws, 2000: 32). In this vein, I would argue that it is the combination of the first two levels in particular—primary and secondary levels of prevention—which offers a realistic prospect of addressing grooming behaviours, breaking cycles of abuse, and targeting and preventing child sexual abuse in the longer term. Moreover, given the costs of treating offenders and victims of child sexual abuse, a proactive approach would be more cost-effective in both financial and human life experience terms than current reactive approaches (Craven, Brown, and Gilchrist, 2007: 68).

While the public health approach may also be premised in part on situational approaches to crime prevention (Wortley and Smallbone, 2006; Smallbone, Marshall, and Wortley, 2008: ch 8), it encompasses a much broader approach to safeguarding and child protection which would address victim vulnerability as well as offender opportunity. The complexity and multifarious nature of the onset of sexual offending against children as highlighted in this book necessitates a multi-layered approach to prevention and protection encompassing a consortium of complementary strategies. Chief among these at the primary level of prevention is a public education and awareness campaign designed to counter the social and cultural misconceptions surrounding child sexual abuse as well as the stigma attached to being either a victim or a perpetrator of sexual abuse. Challenging the shame and stigma attached to child sexual abuse could ultimately prove very powerful both in terms of empowering victims to make disclosures and encouraging sex offenders to seek help.

Primary prevention: public discourses on sex offending against children

With each of the forms of grooming outlined in the course of this study, abuse is made possible by the level of trust placed in offenders. It is our misconceptions about sexual offenders, in large part generated by sensationalist media reporting (Silverman and Wilson, 2002; Greer, 2003), that make us so vulnerable to them. Sex offenders may rely on these mis-assumptions to gain access to children or deflect notice from their activities. Societal acceptance of these myths assists sex offenders by silencing victims and encouraging public denial about the true nature of sexual assaults. This underlines the need for a rigorous public education programme driven by government designed to dispel commonly held mistaken beliefs, and increase public understanding of the real nature of sexual offending, including that against children (Grubin, 1998; Silverman and Wilson, 2002: 54–9; Sanderson, 2004: 305–10). It would also help to shift cultural attitudes and foster a climate which is facilitative of wider public discourse concerning the prevention of sex offending against children.

Public education and awareness campaigns

In engaging children themselves, 'protective knowledge' (Craven, Brown, and Gilchrist, 2007: 70) and skills could usefully be delivered within primary schools as part of a general life skills programme rather than being exclusively focused on child protection. Current programmes delivered in schools across the United Kingdom and the Republic of Ireland around 'keeping safe', however, are almost exclusively focused on 'stranger danger' rather than more sensitive issues concerning safety from violence in the home and identifying appropriate and inappropriate touch (MacIntyre and Carr, 2000; Stephenson, McElearney, and Stead, 2011). Several interviewees in the study commented on the fact that with many such existing programmes, in the words of one treatment professional, 'what that has sort of mutated into in the schools, is into an anti-bullying programme... The actual element of potentially sexually inappropriate behaviours is completely diluted... It is seen as not really grasping what the issues are'.[2]

---

[2] RI 10 (5 July 2011).

The content of a wider preventive programme could include issues such as appropriate behaviour and personal boundaries; self-esteem and respect for others; sexual health; sex and sexuality; and the importance of healthy inter-personal relationships; and consent. The underlying ethos would be to impart information and increase understanding around what is normal and acceptable behaviour, thereby empowering children and young people. Several interviewees were strongly supportive of such a proposal. As one professional who had worked with both offenders and victims commented:

I think it's about educating them to make informed decisions, to understand what is it that we're trying to protect you from, rather than saying don't do...I think we've got to...stop pretending that we can protect them. I think we have to realize, they have access to the information, so now it's about educating them, rather than devising policies and that whole policing of it...And I think we need to help kids decide what is helpful, and open up that conversation.[3]

Targeting children at an earlier age would have a much greater impact in terms of creating a culture of openness concerning potentially harmful behaviours and in protecting children. Aside from any effects of 'grooming', it is the power differential between adults and children in particular which ensures compliance in children (Chapter 4). The widespread use of such programmes would also equip children with the appropriate language and promote a sense of confidence and empowerment so that they feel able to name inappropriate or uncomfortable behaviour. Indeed, self-protection strategies used by victims of child sexual abuse, in particular 'verbal resistance' in the form of saying 'no' to the offender or refusing to have sexual contact, have proven effectiveness in deflecting offender behaviour (Leclerc, Wortley, and Smallbone, 2010, 2011). It may also help to remove some of the barriers to children acknowledging, or disclosing incidences of sexual victimization by encouraging reporting and reducing the shame or guilt concerning sexual victimization and the fear of being disbelieved. As one victim support professional asserted: 'Kids do have a strength and confidence around strangers certainly, but I think it's just being able to pass that on to the next level which is, you know, that if your uncle or

---

[3] NI 2 (23 May 2011). See also the Byron Review progress report (2010) which espoused a similar safety message in relation to children's on-line behaviour.

your aunt or someone says something, or your cousin, then come to me'.[4]

A further strand to the education of children is age appropriate preventive work with young people both in relation to safe on-line activity as well as healthy inter-personal relationships (Wolak, Finkelhor, and Mitchell, 2004). It has been demonstrated that young people may engage in sexually exploitative and abusive practices with each other such as 'peer-to-peer grooming' (Kaufman, Hilliker, and Daleiden, 1996; Kaufman et al, 1998; Barnardo's, 2011; Leclerc, Beauregard, and Proulx, 2008), 'cyber bullying' (Koefed and Ringrose, 2011), and 'sexting' (Livingstone and Helsper, 2009; Ringrose and Erikson Barajas, 2011; Ringrose et al, 2012), where there is often a slight age differential between the parties (Chapter 4). This can not only have a devastating impact on the victim but there may also be life-long legal and personal consequences for the perpetrator if they are charged with the possession or production of sexually explicit materials (Arcabascio, 2010; Sacco et al, 2010). There are ad hoc initiatives in schools run by community safety divisions within some police districts across the United Kingdom as well as the 'Thinkuknow' programme delivered by CEOP ambassadors to 11 to 16-year-olds in England and Wales (Davidson and Martellozzo, 2008a: 279–80; Davidson and Gottschalk, 2010: 150–6). These are based on creating an awareness of 'sexting', indecent images of children and general internet safety as part of 'the traditional focus of "stranger danger" public education campaigns' (Wortley and Smallbone, 2006: 22; see also Budin and Johnson, 1989). Such programmes, however, should be delivered as a core part of the national curriculum as in the United States, New Zealand, and Canada (Davidson and Martellozzo, 2004), and address the range of sexually harmful behaviours towards children. One police officer explained: 'children need to hear this from a variety of sources so that the message is drip-fed through'.[5] Engaging other young people with similar experiences in the delivery of programmes, rather than solely authority figures such as the police, may offer a more effective means of facilitating discourses with young people concerning the risks of sexually harmful behaviour (Ringrose et al, 2012: 55).

[4] RI 1 (11 May 2011).   [5] NI 8 (6 July 2011).

The responsibility for child protection, however, cannot be placed solely on the shoulders of children and young people (Becker and Reilly, 1999; Renk et al, 2002). Children in particular may lack the emotional capacity to protect themselves in situations where they are being abused by someone they know and trust who may also be meeting their emotive needs. In engaging adults, there is a need for a complementary public education scheme (Budin and Johnson, 1989) which addresses the core misplaced notions of risk surrounding sex offending against children. There have been a few notable television and billboard campaigns developed by the voluntary sector which have been based on increasing public awareness of domestic violence (such as those produced by Women's Aid) and to a lesser extent child sexual abuse or sexual exploitation (such as the NSPCC and Barnardo's). For the most part, however, these have focused on scenes of physical violence and abuse. They often contain graphic images of children who have been beaten or neglected. These campaigns, however, miss the crucial point about grooming and abuse which is that much of the underlying behaviour is not immediately obvious to the casual observer. As happened as part of the 'Tackling Sexual Violence & Abuse' strategy in Northern Ireland (DHSSPS, 2008), government-initiated media awareness campaigns should be developed and delivered through television advertisements and related media campaigns. Indeed, the media can be used in a more constructive way than at present to disseminate such information. This, I would argue, should not be a mass undifferentiated strategy which would risk compounding the current confusion which exists around grooming and sexual offending against children, but should be specifically tailored to local communities and contain a number of key messages.

While the enormity of this task cannot be underestimated, some tentative suggestions can be made. Home Office research (Grubin, 1998) suggests that there are a number of critical issues which the community could usefully be educated about including: that contrary to media portrayal and popular belief, the abuser is rarely the 'dirty old man in the raincoat' which we imagine lurking in the corner of the school playground or local park; that the vast majority of sexual abuse, approximately 80 per cent, is committed by people known to the child rather than a predatory stranger; that sex offenders typically offend alone rather than in networks or 'rings'; that sexual abusers are not a homogeneous group—they are men and women and, in a growing number of cases, young people or children; and that there are differing levels of risk and that not all sexual offenders pose the same degree of high risk.

Perhaps one of the most important of these findings is the one highlighted at the outset of this book—that most perpetrators assault children known to them, with these offences taking place in the home of either the offender or the victim. A further interesting study in this respect is another prepared for the Home Office which looked at 94 cases of physical and sexual abuse (Davis et al, 1999). All but one of the complainants knew their alleged abusers, of whom 48 per cent were family members or relations, 20 per cent were family friends or neighbours, 15 per cent were professionals (youth workers, teachers, doctors), and 6 per cent were acquaintances.[6] In view of this stark reality, it is essential that children and all those responsible for them are also made aware that the danger often may not lie with strangers but with those closest to them. In this way, vigilance would be increased and risk and the opportunity for offending reduced (McAlinden, 2006a: 355).

A further key message which has emerged from the primary research in this current study is the complexity of relationships between victims and offenders in some cases and the fact that, in the words of one treatment professional, 'offenders don't all start off the same way in terms of their motivations'.[7] As highlighted in Chapters 4 and 5, some 'preferential' offenders do set out to gain access to children through a conscious process of what could be termed 'grooming'. For other 'situational' or 'opportunist' offenders (Wortley and Smallbone, 2006: 13–18; Smallbone, Marshall, and Wortley, 2008: 160–2), however, there may be no deliberate grooming of the child prior to the first offence. Instead, for some offenders, sexual offending occurs in certain situations or circumstances, particularly when offenders are already proximate to children, and presented with an opportunity to offend. Grooming in such cases may take the form of manipulation of the environment or significant others to provide further opportunities to offend or avoid detection. This also undermines the predatory stranger fallacy and reinforces the greater risk of abuse within intra-familial contexts.

---

[6] See also Sas and Cunningham (1995: 69–70) who report varying percentages: family members or relations (40 per cent); acquaintances (47 per cent); professionals (7 per cent); and strangers (8 per cent).

[7] SC 7 (23 August 2011).

In relation to victims specifically, as another treatment professional explained:

We are quite attached to the idea of the ideal victim . . . this innocent person
that doesn't behave in a sexual way at all, and then is snatched like the
stereotypical grooming. And therefore we find it quite hard to reconcile the
fact that the ideal victim doesn't really happen very often and that most
often it's going to be someone that quite likes their perpetrator, their abuser,
and might even initiate that sexual contact sometimes themselves.[8]

In particular, some victims of intra-familial abuse, in common with
domestic abuse victims (Carbonatto, 1995; Hoyle, 1998; Morris
and Gelsthorpe, 2000: 421), may want to continue contact with
their abuser (Sauzier, 1989; Berliner and Conte, 1995; Hudson,
2002: 622; McAlinden, 2007a: 204–5). In essence, distorted cultural attitudes concerning victimhood and offending identities
must be addressed as part of the process of countering the dominant stereotypes surrounding grooming and its role in child sexual
abuse and the emotionally charged social and political response to
sexual offending against children.

A final key message is that the legal system and its agents are
limited in their ability to protect children in the widest possible
sense, since they only become involved usually once harm has
already occurred. This fact also points to a further primary construct—a real sea change so that every adult in society recognizes
that child protection is the responsibility of all, and not just the
preserve of statutory and voluntary agencies (Sanderson, 2004:
ch 10; Montgomery-Devlin, 2008). The distribution of such information may encourage and empower people to act on concerns
about abusive or potentially abusive behaviour, particularly where
children may be at risk.

Stop it Now!

One such initiative which embodies both primary and secondary
preventive approaches is the Stop it Now! programme. This scheme
was first established in Vermont in the United States by Fran Henry,
a survivor of sexual abuse. The programme aims to promote
community engagement around child sexual abuse—to educate
the public about child sexual abuse and change attitudes and
behaviour so that people are more open about abuse and can take

---

[8] EW 4 (12 September 2011).

appropriate steps to prevent it. It seeks to stop child sexual abuse by encouraging abusers and potential abusers to recognize their behaviour as abusive and seek help, and by giving adults the necessary information to recognize the signs of abuse and to protect children effectively.

As well as raising general awareness about sexual abuse, the programme is targeted at a number of specific groups. These include adults who have abused or are at risk of abusing a child; parents of children and young people with worrying sexual behaviour; and family and friends of abusers to encourage them to support abusers and empower them to confront them when they exhibit inappropriate behaviour (McAlinden, 2007a: 165–8). The programme is delivered through a number of projects which include a website,[9] media campaigns, public information leaflets, training for professionals, information and courses for parents (such as 'Parents Protect'[10] and 'Parents Protect Plus'), public meetings, and a telephone helpline offering advice and support to people who suspect that someone they know presents a risk to a child. A free confidential national helpline, run by the Lucy Faithfull Foundation,[11] also offers support to those abusers seeking help to desist. It aims to encourage offenders to take responsibility for their behaviour and to come forward and be assessed to see if they are suitable to undergo treatment.

Several studies have examined the effectiveness of the programme in encouraging in particular individuals to report for treatment (Tabachnick and Chasan-Taber, 1999; Tabachnick, Chasan-Taber, and McMahon, 2001; Henry and Tabachnick, 2002). The Stop It Now! UK and Ireland helpline received a total of 8,000 telephone calls and emails between June 2005 and December 2009 of which 50 per cent were from adults concerned about their own behaviour, and 25 per cent of which were from family and friends worried about an adult displaying inappropriate sexual thoughts or behaviour towards children (Stop it Now!, 2010: 4). Of this group, 18 per cent of callers were parents, and 39 per cent were partners (Stop it Now!, 2010: 4). As discussed further below, encouraging offenders to self-refer presents a critical and viable dimension of a public

---

[9] See <http://www.stopitnow.org.uk/> (accessed 23 April 2012).

[10] See <http://www.parentsprotect.co.uk/> (accessed 23 April 2012).

[11] The Lucy Faithfull Foundation is a UK-wide charity dedicated to the prevention of child sexual abuse.

health approach to child sexual abuse. Despite the successes of Stop it Now! UK and Ireland, however, the existence of the initiative and its work is not widely known. A comprehensive survey on public attitudes to sexual offending in Northern Ireland, for example, showed that low numbers of respondents (approximately 20 per cent) had heard of the 'Stop It Now!' campaign (McAlinden, 2007b: 3). As has happened with public education and awareness campaigns around help lines for children such as ChildLine, more needs to be done to highlight the availability and effectiveness of schemes, as part of a wider educational strategy.

Such schemes represent a very positive social response to child sexual abuse and the problem of managing the risk posed by sex offenders in the community (Kemshall, Mackenzie, and Wood, 2004). They also constitute a much more effective response to addressing the grooming of children or preparatory behaviours which precede abuse than legislative or policy frameworks such as vetting or the offence of meeting a child following sexual grooming. They promote understanding about child sexual abuse and abusers and encourage responsible action on the part of the local community. At the same time, they also offer a means of challenging abusers or potential abusers about their offending behaviour and providing them with support in their effort to change. In short, properly resourced public education and awareness has much to contribute to a 'culture of safety' (Busch, 2002: 223) in preventing sexual offending against children.

Secondary prevention: professional discourses on child protection and offender management

At the secondary level of prevention, there are a number of elements which could usefully comprise early identification and intervention. While proposed initiatives at the primary level of prevention are based predominantly on public discourses on sexual offending against children, proposals at the secondary level involve a mix of professional and official discourses on child protection and sex offender management involving work with potential victims, families, and offenders.

Early, staged intervention with children and families

A key part of secondary levels of prevention are timely identification of risks to children and earlier professional intervention where there are apparent concerns about risk of harm. Professional discourses on child sexual abuse over time have been a highly contested field which tend to be characterized by extreme positions (Conte, 1994; Smart, 1999). The waves of 'panic' surrounding high profile cases of child physical and sexual abuse, some of which were outlined in Chapter 3, have resulted in increased levels of professional intervention. These often diminish once the case fades away to become less prominent in both public and professional consciousness until the next high profile case emerges when there is a renewed call for the need for early intervention. There is an ongoing need, however, for a greater professional emphasis on confronting concerns and identifying families in need of support at the earliest opportunity. The need to invest more resources into vulnerable families where children might be at risk was shared by several interviewees in the study. A senior probation professional commented: 'I think that's the failing of the system really is that we don't intervene early enough... I think if we were really serious about preventing sexual abuse, we would put a lot more resources into trying to improve the lives of children in general'.[12] This should extend well beyond the current policy focus on early years support (Goldthorpe, 2004),[13] to improving the lives of all children. As part of this approach, one senior police officer commented on the need for professionals to ask challenging questions:

I think there has to be something about workers on the ground actually challenging behaviour, asking difficult questions. I see this in police officers and I see it in social workers as well, where you go into a home and they don't ask difficult questions... Particularly if they're dealing with people that are professionals, you know, there's almost a fear there, and I see that across all the types of offences against children.[14]

At the same time, however, as argued above, such an approach should also be bolstered by the promotion of responsibility on the part of society and reinforcement of the message that child welfare and protection is the responsibility of all.

One recent development which exemplifies this approach is the forthcoming and long-awaited statutory implementation of the 'Children First: National Guidance' (Department of Children and

---

[12] EW 3 (12 September 2011).

[13] See eg the 'Sure Start' programme in England and Northern Ireland and the 'Getting it Right for Every Child' initiative in Scotland.

[14] NI 7 (30 June 2011).

Youth Affairs, 2011) in the Republic of Ireland.[15] The principal aim of the guidance is to assist professionals and the public in identifying and reporting child abuse and neglect and dealing effectively with concerns. The implementation of this approach will also help to raise the level of public as well as professional awareness of child protection (Jeyes, 2011). As one child services professional commented:

A report doesn't come out of the blue. People are scared to make a report, so if they've made a report there's something happening in their family, and I think we need to take that a little bit more seriously rather than just waiting for the confirmation that it definitely happened ... let's forget about whether it's confirmed or not ... what do those children need to help them? What do their families need? ... Staged interventions, maybe ... so that there's not lots of kids falling through the gaps all the time.[16]

Increased levels of support for children and their families should also help to encourage more victims and their families to come forward and report suspicions or concerns or make a disclosure of child abuse.

Training for professionals

The promotion of earlier, staged intervention should also be accompanied by awareness raising and training for professionals around the dynamics of grooming or the preparatory behaviours which precede abuse (Sanderson, 2004: 319–20; Sutton and Jones, 2004; NSPCC, 2011: 34). Many interviewees in the study were of the opinion that there was a need to bring both the education and health sectors more fully into the process of child welfare and protection. In the words of one senior treatment professional, however, 'children don't see the doctor that much unless there's something physically wrong'.[17] In this vein, I would advocate that all teachers and support staff within schools should receive regular training on child protection (Stephenson, McElearney, and Stead, 2011), including new and emerging forms of sexual exploitation or 'grooming' as highlighted in this study such as 'peer-to-peer' and 'street grooming', to accompany the education and awareness of children. As this same professional commented: 'teachers need to be trained because in many ways they are the ones who are most

---

[15] See the Children First Bill 2012.   [16] RI 1 (11 May 2011).
[17] NI 1 (23 May 2011).

likely to be told about it or to start to see the signs... Teachers are probably the guardians of our children really, in those early years, so they need help and education round that.'[18] Furthermore, schools in this regard also have a particular role in identifying and protecting vulnerable children (Sanderson, 2004: 299–301). A children's services practitioner commented: 'the children who are in perhaps the most vulnerable category... are being excluded from school... and schools know who their vulnerable children are and they could probably find two or three per class'.[19]

Several interviewees in the study also advocated further training around the process and impact of sexual exploitation and abuse for the agencies of law enforcement, including the police, lawyers, and the judiciary to encourage proactive policing and prosecution of such offences (Montgomery-Devlin, 2008; Barnardo's, 2011; Beckett, 2011). This would enable earlier intervention with victims and offenders and identification of potentially harmful behaviour towards children and help to promote consistency in decision-making. In relation to the judiciary, one independent professional commented:

> There is still a lack of understanding by the judiciary. I think the judiciary need to be better informed about it and they just need to really understand that this is what this actually is. It's a bit like nearly having to wait four or five times for the man to stand outside the playground. We know he has a pattern of behaviour... so let's intervene... and give a clear message that grooming is not acceptable.[20]

Others have argued that judges need to be much more cognizant of the treatment needs of sex offenders within the context of their deliberations on sentencing (Edwards and Hensley, 2001b). In this broader vein, I would contend that the judiciary also need further training on the early preparatory behaviours which may precede abuse which may be relevant to the making of a risk of sexual harm order or a sexual offences prevention order (Chapter 3). Similarly, training could also be developed for the legal profession as a whole around issues related to sexual exploitation and abuse, particularly those vested with decision-making powers on prosecution (Choo 2007: 39). A greater understanding of the dynamics of grooming and the inherent features of child sexual abuse and exploitation

---

[18] Ibid.   [19] EW 7 (13 September 2011).
[20] NI 2 (23 May 2011).

which work to secure the victim's silence and, therefore, impinge their credibility as a witness (Chapter 6), may also have beneficial effects in the longer term. It may increase professional willingness to proceed with the case, promote victim engagement with the criminal justice system, and help to reduce overall levels of attrition (NSPCC, 2011: 42).

Work with first-time offenders

Secondary preventive initiatives could also include work which addresses the early commission of offending behaviour (NSPCC, 2011: 48). This would take the form of work with first-time offenders, and particularly young offenders, to identify preparatory or trigger behaviours and prevent them from progressing to more ingrained or generalized patterns of grooming and abuse. Many interviewees acknowledged that 'there is a whole gap in service provision about engaging perpetrators who are outside of the criminal court system',[21] and that 'I don't think we offer enough before the abuse has actually happened'.[22] Most sex offenders are never apprehended or convicted (Salter, 2003; McAlinden, 2007a: 4). Moreover, of those that do come into contact with the criminal justice system, there is the limited availability and effectiveness of prison treatment programmes (Beech and Fisher, 2004; Beech et al, 2005).

As outlined above, evidence from the evaluation of the Stop It Now! programme has shown that 50 per cent of calls to its telephone helpline were from adults worried about their own behaviour. Forty-six per cent of this number had not yet abused a child but wanted help to self-manage their sexual thoughts and more than three-quarters (77 per cent) identified their victim as being known to them as a family member, friend, acquaintance, or neighbour (Stop it Now!, 2010: 4). There is a discernible willingness, therefore, on the part of some offenders to confront their harmful thoughts and behaviour at an early stage in the offending process. The relatively high numbers of offenders or potential offenders self-referring, represents a potent element of a public health approach, essentially by targeting those whose sexually harmful thoughts or offending patterns have not yet become entrenched. Indeed, in an age of cultural pluralism and social complexity in

---

[21] NI 14 (3 August 2011).   [22] RI 4 (13 June 2011).

which many western societies lack social and norm cohesion (Tavuchis, 1991), societal attitudes concerning the wrongness of sexualized relationships between adults and children are surprisingly uniform (Hacking, 1999). Encouraging sex offenders or potential sex offenders to self-refer in order to access perpetrator interventions is something that should be actively encouraged and supported. Society, therefore, needs to find a way of making treatment and intervention both accessible and effective through the further government funding and promotion of initiatives such as Stop It Now![23] This would offer a potential means of making inroads into the unknown 'dark figure' of intra-familial abuse in particular.

Another means of intervention which could be further developed with sex offenders, which was supported by interviewees in the study, is the use of restorative justice approaches, particularly with first-time or young offenders or those who have been considered as 'low' or 'medium' risk of re-offending (McAlinden, 2007a). In Australia, New Zealand, and North Carolina a conferencing-style process in the form of a 'family decision making model' is used as a diversionary response to child sexual abuse (Cashmore and Paxman, 1999; Pennell and Burford, 2001). Circles of Support and Accountability have been piloted in Scotland and developed across England and Wales in particular. These schemes have had considerable success over the last ten years in both protecting communities by challenging pro-offending behaviour and in supporting offenders with pro-social supervision and reintegration (Quaker Peace and Social Witness, 2005; Bates et al, 2007; Wilson, Bates, and Völlm, 2010; Bates et al, 2011; Hanvey, Philpot, and Wilson, 2011: 150–65).[24] The main reasons for the piecemeal application of such schemes to date include lack of resources; a punitive penal culture characterized by the dominance of managerialism; and the lack of public appetite in an era of 'penal excess' (Pratt, 2008a, 2008b) for

---

[23] Other planned initiatives include the Offence Prevention Line to be run jointly by the NSPCC and several Probation Trusts in England and Wales as a 24-hour telephone line for all child sex offenders under probation supervision.

[24] The most extensive evaluations have been carried out in Canada where the programmes originated: Wilson et al (2007a, 2007b). The Republic of Ireland is also considering the feasibility of implementing circles on a pilot basis following the Scottish model where projects are managed by one host organization rather than on an multi-agency basis (Clarke, 2011).

anything which could be regarded as a 'soft' response to what is often a highly emotive and heinous crime (McAlinden, 2011a).

The extension of restorative policies on sex offending throughout the United Kingdom and Ireland as part of existing multi-agency frameworks would provide a further means of managing potential risk before harm or further harm occurs, principally by placing the responsibility for child protection back into the hands of families and communities (McAlinden, 2007a). As one independent professional stated, 'Really because it is within us, it's within the family and the community that abuse occurs, that's why you need restorative approaches.'[25] As noted above, in contrast to the limitations intrinsic to criminal justice interventions, familial and community networks may furnish normative controls on offender behaviour (Brogden and Harkin, 2000) and play a pivotal role in the day-to-day management of the offender (McAlinden, 2005: 388; Braithwaite, 1999). Indeed, the use of circles of support may be particularly beneficial in cases where there is no family involvement by creating what one assessment professional termed 'a quasi family'[26] to hold offenders to account and support them in their efforts to reintegrate into the community.

Work with the offender's family

Timely intervention is also important in the context of work with the families of sex offenders, including work with the partner of offenders getting into new relationships (Studer et al, 2011: 500). In the aftermath of offending, with first-time offenders specifically there is a need to develop programmes with the offender's family as part of the process of reintegration, rehabilitation, and management. In relation to preventing further grooming or abuse, supportive programmes with the non-abusing family members are vital, as one children's services professional stated, in order to address 'the collusion within families which allows sex offending to take place, and the very complex dynamics that happen'.[27]

As Smallbone, Marshall, and Wortley (2008: 172) have argued, however, 'it is in domestic settings where the dangers of implementing counterproductive measures become most acute'. Indeed, the expectation that family members who may well have been groomed

---

[25] NI 4 (1 June 2011).   [26] RI 11 (5 July 2011).
[27] RI 2 (11 May 2011).

themselves (Chapter 4) can automatically change to become a protector of the child is far from being unproblematic. Such difficulties may be particularly heightened where the non-abusing partner has psychological, mental health, or other vulnerabilities which may impede their ability to recognize potentially harmful behaviour or to stop it from occurring. Beyond the intrinsic benefits in terms of offender management and child protection, there is also a need to support the families of sex offenders who may find it very difficult to accept the fact that this person has sexually offended against children, particularly where the victim comes from within their own family. In the words of one senior treatment professional:

It's a very painful thing for a family and it often splits the family right down the middle. And if they can't step away from that awful imprisoning need to either completely collude with the person or to shut the person out completely...if they can manage to hold some middle ground there's huge benefit to be gained in that.[28]

A social services interviewee further explained the difficulties which such families may face: 'the picture in the public is that these men are operating on their own. They're not, they're fathers, they're husbands...they continue to be members of families and these families badly need support to enable them to continue to support this person and cope with what's happened themselves'.[29]

The parents or guardians of young sexual offenders may be involved as an integral part of the process of treatment or intervention based on a 'safer lives' or 'good way' approach (Steen, 1993; Ayland and West, 2006; Geary and Lambie, 2006). Beyond a few isolated examples of best practice,[30] however, service provision for children and young people with sexually harmful behaviour 'is patchy across the UK' (NSPCC, 2011: 26). One probation professional explained the rationale of this approach: 'ultimately, when all the agencies pull away, those are the individuals that will be responsible for standing over whether that adult or young person is applying the learning in their day to day life'.[31] A number of support programmes operate across the United Kingdom and Ireland

---

[28]   RI 5 (14 June 2011).

[29]   RI 4 (13 June 2011).

[30]   See eg Barnardo's Young People's Therapeutic Service in Belfast, the GMAP (Greater Manchester Adolescent Project) and the AIM (Assessment, Intervention, Moving On) Project also based in Manchester.

[31]   NI 12 (26 July 2011).

for the families of adult offenders based on the 'Good Lives Model' (GLM) (Ward, 2002a, 2002b; Ward and Gannon, 2006)[32] which are focused on the actual relationship and family dynamics of the environment into which the offender will be released. Many are delivered in conjunction with the offender's treatment programme and form part of the preparation for reintegration and release. Their delivery, however, is also far from widespread. A concerted effort, therefore, should be made by policy-makers and treatment providers in building this component into treatment programmes for both adult and young sexual abusers as a standardized part of release and reintegration.

As will be discussed further in the next chapter, the 'strengths' or 'needs based' model (Burnett and Maruna, 2006) of sex offender reintegration represents a more effective approach than current risk-based approaches operating alone (Ward and Maruna, 2007; McAlinden, 2011b). One probation professional commented: 'if the need remains unsatisfied, then the risk either remains or goes up as a consequence...if you satisfy the need then you reduce the risk'.[33] Moreover, increasing levels of family support for the offender may remove some of the stigma and fear which attaches to being a sexual offender so that in consequence more offenders may be willing to come out into the open and seek help. As outlined above, initiatives such as Stop it Now! could also be used more effectively by families and friends of offenders as a means of seeking professional help and addressing any concerns they may have about the offender's behaviour.

Organizational issues

As Erooga has stated in a review of the literature on institutional abuse, there is 'no single characteristic or set of characteristics that identify someone as being unsuitable to work with children' (Erooga, 2009a: 10). As with child sexual abuse more generally, it is difficult to identify or predict who is likely to be a risk to children prior to the occurrence of actual harm. As argued throughout this book, the complexity of the onset of sexual offending against chil-

---

[32] The GLM reflects a 'strengths-based' approach (Burnett and Maruna, 2006) to offender reintegration. It is based on the concept of 'primary human goods' (Ward and Gannon, 2006: 79) and aims to enhance the well being of offenders and reduce the risk of further offending by helping offenders adopt more socially integrated and pro-social lifestyles. See also Chapter 8.

[33] RI 6 (14 June 2011).

dren which may variously involve manipulation of other staff, significant others, as well as the surrounding environment makes it difficult to accurately prescribe a defined set of warning signs. In other cases still, organizational abuse may stem from close personal interaction with children in a precise set of circumstances where the motivation to sexually offend only crystallizes once the individual is ensconced within that environment (Chapter 5). Furthermore, encouraging society to look closely for a prototype of sex offending behaviour comprised of easily identifiable risks further masks this complexity and extends the 'othering' process (Becker, 1963; Garland, 2001).

Deterring or preventing sex offenders from joining organizations is not sufficient, therefore, to protect children (McAlinden, 2010a; Erooga, Allnock, and Telford, 2012). Pre-employment vetting and barring schemes are only one element of a broader process of effective organizational recruitment procedures (Fitch, Spencer Chapman, and Hilton, 2007: 7) (Chapter 6). Erooga, Allnock, and Telford (2012: 11–12) have argued '[a]s well as providing appropriate "barriers" by way of selection and screening processes it is also necessary to manage organisational processes so that the possibility of inappropriate or abusive behaviour developing or occurring is minimised'. On this basis, the enhancement of recruitment and selection procedures, such as the adoption of value based interviewing (VBI), has been advocated as part of a 'multi-layered recruitment process' (Erooga, 2009a: 3) and as a further means of distinguishing those who over identify emotionally with children (Erooga, 2009a: 7–9, 2009b: 100–2). The difficulty, however, as noted in Chapter 5, is that emotional congruence with children is at once a desirable characteristic in work with children as well as an early indicator of behaviour which may give potential cause for concern (Sullivan et al, 2011: 70).

The range of public inquiries and reviews in the United Kingdom and the Republic of Ireland (Chapter 5) demonstrate that there is often a situational component to institutional abuse (Smallbone and Wortley, 2000; Terry and Ackerman, 2008). As Erooga (2009b: 28) contends, 'without an appropriate organisational culture of safeguarding, any setting...is vulnerable to the corruption of the ethic of care'. I would argue for the extension of the broader societal culture of safeguarding and a concern for the welfare and protection of children, as outlined above, to child care organizations. One senior voluntary sector interviewee outlined the nature of this wider approach highlighting the dangers of a narrow focus on grooming:

Ultimately, I think it is not about individual behaviour, it is about whole organisational behaviour that will extinguish the possibility of grooming, because other than that it takes us into that trying to spot the sex offender and trying to spot grooming, and I just don't believe, by and large, that is possible. I think it does two things...I think it potentially lulls us into a sense of false security; if we don't identify it, we don't think it could be happening. And equally I think it also leaves the potential that some well meaning, though possibly not terribly wise behaviour could be regarded as grooming behaviour, rather than, this is somebody who needs some help to establish appropriate boundaries...So it's not about managing grooming behaviour more effectively, it is about taking a whole organisation, or a whole public health approach. It incorporates knowing what's appropriate and what are appropriate boundaries, as opposed to being rule bound and it becomes much more child friendly.[34]

In practice, this could be advanced by enhancing staff training around issues specific to offender behaviour, and strengthening external and particularly internal management systems which would maximize 'the features that make organizations safer for children' (Beyer et al, 2005: 106). This would include 'systems of staff support, monitoring, and evaluation to facilitate the identification and effective management of inappropriate behaviour' (Sullivan et al, 2011: 70) and 'a culture of awareness and vigilance' (Erooga, 2009a: 6) which 'promotes open and constructive questioning of practice and relationships' (Shaw 2007: 150).

A safeguarding strategy: integrating victim and offender perspectives

A final strategy to be considered as part of early intervention and identification of risk is the integration of victim and offender perspectives on child sexual abuse. The literature endorses the notion of 'joined-up' thinking (Cowan, Pantazis, and Gilroy, 2001: 439) and 'partnership' (Crawford, 1997; Sullivan, 2002; Gilling, 2007) as part of the multi-agency approach to sex offender risk assessment and management (Kemshall and Maguire, 2001, 2002) as the most effective and efficient means of policy formulation and service delivery (Crawford, 1997: 55–6; Huxham and Vangen, 2005; Stoker, 2003) (Chapter 3). The primary research in this study also

---

[34] EW 1 (1 September 2011).

lent support to this literature (Chapter 6). In this vein, I would argue for the fuller extension of this paradigm to encompass an amalgamation of the child protection and offender management ends of the spectrum of professional interventions with child sexual abuse.

As has happened in England and Wales,[35] though not as yet Scotland, Northern Ireland has introduced a Safeguarding Board Northern Ireland (SBNI) on a statutory footing.[36] The primary agencies to be represented include Health and Social Care (including social services), police, probation, the Youth Justice Agency, education, and library boards, and the NSPCC.[37] The omission of the prison service is a significant shortcoming as it excludes consideration of information pertaining to the effectiveness of treatment programmes both at the individual and general level of offending. While such Boards have a primary function at the tertiary level of prevention in terms of holding a case management review in the event of serious injury or death of a child through abuse or neglect, I would argue that they could also be used at the secondary level of prevention to facilitate knowledge exchange about best practice in relation to child protection as well as offender management.

There is close cooperation between social services and the police in each of the jurisdictions in the United Kingdom and the Republic of Ireland in relation to the joint investigation of child sexual abuse (Chapter 3). For the most part, however, once the offender has been convicted, the issue becomes one of sex offender risk assessment, treatment, and management rather than child protection. One senior social worker stated:

You can't talk about child protection without talking about the offender. The victim and the offender have to be together and that has never been done. We still don't have that in process...the difficulty is there is no one driving that forward. To me it is just very, very clear when I see it...people have a very good understanding of child protection but they don't know how the offender and the risk management fit into that...I think it should be looked at...child protection and offender management as two different sides of the one coin.[38]

---

[35] See the Children Act 2004, Part 2.
[36] See the Safeguarding Board Act (NI) 2011.
[37] Ibid, s 1(3).   [38] SC 10 (24 August 2011).

In this regard, I would argue for the further assimilation of victim/ child protection and offender risk assessment and management approaches as part of a new integrated approach to child sexual abuse involving all of the key agencies, including the prison service. This would enhance inter-agency cooperation in relation to the care and protection of children and could be further facilitated, for example, through specifically tailored knowledge exchange seminars aimed at those on the front-line of child protection and offender management.

Conclusion

Given the difficulties concerning non-disclosure or significant delays in disclosure by child sexual abuse victims (Chapter 2), a reactive legal approach which relies on self-identification by victims has enormous limitations. A highly complex and pervasive societal problem such as child sexual abuse means that it becomes difficult to isolate individual agency and statutory from societal approaches. In essence, there is an overarching imperative to create a moral, cultural, social, and political climate in which society assumes more responsibility, as adults, parents, and government, to identify vulnerable children and situations in which children may be at risk (Sas and Cunningham, 1995: 191). One professional in the study stated: 'that's where a public health approach has such an attraction because it is about a carefully graded, targeted focus, but that starts at a very broad level, which is changing people's perceptions'.[39]

Ultimately, however, an assemblage of societal and professional mechanisms needs to be put in place to effect a holistic and proactive response to sexual offending against children. This spectrum of primary and secondary interventions would be based around education and enforcement (of key messages concerning the realities of sexual offending), control (of the opportunities for abuse), and monitoring (of the risk presented by known offenders) and would encompass constituent interventions with potential victims as well as offenders and families. As the NSPPC (2011: 8) have contended: 'a concerted and organised approach based on a public health model which includes a focus on work with adult sex offenders and

---

[39] EW 1 (1 September 2011).

children and young people with sexually harmful behaviour, as well as with victims offers the best prospect for prevention'.

Current prevention approaches premised around 'stranger danger', 'do not address the dynamics of...sexual exploitation found in the majority of actual cases' (Wolak, Finkehor, and Mitchell, 2004: 431). This also points towards the need to broaden the range of social interventions relating to child sexual abuse. One professional interviewed for the study commented:

It has to start from the parents being strong enough to say these sort of things; and be comfortable in recognising it and I think that's where the grooming can be changed. Because...you're not going to change the individual groomer easily, so it has to be the recipient and anybody around them that can support them...it's getting people the confidence and the knowledge that this is going on and they can do something about it...just putting it back in the hands of the parents and the families...I think it's the only way forward because the social workers aren't going to stop it, the guards aren't going to stop it...If everybody's looking out, just aware of it, it might only be at the back of your heads, but it can happen in your family...Knowledge is power.[40]

As Elliot and colleagues have argued, '[i]ncreased awareness and understanding of how and why child sex abusers target their victims', 'is vital to prevention work with children if...programs are to effectively counteract the methods used by offenders to gain access to children and to ensure their silence' (Elliott, Browne, and Kilcoyne, 1995: 593, 579). The challenges of implementing a public health approach as well as the theoretical and policy implications for contemporary risk-based approaches will be addressed in the next and final chapter.

[40] RI 1 (11 May 2011).

8

Conclusion

> No organization, no bishop, no school principal or what-
> ever can guarantee the protection and welfare of children.
> You can't do it. The best you can do is minimize the possibil-
> ity of abuse happening and if it does happen, you maximize
> the possibility of early detection. That's the best you can do.
> Minimize it happening, maximize early detection. That is
> the best you can do and that is the best we can get society
> to do.[1]

Contemporary public and official responses to 'grooming' have
focused almost exclusively on the dangers of predatory sex offenders procuring victims on-line as well as the risks to children within
child care institutions from those in positions of trust. The essence
of this book's argument is that these responses, however, have been
over simplistic in focus producing a contorted understanding of the
term 'grooming' and its role in child sexual abuse. In particular,
the presentation of 'public and virtual settings' (Ost, 2009: 138) as
the dominant sites of harm, tends to direct attention away from
other situational settings in which children may also be at risk.
Indeed, it has been a central argument of this book that grooming
may occur within intra-familial as well as extra-familial contexts as
part of the normalization of sexually harmful behaviours towards
children.

Regulatory frameworks, common to all four jurisdictions in the
United Kingdom and Ireland, have been designed to pre-emptively
capture sexual risks to children prior to the manifestation of actual
harm (McAlinden, 2010a) (Chapter 3). Vetting and barring schemes
and the respective offences of meeting a child following sexual
grooming, however, are inexorably limited to preventing, targeting,

---

[1] Senior statutory sector interviewee: RI 9 (28 June 2011).

and criminalizing known risks to children—where the offender has already been convicted or, at the very least, significant concerns exist about risk of harm (Chapter 6). This analysis has argued that particularly because of the difficulties of drawing clear boundaries between innocuous and more harmful intentions towards children, criminal law and policy are limited in their response to capturing grooming behaviours. The internet may be 'the new frontier for child protection' (Gillespie, 2002a: 12) in 'a multi-media world' which poses considerable challenges for national and international law enforcement (Martellozzo, 2012). As Gillespie (2004c: 239–40) has also argued, however, 'the grooming of children is neither new nor "hi-tech". Adults have been grooming children for abuse for many years, and it takes place as much offline as it does online'. Indeed, the majority of sexual offending against children takes place within intra-familial settings (Grubin, 1998; Leggett, 2000; McGee et al, 2002) where it often remains hidden and undisclosed whether through active or conscious grooming or the shame-guilt-fear dynamic that is integral to child sexual abuse (Chapter 4). In this respect, I have contended that a wide-reaching public health approach, encompassing all stakeholders in civil society, should be developed to supplement existing legal and policy frameworks: 'The impacts and consequences of child sexual abuse are profound and far reaching, it is a public health problem which requires a co-ordinated, concerted and sustained approach if it is to be effectively addressed' (NSPCC, 2011: 49).

The way ahead has been represented as an enhanced social response which goes well beyond the current narrow focus on grooming to encompass a broader multi-layered approach to child protection and sex offender management. This would be facilitated by the education and engagement of potential victims, potential abusers, and guardians to reduce opportunities for abuse (John Jay College, 2011: 4) (Chapter 7). In presenting this argument, and in light of the literature and the primary research examined in the course of this book, three final issues fall to be addressed: (1) the usefulness of 'grooming' as a concept in understanding sexual offending against children; (2) the theoretical and public policy implications for risks-based approaches; and (3) the societal and policy challenges implicit in implementing a public health approach.

Deconstructing Grooming and its Role in Sexual Offending against Children

We are still very much only at the infancy stages in terms of understanding sexual offending against children, including the process known as 'grooming', and the risk that this behaviour poses to children (McAlinden, 2006a: 356). In deconstructing the term and in critically examining its role in child sexual abuse in institutional, internet as well as familial contexts, it is hoped that this book has significantly extended current discourses and made a further contribution to this field. Existing work has tended to focus on the grooming of the child (Berliner and Conte, 1990; Elliott, Browne, and Kilcoyne, 1995; Salter, 1995; van Dam, 2001), primarily within extra-familial contexts including the internet (O'Connell, 2003; Kierkegaard, 2008; Davidson and Gottschalk, 2010; Webster et al, 2012), and, to a lesser extent, that of families, or communities (Conte, Wolf, and Smith, 1989; Elliott, Browne, and Kilcoyne, 1995; Salter, 2003), primarily as a prelude to abuse. This book has demonstrated that within off-line, face-to-face settings, it is not only the child that is manipulated as part of the preparatory stages of sexual abuse, but quite often other protective adults and the surrounding environment.

The analysis has differentiated intra-familial or quasi-intra-familial settings from extra-familial ones (Chapter 4). Indeed, the purpose of grooming in some cases is also broader than is usually acknowledged. It can be used to both initiate abuse *and* facilitate its continuance. New and emerging forms of grooming have been highlighted including 'street grooming', 'peer-to-peer grooming', and 'self-grooming' by the offender, as well as variations in the offending patterns of young sexual abusers and female sexual offenders (Chapter 4). The study has also examined the onset of sexual offending against children within institutional settings, and the 'grooming' or manipulation of professionals who risk assess, manage, or treat sex offenders (Chapter 5).

In expanding the rubric of grooming into other situational contexts a new, more comprehensive definition has emerged from this analysis which, I would contend, better captures the complexity of the phenomenon: *(1) the use of a variety of manipulative and controlling techniques (2) with a vulnerable subject (3) in a range of inter-personal and social settings (4) in order to establish trust or normalize sexually harmful behaviour (5) with the overall aim of facilitating exploitation and/or prohibiting exposure* (Chapter 2). In examining the complexity of the onset of sexual offending against children and in broadening and deepening the understanding of 'grooming' within a range of offending contexts, there is the danger of contributing to the 'demonizing discourse' (Kemshall and Wood, 2007: 216) and proliferating the 'othering' (Becker, 1963; Garland, 2001) of sex offenders. One senior treatment professional outlined the dangers of what another interviewee described as a 'highly pathologized, very individualized, psychologized notion of deviance':[2]

We need to stop this vehement pathologising, using words like grooming. I think we need to find a different way of talking about this stuff that allows a more human, rather than normative discussion about it. It is harmful, there's no doubt about that but I just think, so long as we keep putting labels like 'deviant', 'groomer' on people, you're just going to close them down and I think it has a completely reverse effect... it drives them into a shame place,... it reduces the potential for therapeutic gain and,... it reduces the potential for compliance in the community.[3]

This study set out to use the language of 'grooming' in keeping with existing academic and policy discourses and in order to retain the integrity of the term. As Montgomery-Devlin (2008: 385) argues, however, '[w]e must recognise the significance of terminology in how we discuss and how we approach the work with these children and those who abuse and exploit them, and, just as important, how this can affect policy and legislative change'. Moreover, in applying the term to a range of social and inter-personal contexts, I am mindful of over-extending its use, thereby diluting the potency and expediency of the term.

In this respect, while 'grooming' has emerged as a useful shorthand reference to describe the onset and/or continuation of sexually harmful behaviour towards children, I have argued that it does not accurately describe the nuances or complexities of abuse in all cases. Indeed, the findings in this research lend support to the 'pathways model' which contends that there may be multiple pathways to offending including both 'approach' and 'avoidant' goals (Ward and Hudson, 1998b) (Chapter 4). Grooming tends to denote a conscious, calculated process and a systematic course of conduct on the part of the offender to gain access to victims. As such, I would

---

[2] RI 7 (20 June 2011).   [3] RI 5 (14 June 2011).

contend that it is more appropriate to use and apply this terminology to extra-familial settings where the offender was previously unknown to the victim or their family and has to deliberately go about 'setting up' an opportunity for abuse (McAlinden, 2006a). This would map on to Wortley and Smallbone's (2006: 13–18; Smallbone, Marshall, and Wortley, 2008:160–2) typology of 'committed' or 'predatory' offenders who seek out and manipulate positions or relationships involving access to children. In particular, the term may be more apt to describe internet abuse of children where offenders intentionally set out to make contact with children for sexual purposes whether or not this eventually results in an off-line meeting and a contact sexual offence.

Within, intra-familial, face-to-face settings, however, I would argue that the conceptual and clinical usefulness of the term 'grooming' is more limited and may be less appropriate prior to the onset of first offending. As others have argued, in many such cases the offender will already be known and physically proximate to the child (Craven, Brown, and Gilchrist, 2006: 293–4). That is, some offenders may be 'opportunistic' (Wortley and Smallbone, 2006: 13–18; Smallbone, Marshall, and Wortley, 2008: 160–2) and seek to exploit the child, significant others or the environment to facilitate offending behaviour. Other 'situational' offenders (Wortley and Smallbone, 2006: 13–18; Smallbone, Marshall, and Wortley, 2008: 160–2), may react to circumstances comprised of close, personal interaction with children, the opportunity to offend, and an underlying sexual proclivity towards children. Others still may manipulate the environment or significant others, rather than the child directly, to normalize sexually inappropriate or harmful behaviours.

For second and subsequent offending, grooming may have a role to play in maintaining the child in a situation of abuse or facilitating further opportunities for abuse, while simultaneously avoiding detection. The same conclusion relating to the absence of a strong harmful motivation from the outset in all cases emerged from the analysis of institutional abuse (Chapter 5) which also reflected the broad split between the 'preferential-situational' dichotomy (Cohen, Seghorn, and Calmas, 1969; Howells, 1981; Groth, Hobson, and Gary, 1982). In sum, I would argue that grooming deserves its place in the lexicon of sexual offending against children. It should, however, be used with a note of caution so that it does not become a 'catch-all' term which masks the complexity of the onset of sex offending against children and in particular the multifarious relationships between victims and offenders.

Implications for Risks-Based Approaches: The Rehabilitation of 'Risk'

The zenith of neo-liberal approaches to crime control, which have underpinned penal policy on sex offending in the United Kingdom (McAlinden, 2012a) as well as the Republic of Ireland over the last few decades, is waning. We have reached the 'dead-end' of penal populism (Simon, 2012) and the peak of regulatory initiatives on sex offending exemplified by pre-emptive approaches to capture 'grooming' and risk of sexual harm before it occurs (Chapter 3). Signs of a regression are already emerging in the form of ECHR challenges to lifetime notification for sex offenders[4] (Chapter 3) and the significant scaling back of the Safeguarding Vulnerable Groups legislation[5] (Chapter 6).

The time is ripe, therefore, for reflection and a radical re-think of 'neo-liberalism' (O'Malley, 2012)[6] which has spawned an industry of expansive regulatory penal policies on risk and to seize the opportunity to retract from the monolithic 'culture of control' (Garland, 2001). At the time of writing, in the early administration of the coalition government in England and Wales, the major policy attention has been directed towards alleviating the economic crisis (Farrall, 2010) which has 'left little room for largely symbolic anti-crime and terror measures' (Simon, 2010: 9). This is a pivotal moment, therefore, in criminal justice policy-making which presents a real opportunity to develop new and innovative policies on child sexual abuse. It offers the prospect of moving away from neo-liberal crime policies which have characterized advanced Western democracies over the last few decades (O'Malley, 1999; Cavadino and Dignan, 2006a) and of returning to welfarist-based principles (Garland, 1985, 1996). These policies would depart from the concern with controlling the 'dangerous classes' (Pratt, 2000a; Garland, 2001) in favour of more inclusionary social and penal

---

[4] R (on the application of F and Thompson) v Secretary of State for the Home Department [2010] UKSC 17.

[5] See the Protection of Freedoms Act 2012, Part 5.

[6] Professor Pat O'Malley was a Visiting Professor at the School of Law at Queen's University Belfast when the book was being completed (May 2012).

policies around sex offending which address more explicitly the interests of victims as well as offenders, and recognize child sexual abuse as a pervasive social problem.

There are two primary failings of pre-emptive risk policies (Zedner, 2009) on sexual offending based on radical prevention (Seddon, 2008), 'preventive governance' (Ashenden, 2002) or 'precautionary logic' (Ericson, 2007) which represent significant challenges in reformulating regulatory discourses on risk. The first of these is that measures such as vetting and the offence of meeting a child following sexual grooming give the 'allure of protection' (Hebenton and Seddon, 2009: 12) or the impression rather than the substance of security (Furedi and Bristow, 2008: 7). The recent pre-emptive and insidious measures on grooming, however, seek to 'govern the ungovernable' (McAlinden, 2006a: 42)—that is they are limited inevitably to known, identifiable, and preventable risks and not the unknown, hidden and therefore the most dangerous ones. The second, as noted throughout this book, is that there is a wider 'politics and culture of fear' (Furedi, 2006a, 2006b) in contemporary society which relates to potential risks to public safety posed by stranger danger and abuse, and grooming in particular, and the need to take ever more stringent precautionary measures against them. It is this politics of culture and fear surrounding sexual offending, created in large part by the media and sustained in turn by public and official responses, which fuels the regulatory regime (McAlinden, 2010a: 41–2).

The complementary public health approach which has been outlined in the previous chapter aims to counteract both of these challenges. It offers a means of proactively addressing harms to children within intra-familial as well as extra-familial contexts primarily by encouraging a culture of openness and accountability concerning child sexual abuse. It also offers a viable means of engaging the public in informed and measured discourses concerning sexual offending against children. This approach has the potential to make children safer on a wider scale, not only on the internet and within child care institutions, but also crucially within their own families where they may be most at risk. To date, policy makers have failed to exploit the full range of preventive opportunities presented by the public health model (McMahon and Puett, 1999; Smallbone, Marshall, and Wortley, 2008: 47). As Ost (2009: 242) has argued, however, 'strategies of situational crime prevention may offer a better way forward than increased criminalization'.

This 'new' risk discourse would represent a distinct move away from 'governing through crime' (Simon, 2007) where risk would be configured very differently than at present. In particular, concerns about sexual abuse as a 'crime' and the omnipresence of sexual offenders in the community would be tempered by broader concerns with the welfare and safety of children. It would also entail a distinct move away from current *offender*-focused strategies to also incorporate *offence*-focused strategies. Moreover, this discourse would counter current constructions of risk as 'external' and 'other' and address the realities of risk concerning child sexual abuse—they most often occur in the private sphere and lie within families rather than outside them. In practice, the collective, societal management of risk would involve the community and the rolling out of a tapestry of services tailored to the needs of victims, offenders and families affected by child sexual abuse, Risk, therefore, would be minimized and managed through bottom-up as well as top-down approaches which would represent proactive and anticipatory responses to child protection and not just reactive responses after specific problems occur.

'Risk technologies' within contemporary governing frameworks may be the subject of multiple configurations, with attendant implications for the selection of regulatory and social interventions with sex offending (O'Malley, 2004: 6). The way forward is encapsulated in Kemshall's (2008: 133) phrase of 'blended protection' which synthesiszes protective and reintegrative strategies. It is presented as a departure from contemporary dichotomous discourses on sexual offending which tend to polarize victims and offender issues, as well as management and reintegration issues. This view was shared by several interviewees in the study where one senior probation interviewee phrased the issue rhetorically: 'how do we couple monitoring, management and the building in of protective factors?'[7]

This re-formulated paradigm of risk would be orientated towards, what I would term, a 'panoptican of the victim' and the environment rather than the situational risk management of the offender. This necessitates a fundamental shift in focus away from applying 'checklists' in recognizing patterns of grooming behaviour as others have advocated (van Dam, 2001; Salter, 2003; Sanderson, 2004 Powell, 2007), towards broadening protective

---

[7] RI 8 (23 June 2011).

efforts around victims, offenders, and communities. A wider professional, political, and social culture of safeguarding would comprise mechanisms to address pro-offending behaviour as well as timely intervention with victims. A public health approach to child sexual abuse focuses efforts on 'decreasing risk' related to offenders as well as 'bolstering protective and resilience factors' relating to victims (NSPCC, 2011: 30). This post-modern application of panoptic principles (Foucault, 1977; Bentham, 1995), where surveillance is used as a form of social control, could potentially capture a broader range of potential harms to children than concentrating resources solely on offenders and in particular the 'critical few'. Risk management approaches around offenders would also be supplemented by 'strengths-based' approaches (Burnett and Maruna, 2006) as part of a 'good lives' approach (Ward, 2002a, 2002b; Ward and Gannon, 2006). These would address the limitations of risk-based approaches and represent a more effective approach to offender reintegration and a better balance between risk management and rehabilitation (Ward and Maruna, 2007; McAlinden, 2011b).

As the introductory quotation conveys, no system can eliminate risk entirely (McAlinden, 2010a: 41). There will always be high profile cases of abuse by predatory strangers that are one-off and random and perhaps not that easily preventable. Increasing awareness of the dynamics and complexities of grooming, however, has broader policy implications for better understanding how child sexual abuse and exploitation occurs, how it often goes undetected and how ultimately it may be prevented. Educating parents and carers and children themselves to be wary would increase societal vigilance about 'risky behaviour' beyond the current narrow legalistic focus on known 'risky individuals' (McAlinden, 2006a: 355). It would also go some way towards addressing unknown risks (Soothill, 2005; Soothill et al, 2005a, 2005b) and simultaneously reducing opportunities for 'grooming' behaviour prior to the onset of child sexual abuse.

Enhanced knowledge of how sex offenders operate may also provide specific and practical assistance to policy-makers and practitioners in the area of child protection and sex offender treatment and management by enhancing the efficacy of targeted interventions with offenders and the skills of those professionals who work within them. In this respect, there was a split in the views of interviewees regarding the relevance of an examination of grooming and the preparatory behaviours which precede abuse to treatment interventions with sex offenders. On the one hand, several assessment and treatment professionals shared the following viewpoint: 'I think we need to have a very sensitized and nuanced view of grooming and we need to spend our time looking at the seemingly insignificant decisions made by offenders'.[8] For other treatment professionals, however, 'If you don't concentrate on the skills and strengths and other things, then I think all we are doing is reinforcing an offender's negative views of himself'.[9] At the time of writing, each of the jurisdictions in the United Kingdom along with the Republic of Ireland were beginning to re-formulate their treatment programmes. The new ethos of these programmes was outlined by one senior probation professional:

At the moment we spend an awful lot of time looking in great detail at a person's modus operandi...how they engaged in grooming and so on...which has been termed a confessional approach because it is about encouraging people to confess. We are moving towards what we are calling a bio-psycho social approach, which is about recognising that there are not just psychological elements to a person's offending, but also things to do with a person's biology...which we probably can't address in a treatment programme. The new programme is more about developing strengths and putting in place things that people need to become part of society and live decent lives, rather than constantly being on the lookout for risky situations.[10]

In my view, however, there is a need to ensure that policy developments in this area do not become too future focused to the neglect of pre-offence behaviour and the triggers that led to offending in the first place. In this respect, research has also shown that there is a positive correlation between grooming and recidivist behaviour (McGrath, 1991; Scalora and Garbin, 2003). In Scalora and Garbin's (2003) multi-variate analysis of sex offender recidivism, for example, one of the key characteristics of repeat offending was, inter alia, the engagement in more grooming of victims or less violent behaviour in order to overcome the victim's resistance to the assault. Treatment interventions, therefore, should be assiduous of not only the nuances of victim-offender interaction, but also self-grooming strategies employed by offenders pre- and post-offence

---

[8] RI 11 (5 July 2011).   [9] SC 11 (7 September 2011).
[10] EW 3 (12 September 2011).

and, additionally, the dynamics of relationships between offenders within treatment programmes and between offenders and professionals tasked with their assessment, treatment, and management. Offenders in particular need to be equipped to identify these risks and put in place strategies to self-manage or prevent them.

Challenges for Public Health Approaches

While there may be general awareness about the risks of child sexual victimization by strangers, the onset of sexual abuse can be such a subtle, refined, and sophisticated process that families, communities, and organizations are unable to pinpoint concerns or to recognize it. Indeed, people are not fully cognizant of such risks essentially because, in the words of one independent professional: 'people have an image about abuse, that it's only done by people who really are different from the rest of us, as opposed to the fact that offenders are exactly the same as the rest of us'.[11] Similarly, in the words of a victim support interviewee: 'the main difficulty is…getting society to recognize that it happens with close people and…I think the more we can get people to recognize it could happen within their family then I think that's the biggest step forward we can make'.[12] As noted earlier, the failure to recognize that sex offenders are 'ordinary people' known to the child can leave children more susceptible to abuse (Sutton and Jones, 2004: 21). Challenging the media's image that sex offences are committed exclusively by strangers, however, and promoting a culture of openness and public discourses around this fact, raises a number of difficult issues.

Grooming has been the subject of a 'moral panic' (see Cohen, 1972) in the media and amongst polticians, and the recent legislation common to many jurisdictions is in part a reflection of this. In extending the public understanding of grooming to familial contexts, there is a danger of simply increasing levels of suspicion, mistrust, and surveillance (Foucault, 1977). If society is encouraged to look very closely for abuse, there might be an associated danger of undermining trust rather than seeking to safeguard it. This might further heighten the moral panic surrounding sexual crime creating a society where no one trusts anyone (Hudson, 2005: 183). Care

---

[11] NI 4 (1 June 2011).   [12] RI 1 (11 May 2011).

will need to be taken in particular that vigilance does not mutate into vigilantism thereby exacerbating the difficulties sex offenders face in seeking rehabilitation and reintegration into society.

Parents in particular may be reluctant to allow their children to engage in education and awareness programmes due to the fear of frightening children about the insidious nature of sex offending in society and undermining their innocence. One senior social worker articulated this problem as follows: 'it can be very, very difficult in terms of balancing protection and the understanding of the public. You don't want them to go to the extreme...and you don't want children to be frightened, but you do want them to have an understanding of what's uncomfortable...and appropriateness.'[13] If parents, however, can be persuaded that this approach could deliver some tangible benefit in the form of managing sex offender risk and reducing future offending behaviour and that this is the most effective way to protect their children from the risk they feel sex offenders pose, then more parents may be willing to facilitate their children's involvement in such schemes.

There is a related danger that imparting such information may further damage normal, healthy child-adult inter-personal relationships, which are 'a constant feature of human life' (Khan, 2004: 224; see also Furedi and Bristow, 2008). This particular tension between increasing public cognizance of potential risks without over inflating them was articulated by several interviewees in the study. One social services professional stated: 'we need to work out how to put out that information to make people aware without stigmatizing people who are genuinely caring about children. I think it's really, really hard for men these days to have a relationship with their own child without people thinking that certain behaviours might be a bit suspect.'[14] Inflated public concerns about the risk posed by sex offenders also have an impact at the macro-level on organizations as well as individuals. A senior treatment professional commented:

It's really, really discouraging men from having any kind of close contact with children. It's just completely distorting things, you know. I think that's really scary. I think when you see a man hugging a child now, the first question in your mind is, is he up to no good? So I think some sort of public programme would have to be terribly careful that it didn't incite that

---

[13] SC 10 (24 August 2011).   [14] RI 4 (13 June 2011).

further. Because you've got whole care organisations now that are absolutely run and managed by women, because men won't go anywhere near them.[15]

As noted in Chapter 6, the perpetuation of public fears and anxieties concerning the pervasiveness of sexual offending against children helps to further mask 'unknown risks' until they manifest themselves in the form of actual harm to children. A social and political retraction from this position is essential because heightened levels of fear, suspicion, and mistrust which attach to all those who come into contact with our children (Furedi and Bristow, 2008) may undermine our latent ability to make discerning judgments about those who genuinely pose a risk (McAlinden, 2010a: 41).

Given the problems of accurately defining 'grooming' or positively identifying potential risk to children prior to actual harm (Gillespie, 2002a, 2004a; Ost, 2004) (Chapters 2 and 6), there are related challenges in pinpointing at what level concerns crystallize where parents or children should act on suspicions or instincts (see Chapter 6). This is particularly applicable within the intra-familial context where much of what precedes actual abuse and what could be termed 'grooming' constitutes 'normal' parental behaviour or at least that which has become normalized within a particular family (see Chapter 4). The fact that grooming can be such a gradual scale and that much of what could be termed 'grooming' with the benefit of contextual hindsight actually constitutes routine interaction with children, particularly at the early stages of the process, is also something which must be addressed within education and awareness programmes.

There are two further contemporary social and cultural constructs surrounding sex offending against children which do not sit easily with each other or the adoption of a public health approach. On one level, the wholesale adoption of such an approach may be initially hard to reconcile with penal populism (Bottoms, 1995; Johnstone, 2000) as outlined in the first part of the book. Such discourses tend to characterize the identities of child victims as 'innocents' which must be protected at all costs (Jackson and Scott, 1999: 86) and adult offenders as the ultimate 'wrongdoers'. This belies the complexities of the relationships between victims and

---

[15] RI 5 (14 June 2011).

offenders in many cases as highlighted throughout this book. On another level, strong cultural and political views concerning the need to protect children from sex offenders are fundamentally at odds with many forms of contemporary popular culture which tend to sexualize children (Durham, 2009; Levin and Kilbourne, 2009; Papadopoulos, 2010). One interviewee involved in work with offenders commented on the current barrage of mixed messages regarding children's sexuality and appropriate behaviour:

I think that the world that we live in is incredibly sexualized now and that is normalized and...a lot of things are being driven by the consumer society that we live in...And it's just all kind of out of whack with what is normal. There's kind of no boundaries...I just think that we are giving out the wrong messages and we're going to have to rewind and recoil all that back in again. And then if we add on things like, the internet and technology and how we communicate now, it becomes terrifying...And these little children aren't meaning to be overly sexual in their behaviour, they are just being little kids, but they've got access to all this stuff that other generations didn't have, so there's no boundaries on them.[16]

Indeed, concerns about the sexualization of children have also been recognized in England and Wales and Scotland at public policy level (Buckingham et al, 2010; Papadopoulos, 2010; HM Government, 2010; Bailey, 2011). The critical tension between these two constructs—that society simultaneously regards children as erotic and an erotic response to children as criminally unimaginable (Kincaid, 1998: 20)—also needs to be confronted in designing and implementing public health approaches to child sexual abuse.

One of the greatest challenges, however, is in using such information to proactively address and manage the risk of abuse within intra-familial or quasi-intra-familial environments (Smallbone, Marshall, and Wortley, 2008: 172). This task may be considerably more complex in certain environments where children are more vulnerable to abuse. One victim support interviewee pinpointed this challenge in terms of families who may be affected by abuse:

Given that we know that most children who are abused are abused at home, the difficulty is (a) in facilitating as a society our engagement in the fact that families are not always the safest place for children, and then (b) in helping a child protect themselves when they are being abused in what should be the safest place of all, at home.[17]

---

[16] SC 6 (22 August 2011).   [17] RI 2 (11 May 2011).

Other interviewees framed this challenge in terms of society as a whole:

It is fairly difficult to recognize someone we know, we love, we care about, we drink a beer with, who is our boss... to see them as a potential sex offender, and therefore we dismiss their behaviour that we might ought to have recognized. And that is part of what we need to do... help people recognize behaviours and not be put off because they like... the person that is doing it.[18]

In this vein, it has been argued that the public already accepts that the risk of sexual victimization by a stranger is slight but is reluctant to visualize the risk in domestic terms (Greer, 2003). They deliberately choose to construct 'sites of danger' as being located within the public sphere and associated with predatory strangers which are perceived as more damaging or threatening. Any alternative is considered unpalatable and undermines the traditional views of the family and home as the accepted realm of safety and protection (Saraga, 2001). In short, information will need to be delivered in a sensitive and responsible way so as to avoid a compounding of current problems and, above all, to make sure that one panic about sex offending is not simply replaced by another (McAlinden, 2006a: 356).

In relation to children themselves, the long-term consequences of grooming behaviours for victims of intra-familial abuse have been considered in Chapter 4. In the short-term, there are also related difficulties in engaging children in public health approaches and increasing their understanding of appropriate behaviours and boundaries. There are acknowledged boundary confusions concerning acceptable and innocuous behaviour towards children and that which begins to denote a more sinister intention or the onset of an abusive process. Such difficulties become especially significant when one considers that children may unwittingly facilitate such behaviour as the willing recipients of increased attention, affection, or gift giving. Several interviewees in the study conceded that children may 'enjoy' being groomed, albeit they do not recognize the behaviour as abusive. In the words of one treatment professional, also noted in the previous chapter: 'the ideal victim doesn't really happen very often and that most often it's going to be someone that quite likes their perpetrator, their abuser, and might even initiate

---

[18] EW 13 (22 September 2011).

that sexual contact sometimes themselves'.[19] Such boundary issues become even more problematic in relation to peer-to-peer grooming or children on children abuse and in ascertaining in particular how much of this behaviour is innocent exploration as opposed to early indicators of a more sexually harmful motivation. In short, there are obvious difficulties in encouraging children to report matters which they do not particularly regard as unwelcome. Such challenges are made even more manifest by the enhanced sexualization of children in contemporary culture as outlined above. As outlined in the previous chapter, however, educating children in schools about a range of issues relating to consent, sexual health, and healthy inter-personal relationships, via peers as well as traditional authority figures, represents the most viable means of engaging children in discourses around grooming and sexual exploitation and abuse.

Perhaps the most fundamental barrier for society in protecting children from sex offenders is the seismic cultural shift needed to overcome the stigmatization which surrounds sex offending against children and recognize it as fairly ubiquitous. While schools have been identified in the previous chapter as the most likely vehicle for educating children and their parents and carers about abuse, how to engage other adults is a pertinent issue. As one senior voluntary sector interviewee explained: 'a critical starting point is, "believe it can happen here. If you don't believe it can happen here, you are not going to recognize the signs when it is, and you're not going to do something"'.[20] This very potent implication was articulated further by another senior voluntary sector interviewee as a critical stumbling block for society:

It is very comfortable to identify, name and shame paedophiles, rather than acknowledge that we actually don't know who is potentially a risk. And therefore I think that is a real barrier to protecting children because we want to identify individuals who are risky, rather than say...an awful lot of people have the potential in certain circumstances, to abuse. And we don't know who they are and they don't know who they are and until those circumstances arise...it couldn't be known. And I think that's a really frightening, quite contentious, and deeply uncomfortable but seems to be a rather hard reality.[21]

---

[19] EW 4 (12 September 2011).   [20] EW 13 (22 September 2011).
[21] EW 1 (1st September 2011).

In short, the future development of effective social policies to safeguard children, support families, and address pro-offending behaviour, may effectively reduce the potential for grooming and abuse to occur in the longer term, but only if we, as a society, can accept the possibility of it occurring in the first place.

Appendix 1
Research Methodology

Sampling

Interviewees were selected on the basis of 'purposeful sampling' using a range of criteria including knowledge and experience of working on sexual offence cases, and comprised those at the 'elite', managerial or policy level as well as those directly involved with offenders and victims in the field. Initial contacts were known professional associates of the author. Further participants were identified and recruited on a 'snowballing' basis using professional referrals to other colleagues. Additionally, where research permissions were sought formally from the research governance department at a central agency level, the author was provided by the agency with the names and contact details of participants who matched the sampling criteria.

The author did not interview children or their families. There is no ethical justification for research that would risk further traumatization of child victims and their families. Further, previous studies have examined the perspectives of children and their families in the context of the disclosure process. This study, however, presents a comprehensive and systematic review of these relevant literatures on grooming (eg Berliner and Conte, 1990; Salter, 1995, 2003; Gallagher, 1998; Gallagher et al, 2003; Gillespie, 2004a). As noted above, a unique contribution of the study is an examination of 'grooming' from an institutional perspective. As such, the perspectives of children and their families were examined through the prism of professional agencies as well as advocacy groups.

Interview schedule and procedure

Semi-structured in-depth interviews were conducted on a one-to-one basis for a minimum of 45 minutes, with nearly all extending well beyond an hour.[1] Interview questions were framed around the key themes from the secondary literature on grooming and sexual offending more generally. Participants, however, were encouraged to go beyond these questions to address other issues which they felt were important to tackling the

---

[1] A small number of interviews (five) were conducted by telephone where participants had to cancel the pre-arranged interview at short notice, and it was not otherwise possible to re-arrange.

grooming process. Additionally, a set of subsidiary themes related to policy and practice were also addressed during the course of the interviews. These included a comparison of legal and policy frameworks and in particular the issue of inter-agency cooperation both within and across jurisdictions which has been a key feature of recent discourses on sex offender treatment and management (Kemshall and Maguire, 2001). Brief notes were taken by the author during the interview. All interviews were taped and fully transcribed. The transcripts were analysed by the author in conjunction with similarities or departures from the key themes arising from the secondary literature on grooming.[2]

---

[2] Data analysis was initially conducted manually as well as subsequently through the use of the NVivo software (Version 7.0).

Appendix 2
Interview Schedule

Preliminary Issues

1. About myself
2. Participant Information Sheet and Informed Consent Forms (for signature)
3. The form of the interview (eg I'd like to ask you a number of questions, but we can talk about related issues if something comes to mind)

Can you tell me, very briefly, a little bit about your career history and what your current job involves?

Research Questions

The primary research questions relate to four core themes (A–D):

(A) The Nature and Extent of Sexual Grooming:

(1) What do you understand by the term 'grooming'?
(2) What is the purpose of grooming and what does the process involve?
(3) What are some of the key variables in the grooming process?

eg what sort of techniques do would-be offenders employ?

(4) What about the following forms of grooming—which, if any, of these terms have you come across before?

- 'on-line grooming'?
- 'off-line/face-to-face grooming'?
- 'familial grooming'?
- 'societal grooming'?
- 'institutional grooming'?
- 'street/on-street grooming'?
- 'peer-to-peer grooming'?
- 'self-grooming'?

(5) What is the nature of grooming as witnessed and experienced in the course of your area of work?

eg what are the most common forms you have come across?
eg are some more prevalent than others?

(6) How does that compare with current public/popular images of 'grooming'?

eg as portrayed by the media, for example, and as commonly understood by the wider public?

(7) Are there any problems with current contemporary constructions of grooming either from an official or popular stand-point?

(8) How important a role does grooming play in the onset of sexual offending against children? What about against adults?

(9) How important is victim identification/selection as part of the grooming process?

eg are particular children, families, or institutions targeted?

If so, what are some of the key variables which might inform victim selection?

(10) How effective is grooming behaviour?

eg with children, families, communities, within organizations?

(11) Has the role of grooming in sexual abuse cases been in any way overstated?

eg one academic has claimed that 'grooming is a ubiquitous feature of the sexual abuse of children'.[1] Would you agree with that statement?

(12) What is the overall general extent of grooming in cases of sexual offending?

eg how common is grooming behaviour as a whole in the onset of sexual offending behaviour/in the cycle of sexual abuse/in re-offending behaviours?

(13) How does grooming impact upon your work?

(14) What is the main source of your current knowledge about the grooming process?

eg where does your knowledge of grooming come from—involvement in individual cases?; studies of the disclosure process?; data from treatment programmes?; published statistics?; the media; other?

(B) Institutional Grooming

One of the specific focuses of this study is to look at grooming within an institutional context.

(15) Does sexual grooming have particular resonance in an institutional context, for example within the context of child care organizations such as care homes?

[1] Thornton (2003).

eg offenders who use their employment status/position as a vehicle to abuse children?

(16) If so, are there any special features or dynamics when grooming occurs within organizations rather than with specific individuals?

eg vulnerability, trust etc;?

(17) Do modes of 'institutional grooming' ever occur with professionals within the context of interviews with suspect sex offenders or within the course of sex offender treatment and management programmes?

eg where sex offenders appear to give what they perceive as the 'right' responses to professionals in order to convince them that they pose no risk to children or of their compliance with treatment or management protocols?

(18) How prevalent is the concept of 'self-grooming' that sex offenders, via denial and minimization techniques, may groom themselves into normalizing sexually deviant behaviour or into thinking that they pose no risk to children?

eg does this ever manifest itself in terms of non-engagement with treatment and management systems put in place for offenders?

(19) Are grooming behaviours and the tactics used by offenders to gain access to children specifically addressed within the context of offender treatment or management programmes?

(20) Does grooming ever have an impact on the effectiveness or outcomes of treatment or management programmes?

(21) How could child protection/offender treatment and management systems be enhanced to better target and more effectively address grooming behaviour?

(C) Protective Policies and Procedures

(22) What are the main difficulties in trying to protect children from sexual exploitation in general?

(23) What are some of the major problems involved in responding to grooming behaviour in particular?

eg the difficulties in managing or 'policing' such behaviour?

(24) Are some forms of grooming, in this respect, more problematic than others?

See question (4) above for list of different forms of grooming.

(25) What are the main legislative or policy responses which target grooming within your jurisdiction and what impact have they had on child protection/sex offender treatment or management?

eg the offence of meeting a child following sexual grooming/certain preliminary contact/for the purpose of sexual exploitation?
eg pre-employment vetting and barring schemes?
eg child abduction legislation
eg any others?

(26) **How effective are these current laws and policies in preventing and targeting grooming behaviour?**

eg prior to the occurrence of actual harm?/identifying harmful behaviour early on?

(27) **How effective are current laws in criminalizing grooming behaviour?**

eg are there any major problems with the legislation—evidential difficulties in proving intention for the offence of meeting a child following grooming etc?

(28) **Does grooming ever have an impact on the effectiveness of pre-employment vetting and barring schemes?**

eg sex offenders trying to by-pass/circumvent vetting systems?

(29) **How can grooming be more effectively targeted prior to the occurrence of actual harm?**

eg are there any amendments/changes to the law or policy or procedures which you would advocate as a protective or preventive measure which would make legislative or policy responses to grooming more effective?

(30) **What do you think of developing a coordinated public health approach to grooming to complement the legal and policy framework? eg public education and awareness programmes?**

eg do you see any problems with such an approach?

(31) **In a similar vein, what do you think of developing an organized social response to grooming?**

eg children's babysitting clubs
eg or more formally, community engagement programmes such as 'StopItNow!' or Circles of Support and Accountability?

(32) **How do you see child protection, or sex offender/treatment and management systems in the future generally?**

eg will it/they remain the same or change in some ways?

(33) **Are there any alternative measures which you would consider in order to reduce opportunities for child sexual exploitation and grooming in particular?**

(D) The Inter-agency Context

(34) Does grooming ever have resonance in an inter-agency context?

(35) Does grooming ever have resonance in a cross-jurisdictional context in cases involving cross-jurisdictional cooperation?

eg if an offender living in one jurisdiction communicates with a child on-line and then travels to another jurisdiction to meet with them?

(36) What are the additional difficulties in targeting grooming behaviour when cases involve a cross-jurisdictional element?

(37) Are inter-agency structures effective in targeting and preventing grooming behaviour?

(38) Are there any problems relating to grooming behaviour, how it occurs, how it is addressed within legal or policy frameworks which you consider are unique to your jurisdiction?

eg types of cases?
eg the size of the jurisdiction?
eg ease of cross border access etc?

Any other comments which you would like to make which were not specifically addressed?

Bibliography

Abel, G.G, Becker, J.V., Mittleman, M.S., Rouleau, J.L., and Murphy, W. (1987), 'Self-reported Sex Crimes of Non-incarcerated Paraphiliacs', 2 *Journal of Interpersonal Violence* 3.

Abel, G., Lawry, S., Karlstrom, E., Osborn, C., and Gillespie, C. (1994), 'Screening Tests for Pedophilia', 21 *Criminal Justice and Behaviour* 115.

Abrams, L. (1998), *The Orphan Country* (Edinburgh: John Donald Publishers).

Adam, A. (2002), 'Cyberstalking and Internet Pornography: Gender and the Gaze', 4 *Ethics and Information Technology* 133.

Adler, F. (1983), *Nations Not Obsessed with Crime* (Littleton, CO: FB Rothman).

Agamben, G. (2005), *State of Exception* (Chicago: University of Chicago Press).

Akdeniz, Y. (2008), *Internet Child Pornography and the Law* (Aldershot: Ashgate).

Alexander, S., Meuwese, S., and Wolthuis, A. (2000), 'Policies and Developments Relating to the Sexual Exploitation of Children: The Legacy of the Stockholm Conference', 8 *European Journal on Criminal Policy Research* 479.

Allnock, D. (2010), *Children and Young People Disclosing Abuse: A Research Briefing* (London: NSPCC).

American Psychiatric Association (2000), *Diagnostic and Statistical Manual of Mental Disorders* (4th edn, text revised) (Washington DC: American Psychiatric Association).

Amroliwala, D. (2007), *Report of the Enquiry into the Handling by Home Office Officials of Notifications, by Other European Countries, of Criminal Convictions for UK Citizens* (London: The Home Office).

Anderson, B. (1983), *Imagined Communities* (London and New York: Verso).

Arcabascio, C. (2010), 'OMG R U Going 2 Jail???', 16 *Richmond Journal of Law and Technology* 1.

Arnold, B. (2009), *The Irish Gulag: How the State Betrayed its Innocent Children* (Dublin: Gill & Macmillan).

Ashenden, A. (2002), 'Policing Perversion: The Contemporary Governance of Paedophilia', 6 *Cultural Values* 197.

——(2004), *Governing Child Sexual Abuse: Negotiating the Boundaries of Public and Private, Law and Science* (London: Routledge).

Ashfield, S., Brotherston, S., Eldridge, H., and Elliott, I. (2010), 'Working with Female Sexual Offenders: Therapeutic Process Issues', in T.A. Gannon and F. Cortoni (eds), *Female Sexual Offenders: Theory, Assessment and Treatment* (Chichester: Wiley-Blackwell).

Ashurst, L. (2011), 'Emotional Intelligence and the Practitioner Working with Sexually Harmful Behaviour', in M.C. Calder (ed), *Contemporary Practice With Young People Who Sexually Abuse: Evidence-based Developments* (Dorset: Russell House Publishing).

Ashworth, A. (2002), 'Re-drawing the Boundaries of Entrapment', *Criminal Law Review* 161.

Ayland, L. and West, B. (2006), 'The Good Way Model: A Strengths-based Approach for Working with Young People, Especially those with Intellectual Difficulties, who have Sexually Abusive Behaviour', 12 *Journal of Sexual Aggression* 189.

Bagley, C. and King, K. (1990), *Child Sexual Abuse: The Search for Healing* (London and New York: Tavistock, Routledge).

Bagley, C. and Ramsey, R. (1986), 'Sexual Abuse in Childhood: Psycho-Social Outcomes and Implications for Social Work Practice', 4 *Journal of Social Work and Human Sexuality* 33.

Bailey, R. (2011), *Letting Children be Children: Report of an Independent Review of the Commercialisation and Sexualisation of Childhood* (London: Department for Education).

Baker, A.W. and Duncan, S.P. (1985), 'Child Sexual Abuse: A Study of Prevalence in Great Britain', 9 *Child Abuse and Neglect* 457.

Barnardo's (2009), *Whose Child Now? Fifteen Years of Working to Prevent Sexual Exploitation of Children in the UK* (Barkingside, Ilford: Barnardo's).

——(2011), *Puppet on a String: The Urgent Need to Cut Children Free from Sexual Exploitation* (Barkingside, Ilford: Barnardo's).

Barter, C. (1999), 'Practitioners' Experiences and Perceptions of Investigating Allegations of Institutional Abuse', 4 *Child Abuse Review* 392.

——(2007), 'Prioritising Young People's Concerns in Residential Care: Responding to Peer Violence', in A. Kendrick (ed), *Residential Child Care: Prospects and Challenges* (London: Jessica Kingsley Publishers).

Barter, C., McCarry, M., Berridge, D., and Evans, K. (2009), *Partner Exploitation and Violence in Teenage Intimate Relationships*, available at <http://www.nspcc.org.uk/Inform/research/findings/partner_exploitation_and_violence_report_wdf70129.pdf> (NSPCC) (accessed 7 May 2012).

Bates, A., Macrae, R., Williams, D., and Webb, C. (2011), 'Ever-increasing Circles: A Descriptive Study of Hampshire and Thames Valley Circles of Support and Accountability 2002–09', *Journal of Sexual Aggression*, 1–19, iFirst.

Bates, A., Saunders, R., and Wilson, C. (2007), 'Doing Something About It: A Follow-up Study of Sex Offenders Participating in Thames Valley

Circles of Support and Accountability', 5 *British Journal of Community Justice* 19.

Bates-Gaston, J. (2003), 'Terrorism and Imprisonment in Northern Ireland: A Psychological Perspective', in A. Silke (ed), *Terrorists, Victims and Society: Psychological Perspectives on Terrorism and its Consequences* (Chichester: Wiley).

Beck, U. (1992), *Risk Society: Towards a New Modernity* (London: Sage).

Becker, H. (1963), *Outsiders: Studies in the Sociology of Deviance* (New York: The Free Press of Glencoe).

Becker, J.V. and Reilly, D.W. (1999), 'Preventing Sexual Abuse and Assault', 11 *Sexual Abuse: A Journal of Research and Treatment* 267.

Beckett, H. (2011), *Not a World Away: The Sexual Exploitation of Children and Young People in Northern Ireland* (Barnardo's Northern Ireland), available at <http://www.barnardos.org.uk/13932_not_a_world_away_full_report.pdf> (accessed 28 November 2011).

Beckett, R.C., Beech, A., Fisher, D., and Fordham, A.S. (2004), *Community Based Treatment for Sex Offenders: An Evaluation of Seven Treatment Programmes* (London: Home Office).

Beech, A.R. (1998), 'A Psychometric Typology of Child Abusers', 42 *International Journal of Offender Therapy and Comparative Criminology* 319.

Beech, A.R. and Elliott, I.A. (2011), 'Understanding the Emergence of the Internet Sex Offender: How Useful are Current Theories in Understanding the Problem?', in E. Quayle and K. Ribisl (eds), *Understanding and Preventing Online Sexual Exploitation of Children* (Oxford: Routledge).

Beech, A.R. and Fisher, D.D. (2004), 'Treatment of Sex Offenders in the UK in Prison and Probation Settings', in H. Kemshall and G. McIvor (eds), *Managing Sex Offender Risk* (London: Jessica Kingsley).

Beech, A.R., Oliver, C., Fisher, D., and Beckett, R. (2005), 'STEP 4: The Sex Offender Treatment Programme in Prison: Addressing the Offending Behaviour of Rapists and Sexual Murderers', available at <http://www.hmprisonservice.gov.uk/assets/documents/100013DBStep_4_SOTP_report_2005.pdf> (accessed 30 April 2012).

Benneworth, K. (2009), 'Police Interviews with Suspected Pedophiles: A Discourse Analysis', 20 *Discourse Society* 555.

Bentham, J. (1995), 'Panoptican', in M. Bozovic (ed), *The Panopticon Writings* (London: Verso).

Ben-Yehuda, N. (2001), *Betrayal and Treason: Violations of Trust and Loyalty* (Boulder: Colorado: Westview).

Berliner, L. (2002), 'Introduction: Confronting an Uncomfortable Reality', 14 *American Professional Society on the Abuse of Children Advisor* 2.

Berliner, L. and Conte, J.R. (1990), 'The Process of Victimisation: The Victims' Perspective', 14 *Child Abuse and Neglect* 29.

——(1995), 'The Effects of Disclosure and Intervention on Sexually Abused Children', 19 *Child Abuse and Neglect* 371.

Berridge, D. and Brodie, I. (1996), 'Residential Child Care in England and Wales: The Inquiries and After', in M. Hill and J. Aldgate (eds), *Child Welfare Services: Developments in Law, Policy, Practice and Research* (London: Jessica Kingsley).

Berry, J. (1992), *Lead Us Not Into Temptation: Catholic Priests and the Sexual Abuse of Children* (New York: Doubleday).

Best, J. (1990), *Threatened Children: The Rhetoric of Child Victims* (Chicago: University of Chicago Press).

Beyer, L., Higgins, D., and Bromfield, L. (2005), *Understanding Organizational Risk Factors for Child Maltreatment: A Review of Literature* (Melbourne: National Child Protection Clearinghouse, Australian Institute of Family Studies).

Bichard, Sir M. (2004), *The Bichard Inquiry Report* (London: Home Office).

Bickley, J. and Beech, A.R. (2001), 'Classifying Child Abusers: Its Relevance to Theory and Clinical Practice', 45 *International Journal of Offender Therapy and Comparative Criminology* 51.

——(2002), 'An Investigation of the Ward and Hudson Pathways Model of the Sexual Offense Process with Child Abusers', 17 *Journal of Interpersonal Violence* 371.

Birrell, D. and Murie, A. (1980), *Policy and Government in Northern Ireland: Lessons of Devolution* (Dublin: Gill and Macmillan).

Bithell, S. (1991), *Educator Sexual Abuse: A Guide for Prevention in the Schools* (Boise, ID: Tudor House Publishing Co).

Black, A. and Williams, C. (2002), *Fife Council Independent Enquiry Established by the Chief Executive following the Conviction of David Logan Murphy for the Sexual Abuse of Children* (Kirklady: Fife Council).

Blagg, H., Pearson, G., Sampson, A., Smith, D., and Stubbs, P. (1988), 'Inter-agency Co-operation and Reality', in T. Hope and M. Shaw (eds), *Communities and Crime Reduction* (London: HMSO).

Boer, D.P., Eher, R., Craig, L.A., Miner, M.H., and Pfäfflin, F. (2011), *International Perspectives on the Assessment and Treatment of Sexual Offenders: Theory, Practice and Research* (Chichester: Wiley-Blackwell).

Bohlander, M. (2005), 'The Sexual Offences Act 2003 and the Tyrell Principle—Criminalising the Victims?', *Criminal Law Review* 701.

Boney-McCoy, S. and Finkelhor, D. (1995), 'Prior Victimization: A Risk Factor for Child Sexual Abuse and for PTSD-related Symptomatology among Sexually Abused Youth', 19 *Child Abuse and Neglect* 1401.

Bordin, E. (1994), 'Theory and Research on the Therapeutic Alliance: New Directions', in A.O. Horvath and L.S. Greenberg (eds), *The Working Alliance: Theory, Research, and Practice* (New York: John Wiley and Sons).

Bottoms, A.E. (1995), 'The Philosophy and Politics of Punishment and Sentencing', in C. Clarkson and R. Morgan (eds), *The Politics of Sentencing Reform* (Oxford: Oxford University Press).

Bovard-Johns, R.M. (2009), *Juvenile Sex Offenders and Therapeutic Alliance: The Intricate Dynamics of Alliance in Relation to Attachment, Trauma and Religion.* Unpublished study (Northampton, MA: Smith College School for Social Work).

Brackenridge, C.H. (1997), '"He Owned Me Basically": Women's Experience of Sexual Abuse in Sport', 32 *International Review for the Sociology of Sport* 115.

——(2001), *Spoilsports: Understanding and Preventing Sexual Exploitation in Sport* (London: Routlege).

Brackenridge, C.H. and Fasting, K. (2005), 'The Grooming Process in Sport: Narratives of Sexual Harassment and Abuse', 13 *Autobiography* 33.

Brackenridge, C.H. and Kirby, S. (1997), 'Playing Safe? Assessing the Risk of Sexual Abuse to Young Elite Athletes', 32 *International Review for the Sociology of Sport* 407.

Braithwaite, J. (1989), *Crime, Shame and Reintegration* (Sydney: Cambridge University Press).

——(1999), 'Restorative Justice: Assessing Optimistic and Pessimistic Accounts', in M. Tonry (ed), 25 *Crime and Justice: A Review of Research* 1.

——(2000), 'The New Regulatory State and the Transformation of Criminology', 40 *British Journal of Criminology* 222.

Brannan, C., Jones, R., and Murch, J. (1993), *Castle Hill Report: Practice Guide* (Shropshire: Shropshire County Council).

Brehm, S. and Kassin, S. (1993), *Social Psychology* (Boston, MA: Houghton Mifflin Co).

Brennan, C. (2007), 'Facing What Cannot Be Changed: The Irish Experience of Confronting Institutional Child Abuse', 29 *Journal of Social Welfare and Family Law* 245.

Brogden, M. and Harkin, S. (2000), 'Community Rules Preventing Reoffending by Child Sex Abusers: A Life History Approach', 28 *International Journal of the Sociology of Law* 45.

Browne, A. and Finkelhor, D. (1986), 'Impact of Child Sexual Abuse: A Review of the Research', 9 *Psychological Bulletin* 66.

Brownlee, I. (1998), 'New Labour—New Penology? Punitive Rhetoric and the Limits of Managerialism in Criminal Justice Policy', 25 *Journal of Law and Society* 313.

Browne, K. and Lynch, M.A. (1999), 'The Experiences of Children in Public Care', 8 *Child Abuse Review* 353.

Bryan, T. and Doyle, P. (2003), 'Developing Multi-Agency Public Protection Arrangements', in A. Matravers (ed), *Sex Offenders in the Community: Managing and Reducing the Risks* (Cullompton, Devon: Willan Publishing, Cambridge Criminal Justice Series).

Buckingham, D., Bragg, S., Russell, R., and Willett, R. (2010), *Sexualised Goods aimed at Children*, Research Report (Edinburgh: Scottish Parliament).

Budin, L. and Johnson, C. (1989), 'Sex Abuse Prevention Programs: Offenders' Attitudes about their Efficacy', 13 *Child Abuse and Neglect* 77.

Buhrmester, D. (1996), 'Need Fulfilment, Interpersonal Competence, and the Developmental Contexts of Early Adolescent Friendship', in W.M. Bukowski, A.F. Newcomb, and W.W. Hartup (eds), *The Company They Keep: Friendship in Childhood and Adolescence* (Cambridge: Cambridge University Press).

Bunting, L. (2005), *Females who Sexually Offend Against Children: Responses of the Child Protection and Criminal Justice Systems* (London: NSPCC).

——(2007), 'Dealing with a Problem that Doesn't Exist? Professional Responses to Female Perpetrated Child Sexual Abuse', 16 *Child Abuse Review* 252.

Burke, A., Sowerbutts, S., Blundell, B., and Sherry, M. (2002), 'Child Pornography and the Internet: Policing and Treatment Issues', 9 *Psychiatry, Psychology and Law* 79.

Burnett, R. and Appleton, C. (2004), *Joined-Up Youth Justice: Tackling Youth Crime in Partnership* (London: Russell House Publishing Ltd).

Burnett, R. and Maruna, S. (2006), 'The Kindness of Prisoners: Strengths-based Resettlement in Theory and in Action', 6 *Criminology and Criminal Justice* 83.

Busch, R. (2002), 'Domestic Violence and Restorative Justice Initiatives: Who Pays if We Get it Wrong?', in H. Strang and J. Braithwaite (eds), *Restorative Justice and Family Violence* (Melbourne: Cambridge University Press).

Butler-Sloss, E. (1988), *Report of the Inquiry into Child Abuse in Cleveland* (The Butler-Sloss Report), Cmnd 412 (London: HMSO).

Byron, T. (2010), *Do We Have Safer Children in A Digital World? A Review of Progress Since the 2008 Byron Review* (Department of Children, Schools and Families), available at <https://www.education.gov.uk/publications/eOrderingDownload/DCSF-00290-2010.pdf> (accessed 7 May 2012).

Calder, M.C. (2004), *Child Sexual Abuse and the Internet: Tackling the New Frontier* (Dorset: Russell House Publishing).

Canter, D., Hughes, D., and Kirby, S. (1998), 'Paedophilia, Pathology, Criminality, or Both? The Development of a Multivariate Model of

Offence Behaviour in Child Sexual Abuse', 9 *Journal of Forensic Psychiatry* 532.

Carbonatto, H. (1995), *Expanding Intervention Options for Spousal Abuse: The Use of Restorative Justice*, Occasional Papers in Criminology New Series: No 4 (Wellington, New Zealand: Institute of Criminology, Victoria University of Wellington).

Carr, J. (2004), *Child Abuse, Child Pornography and the Internet* (NCH: London).

Cashmore, J. and Paxman, M. (1999), *Family Decision Making: A Pilot Project by Burnside and DoCS, Evaluation Report* (New South Wales: Social Policy and Research Centre, University of New South Wales).

Castel, R. (1991), 'From Dangerousness to Risk', in G. Burchell, C. Gordon, and P. Miller (eds), *The Foucault Effect: Studies in Govermentality* (Chicago: University of Chicago Press).

Cavadino, M. and Dignan, J. (2006a), 'Penal Policy and Political Economy', 6 *Criminology and Criminal Justice* 435.

—— (2006b), *Penal Systems: A Comparative Approach* (London: Sage).

Cawson, P., Wattam, C., Brooker, S., and Kelly, G. (2000), *Child Maltreatment in the United Kingdom* (London: NSPCC).

Cense, M. (1997), *Red Card or Carte Blanche: Risk Factors for Sexual Harassment and Sexual Abuse in Sport: Summary, Conclusions and Recommendation* (Arnhem: NOC and NSF).

Chambers, J.C., Ward, T., Eccleston, L., and Brown, M. (2009), 'The Pathways Model of Assault: A Qualitative Analysis of the Assault Offender and Offense', 24 *Journal of Interpersonal Violence* 1423.

Chan, V., Homes, A., Murray, L., Treanor, S., and Ipsos Mori Scotland (2010), *Evaluation of the Sex Offender Community Disclosure Pilot* (Scottish Government Social Research), available at <http://www.scotland.gov.uk/socialresearch> (accessed 20 April 2011).

Chase, E. and Statham, J. (2005), 'Commercial and Sexual Exploitation of Children and Young People in the UK: A Review', 14 *Child Abuse Review* 4.

Child Exploitation and Online Protection Centre (CEOP) (2007), 'Most Wanted Special Edition', *E-bulletin* issue 13 November.

—— (2010), *Strategic Overview 2009–2010* (London: CEOP), available at <http://www.ceop.police.uk/Documents/Strategic_Overview_2009-10_(Unclassified).pdf> (accessed 5 April 2011).

—— (2011a), *Out of Mind, Out of Sight. Breaking Down the Barriers to Understanding Child Sexual Exploitation* (London: CEOP), available at <http://ceop.police.uk/Documents/ceopdocs/ceop_thematic_assessment_executive_summary.pdf> (accessed 28 November 2011).

—— (2011b), *Annual Review 2010–11 and Centre Plan 2011–12* (London: CEOP), available at <http://ceop.police.uk/Documents/ceopdocs/Annual%20Rev2011_FINAL.pdf> (accessed 28 November 2011).

Choo, K.-K.R. (2009), 'Online Child Grooming: A Literature Review on the Misuse of Social Networking Sites for Grooming Children for Sexual Offences', AIC Reports Research and Public Policy Series 103 (Canberra: Australian Institute of Criminology).

Christiansen, J. and Blake, R. (1990), 'The Grooming Process in Father-Daughter Incest', in A. Horton, B. Johnson, L. Roundy, and D. Williams (eds), *The Incest Perpetrator: A Family Member No One Wants to Treat* (Newbury Park: Sage).

Christie, N. (2000), *Crime Control as Industry* (3rd edn) (London: Routledge).

Clarke, A. (2011), *Feasibility Study into Circles of Support and Accountability (COSA) For Ireland: Final Report*, Report Commissioned by the Probation Service, available at <http://www.iprt.ie/contents/2256> (accessed 23 April 2012).

Cleland, A. (2005), 'Protection is Better than Cure', 36 *Scots Law Times* 201.

Clyde Committee (1946), *Report of the Committee on Homeless Children*, Cmd 6911 (Edinburgh: HMSO).

Clyde Report (1992), *The Orkney Inquiry: Report of Inquiry into the Removal of Children from Orkney in February 1991* (Edinburgh: HMSO).

Cobley, C. (2000/05), *Sex Offenders: Law, Policy and Practice* (Bristol: Jordans).

Cohen, L.E. and Felson, M. (1979), 'Social Change and Crime Rate Trends: A Routine Activities Approach', 44 *American Sociological Review* 588.

Cohen, S. (1972), *Folk Devils and Moral Panics* (London: Paladin).

Cohen, S. (2001), *States of Denial: Knowing About Atrocities and Suffering* (Cambridge: Polity Press).

Cohen, M., Seghorn, T., and Calmas, W. (1969), 'Sociometric Study of the Sex Offender', 74 *Journal of Abnormal Psychology* 249.

Coleman, J.S. (1990), *Foundations of Social Theory* (Cambridge, Massachusetts: Harvard University Press).

Colton, M. (2002), 'Factors Associated with Abuse in Residential Child Care Institutions', 16 *Children and Society* 33.

Colton, M. and Vanstone, M. (1996), *Betrayal of Trust: Sexual Abuse by Men who Work with Children: In Their Own Words* (London: Free Association Books).

Colton, M., Vanstone, M., and Walby, C. (2002), 'Victimization, Care and Justice: Reflections on the Experience of Victims/Survivors involved in Large-scale Historical Investigations of Child Sexual Abuse in Residential Institutions', 32 *British Journal of Social Work* 541.

Commission to Inquire Into Child Abuse (2009), *Report of the Commission to Inquire Into Child Abuse* (Chair: Judge Séan Ryan) (May, 2009), available at <http://www.childabusecommission.ie/> (accessed 21 February 2011).

Commission of Investigation (2009), *Report into the Catholic Archdiocese of Dublin* (Chair: Judge Yvonne Murphy) (November, 2009) (Dublin: Department of Justice and Law Reform). Also available at <http://www.dacoi.ie/> (accessed 21 February 2011).

Connelly, C. and Williamson, S. (2000), *Review of the Research Literature on Serious Violent and Sexual Offenders*, Crime and Criminal Justice Research Findings No 46 (Edinburgh: Scottish Executive Central Research Unit).

Constantin, S. (2008), *Towards a European Criminal Record* (Cambridge: Cambridge University Press).

Conte, J.R. (1994), 'Child Sexual Abuse: Awareness and Backlash', 4 *The Future of Children* 224.

Conte, J.R., Wolf, S., and Smith, T. (1989), 'What Sexual Offenders Tell Us About Prevention Strategies', 13 *Child Abuse and Neglect* 293.

Cook, J. and Wall, T. (1980), 'New York Attitude Measures of Trust, Organization, Commitment, and Personal Need Non-fulfilment', 53 *Journal of Occupational Psychology* 39.

Cooper, A., McLoughlin, I.P., and Campbell, K.M. (2000), 'Sexuality in Cyberspace: Update for the 21st Century', 3 *Cyber Psychology and Behaviour* 521.

Corby, B., Doig, A., and Roberts, V. (2001), *Public Inquiries into Abuse of Children in Residential Care* (London: Jessica Kingsley).

Cortoni, F. and Hanson, R.K. (2005), *A Review of the Recidivism Rates of Adult Female Sexual Offenders*, Research Report No R-169 (Ottawa, Ontario: Correctional Service of Canada).

Council of Europe (2011), *Council of Europe Annual Penal Statistics— SPACE I—2009*, available at <http://www.coe.int/t/dghl/standardsetting/cdpc/Bureau%20documents/PC-CP(2011)3%20E%20-%20SPACE%20I%202009.pdf> (accessed 13 October 2011).

Cowan, D., Pantazis, C., and Gilroy, R. (2001), 'Social Housing as Crime Control: An Examination of the Role of Housing Management in Policing Sex Offenders', 10 *Social and Legal Studies* 435.

—— (2011), *Report into the Catholic Archdiocese of Cloyne* (Chair: Judge Yvonne Murphy) (July, 2011) (Dublin: Department of Justice and Law Reform). Also available at <http://www.dacoi.ie/> (accessed 5 September 2011).

Cowburn, M., Wilson, C., and Loewenstein, P. (1992), *Changing Men: A Practice Guide to Working with Adult Male Sex Offenders* (Nottingham: Nottinghamshire Probation Service).

Craissati, J., McClurg, G., and Browne, K. (2002), 'Characteristics of Perpetrators of Child Sexual Abuse who have been Sexually Victimized as Children', 14 *Sexual Abuse: Journal of Research and Treatment* 225.

Craven, S., Brown, S., and Gilchrist, E. (2006), 'Sexual Grooming of Children: Review of the Literature and Theoretical Considerations', 12 *Journal of Sexual Aggression* 287.

——(2007), 'Current Responses to Sexual Grooming: Implication for Prevention', 46 *Howard Journal of Criminal Justice* 60.

Crawford, A. (1997), *The Local Governance of Crime: Appeals to Community and Partnership* (Oxford: Clarendon Press).

——(2001), 'Joined-Up but Fragmented: Contradiction, Ambiguity and Ambivalence at the Heart of New Labour's "The Third Way"', in R. Matthews and J. Pitts (eds), *Crime, Disorder and Community Safety: A New Agenda* (London: Routledge).

——(2003), 'Contractual Governance of Deviant Behaviour', 30 *Journal of Law and Society* 479.

——(2006), 'Networked Governance and the Post-Regulatory State? Steering, Rowing and Anchoring the Provision of Policing and Security', 10 *Theoretical Criminology* 449.

Crawford, A. and Jones, M. (1995), 'Inter-agency Co-operation and Community-Based Crime Prevention: Some Reflections on the Work of Pearson and Colleagues', 35 *British Journal of Criminology* 17.

Criminal Justice Inspection Northern Ireland (2010), *An Inspection of the Handling of Sexual Offence Cases by the Justice System in Northern Ireland: Donagh Sexual Abuse Cases Inspection* (Belfast: Criminal Justice Inspection Northern Ireland), available at <http://www.dojni.gov.uk/index/publications/publication-categories/pubs-criminal-justice/cji_-_donagh_sexual_abuse_cases_inspection_-_november_2010.pdf> (accessed 25 January 2012).

Criminal Justice Review Group (2000), *Review of the Criminal Justice System in Northern Ireland* (Belfast: HMSO).

Croall, H. (2006), 'Criminal Justice in Post-devolutionary Scotland', 26 *Critical Social Policy* 587.

Croall, H., Mooney, G., and Munro, M. (2010), *Criminal Justice in Scotland* (Oxon: Willan Publishing).

Curry, T. (1991), 'Fraternal Bonding in the Locker Room: A Profeminist Analysis of Talk About Competition and Women', 8 *Sociology of Sport Journal* 119.

Cussen Commission (1936), *Report of the Commission of Inquiry into the Reformatory and Industrial School System, 1934–1936* (the Cussen Report) (Dublin: The Stationery Office).

Danet, B. (1998), 'Text as Mask: Gender, Play and Performance on the Internet', in S.G. Jones (ed), *Cybersociety 2.0: Revisiting Computer-mediated Community* (Thousand Oaks, CA: Sage).

Darjee, R. and Russell, K. (2011), 'The Assessment and Sentencing of High-Risk Offenders in Scotland: A Forensic Clinical Perspective', in B. McSherry and P. Keyzer (eds), *Dangerous People: Policy, Prediction and Practice*, International Perspectives on Forensic Mental Health Series (London and New York: Routledge).

Darroch, D. (2011), 'OLR Offenders: Issues and Challenges', paper presented at 'Serious Sexual and Violent Offenders in Scotland: Current Issues and Challenges', Mackay Hannah One Day Conference, 8 June (Edinburgh).

Dasgupta, P. (1988), 'Trust as Commodity', in D. Gambetta (ed), *Trust: Making and Breaking Co-operative Relations* (Oxford: Basil Blackwell).

Davidson, J. (2004), 'Child Sexual Abuse Prevention Programmes: The Role of Schools', in O. Giotakos, R. Eher, and F. Plafflin (eds), *Sex Offending is Everybody's Business*, 8th International Conference of the International Association for the Treatment of Sexual Offenders, 6–9 October (Pabst: Lengerich).

Davidson, J. and Gottschalk, P. (2010), *Online Groomers: Profiling, Policing and Prevention* (Dorset: Russell House Publishing).

—— (2011), *Internet Child Abuse: Current Research and Policy* (London: Routledge).

Davidson, J.C. and Martellozzo, E. (2004), *Educating Children About Sexual Abuse and Evaluating the Metropolitan Police Safer Surfing Programme*, available at <http://www.saferschoolpartnerships.org/ssp-topics/evaluations/documents/ssfindingsreport.pdf> (accessed 30 April 2012).

—— (2005), 'Policing the Internet and Protecting Children from Sex Offenders Online: When Strangers Become "Virtual Friends"', paper presented at the Cybersafety Conference, University of Oxford, 8–10 September, available at <http://www.childcentre.info/robert/extensions/robert/doc/c346d88f5786691dbb85040d651e8255.pdf> (accessed 8 July 2011).

—— (2008a), 'Protecting Vulnerable Young People in Cyberspace from Sexual Abuse: Raising Awareness and Responding Globally', 9 *Police Practice and Research* 277.

—— (2008b), 'Protecting Children Online Towards a Safer Internet', in G. Letherby, K. Williams, P. Birch, and M. Cain (eds), *Sex as Crime?* (Cullompton, Devon: Willan Publishing).

Davidson, N., Miller, D., and McCafferty, T. (eds) (2010), *Neoliberal Scotland* (Newcastle: Cambridge Scholars Press).

Davis, G., Hoyano, L., Keenan, C., Maitland, L., and Morgan, R. (1999), *An Assessment of the Admissibility and Sufficiency of Evidence in Child Abuse Prosecutions*, A Report for the Home Office by the Department of Law, University of Bristol (London: Home Office).

Davis, L.F. (1980), 'Sex and the Residential Setting', in R.G. Walton and D. Elliott (eds), *Residential Care: A Reader in Current Theory and Practice* (Oxford: Pergamon).

Dawson, R. (1983), *The Abuse of Children in Foster Care: Summary Report* (Ontario: Ontario Family and Children's Services of Oxford County).

Demetriou, C. and Silke, A. (2003), 'A Criminological Internet Sting: Experimental Evidence of Illegal and Deviant Visits to a Website Trap', 43 *British Journal of Criminology* 213.

Denov, M. (2004), *Perspectives on Female Sex Offending: A Culture of Denial* (Hampshire, England: Ashgate Publishing).

Denyer, R.L. (2009), 'Proving Bad Character', *Criminal Law Review* 562.

Department of Children and Youth Affairs (2011), *Children First: National Guidance for the Protection and Welfare of Children* (Dublin: Department of Children and Youth Affairs), available at <http://www.dcya. gov.ie/documents/child_welfare_protection/ChildrenFirst.pdf> (accessed 23 April 2012).

Department for Education for Northern Ireland (DENI) (1999), *Pastoral Care in Schools: Child Protection* (Belfast: DENI).

Department of Health and Social Services (Northern Ireland) (DHSS (NI)) (1982), *Report on Homes and Hostels for Children and Young People in Northern Ireland* (the Sheridan Report) (Belfast: DHSS).

Department of Health, Social Services and Public Safety (DHSSPS) (2008), *Tackling Sexual Violence and Abuse: A Regional Strategy 2008–2013* (Belfast: DHSSPS), available at <http://www.dhsspsni.gov.uk/sexualviolencestrategy08.pdf> (accessed 7 May 2012).

Department of Justice and Law Reform (2009), *The Management of Sex Offenders: A Discussion Document*, available at <http://www.inis.gov. ie/en/JELR/Pages/PB09000022> (accessed 6 March 2012).

Dessecker, A. (2008), *Dangerousness, Long Prison Terms, and Preventive Measures in Germany*, Séminaire GERN. Longues Peines et Peines Indéfinies. Punir la dangerosité. Paris, 21 March 2008, available at <http://champpenal.revues.org/7508> (accessed 19 May 2011).

Devereux, G. (1967), *From Anxiety to Method in the Behavioural Sciences* (The Hague: Mouton).

de Young, M. (1988), 'The Indignant Page: Techniques of Neutralization in the Publications of Pedophilia Organizations', 12 *Child Abuse and Neglect* 583.

Dickson, B. (2001), *The Legal System of Northern Ireland* (4th edn) (Belfast: SLS Publications).

Döring, N.A. (2000), 'Feminist Views of Cybersex: Victimisation, Liberation and Empowerment', 3 *Cyber Psychology* 863.

Douglas, M. (1986), *How Institutions Think* (New York: Syracuse University Press).

Downes, D. (1988), *Contrasts in Tolerance: Post-War Penal Policy in the Netherlands and England and Wales* (Oxford: Oxford University Press).

Doyle, P. (1989), *The God Squad* (London: Corgi Books).

Doyle, T.P., Swipe, A.W.R., and Wall, P.J. (2006), *Sex, Priests and Secret Codes. The Catholic Church's 2000-year Paper Trail of Sexual Abuse* (Los Angeles: Volt Press).

Drake, D., Muncie, J., and Westmarland, L. (eds) (2010), *Criminal Justice: Local and Global* (Cullompton, Devon: Willan Publishing).

Dudai, R. (2012), 'Informers and the Transition in Northern Ireland', 52 *British Journal of Criminology* 32.

Duff, P. and Hutton, N. (eds) (1999), *Criminal Justice in Scotland* (Aldershot: Ashgate).

Duff, R.A. and Garland, D. (1994), 'Introduction: Thinking About Punishment', in R.A. Duff and D. Garland (eds), *A Reader on Punishment* (Oxford: Oxford University Press).

Durham, M.G. (2009), *The Lolita Effect: The Media Sexualization of Young Girls and What We Can Do About It* (London/New York: Duckworth Overlook).

Durkin, K. (1997), 'Misuse of the Internet by Pedophiles: Implications for Law Enforcement and Probation Practice', 61 *Federal Probation* 14.

Durkin, K. and Bryant, C. (1999), 'Propagandising Pederasty: A Thematic Analysis of the Online Exculpatory Accounts of Unrepentant Pedophiles', 20 *Deviant Behaviour: An Interdisciplinary Journal* 103.

ECPAT (2012), *NGO Monitoring Report : ECPAT Sweden*, <http://www.crin.org/docs/resources/treaties/crc.38/Sweden_ECPAT_ngo_report.pdf> (accessed 7 May 2012).

Edwards, S. (2002), 'Prosecuting Child Pornography Possession and Taking Indecent Photographs of Children', 22 *Journal of Social Welfare and Family Law* 1.

Edwards, W. and Hensley, C. (2001a), 'Contextualising Sex Offender Management Legislation and Policy: Evaluating the Problem of Latent Consequences in Community Notification Laws', 45 *International Journal of Offender Therapy and Comparative Criminology* 83.

——(2001b), 'Restructuring Sex Offender Sentencing: A Therapeutic Jurisprudence Approach to the Criminal Justice Process', 45 *International Journal of Offender Therapy and Comparative Criminology* 646.

Eher, R. and Ross, T. (2006), 'Reconsidering Risk for Re-offense in Intrafamilial Child Molesters: New Aspects on Clinical and Criminological Issues', 1 *Sexual Offender Treatment* 1.

Elliott, I.A., Beech, A.R., Mandeville-Norden, R., and Hayes, E. (2009), 'Psychological Profiles of Internet Sexual Offenders: Comparisons with Contact Sexual Offenders', 21 *Journal of Research and Treatment* 76.

Elliott, M., Browne, K., and Kilcoyne, J. (1995), 'Child Abuse Prevention: What Offenders Tell Us', 19 *Child Abuse and Neglect* 579.

eMarketer (2007), 'The Promise of Social Network Advertising', *Media Release* 14 December, available at <http://www.emarketer.com/Article.aspx?R=1005688> (accessed 7 April 2011).

Ericson, R. (2007), *Crime in an Insecure World* (Cambridge: Polity Press).

Ericson, R.V. and Haggerty, K.D. (1997), *Policing the Risk Society* (Oxford: Clarendon Press).

Erooga, M. (2009a), *Towards Safer Organisations: Adults Who Pose a Risk to Children in the Workplace and Implications for Recruitment and Selection*. Executive Summary (February) (NSPCC), available at <http://www.nspcc.org.uk/Inform/research/findings/towardssaferorganisationssummary_wdf63929.pdf> (accessed 22 August 2009).

——(2009b), *Towards Safer Organisations: Adults Who Pose a Risk to Children in the Workplace and Implications for Recruitment and Selection*. Full Report (July) (NSPCC), available at <http://www.nspcc.org.uk/Inform/research/findings/towardssaferorganisationsreport_wdf72972.pdf> (accessed 22 August 2009).

Erooga, M., Allnock, D., and Telford, P. (2012), *Towards Safer Organisations II: Using the Perspectives of Convicted Sex Offenders to Inform Organisational Safeguarding of Children* (London: NSPCC).

Erooga, M., Clark, P., and Bentley, M. (1990), 'Protection, Control, Treatment: Groupwork with Child Sexual Abuse Perpetrators', 3 *Groupwork* 172.

European Commission (2007), *Safer Internet for Children: Qualitative Study in 29 European Countries—Summary Report* (European Commission).

Fahey, T., Russell, H., and Whelan, C.T. (eds) (2007), *Best of Times? The Social Impact of the Celtic Tiger* (Dublin: Institute of Public Administration).

Falshaw, L., Friendship, C., and Bates, A. (2003), *Sexual Offenders—Measuring Reconviction, Reoffending and Recidivism*, Home Office Research Findings, No 183 (London: Home Office).

Farrall, S. (2010), 'What Criminal Justice Policies Might the Lib Dem-Con Government Pursue?', 66 *British Society of Criminology Newsletter* 5.

Fasting, K., Brackenridge, C.H., and Walseth, K. (2002), 'Coping with Sexual Harassment in Sport—Experiences of Elite Female Athletes', in C. Brackenridge and K. Fasting (eds), *Sexual Harassment and Abuse in Sport—International Research and Policy Perspectives*, Special issue, 8 *Journal of Sexual Aggression* 37.

Feeley, M. and Simon, J. (1992), 'The New Penology: Notes on the Emerging Strategy of Corrections and Its Implications', 30 *Criminology* 449.

——(1994), 'Actuarial Justice: the Emerging New Criminal Law', in D. Nelken (ed), *The Futures of Criminology* (London: Sage).

Fenske, A.G. (2007), *Measuring Empathy, Feedback, Therapeutic Alliance and Outcome with Sexual Offenders*. Unpublished study (Newberg, OR: Graduate Department of Clinical Psychology George Fox University).

Fergusson, D.M. and Mullen, P.E. (1999), 'Childhood Sexual Abuse: An Evidence-based Perspective', 40 *Developmental Clinical Psychology and Psychiatry* 581.

Ferguson, H. (1995), 'The Paedophile Priest: A Deconstruction', 84 *Studies* 247.

Fernandez, Y.M. (2006), 'Focusing on the Positive and Avoiding Negativity in Sexual Offender Treatment', in W.L. Marshall, Y.M. Fernandez, L.E. Marshall, and G.A. Serran (eds), *Sexual Offender Treatment: Controversial Issues* (West Sussex: John Wiley and Sons Ltd).

Ferriter, D. (2005), *The Transformation of Ireland, 1900–2000* (London: Profile Books).

Festinger, L. (1957), *A Theory of Cognitive Dissonance* (New York: Harper and Row).

Finkelhor, D. (1979), Sexually Victimized Children (New York: Sage).

—— (1984), *Child Sexual Abuse: New Theory and Research* (New York: The Free Press).

—— (1988), 'The Trauma of Child Sexual Abuse: Two Models', in G.J. Powell (ed), *The Lasting Effects of Child Sexual Abuse* (Newbury Park, Ca: Sage).

Finkelhor, D. and Dziuba-Leatherman, J. (1995), 'Victimization Prevention Programs: A National Survey of Children's Exposure and Reactions', 19 *Child Abuse and Neglect* 129.

Finkelhor, D., Hotaling, G., Lewis, I.A., and Smith, C. (1990), 'Sexual Abuse in a National Survey of Adult Men and Women: Prevalence Characteristics and Risk Factors', 14 *Child Abuse and Neglect* 19.

Finkelhor, D., Mitchell, K.J., and Wolak, J. (2000), *Online Vicimization: A Report on the Nation's Youth* (Alexandria, VA: National Center for Missing and Exploited Children), available at <http://www.missingkids.com/en_US/publications/NC62.pdf> (accessed 29 March 2011).

Finkelhor, D., Williams, L., and Burns, N. (1988), *Nursery Crimes: A Study of Sexual Abuse in Day Care* (Newbury Park, CA: Sage).

Fisher, E. (2002), 'Precaution, Precaution Everywhere: Developing a "Common Understanding" of the Precautionary Principle in the European Community', 9 *Maastricht Journal of European and Comparative Law* 7.

Fitch, K., Spencer Chapman, K., and Hilton, Z. (2007), *Protecting Children from Sexual Abuse: Safer Recruitment of Workers in a Border-free Europe* (London: NSPCC), available at <http://www.nspcc.org.uk/Inform/publications/downloads/protectingchildrenfromsexualabuseineuropefullreport_wdf54737.pdf> (accessed 28 November 2011).

Forde, L. (1999), *The Commission of Inquiry into Abuse of Children in Queensland Institutions—Final Report* (Brisbane: Government of Queensland).

Formicola, J.R. (2004), 'The Vatican, the American Bishops, and the Church-State Ramifications of Clerical Sexual Abuse', 46 *Journal of Church and State* 479.

Foucault, M. (1977), *Discipline and Punish: The Birth of the Prison* (London: Penguin).

Francis, P. and Turner, N. (1995), 'Sexual Misconduct Within the Christian Church: Who are the Perpetrators and Those They Abuse?', 39 *Counselling and Values* 218.

Frawley-O'Dea, M.G. (2007), *Perversion of Power: Sexual Abuse in the Catholic Church* (Nashville, Tennessee: Vanderbilt University Press).

Frey, L.L. (2010), 'The Juvenile Female Sexual Offenders: Characteristics, Treatment and Research', in T.A. Gannon and F. Cortoni (eds), *Female Sexual Offenders: Theory, Assessment and Treatment* (Chichester: Wiley-Blackwell).

Friedrichs, D.O. (1996), *Trusted Criminals: White-Collar Crime in Contemporary Society* (New York: Wadsworth Publishing Co).

Friendship, C. and Thornton, D. (2001), 'Sexual Reconviction for Sexual Offenders Discharged From Prison in England and Wales: Implications for Evaluating Treatment', 41 *British Society of Criminology* 285.

Frizell, E. (2009), *Independent Inquiry into Abuse at Kerelaw Residential School and Secure Unit*, jointly commissioned by the Scottish Government and Glasgow City Council (Edinburgh: The Scottish Government).

Frost, A. (2011), 'Bringing "Good Lives" to Life: Applying Social Therapy to Working with Sexual Offenders', in D.P. Boer, R. Eher, L.A. Craig, M.H. Miner, and F. Pfäfflin (eds), *International Perspectives on the Assessment and Treatment of Sexual Offenders* (Chichester: Wiley-Blackwell).

Fulda, J.S. (2007), 'Internet Stings Directed at Pedophiles: A Study in Philosophy and Law', 11 *Sexuality and Culture* 52.

Furedi, F. (2006a), *Politics of Fear: Beyond Left and Right* (2nd edn) (London: Continnum International Publishing Group Ltd).

——(2006b), *Culture of Fear Revisited* (2nd rev edn) (London: Continnum International Publishing Group Ltd).

Furedi, F. and Bristow, J. (2008), *Licensed to Hug: How Child Protection Policies are Poisoning the Relationship between the Generations* (London: Civitas).

Gallagher, B. (1998), *Grappling With Smoke: Investigating and Managing Organised Abuse—A Good Practice Guide* (London: NSPCC).

——(1999), 'Institutional Abuse', in N. Parton and C. Wattam (eds), *Child Sexual Abuse: Responding to the Experiences of Children* (New York: Wiley Publishers).

——(2000), 'The Extent and Nature of Known Cases of Institutional Child Sexual Abuse', 30 *British Journal of Social Work* 795.

Gallagher, B., Christmann, K., Fraser, C., and Hodgson, B. (2003), 'International and Internet Child Sexual Abuse and Exploitation: Issues Emerging From Research', 15 *Child and Family Law Quarterly* 353.

——(2006), *International and Internet Child Sexual Abuse and Exploitation*, Research Report (Huddersfield: University of Huddersfield, Centre for Applied Childhood Studies).

Gambetta, D. (1988), 'Can We Trust Trust?', in D. Gambetta (ed), *Trust: Making and Breaking Co-operative Relations* (Oxford: Basil Blackwell).

Gannon, T.A. and Cortoni, F. (eds) (2010), *Female Sexual Offenders: Theory, Assessment and Treatment* (Chichester: Wiley-Blackwell).

Gannon, T.A., Rose, M.R., and Ward, T. (2008), 'Pathways to Female Sexual Offending: Approach or Avoidance?', 20 *Sexual Abuse: A Journal of Research and Treatment* 352.

Garland, D. (1985), *Punishment and Welfare: A History of Penal Strategies* (Aldershot: Gower).

——(1990), *Punishment and Modern Society* (Oxford: Clarendon Press).

——(1996), 'The Limits of the Sovereign State: Strategies of Crime Control in Contemporary Society', 36 *British Journal of Criminology* 445.

——(1999a), 'The Commonplace and the Catastrophic: Interpretations of Crime in Late Modernity', 3 *Theoretical Criminology* 353.

——(1999b), 'Preface', in P. Duff and N. Hutton (eds), *Criminal Justice in Scotland* (Aldershot: Ashgate).

——(2001), *The Culture of Control: Crime and Social Order in Contemporary Society* (Oxford: Oxford University Press).

Garland, D. and Sparks, R. (2000), 'Criminology Social Theory and the Challenge of Our Times', 40 *British Journal of Criminology* 189.

Garlick, R. (1994), 'Male and Female Responses to Ambiguous Instructor Behaviours', 30 *Sex Roles* 135.

Geary, J. and Lambie, I. (2006), *Turning Lives Around: A Process Evaluation of Community Adolescent Sexual Offender Treatment Programmes in New Zealand*. Report commissioned by the Department of Child Youth and Family (Auckland: Auckland Uniservices Ltd).

Gelles, R. (1986), *Family Violence* (Thousand Oaks, CA: Sage Publications).

Giaretto, H. (1978), 'Humanistic Treatment of Father/Daughter Incest', 18 *Journal of Humanistic Psychology* 59.

Gilbert, R., Widom, C.S., Browne, K., Fergusson, D., Webb, E., and Janson, S. (2009), 'Burden and Consequences of Child Maltreatment in High-income Countries', 373 *Lancet* 68.

Gillespie, A.A. (2001), 'Children, Chatrooms and the Law', *Criminal Law Review* 435.

——(2002a), 'Child Protection on the Internet—Challenges for Criminal Law', 14 *Child and Family Law Quarterly* 411.

——(2002b), 'Entrapment on the "Net"', 7 *Journal of Civil Liberties* 143.

——(2004a), '"Grooming": Definitions and the Law', 154 *New Law Journal* 586.

——(2004b), 'Internet Grooming: The New Law', 204 *Childright* 10.

——(2004c), 'Tackling Grooming', 77 *The Police Journal* 239.

——(2005), 'Tackling Child Grooming on the Internet: The UK Approach', 10 *Bar Review* 4.

——(2006), 'Enticing Children on the Internet: The Response of the Criminal Law', 3 *Juridical Review* 229.

——(2007a), 'Barring Teachers: The New Vetting Arrangements', 19 *Education and the* Law 1.

——(2007b), 'The Future of Child Protection and the Criminal Law', 17 *Irish Criminal Law Journal* 2.

——(2008), 'Cyber-Stings: Policing Sex Offences on the Internet', 81 *The Police Journal* 196.

Gilligan, P. and Ahktar, S. (2006), 'Cultural Barriers to Disclosure of Child Sexual Abuse in Asian Communities: What Women Say', 36 *British Journal of Social Work* 1361.

Gilling, D. (2007), *Crime Reduction and Community Safety: Labour and the Politics of Local Crime Control* (Cullompton, Devon: Willan Publishing).

Giroux, H.A. (2002), 'Democracy and the Politics of Terrorism: Community, Fear, and the Suppression of Dissent', 2 *Cultural Studies* 334.

Glaser, B. and Straus, A. (1967), *The Discovery of Grounded Theory: Strategies for Qualitative Research* (New York: Aldine Publishing Co).

Goldthorpe, L. (2004), 'Every Child Matters: A Legal Perspective', 13 *Child Abuse* 115.

Good, D. (1988), 'Individuals, Interpersonal Relations and Trust', in D. Gambetta (ed), *Trust: Making and Breaking Co-operative Relations* (Oxford: Basil Blackwell).

Goodstein, A. (2007), *Totally Wired: What Teens and Tweens are Really Doing Online* (New York, NY: St Martin's Press).

Gottschalk, P. (2011), 'Stage Model for Online Grooming Offenders', in J. Davidson and P. Gottschalk (eds), *Internet Child Abuse: Current Research and Policy* (Abingdon: Routledge).

Greer, C. (2003), *Sex Crime and the Media: Sex Offending and the Press in a Divided Society* (Cullompton, Devon: Willan Publishing).

Griffith, G. and Roth, L. (2007), 'Protecting Children from Online Sexual Predators', *NSW Parliamentary Library Briefing Paper No 10/07* (Sydney: NSW Parliamentary Library).

Grimshaw, R. (2004), 'Whose Justice? Principal Drivers of Criminal Justice Policy, Their Implications for Stakeholders, and Some Foundations for Critical Policy Departures', Papers Presented at the *British Society of Criminology Conference*, vol 7.

Groth, A.N., Hobson, W.F., and Gary, T.S. (1982), 'The Child Molester: Clinical Observations', in J. Conte and D. Shored (eds), *Social Work and Child Sexual Abuse* (New York: Haworth).

Groth, A.N., Longo, R.E., and McFadin, J.B. (1982), 'Undetected Recidivism among Rapists and Child Molesters', 23 *Crime and Delinquency* 450.

Gruber, K.J. and Jones, R.J. (1983), 'Identifying Determinants of Risk of Sexual Victimization of Youth', 7 *Child Abuse and Neglect* 17.

Grubin, D. (1998), *Sex Offending Against Children: Understanding the Risk*, Police Research Series Paper 99 (London: Home Office).

Grubin, D.H. and Thornton, D. (1994), 'A National Programme for the Assessment and Treatment of Sex Offenders in the English Prison System', 21 *Criminal Justice and Behaviour* 55.

Hacking, I. (1999), *The Social Construction of What?* (Cambridge, MA: Harvard University Press).

Hall, G.C. and Hirschman, R. (1992), 'Sexual Aggression against Children: A Conceptual Perspective of Etiology', 19 *Criminal Justice and Behaviour* 8.

Hall, M. (2000), 'After Waterhouse: Vicarious Liability and the Tort of Institutional Abuse', 22 *Journal of Social Welfare and Family Law* 159.

Halpern, J. (2003), 'What is Clinical Empathy?', 18 *Journal of Intern Medicine* 670.

Hanson, R.F., Resnick, H.S., Kilpatrick, D.G., and Best, C. (1999), 'Factors Related to the Reporting of Childhood Rape', 23 *Child Abuse and Neglect* 559.

Hanvey, S., Philpot, T., and Wilson, C. (2011), *A Community-Based Approach to the Reduction of Sexual Offending: Circles of Support and Accountability* (London and Philadelphia: Jessica Kingsley Publishers).

Hare, R.D. and Hart, S.D. (1993), 'Psychopathy, Mental Disorder and Crime', in S. Hogdson (ed), *Mental Disorder and Crime* (Thousand Oaks, CA: Sage Publications).

Harris, A.R. and Hanson, R.K. (2004), 'Sex Offender Recidivism—A Simple Question. Public Safety and Emergency Preparedness Canada', available at <http://www.publicsafety.gc.ca/res/cor/rep/2004-03-se-off-eng.aspx> (accessed 23 January 2012).

Harris, D.A. (2010), 'Theories of Female Sexual Offending', in T.A. Gannon and F. Cortoni (eds), *Female Sexual Offenders: Theory, Assessment and Treatment* (Chichester: Wiley-Blackwell).

Harrison, C. (2006), 'Cyberspace and Child Abuse Images: A Feminist Perspective', 21 *Affilia: Journal of Women and Social Work* 365–79.

Harrison, F. (1977), *The Dark Angel: Aspects of Victorian Sexuality* (London: Sheldon Press).

Harrison, K. (2011), *Dangerousness, Risk and the Governance of Serious Sexual and Violent Offenders* (London: Routledge).

Harrison, K., Manning, R., and McCartan, K.F. (2010), 'Current Multidisciplinary Definitions and Understandings of "Paedophilia"', 19 *Social and Legal Studies* 481.

Harvie, P. and Manzi, T. (2011), 'Interpreting Multi-Agency Partnerships: Ideology, Discourse and Domestic Violence', 20 *Social and Legal Studies* 79.

Hasebrink, U., Livingstone, S., and Haddon, L. (2008), *Comparing Children's Online Opportunities and Risks Across Europe: Cross-national Comparisons for EU Kids* (London: EU Kids On-line).

Haugaard, J.J. and Reppucci, N.D. (1988), *The Sexual Abuse of Children: A Comprehensive Guide to Current Knowledge and Intervention Strategies* (San Francisco and London: Jossey-Boss Publishers).

Haywood, T., Kravitz, H., Grossman, L., Wasyliw, O., and Hardy, D. (1996), 'Psychological Aspects of Sexual Functioning among Cleric and Noncleric Alleged Sex Offenders', 20 *Child Abuse and Neglect* 527.

Hebenton, B. and Thomas, T. (1996), 'Tracking Sex Offenders', 35 *The Howard Journal of Criminal Justice* 97.

Hebenton, B. and Seddon, T. (2009), 'From Dangerousness to Precaution: Managing Sexual and Violent Offenders in an Insecure and Uncertain Age', 49 *British Journal of Criminology* 343.

Hendrick, H. (2003), *Child Welfare: Historical Dimensions, Contemporary Debate* (Bristol: Policy Press).

Henry, F. and Tabachnick, J. (2002), 'Stop it Now!: The Campaign to Prevent Child Sexual Abuse', in B. Schwartz (ed), *The Sex Offender: Vol 4* (Kingston: New Jersey, Civic Research Institute).

Her Majesty's (HM) Government (2010), *Call to End Violence against Women and Girls* (London: Home Office).

Her Majesty's Stationery Office (HMSO) (1985), *Report of the Committee of Inquiry into Children's Homes and Hostels* (the Hughes Report) (London: HMSO).

Herman, J.L. (1981), *Father-Daughter Incest* (Cambridge, Massachusetts: Harvard University Press).

—— (1997), *Trauma and Recovery* (New York: Basic Books).

Hershkowitz, I., Lanes, O., and Lamb, M.E. (2007), 'Exploring the Disclosure of Child Sexual Abuse with Alleged Victims and their Parents', 31 *Child Abuse and Neglect* 111.

Hetherton, J. (1999), 'The Idealisation of Women: Its Role in the Minimisation of Child Sexual Abuse by Females', 23 *Child Abuse and Neglect* 161.

Hofmeyr, K. (2006), 'The Problem of Private Entrapment', *Criminal Law Review* 319.

Hogan, G. (2005), 'De Valera, the Constitution and the Historians', 40 *Irish Jurist* 293.

Hogue, T.E. and Peebles, J. (1997), 'The Influence of Remorse, Intent and Attitudes Toward Sex Offenders on Judgments of a Rapist', 3 *Psychology, Crime and Law* 249.

Hollin, C.R. and Howells, K. (1991), *Clinical Approaches to Sex Offenders and their Victims* (Chichester: Wiley).

Holman, B. (1996), *The Corporate Parent, Manchester Children's Department 1948–1971* (London: National Institute for Social Work).

Holt, T., Blevins, K., and Burkert, N. (2010), 'Considering the Pedophile Subculture Online', 22 *Sexual Abuse: A Journal of Research and Treatment* 3.

Home Office (1996), *Protecting the Public: The Government's Strategy on Crime in England and Wales* (Cm 3190) (London: HMSO).

——(1997), *The Sex Offenders Act 1997, Home Office* Circular 39/97 (London: Home Office).

——(2000), *Setting the Boundaries: Reforming the Law on Sex Offences* (London: Home Office).

——(2002), *Protecting the Public: Strengthening Protection Against Sex Offenders and Reforming the Law on Sexual Offences*, Cm 5668 (London: HMSO).

Hope, T. and Murphy, D.J.I. (1983), 'Problems of Implementing Crime Prevention: The Experience of a Demonstration Project', 22 *Howard Journal* 38.

Horgan, G. (2006), 'Devolution, Direct Rule and Neo-liberal Reconstruction in Northern Ireland', 26 *Critical Social Policy* 656.

Hörnle, J. (2011), 'Countering the Dangers of Online Pornography—Shrewd Regulation of Lewd Content', 2 *European Journal of Law and Technology* 1.

Hough, M., Millie, A., and Jacobson, J. (2005), *Anti-social Behaviour Strategies: Finding a Balance* (Bristol: Policy Press).

Howard, C.A. (1993), 'Factors Influencing a Mother's Response to her Child's Disclosure of Incest', 24 *Professional Psychology: Research and Practice* 176.

Howells, K. (1981), 'Adult Sexual Interest in Children: Considerations Relevant to Theories of Etiology', in M. Cook and K. Howells (eds), *Adult Sexual Interest in Children* (London: Academic Press).

Howitt, D. (1995), *Paedophiles and Sexual Offences Against Children* (Oxford: John Wiley and Sons).

Hoyle, C. (1998), *Negotiating Domestic Violence: Police, Criminal Justice and Victims* (Oxford: Oxford University Press).

Hudson, B. (2002), 'Restorative Justice and Gendered Violence: Diversion or Effective Justice?', 42 *British Journal of Criminology* 616.

Hudson, K. (2005), *Offending Identities: Sex Offenders' Perspectives on their Treatment and Management* (Cullompton, Devon: Willan Publishing).

Hughes, B., Parker, H., and Gallagher, B. (1996), *Policing Child Sexual Abuse: The View from Police Practitioners* (London: Home Office Police Research Group Report).

Hunt, P. (1994), *Report of the Inquiry into Multiple Abuse in Nursery Classes in Newcastle Upon Tyne* (Newcastle Upon Tyne: City Council of Newcastle Upon Tyne).

Hunter, J.A., Goodwin, D.W., and Wilson, R.J. (1992), 'Attributions of Blame in Child Sexual Abuse Victims: An Analysis of Age and Gender Influences', 1 *Journal of Child Sexual Abuse* 75.

Huxham, C. and Vangen, S. (2005), *Managing to Collaborate: The Theory and Practice of Collaborative Advantage* (London: Routledge).

Inglis, T. (1998), *Moral Monopoly: The Rise and Fall of the Catholic Church in Ireland* (2nd edn) (Dublin: University College Dublin Press).

——(2005), 'Origins and Legacies of Irish Prudery: Sexuality and Social Control in Modern Ireland', 40 *Éire-Ireland* 9.

Innes, M. (2004), 'Signal Crimes and Signal Disorders: Notes on Deviance as Communicative Action', 55 *British Journal of Sociology* 335.

Internet Crime Forum (ICF) (2001), *Chat Wise Street Wise* (Internet Crime Forum), available at <http://www.internetcrimeforum.org.uk/chatwise_streetwise.html> (accessed 18 February 2011).

Itzin, C. (ed) (2000), *Home Truths About Child Sexual Abuse, Influencing Policy and Practice: A Reader* (London and New York: Routledge).

——(2001), 'Incest, Paedophila, Pornography and Prostitution: Making Familial Males More Visible as the Abusers', 10 *Child Abuse Review* 35.

Jacobs, J.B. and Blitsa, D. (2008), 'Major "minor" Progress Under the Third Pillar: EU Institutions Building in the Sharing of Criminal Record Information', 8 *Chicago-Kent Journal of International and Comparative Law* 111.

Jacobson, J. and Hough, M. (2010), *Unjust Deserts: Imprisonment for Public Protection* (London: Prison Reform Trust).

Jackson, S. and Scott, S. (1999), 'Risk Anxiety and the Social Construction of Childhood', in D. Lupton (ed), *Risk and Socio-cultural Theory: New Directions and Perspectives* (Cambridge: Cambridge University Press).

Jenkins, P. (1996), Paedophiles and Priests: Anatomy of a Contemporary Crisis (Oxford: Oxford University Press).

——(2001), 'How Europe Discovered Its Sex Offender Crisis', in J. Best (ed), *How Claims Spread: Cross-National Diffusion of Social Problems* (New York: De Gruyter).

Jeyes, G. (2011), 'Protecting Children: A Community Responsibility', 7 *Health Matters* 55.

John Jay College (2004), *The Nature and Scope of Sexual Abuse of Minors by Catholic Priests and Deacons in the United States, 1950–2002* (Washington, DC: United States Conference of Catholic Bishops).

——(2011), *The Causes and Context of Sexual Abuse of Minors by Catholic Priests in the United States, 1950–2010, A Report Presented to the United States Conference of Catholic Bishops by the John Jay College Research Team* (Washington, DC: United States Conference of Catholic Bishops).

Johnson-George, C. and Swap, W. (1982), 'Measurement of Specific Interpersonal Trust: Construction and Validation of a Scale to Assess Trust in a Specific Other', 43 *Journal of Personality and Social Psychology* 1306.

Johnstone, G. (2000), 'Penal Policy Making: Elitist, Populist or Participatory?', 2 *Punishment and Society* 161.

Jones, T. and Newburn, T. (2005), 'Pressure Groups, Politics and Comparative Penal Reform: Sex Offender Registration and Notification in the USA and UK', Paper presented at the annual meeting of the American Society of Criminology, Toronto, November.

——(2006), 'Three Strikes and You're Out: Exploring Symbol and Substance in American and British Crime Control Politics', 46 *British Journal of Criminology* 781.

Kahan, B. (2000). 'Residential Child Care After Waterhouse', *Children Webmag,* March, available at <http://www.davidlane.org/children/chukmar/index.htm> (accessed 16 August 2011).

Kaufman, K.L., Hilliker, D.R., and Daleiden, E.L. (1996), 'Sub group Differences in the Modus Operandi of Adolescent Sexual Offenders', 1 *Child Maltreatment* 17.

Kaufman, K.L., Holmberg, J.K., Orts, K.A., McCrady, F.E., Rotzien, A.L., and Daleiden, E.L., and Hilliker, D.R. (eds) (1998), 'Factors Influencing Sexual Offenders' Modus Operandi: An Examination of Victim-Offender Relatedness and Age', 3 *Child Maltreatment* 349.

Kaufman, K.L., Wallace, A.M., Johnson, C.F., and Reeder, M.L. (1995), 'Comparing Female and Male Perpetrators' Modus Operandi: Victims' Reports of Sexual Abuse', 10 *Journal of Interpersonal Violence* 322.

Keary, K. and Fitzpatrick, C. (1994), 'Children's Disclosure of Sexual Abuse during Formal Investigation', 18 *Child Abuse and Neglect* 543.

Keating, M. (ed) (2007), *Scottish Social Democracy: Progressive Ideas for Public Policy* (Brussels: Peter Lang).

Kee, H.W. and Knox, R.E. (1970), 'Conceptual and Methodological Considerations in the Study of Trust', 14 *Journal of Conflict Resolution* 357.

Keenan, M. (2006), 'The Institution and the Individual', 57 *The Furrow* 3.

——(2011), *Child Sexual Abuse and the Catholic Church: Gender, Power and Organizational Culture* (New York: Oxford University Press).

Kelly, G. (1990), *Pattern of Child-Care Careers and the Decisions That Shape Them* (Belfast: Queen's University, Department of Social Studies).

Kelly, G. and Pinkerton, J. (1996), 'The Children (Northern Ireland) Order 1995: Prospects for Progress?', in M. Hill, and J. Aldgate (eds), Child Welfare Services: Developments in Law, Policy, Practice and Research (London: Jessica Kingsley Publishers).

Kelly, L. (1988), *Surviving Sexual Violence* (Cambridge: Polity Press).

Kelly, L., Regan, L., and Burton, S. (2000), 'Sexual Exploitation: A New Discovery of One Part of the Continuum of Sexual Abuse in Childhood', in C. Itzin (ed), *Home Truths About Child Sexual Abuse: Influencing Policy and Practice—A Reader* (London: Routledge).

Kempe, H. (1978), 'Sexual Abuse: Another Hidden Pediatric Problem', 62 *Pediatrics* 382.

Kemshall, H. (2001), *Risk Assessment and Management of Known Sexual and Violent Offenders: A Review of Current Issues*, Police Research Series Paper No 140 (London: Home Office).

——(2004), 'Female Sex Offenders', in H. Kemshall and G. McIvor (eds), *Managing Sex Offender Risk* (London: Jessica Kingsley Publishers).

——(2008), *Understanding the Community Management of High Risk Offenders* (Maidenhead: Open University Press).

Kemshall, H., Mackenzie, G., and Wood J. (2004), *Stop it Now! UK and Ireland: An Evaluation* (Leicester: De Monfort University and London: Stop it Now!).

Kemshall, H. and Maguire, M. (2001), 'Public Protection, Partnership and Risk Penalty: The Multi-agency Risk Management of Sexual and Violent Offenders', 3 *Punishment and Society* 237.

——(2002), 'Community Justice, Risk Management and the Role of Multi-Agency Public Protection Panels', 1 *British Journal of Community Justice* 11.

——(2003), 'Sex Offenders, Risk Penality and the Problem of Disclosure', in A. Matravers (ed), *Sex Offenders in the Community: Managing and Reducing the Risks* (Cullompton, Devon: Willan Publishing).

Kemshall, H. and McIvor, G. (eds) (2004), *Managing Sex Offender Risk* (London: Jessica Kingsley Publishers).

Kemshall, H., Parton, N., Walsh, M., and Waterson, J. (1997), 'Concepts of Risk in Relation to the Organisational Structure and Functioning within the Personal Social Services and Probation', 31 *Social Policy and Administration* 213.

Kemshall, H. and Wood, J. (2007), 'Beyond Public Protection: An Examination of Community Protection and Public Health Approaches to High-Risk Offenders', 7 *Criminology and Criminal Justice* 203.

Kemshall, H., Wood, J., Westwood, S., Stout, B., Wilkinson, B., Kelly, G., and Mackenzie, G. (2010), *Child Sex Offender Review* (CSOR) *Public Disclosure Pilots: A Process Evaluation* (4th edn) (London: Home Office).

Kendrick, A. (1995), *Residential Care in the Integration of Child Care Services* (Edinburgh: The Scottish Office Central Research Unit).

—— (2005), 'Social Exclusion and Social Inclusion: Themes and Issues in Residential Child Care', in D. Crimmens and I. Milligan (eds), *Facing Forward: Residential Child Care in the 21st Century* (Lyme Regis: Russell House Publishing).

Kennedy Commission (1970), *Reformatory and Industrial Schools System Report* (the Kennedy Report) (Dublin: The Stationery Office).

Kent, R. (1997), *Children's Safeguards Review* (Edinburgh: Scottish Office).

Keogh, D. and McCarthy, A. (2007), *The Making of the Irish Constitution* (Cork: Mercier Press).

Kerr, A. (1999), *Protecting Disabled Children and Adults in Sport and Recreation: The Guide* (Leeds: National Coaching Foundation).

Khan, A. (2004), 'Sexual Offences Act 2003', 68 *Journal of Criminal Law* 220.

Kierkegaard, S. (2008), 'Cybering, Online Grooming and Ageplay', 24 *Computer Law and Security Report* 41.

Kiesler, S.J., Siegel, J., and McGuire, T.W. (1984), 'Social Psychological Aspects of Computer-mediated Communications', 39 *American Psychologist* 1123.

Kilbrandon Committee (1964), *Children and Young Persons in Scotland: Report by the Committee appointed by the Secretary of State for Scotland*, Cmnd 2306 (Edinburgh: HMSO).

Kilcommins, S., O'Donnell, I., O'Sullivan, E., and Vaughan, B. (2004), *Crime, Punishment and the Search for Order in Ireland* (Dublin: Institute of Public Administration).

Kincaid, J.R. (1998), *Erotic Innocence: The Culture of Child Molesting* (Durham and London: Duke University Press).

Kirby, S., Francis, B., Harman, J., and Soothill, K. (2005), 'Identifying Future Repeat Danger from Sexual Offenders Against Children: A Focus on those Convicted and those Strongly Suspected of Such Crime', 16 *Journal of Forensic Psychiatry and Psychology* 225.

Kirby, S. and Greaves, L. (1996), 'Foul Play: Sexual Abuse and Harrassment in Sport', paper presented to the Pre-Olympic Scientific Congress, Dallas, United States, 11–14 July.

Kirkwood, A. (1993), *The Report of the Inquiry into Aspects of the Management of Children's Homes in Leicestershire between 1973 and 1986* (Leicester: Leicestershire County Council).

Kleinhans, M.M. (2002), 'Criminal Justice Approaches to Paedophilic Sex Offenders', 11 *Social and Legal Studies* 233.

Kline, P.M., McMackin, R., and Lezotte, E. (2008), 'The Impact of the Clergy Sexual Abuse Scandal on Parish Communities', 17 *Journal of Child Sexual Abuse* 290.

Knox, C. (2002), 'See No Evil, Hear No Evil: Insidious Paramilitary Violence in Northern Ireland', 42 *British Journal of Criminology* 164.

Koefed, J. and Ringrose, J. (2011), 'Travelling and Sticky Affects: Exploring Teens and Sexualized Cyberbullying through a Butlerian-Deleuzian-Guattarian Lens', 33 *Discourse: Studies in the Cultural Politics of Education* 1.

Kool, R. (2011), 'Prevention by All Means: A Legal Comparison of the Crimininalization of Online grooming and its Enforcement', 7 *Utrecht Law Review* 46.

Kosaraju, A. (2008), 'Grooming: The Myth and Reality of Child Sexual Exploitation', 246 *Childright* 14.

Kramer, R.M., Brewer, M.B., and Hanna B. (1996), 'Collective Trust and Collective Action: Trust as a Social Decision', in R. Kramer and T. Tyler (eds), *Trust in Organisations* (Thousand Oaks, CA: Sage Publications).

Krone, T. (2005), 'International Police Operations against Online Child Pornography', 296 *Trends and Issues in Crime and Criminal Justice* 1.

Lacey, N. (1987), 'A Clear Concept of Intention: Elusive or Illusory?', 56 *Modern Law Review* 621.

——(2004), 'Criminalisation as Regulation', in C. Parker, C. Scott, N. Lacey, and J. Braithwaite (eds), *Regulating Law* (Oxford: Oxford University Press).

La Fontaine, J. (1990), *Child Sexual Abuse* (Cambridge: Polity Press).

La Fontaine, J. and Morris, S. (1991), *The Boarding School Line: January–July 1991. A Report from ChildLine to the DES* (London: ChildLine).

Lamb, M. (1998), 'Cybersex: Research Notes on the Characteristics of Visitors to Online Chat rooms', 19 *Deviant Behaviour: An Interdisciplinary Journal* 121.

Lamb, M.E. and Brown, D.A. (2006), 'Conversational Apprentices: Helping Children Become Competent Informants about their Own Experiences', 24 *British Journal of Development Psychology* 215.

Lang, R.A. and Frenzel, R.R. (1988), 'How Sex Offenders Lure Children', 1 *Annals of Sex Research* 303.

Langevin, R., Curnoe, S., and Bain, J. (2000), 'A Study of Clerics who Commit Sexual Offenses: Are They Different from other Sex Offenders?', 24 *Child Abuse and Neglect* 535.

Lanning, K.V. (1998), 'Cyber "Pedophiles": A Behavioural Perspective', 11 *American Professional Society on the Abuse of Children Advisor* 12.

Lanning, K.V. (2002), 'Law Enforcement Perspective on the Compliant Child Victim', 14 *American Professional Society on the Abuse of Children Advisor* 4.

Law, A. (2005), 'Welfare Nationalism: Social Justice and/or Entrepreneurial Scotland', in G. Mooney and G. Scott (eds), *Exploring Social Policy in the 'New' Scotland* (Bristol: Policy Press).

Law Commission of Canada (2000), *Restoring Dignity: Responding to Child Abuse in Canadian Institutions* (Canada: Law Commission of Canada).

Law Reform Commission (LRC) (2010), *Consultation Paper on Hearsay in Civil and Criminal Cases*, LRC CP 60–2010 (Dublin: Law Reform Commission).

Laws, D.R. (1996), 'Relapse Prevention or Harm Reduction?', 8 *Sexual Abuse: A Journal of Research and Treatment* 243.

——(2000), 'Sexual Offending as a Public Health Problem: A North American Perspective', 8 *Journal of Research and Treatment* 243.

——(2008), 'The Public Health Approach: A Way Forward?', in D.R. Laws and W.T. O'Donohue (eds), *Sexual Deviance: Theory, Assessment and Treatment* (New York: Guildford Press).

Leahy, T., Pretty, G., and Tenenbaum, G. (2002), 'Prevalence of Sexual Abuse in Organised Competitive Sport in Australia', 8 *Journal of Sexual Aggression* 16.

Leberg, E. (1997), *Understanding Child Molesters: Taking Charge* (Thousand Oaks, CA: Sage Publications).

Leclerc, B., Beauregard, E., and Proulx, J. (2008), 'Modus Operandi and Situational Aspects in Adolescent Sexual Offenses Against Children: A Further Examination', 52 *International Journal of Offender Therapy and Comparative Criminology* 46.

Leclerc, B., Proulx, J., and McKibben, A. (2005), 'Modus Operandi of Sexual Offenders Working or Doing Voluntary Work with Children and Adolescents', 11 *Journal of Sexual Aggression* 187.

Leclerc, B., Wortley, R., and Smalbone, S. (2010), 'An Exploratory Study of Victim Resistance in Child Sexual Abuse: Offender Modus Operandi and Victim Characteristics', 22 *Sexual Abuse: A Journal of Research and Treatment* 25.

——(2011), 'Victim Resistance in Child Sexual Abuse: A Look into the Efficacy of Self-Protection Strategies Based on the Offender's Experience', 26 *Journal of Interpersonal Violence* 1868.

Leggett, S. (2000), 'Paedophiles and Other Child Abusers', 5 *The Ulster Humanist* 7.

Lenhart, A. (2009), 'Teens and Sexting: How and Why Minor Teens are Sending Sexually Suggestive Nude or Nearly Nude Images via Text Messaging', Pew Research Centre Report, available at <http://pewresearch.org/assets/pdf/teens-and-sexting.pdf> (accessed 7 May 2012).

Lenhart, A. and Madden, M. (2007), *Social Networking Websites and Teens: An Overview* (Washington DC: Pew Internet and American Life Project), available at <http://www.pewinternet.org/Reports/2007/Social-Networking-Websites-and-Teens.aspx> (accessed 7 April 2011).

Levenson, J.S., Brannon, Y.N., Fortney, T., and Baker, J. (2007), 'Public Perceptions about Sexual Offenders and Community Protection Policies', 7 *Analyses of Social Issues and Public Policy* 1.

Levin, D.E. and Kilbourne, J. (2009), *So Sexy So Soon: The New Sexualized Childhood and What Parents Can do to Protect their Kids* (New York: Ballantine books).

Levy, A. and Kahan, B. (1991), *The Pindown Experience and the Protection of Children: the Report of the Staffordshire Child Care Inquiry 1990* (Stafford: Staffordshire County Council).

Levy, N. (2002), 'In Defence of Entrapment in Journalism (and Beyond)', 19 *Journal of Applied Philosophy* 121.

Lewis, P. and Mullis, A. (1999), 'Delayed Prosecution for Childhood Sexual Abuse', 115 *Law Quarterly Review* 265.

Liberty (2003), *Liberty's Second Reading Briefing on the Sex Offences Bill in the House of Lords*, available at <http://www.liberty-human-rights.org.uk/pdfs/policy03/sex-offences-bill-2nd-reading-lords.pdf> (accessed 28 November 2011).

Lieb, R. (2000), 'Social Policy and Sexual Offenders: Contrasting United States and European Policies', 8 *European Journal on Criminal Policy and Research* 423.

Lieb, R. (2003), 'Joined-up Worrying: the Multi-Agency Public Protection Panels', in A. Matravers (ed), *Sex Offenders in the Community: Managing and Reducing the Risks* (Cullompton, Devon: Willan Publishing, Cambridge Criminal Justice Series).

Liddle, A.M. and Gelsthorpe, L.R. (1994), *Inter-agency Crime Prevention: Organising Local Delivery*, Police Research Group, Crime Prevention Unit Series Paper No 52 (London: Home Office).

Lippert, T., Cross, T.P., Jones, L., and Walsh, W. (2010), 'Suspect Confession of Child Sexual Abuse to Investigators', 15 *Child Maltreatment* 161.

Livingstone, S. (2005), *UK Children Go Online: Emerging Opportunities and Dangers* (London: London School of Economics).

—— (2009), *Children and the Internet: Great Expectations and Challenging Realities* (Cambridge: Polity).

Livingstone, S. and Bober, M. (2004), *UK Children Go Online: Surveying the Experiences of Young People and their Parents* (London: London School of Economics).

—— (2005), *Internet Literacy among Children and Young People* (London: London School of Economics).

Livingstone, S. and Hadden, L. (2009), *Kids Online: Opportunities and Risks for Children* (Bristol: Policy Press).

Livingstone, S. and Helsper, E. (2007), 'Taking Risks when Communicating on the Internet: The Role of Offline Social-psychological Factors in Young People's Vulnerability to Online Risks', 10 *Information, Communication and Society* 619.

—— (2009), 'Balancing Opportunities and Risks in Teenagers' Use of the Internet: The Role of Online Skills and Internet Self-efficacy', 12 *New Media and Society* 309.

Llewellyn, J. (2002), 'Dealing with the Legacy of Native Residential School Abuse in Canada: Litigation, ADR and Restorative Justice', 52 *University of Toronto Law Journal* 253.

Loader, I. and Walker, N. (2007), *Civilizing Security* (Cambridge: Cambridge University Press).

Loftus, J. and Camargo, R. (1993), 'Treating the Clergy', 6 *Annals of Sex Research* 287.

Long, B. and McLachlan, B. (2002), *The Hunt for Britain's Paedophiles* (London: Hodder and Stoughton).

Lounsbury, K., Mitchell, K., and Finkelhor, D. (2011), 'The True Prevalence of "Sexting"', Crimes against Children Research Centre, available at <https://www.unh.edu/ccrc/pdf/Sexting%20Fact%20Sheet%20 4_29_11.pdf> (accessed 7 May 2012).

Luhmann, N. (1988), 'Family, Confidence, Trust: Problems and Alternatives', in D. Gambetta (ed), *Trust: Making and Breaking Co-operative Relations* (Oxford: Basil Blackwell).

Lussier, P. and Davies. G. (2011), 'A Person-Oriented Perspective On Sexual Offenders, Offending Trajectories, and Risk of Recidivism: A New Challenge for Policymakers, Risk Assessors, and Actuarial Prediction?', 17 *Psychology, Public Policy, and Law* 530.

MacIntyre, D. and Carr, A. (2000), *Prevention of Child Sexual Abuse in Ireland: The Development and Evaluation of The Stay Safe Programme*, Studies in Health and Human Services, vol 3 (Lewiston, Queeston, and Lampeter: The Edwin Mellen Press).

MacLeod, M. (1999), 'The Abuse of Children in Institutional Settings: Children's Perspectives', in N. Stanley, J. Manthorpe, and B. Penhale (eds), *Institutional Abuse: Perspectives Across the Life Course* (London: Routledge).

Magee, Sir I. (2008), *Review of Criminality Information* (London: Home Office).

Magnusson, A. (1984), *The Village: A History of Quarrier's* (Bridge of Weir: Quarrier's Homes).

Maguire, M. (2007), 'Crime Data and Statistics', in M. Maguire, R. Morgan, and R. Reiner (eds), *The Oxford Handbook of Criminology* (4th edn) (Oxford: Clarendon Press).

Maguire, M. and Kemshall, H. (2004), 'Multi-Agency Public Protection Arrangements: Key Issues', in H. Kemshall and G. McIvor (eds), *Managing Sex Offender Risk* (London: Jessica Kingsley Publishers).

Maguire, M., Kemshall, H., Noakes, L., Wincup, E., and Sharpe, K. (2001), *Risk Management of Sexual and Violent Offenders: The Work of Public Protection Panels*, Police Research Series Paper No 13 (London: Home Office).

Majone, G. (1994), 'The Rise of the Regulatory State in Western Europe', 17 *West European Politics* 77.

Malesky, L.A. and Ennis, L. (2004), 'Supportive Distortions: An Analysis of Posts on a Pedophile Internet Message Board', 24 *Journal of Addictions and Offender Counselling* 92.

Mann, R.E. and Thornton, D. (1998), 'The Evolution of a Multisite Sexual Offender Treatment Program', in W.L. Marshall, Y.M. Fernandez, S.M. Hudson, and T. Ward (eds), *Sourcebook of Treatment Programs for Sexual Offenders* (New York and London: Plenum Press).

Mantovani, F. (2001), 'Networked Seduction: A Test-bed for the Study of Strategic Communication on the Internet', 4 *Cyber Psychology and Behaviour* 147.

Marshall, K., Jamieson, C., and Finlayson, A. (1999), *Edinburgh's Children: The Report of the Edinburgh Inquiry into Abuse and Protection of Children in Care* (Edinburgh: City of Edinburgh Council).

Marshall, W.L., Anderson, D., and Champagne, F. (1997), 'Self-esteem and its Relationship to Sexual Offending Psychology', 3 *Crime and Law* 161.

Marshall, W.L. and Barbaree, H.E. (1990), 'An Integrated Theory of the Etiology of Sexual Offending', in W.L. Marshall, D.R. Laws, and H.E. Barbaree (eds), *Handbook of Sexual Assault: Issues, Theories, and Treatment of the Offender* (New York: Plenum Press).

Marshall, W.L. and Marshall, L.E. (2011), 'The Future of Sexual Offender Treatment Programs', in D.P. Boer, R. Eher, L.A. Craig, M.H. Miner, and F. Pfäfflin (eds), *International Perspectives on the Assessment and Treatment of Sexual Offenders: Theory, Practice and Research* (Chichester: Wiley-Blackwell).

Marshall, W.L., Serran, G.A., and Cortoni, F.A. (2000), 'Childhood Attachments and Sexual Abuse and their Relationship to Coping in Child Molesters', 12 *Sexual Abuse: A Journal of Research and Treatment* 17.

Martellozzo, E. (2011), 'Understanding the Perpetrators' Online Behaviour', in J. Davidson and P. Gottschalk (eds), *Internet Child Abuse: Current Research and Policy* (Abingdon: Routledge).

——(2012), *Online Child Sexual Abuse: Grooming, Policing and Child Protection in a Multi-Media World* (London and New York: Routledge).

Maruna, S. (2001), *Making Good: How Ex-Convicts Reform and Rebuild Their Lives* (Washington DC: APA Books).

Mason, S. (2011), *A Managed Approach: Part One of the Review of the Criminal Records Regime in Northern Ireland*, available at <http://www.dojni.gov.uk/index/publications/publication-categories/pubs-policing-community-safety/a_managed_approach.pdf> (accessed 7 May 2012).

——(2012), *A Managed Approach: Part Two of the Review of the Criminal Records Regime in Northern Ireland*, available at <http://www.dojni.gov.uk/index/publications/publication-categories/pubs-policing-community-safety/a-managed-approach---a-review-of-the-criminal-records-regime-in-northern-ireland.pdf> (accessed 7 May 2012).

Masson, H. (2004), 'Young Sex Offenders', in H. Kemshall and G. McIvor (eds), *Managing Sex Offender Risk* (London: Jessica Kingsley Publishers).

Matravers, A (ed) (2003), *Sex Offenders in the Community: Managing and Reducing the Risks* (Cullompton, Devon: Willan Publishing, Cambridge Criminal Justice Series).

Mathews, J. (1998), 'An 11-year Perspective of Working with Female Sexual Offenders', in W. L. Marshall, T. Ward, and S.M. Hudson (eds), *Sourcebook of Treatment Programs for Sexual Offenders* (New York, NY: Plenum Press).

Matthews, R. (2005), 'The Myth of Punitiveness', 9 *Theoretical Criminology* 175.

Mathews, R., Matthews, J.K., and Speltz, K. (1989), *Female Sexual Offenders: An Exploratory Study* (Brandon, VT: Safer Society Press).

McAlinden, A. (2000), 'Sex Offender Registration: Implications and Difficulties for Ireland' (Special Issue: Crime and Policing), 10 *Irish Journal of Sociology* 75.

——(2005), 'The Use of "Shame" with Sexual Offenders', 45 *British Journal of Criminology* 373.

——(2006a), '"Setting 'Em Up": Personal, Familial and Institutional Grooming in the Sexual Abuse of Children', 15 *Social and Legal Studies* 339.

——(2006b), 'Managing Risk: From Regulation to the Reintegration of Sexual Offenders', 6 *Criminology and Criminal Justice* 197.

——(2007a), *The Shaming of Sexual Offenders: Risk, Retribution and Reintegration* (Oxford: Hart Publishing).

——(2007b), 'Public Attitudes Towards Sex Offenders in Northern Ireland', *Research and Statistical Bulletin 6/2007* (Belfast: Northern Ireland Office, Statistics and Research Branch).

——(2009), 'Employment Opportunities and the Community Reintegration of Sex Offenders', NIO Statistical and Research Series Report No 20 (Belfast: Northern Ireland Office).

——(2010a), 'Vetting Sexual Offenders: State Over-extension, the Punishment Deficit and the Failure to Manage Risk', 19 *Social and Legal Studies* 25.

——(2010b), 'Punitive Policies on Sexual Offending: From Public Shaming to Public Protection', in A. Williams and M. Nash (eds), *Handbook of Public Protection* (Cullompton, Devon: Willan Publishing).

——(2011a), '"Transforming Justice": Challenges for Restorative Justice in an Era of Punishment-based Corrections' (Special Issue: Essays in Celebration of the 35th Anniversary of Restorative Justice), 14 *Contemporary Justice Review* 383.

——(2011b), 'The Reintegration of Sexual Offenders: From a "Risks" to a "Strengths-based" Model of Offender Resettlement', in S. Farrall,

R. Sparks, S. Maruna, and M. Hough (eds), *Escape Routes: Contemporary Perspectives on Life After Punishment* (New York and London: Routledge).

—— (2012a), 'The Governance of Sexual Offending Across Europe: Penal Policies, Political Economies and the Institutionalisation of Risk', 14 *Punishment and Society* 166.

—— (2012b), 'An Inconvenient Truth: Barriers to Truth Recovery in the Aftermath of Institutional Child Abuse in Ireland', *Legal Studies*, Article first published online: 13 June 2012 | DOI: 10.1111/j.1748-121X.2012.00243.x.

McAra, L. (2007), 'Welfarism in Crisis: Crime Control and Penal Practice in Post-Devolution Scotland', in M. Keating (ed), *Scottish Social Democracy: Progressive Ideas for Public Policy* (Brussels: Peter Lang).

—— (2008), 'Crime, Criminology and Criminal Justice in Scotland', 5 *European Journal of Criminology* 481.

McCabe, K.A. and Manian, S. (2010), *Sex Trafficking: A Global Perspective* (Lanham, MD: Lexington Books).

McCarthy, J. (2010), *Deep Deception: Ireland's Swimming Scandals* (Dublin: The O'Brien Press Ltd).

McCold, P. (1996), 'Restorative Justice and the Role of the Community', in B. Galaway and J. Hudson (eds), *Restorative Justice: International Perspectives* (Monsey, NY: Criminal Justice Press).

McCrone, D. (2001), *Understanding Scotland: The Sociology of a Nation* (2nd edn) (London: Routledge).

McGee, H., Garavan, R., de Barra, M., Byrne, J., and Conroy, R. (2002), *The SAVI Report: Sexual Abuse and Violence in Ireland* (Dublin: The Liffey Press in Association with the Dublin Rape Crisis Centre).

McGrath, R.J. (1991), 'Sex-Offender Risk Assessment and Disposition Planning: A Review of Empirical and Clinical Findings', 35 *International Journal of Offender Therapy and Comparative Criminology* 328.

McGuinness, C. (1993), *The Report of the Kilkenny Incest Investigation* (Dublin: The Stationery Office).

McIvor, G. and McNeill, F. (2007), 'Probation in Scotland: Past, Present and Future', in L. Geslthorpe and R. Morgan (eds), *Handbook of Probation* (Cullompton, Devon: Willan Publishing).

McLaughlin, E. (2005), 'Governance and Social Policy in Northern Ireland (1999–2004): the Devolution Years and Postscript', in M. Powell, L. Bauld, and K. Clarke (eds), *Social Policy Review 17* (Bristol: Policy Press/Social Policy Association).

McLaughlin, S. (2009), 'Online Sexual Grooming of Children and the Law', 14 *Communications Law* 8.

McMahon, P.M. (2000), 'The Public Health Approach to the Prevention of Sexual Violence', 12 *Sexual Abuse: A Journal of Research and Treatment* 27.

McMahon, P.M. and Puett, R.C. (1999), 'Child Sexual Abuse as a Public Health Issue: Recommendations of an Expert Panel', 11 *Sexual Abuse: A Journal of Research and Treatment* 257.

McNeill, F. and Whyte, B. (2007), *Reducing Re-offending: Social Work and Community Justice in Scotland* (Cullompton, Devon: Willan Publishing).

McSherry, B. and Keyzer, P. (2009), *Sex Offenders and Preventive Detention: Politics, Policy and Practice* (Sydney: The Federation Press).

—— (2011), *Dangerous People: Policy, Prediction, and Practice* (New York and London: Routledge).

Melossi, D. (2001), 'The Cultural Embeddedness of Social Control: Reflections on the Comparison of Italian and North-American Cultures Concerning Punishment', 5 *Punishment and Society* 403.

Mercado, C.C., Merdian, H.L., and Egg, R. (2011), 'The Internet and Sexual Offending: An International Perspective', in D.P. Boer, R. Eher, L.A. Craig, M.H. Miner, and F. Pfäfflin (eds), *International Perspectives on the Assessment and Treatment of Sexual Offenders: Theory, Practice and Research* (Chichester: Wiley-Blackwell).

Mercado, C.C., Tallon, J.A., and Terry, K. (2008), 'Persistent Sexual Abusers in the Catholic Church: An Examination of Characteristics and Offense Patterns', 35 *Criminal Justice and Behavior* 629.

Mercado, C.C., Terry, K., and Perillo, A.D. (2011), 'Sexual Abuse in the Catholic Church and other Youth Serving Organisations', in D.P. Boer, R. Eher, L.A. Craig, M.H. Miner, and F. Pfäfflin (eds), *International Perspectives on the Assessment and Treatment of Sexual Offenders: Theory, Practice and Research* (Chichester: Wiley-Blackwell).

Mercy, J.A. (1999), 'Having New Eyes: Viewing Child Sexual Abuse as a Public Health Problem', 11 *Sexual Abuse: A Journal of Research and Treatment* 317.

Messner, M. (1992), *Power at Play: Sports and the Problem of Masculinity* (Boston: Beacon Press).

Messner, M. and Sabo, D. (1990), *Sport, Men and the Gender Order* (Champion, IL: Human Kenetics).

Middleton, D. (2004), 'Current Treatment Approaches', in M.C. Calder (ed), *Child Sexual Abuse and the Internet: Tackling the New Frontier* (Dorset: Russell House Publishing).

Middleton, D., Elliott, I., Mandeville-Norden, R., and Beech, A. (2006), 'An Investigation into the Applicability of the Ward and Siegert Pathways Model of Child Sexual Abuse with Internet Offenders', 12 *Psychology, Crime and Law* 589.

Mitchell, K.J., Finkelhor, D., and Wolak, J. (2001), 'Risk Factors for and Impact of Online Sexual Solicitation of Youth', 285 *Journal of the American Medical Association* 3011.

—— (2005), 'The Internet and Family and Acquaintance Sexual Abuse', 10 *Child Maltreatment* 49.

—— (2007), 'Youth Internet Users at Risk for the Most Serious Online Sexual Solicitations', 32 *American Journal of Preventive Medicine* 532.

Mitchell, K.J., Wolak, J., and Finkelhor, D. (2005), 'Police Posing as Juveniles Online to Catch Sex Offenders: Is it Working?', 17 *Journal of Research and Treatment* 241.

Montgomery-Devlin, J. (2008), 'The Sexual Exploitation of Children and Young People in Northern Ireland: Overview from the Barnardo's Beyond the Shadows Service', 14 *Child Care in Practice* 381.

Mooney, G. and Poole, L. (2004), '"A Land of Milk and Honey"? Social Policy in Scotland After Devolution', 24 *Critical Social Policy* 458.

Moore, C. (1995), *Betrayal of Trust: The Father Brendan Smyth Affair and the Catholic Church* (Dublin: Marino).

Moore, C. (1996), *Kincora Scandal: Political Cover-up and Intrigue in Ulster* (Dublin: Marino).

Moore, R., Lee, T., and Hunt, R. (2007), 'Entrapped on the Web? Applying the Entrapment Defense to Cases Involving On-line Sting Operations', 32 *American Journal of Criminal Justice* 87.

Moran, M. (2001), 'The Rise of the Regulatory State in Britain', 5 *Parliamentary Affairs* 19.

—— (2003), *The British Regulatory State: High Modernism and Hyper Innovation* (Oxford: Oxford University Press).

Morris, A. and Gelsthorpe, L. (2000), 'Re-visioning Men's Violence Against Female Partners', 39 *The Howard Journal* 412.

Morrison, T., Erooga, M., and Beckett, R.C. (1994), *Sexual Offending Against Children: Assessment and Treatment of Males* (London: Routledge).

Moulden, H.M., Firestone, P., and Wexler, A.F. (2007), 'Child Care Providers Who Commit Sexual Offences: A Description of Offender, Offence, and Victim Characteristics', 51 *International Journal of Offender Therapy and Comparative Criminology* 384.

Mowen, M. (2011), 'Community Perspective on Reintegration—Donagh Community Forum: The McDermott Brothers Case', paper presented at the NOTA Conference, 'Sexual Violence: Facilitating Reintegration and Preventing Recidivism', Belfast, 9 November.

Mrazek, P.J., Lynch, M.A., and Bentovim, A. (1983), 'Sexual Abuse of Children in the United Kingdom', 7 *Child Abuse and Neglect* 147.

Muncie, J. (2005), 'The Globalization of Crime Control—The Case of Youth and Juvenile Justice: Neo-liberalism, Policy Convergence and International Conventions', 9 *Theoretical Criminology* 35.

Muncie, J. (2009), *Youth and Crime* (London: Sage Publications).

Munro, M. and McNeill, F. (2010), 'Fines, Community Sanctions and Measures in Scotland', in H. Croall, G. Mooney, and M. Munro (eds), *Criminal Justice in Scotland* (Abingdon: Willan Publishing).

Murphy, F.D., Buckley, H., and Joyce, L. (2005), *The Ferns Report*, presented by the Ferns Inquiry to the Minister for Health and Children (Dublin: Government Publications).

Murphy, J. (1992), *British Social Services: The Scottish Dimension* (Edinburgh: Scottish Academic Press).

Murphy, R. (1998), *Report of the Independent Inquiry into Matters Relating to Child Sexual Abuse in Swimming* (Dublin: Department for Tourism, Sport, and Recreation).

Myers, J. and Barrett, B. (2002), *In at the Deep End* (London: NSPCC).

Nair, A. (2006), 'Mobile Phones and the Internet: Legal Issues in the Protection of Children', 20 *International Review of Law and Computers* 177.

Nathan, P. and Ward, T. (2002), 'Female Sex Offenders: Clinical and Demographic Features', 8 *The Journal of Sexual Aggression* 21.

National Center for Missing and Exploited Children (NCMEC) (2007), *CyberTipline Annual Report Totals* (Alexandria, VA: NCMEC), available at <http://www.cybertipline.com/en_US/documents/CyberTipline ReportTotals.pdf> (accessed 29 March 2011).

National Criminal Intelligence Service (NCIS) (2003), *United Kingdom Threat Assessment of Serious and Organised Crime* (London: NCIS).

National Society for the Prevention of Cruelty to Children (NSPCC) (2010), *A Briefing Paper on Abuse of Trust in Sport by NSPCC Northern Ireland*, available at <http://www.nspcc.org.uk/Inform/ policyandpublicaffairs/northernireland/briefings/abuse_of_trust_in_ sport_wdf70532.pdf> (accessed 28 November 2011).

—— (2011), *Sexual Abuse: A Public Health Challenge*, available at <http:// www.nspcc.org.uk/inform/resourcesforprofessionals/sexualabuse/evidence-review-pdf_wdf87818.pdf> (accessed 7 May 2012).

Nelken, D. (2000), *Contrasting Criminal Justice: Getting From Here to There* (Aldershot: Dartmouth).

—— (2007), 'Comparing Criminal Justice', in M. Maguire, R. Morgan, and R. Reiner (eds), *The Oxford Handbook of Criminology* (4th edn) (Oxford: Oxford University Press).

Newburn, T. (2002), 'Atlantic Crossings: "Policy Transfer" and Crime Control in the USA and Britain', 4 *Punishment and Society* 165.

—— (2010), 'Diffusion, Differentiation and Resistance in Comparative Penality', 10 *Criminology and Criminal Justice* 341.

Newburn, T. and Sparks, R. (eds) (2004), *Criminal Justice and Political Cultures: National and International Dimensions of Crime Control* (Cullompton, Devon: Willan Publishing).

Newman, G.R. (2007), 'Sting Operations', *Problem Orientated Guides for Police Response Guides Series* No 6. (Washington, DC: US Department of Justice, Office of Community Oriented Policing Services).

Nicholas, S., Kershaw, C., and Walker, A. (2007), *Crime in England and Wales* 2006/07 (London: Home Office).

Nolan, B., O'Connell, P., and Whelan, C.T. (eds) (2000), *Bust to Boom: The Irish Experience of Growth and Inequality* (Dublin: Institute of Public Administration).

Nolan, L. (2001), *Report of the Review on Child Protection in the Catholic Church in England and Wales: A Programme for Action* (2001), available at <http://www.cathcom.org/mysharedaccounts/cumberlege/finalnolan1.htm> (accessed 21 February 2011).

Norrie, K.McK., Sutherland, E.E., and Cleland, A. (2004), *Stair Memorial Encyclopaedia, Reissue Volume: Child and Family Law* (Edinburgh: LexisNexus/Butterworths).

Norrie, K. (2005), 'Prevention as the Cure', 50 *Journal of the Law Society of Scotland* 20.

Northern Ireland Assembly Research and Library Service (2010a), *Safeguarding Children Between the Jurisdictions of Northern Ireland, Great Britain and the Republic of Ireland*, Assembly Briefing Note 73/10, available at <http://www.niassembly.gov.uk/researchandlibrary/2010/7310.pdf> (accessed 19 April 2011).

—— (2010b), *Positions of Trust Legislation and Sports Coaches*, Assembly Briefing Note 138/10, available at <http://www.niassembly.gov.uk/researchandlibrary/2010/13810.pdf> (accessed 28 November 2011).

Northern Ireland Association for the Care and Resettlement of Offenders (NIACRO) (2008), *NIACRO's Response to Consultation Paper: Proposed Draft Sexual Offences (NI) Order 2007*, available at <http://www.niacro.co.uk/current-issues/34/niacros-response-to-the-nio-draft-sexual-offences-ni-order-20/> (accessed 28 November 2011).

North Western Health Board (1998), *Report of the Inquiry into the West of Ireland Farmer Case* (Manorhamilton: North Western Health Board).

Obokata, T. (2006), *Trafficking of Human Beings from a Human Rights Perspective: Towards a Holistic Approach* (The Netherlands: Martinus Nijhoff Publishers).

O'Connell, R. (2003), *A Typology of Child Cybersexploitation and Online Grooming Practices*, available at <http://image.guardian.co.uk/sysfiles/Society/documents/2003/07/24/Netpaedoreport.pdf> (accessed 18 February 2011).

O'Donnell, I. (2005), 'Crime and Justice in the Republic of Ireland', 2 *European Journal of Criminology* 99.

—— (2008), 'Stagnation and Change in Irish Penal Policy', 47 *Howard Journal of Criminal Justice* 121.

O'Donnell, I., Baumer, E.P., and Hughes, N. (2008), 'Recidivism in the Republic of Ireland', 8 *Criminology and Criminal Justice* 123.

O'Donnell, I. and Milner, C. (2007), *Child Pornography: Crime, Computer and Society* (Cullompton, Devon: Willan Publishing).

O'Gorman, C. (2009), *Beyond Belief* (London: Hodder and Stoughton).

O'Malley, P. (1999), 'Volatile Punishments: Contemporary Penality and the Neo-Liberal Government', 3 *Theoretical Criminology* 175.

——(2004), *Risk, Uncertainty and Government* (London: Glasshouse Press).

—— (2010), *Crime and Risk* (London: Sage Publications Ltd).

—— (2012), 'Is it Time to Ditch Neoliberalism from Criminological Theory', Brown Bag Seminar, 21 May, School of Law, Queen's University Belfast.

O'Malley, T. (2009), 'Responding to Institutional Abuse: The Law and Its Limits', in T. Flannery (ed), *Responding to the Ryan Report* (Dublin: Columba Press).

Oliver, A.L. (1997), 'On the Nexus of Organizations and Professions: Networking through Trust', 67 *Sociological Inquiry* 227.

Olson, L.N., Daggs, J.L., Ellevold, B.L., and Rogers, T.K.K. (2007), 'Entrapping the Innocent: Toward a Theory of Child Sexual Predators' Luring Communication', 17 *Communication Theory* 231.

Ormerod, D. (2011), 'Case Comment—Sexual Offences: Meeting a Child Following Grooming', *Criminal Law Review* 340.

Orwell, G. (1949), *Nineteen Eighty Four: A Novel* (London: Secker and Warburg).

Ost, S. (2002), 'Children at Risk: Legal and Societal Perceptions of the Potential Threat that the Possession of Child Pornography Poses to Society', 29 *Journal of Law and Society* 436.

——(2004), 'Getting to Grips with Sexual Grooming? The New Offence under the Sexual Offences Act 2003', 26 *Journal of Social Welfare and Family* 147.

——(2009), *Child Pornography and Sexual Grooming: Legal and Societal Responses* (Cambridge: Cambridge University Press).

Owen, C. and Statham, J. (2009), *Disproportionality in Child Welfare: The Prevalence of Black and Ethnic Minority Children in 'Looked After' and 'Children in Need' Populations and on Child Protection Registers in England* (London: Department of Children, Schools and Families).

Palmer, T. (2001), *No Son of Mine! Children Abused Through Prostitution* (Barkingside, UK: Barnardo's).

Palmer, T. and Stacey, L. (2004), *Just One Click: Sexual Abuse of Children and Young People through the Internet and Mobile Phone Technology* (Barkingside, UK: Barnardo's).

Papadopoulos, L. (2010), *Sexualisation of Young People Review*, available at <http://www.wrc.org.uk/includes/documents/cm_docs/2010/s/sexualisationyoungpeople.pdf> (accessed 30 April 2012).

Parkinson, P., Oats, K., and Jayakody, A. (2009), *A Study of Reported Sexual Abuse in the Anglican Church*, available at <http://www.apo.org.au/research/study-reported-child-sexual-abuse-anglican-church> (accessed 29 September 2011).

Parton, N. (1985), *The Politics of Child Abuse* (Basingstoke: Macmillan).

——(2004), 'From Maria Colwell to Victoria Climbié: Reflections on Public Inquiries into Child Abuse A Generation Apart', 13 *Child Abuse Review* 80.

——(2006), *Safeguarding Childhood: Early Intervention and Surveillance in a Late Modern Society* (London: Palgrave/Macmillan).

Parton, N., Thorpe, D., and Wattam, C. (1997), *Child Protection: Risk and the Moral Order* (Hampshire: Macmillan).

Pearson, G., Blagg, H., Smith, D., Sampson, A., and Stubbs, P. (1992), 'Crime, Community and Conflict: The Multi-Agency Approach', in D. Downes (ed), *Unravelling Criminal Justice* (London: Macmillan).

Pennell, J. and Burford, G. (2001), 'Family Group Decision Making: Resolving Child Sexual Abuse', in G. Burford (ed), *Broken Icons* (St John's, NF: Jesperson Press).

Petrunik, M. and Deutschmann, L. (2008), 'The Exclusion-Inclusion Spectrum in State and Community Response to Sex Offenders in Anglo-American and European Jurisdictions', 52 *International Journal of Offender Therapy and Comparative Criminology* 499.

Pfeiffer, C., Windizio, M., and Kleimann, M. (2005), 'Media Use and Its Impacts on Crime Perception, Sentencing Attitudes and Crime Policy', 2 *European Journal of Criminology* 259.

Phelan, P. (1995), 'Incest and Its Meaning: The Perspectives of Fathers and Daughters', 19 *Child Abuse and Neglect* 7.

Pickett, C.L., Gardner, W.L., and Knowles, M. (2004), 'Getting a Cue: The Need to Belong and Enhanced Sensitivity to Social Cues', 30 *Personality and Social Psychology* 1095.

Pinkerton, J. (1994), *In Care At Home: Parenting, The State and Civil Society* (Aldershot: Avebury).

Plante, T.G. (ed) (2004), *Sin Against the Innocents: Sexual Abuse by Priests and the Role of the Catholic Church* (Westport, Connecticut: Praeger Publishers).

Plymouth Safeguarding Children Board (2010), *Serious Case Review, Overview Report, Executive Summary in Respect of Nursery Z*, available at <http://www.plymouth.gov.uk/serious_case_review_nursery_z.pdf> (accessed 20 July 2011).

Povey, D. (ed), Coleman, K., Kaiza, P., and Roe, S. (2009), *Homicides, Firearm Offences and Intimate Violence 2007/08 (Supplementary Volume 2 to Crime in England and Wales 2007/08)*. Home Office Statistical Bulletin 02/09 (London: Home Office).

Powell, A. (2007), *Paedophiles, Child Abuse and the Internet* (Oxford: Radcliffe Publishing).

Power, H. (2003), 'Disclosing Information on Sex Offenders: The Human Rights Implications', in A. Matravers (ed), *Sex Offenders in the Community: Managing and Reducing the Risks* (Cullompton, Devon: Willan Publishing, Cambridge Criminal Justice Series).

Pratt, J. (2000a), 'The Return of the Wheelbarrow Men; or the Arrival of Postmodern Penality', 40 *British Journal of Criminology* 127.

——(2000b), 'Emotive and Ostentatious Punishment: Its Decline and Resurgence in Modern Society', 2 *Punishment and Society* 417.

——(2008a), 'Scandinavian Exceptionalism in an Era of Penal Excess: Part I: The Nature and Roots of Scandinavian Exceptionalism', 48 *British Journal of Criminology* 127.

——(2008b), 'Scandinavian Exceptionalism in an Era of Penal Excess: Part 2: Does Scandinavian Exceptionalism Have a Future?', 48 *British Journal of Criminology* 275.

Prentky, R.A. (1999), 'Child Sexual Molestation', in V. van Hasselt and M. Hersen (eds), *Handbook of Psychological Approaches with Violent Offenders: Contemporary Strategies and Issues* (New York: Kluwer Academic/Plenum).

Pringle, K. (1993), 'Sexual Abuse Perpetrated by Welfare Personnel and the Problem of Men', 36 *Critical Social Policy* 4.

Prison Reform Trust (2004), 'England and Wales: Europe's Lifer Capital', available at <http://www.prisonreformtrust.org.uk/subsection.asp?id=352> (accessed 1 October 2010).

Prosser, T. (1995), 'The State, Constitutions and Implementing Economic Policy: Privatization and Regulation in the UK, France and the USA', 4 *Social and Legal Studies* 507.

Pryor, D.W. (1996), *Unspeakable Acts: Why Men Sexually Abuse Children* (New York: New York University Press).

Quaker Peace and Social Witness (2005), *Circles of Support and Accountability in the Thames Valley: The First three Years—April 2002 to March 2005* (London: Quaker Communications).

Quayle, E. and Taylor, M. (2001), 'Child Seduction and Self-Representation on the Internet', 4 *CyberPsychology and Behaviour* 597.

——(2005), *Viewing Child Pornography on the Internet* (Dorset: Russell House Publishing).

Raftery, M. and O'Sullivan, E. (1999), *Suffer the Little Children: The Inside Story of Ireland's Industrial Schools* (Dublin: New Island).

Ramage, S. (2007), 'Data Protection and Criminal Justice: Some Recent Developments in EU and Domestic Law', 169 *Criminal Lawyer* 7.

Ramm, M. (2011), 'Violent Offenders with Mental Disorders: Current Issues and Challenges', paper presented at the 'Serious Violent and Sexual Offenders in Scotland: Current Issues and Challenges' Conference, Edinburgh, 8 June.

Reder, P., Duncan, S., and Gray, M. (1993), *Beyond Blame: Child Abuse Tragedies Revisited* (London: Routledge).

Reichel, P. (2008), *Comparative Criminal Justice Systems: A Topical Approach* (4th edn) (Englewood Cliffs, NJ: Prentice Hall).

Reiss, A. (1989), 'The Institutionalisation of Risk', 11 *Law and Policy* 392.

Renk, K., Liljequist, L., Steinberg, A., Bosco, G., and Phares, V. (2000), 'Prevention of Child Sexual Abuse: Are We Doing Enough?', 3 *Trauma, Violence and Abuse* 68.

Richardson, G., Kelly, T.P., Bhate, S.R., and Graham, F. (1997), 'Group Differences in Abuser and Abuse Characteristics in a British Sample of Sexually Abusive Adolescents', 9 *Sexual Abuse: A Journal of Research and Treatment* 239.

Ringrose, J. and Eriksson Barajas, K. (2011), 'Gendered Risks and Opportunities? Exploring Teen Girls' Digital Sexual Identity in Postfeminist Media Contexts' (Special Issue: Postfeminism and the Mediation of Sex), 7 *International Journal of Media and Cultural Politics* 121.

Ringrose, J., Gill, R., Livingstone, S., and Harvey, L. (2012), *A Qualitative Study of Children, Young People and 'Sexting'*, A Report Prepared for the NSPCC (NSPCC), available at <http://www.nspcc.org.uk/Inform/resourcesforprofessionals/sexualabuse/sexting-research_wda89260.html> (accessed 14 May 2012).

Ritchie, G. (2001), *Study on Disqualification from Working with Children Within the EU* (London: Institute of Advanced Legal Studies).

Robben, A.C.G.M. (1995), 'The Politics of Truth and Emotion among Victims and Perpetrators of Violence', in C. Nordstrom and A.C.G.M. Robben (eds), *Fieldwork Under Fire: Contemporary Studies of Violence and Survival* (Berkeley: University of California Press).

Robbins, P. and Darlington, R. (2003), 'The Role of the Industry and the Internet Watch Foundation', in A. MacVean and P. Spindler (eds), *Policing Paedophiles on the Internet* (Bristol: Benson Publications).

Roberts, A. (2000), 'Crime Creation? Some Questions of Fairness and Efficacy in Covert Operations', 73 *The Police Journal* 263.

Roberts, J.V., Stalans, L., Indermaur, D., and Hough, M. (2003), *Penal Populism and Public Opinion: Findings from Five Countries* (New York: Oxford University Press).

Roberts, P. (2002), 'On Method: The Ascent of Comparative Criminal Justice', 22 *Oxford Journal of Legal Studies* 517.

Robinson, L. (1998), *Crossing the Line: Sexual Harassment and Abuse in Canada's National Sport* (Toronto: McClelland and Steward Inc).

Room, S. (2004), 'Meeting the Challenges of Climbié and Soham: Part 3', 154 *New Law Journal* 590.

Ropelato, J. (2007), 'Internet Pornography Statistics', available at <http://internet-filter-review.toptenreviews.com/internet-pornography-statistics.html> (accessed 4 April 2010).

Rose, N. (2000), 'Government and Control', 40 *British Journal of Criminology* 321.

Rosetti, S.J. (ed) (1990), *Slayer of the Soul: Child Sexual Abuse and the Catholic Church* (Mystic CT: Twenty-third Publications).

—— (1995), 'The Impact of Child Sexual Abuse on Attitudes Toward God and the Catholic Church', 19 *Child Abuse and Neglect* 1469.

Ross, E.C., Polaschek, D.L.L., and Ward, T. (2008), 'The Therapeutic Alliance: A Theoretical Revision for Offender Rehabilitation', 13 *Aggression and Violent Behaviour* 462.

Ruggiero, V., Ryan, M., and Sim, J. (eds) (1993), *Western European Penal Systems* (London: Sage).

Russell, D.E.H. (1986), *The Secret Trauma: Incest in the Lives of Girls and Women* (New York: Basic Books).

Russell, P. (1996), 'Children with Disabilities', in H. Kemshall and J. Pritchard (eds), *Good Practice in Risk Assessment and Management* (London: Jessica Kingsley).

Sacco, D., Argudin, R., Maguire, J., and Tallon, K. (2010), *Sexting: Youth Practices and Legal Implications*. Berkman Center Research Publication No 2010–8, available at <http://papers.ssrn.com/sol3/papers.cfm?abstract_id=1661343> (accessed 14 May 2012).

Salter, A. (1995), *Transforming Trauma: A Guide to Understanding and Treating Adult Survivors of Child Sexual Abuse* (Newbury Park, California: Sage).

Salter, A. (2003), *Predators, Pedophiles, Rapists, and Other Sex Offenders: Who They Are, How They Operate, and How We Can Protect Ourselves and Our Children* (New York: Basic Books).

Sampson, A. (1994), *Acts of Abuse: Sex Offenders and the Criminal Justice System* (London: Routledge).

Sampson, A., Smith, D., Pearson, G., Blagg, H., and Stubbs, P. (1991), 'Gender Issues in Inter-agency Relations: Police, Probation and Social Services', in P. Abbott and C. Wallace (eds), *Gender, Power and Sexuality* (Basingstoke: Macmillan).

Sampson, A., Stubbs, P., Smith, D., Pearson, G., and Blagg, H. (1988), 'Crime, Localities and the Multi-Agency Approach', 28 *British Journal of Criminology* 478.

Sanderson, C. (2004), *The Seduction of Children: Empowering Parents and Teachers to Protect Children From Sexual Abuse* (London and Philadelphia: Jessica Kingsley Publishers).

Sanford, L.T. (1982), *The Silent Children: A Parent's Guide to the Prevention of Child Sexual Abuse* (New York: McGraw-Hill).

Saraga, E. (2001), 'Dangerous Places: The Family as a Site of Crime', in J. Muncie and E. McLaughlin (eds), *The Problem of Crime* (2nd edn) (London: Sage).

Sas, L.D. and Cunningham, A.H. (1995), *Tipping the Balance to Tell the Secret: The Public Discovery of Child Sexual Abuse* (London and Ontario: London Family Court Clinic).

Sauzier, M. (1989), 'Disclosure of Child Sexual Abuse: For Better for Worse', 12 *Psychiatric Clinics of North America* 455.

Savelsberg, J.J. (1999), 'Knowledge, Domination and Criminal Punishment Revisited', 1 *Punishment and Society* 45.

Scalora, M.J. and Garbin, C. (2003), 'A Multivariate Analysis of Sex Offender Recidivism', 47 *International Journal of Offender Therapy and Comparative Criminology* 309.

Scarpa, S. (2008), *Trafficking in Human Beings: Modern Slavery* (Oxford: Oxford University Press).

Scott, S. and Skidmore, P. (2006), *Reducing the Risk: Barnardo's Support for Sexually Exploited Young People: A Two Year Evaluation* (Essex: Barnardo's).

Scottish Law Commission (SLC) (2010), *Discussion Paper on Similar Fact Evidence and the Moorov Doctrine* DP 145 (Edinburgh: The Stationery Office).

Seddon, T. (2008), 'Dangerous Liaisons: Personality Disorder and the Politics of Risk', 10 *Punishment and Society* 301.

Sgori, S.M. (ed) (1982), *Handbook of Clinical Intervention in Child Sexual Abuse* (Lexington, MA: Lexington Books).

Shannon, G. (2007), *Report of the Special Rapporteur on Child Protection: A Report Submitted to the Oireachtas*, available at <http://www.dcya.gov.ie/documents/child_welfare_protection/Report_of_Special_Rapporteur_on_Child_Protection_Geoffrey_Shannon.PDF> (accessed 28 November 2011).

Shaw, T. (2007), *Historical Abuse Systemic Review: Residential Schools and Children's Homes in Scotland 1950–1995* (Edinburgh: The Scottish Government), available at <http://www.scotland.gov.uk/Publications/2007/11/20104729/0> (accessed 19 July 2011).

——(2011), *Time to Be Heard: A Pilot Forum*, an independent report by Tom Shaw Commissioned by the Scottish Government (Edinburgh: The Scottish Government).

Shearing, C. (2000), 'Punishment and the Changing Face of Governance', 3 *Punishment and Society* 203.

Sheldon, K, and Howitt, D. (2007), *Sex Offenders and the Internet* (Chichester: Wiley).

Shelley, L. (2010), *Human Trafficking: A Global Perspective* (Cambridge: Cambridge University Press).

Sher, J. (2007), *Caught in the Web: Inside the Police Hunt to Rescue Children From Online Predators* (New York: Carroll & Graf Publishers).

Short, J., Williams, E., and Christie, B. (1976), *The Social Psychology of Telecommunications* (Chichester: Wiley).

Shute, S. (2004), 'The Sexual Offences Act 2003: (4) New Civil Preventative Orders—Sexual Offences Prevention Orders; Foreign Travel Orders; Risk of Sexual Harm Orders', *Criminal Law Review* 417.

Silva, D.C. (1990), 'Pedophilia: An Autobiography', in J.R. Feierman (ed), *Pedophilia: Biosocial Dimensions* (New York: Springer-Verlag).

Silverman, J. and Wilson, D. (2002), *Innocence Betrayed: Paedophilia, the Media and Society* (Cambridge: Polity Press).

Simester, A.P. and Chan, W. (1997), 'Intention Thus Far', *Criminal Law Review* 704.

Simon, J. (1998), 'Managing the Monstrous: Sex Offenders and the New Penology', 4 *Psychology, Public Policy and Law* 452.

—— (2007), *Governing Through Crime: How the War on Crime Transformed American Democracy and Created a Culture of Fear* (New York: Oxford University Press).

—— (2010), 'Crime and the New Politics: Will Cameron and Clegg Govern Through Crime?', 66 *British Society of Criminology Newsletter* 8.

—— (2012), *Mass Incarceration on Trial: America's Courts and the Future of Imprisonment* (New York: The New Press) (in press).

Siskind, A. (1986), 'Issues in Institutional Child Sexual Abuse: The Abused, the Abuser and the System', 4 *Residential Treatment for Children and Youth* 9.

Skinner, A. (1992), *Another Kind of Home: A Review of Residential Child Care* (Edinburgh: Scottish Office).

Smallbone, S., Marshall, W.L., and Wortley, R. (2008), *Preventing Child Sexual Abuse: Evidence, Policy and Practice* (Cullompton, Devon: Willan Publishing).

Smallbone, S.W. and Wortley, R.K. (2000), *Child Sexual Abuse in Queensland: Offender Characteristics and Modus Operandi* (Brisbane: Queensland Crime Commission).

Smart, C. (1999), 'A History of Ambivalence and Conflict in the Discursive Construction of the "Child Victim" of Sexual Abuse', 8 *Social and Legal Studies* 391.

Smith, D.R. (1993), *Safe From Harm: A Code of Practice for Safeguarding the Welfare of Children in Voluntary Organisations in England and Wales* (London: Home Office).

Smith, D.W., Letourneau, E.J., Saunders, B.E., Kilpatrick, D.G., Resnick, H.S., and Best, C.L. (2000), 'Delay in Disclosure of Childhood Rape: Results from a National Survey', 24 *Child Abuse and Neglect* 273.

Smith, K. (ed), Coleman, K., Eder, S., and Hall, P. (2011), *Homicides, Firearm Offences and Intimate Violence 2007/08 (Supplementary Volume 2 to Crime in England and Wales 2009/10)*. Home Office Statistical Bulletin 01/11 (London: Home Office).

Smith, R.G., Grabosky, P., and Urbas, G. (2004), *Cyber Criminals on Trial* (Cambridge: Cambridge University Press).

Social Services Inspectorate (SSI) (1993), *An Abuse of Trust: The Report of the Social Services Inspectorate into the case of Martin Huston* (Belfast: DHSS (SSI)).

Sommer, P. (2002), 'Evidence in Internet Paedophilia Cases', 8 *Computer and Telecommunications Law Review* 176.

Somners, M. (2008), *The Dangers of Online Predators* (New York: Rosen Publishing).

Soothill, K. (ed) (1999), *Criminal Conversations: An Anthology of the Work of Tony Parker* (Abingdon and New York: Routledge).

Soothill, K. (2005), 'Strongly Suspected of Serious Sex Crime and Future Danger', 16 *Journal of Forensic Psychiatry and Psychology* 221.

Soothill, K., Francis, B., Sanderson, B., and Ackerley, E. (2000), 'Sex Offenders: Specialists, Generalists—or Both? A 32-year Criminological Study', 40 *British Journal of Criminology* 56.

Soothill, K. Harman, J. Francis, B., and Kirby, S. (2005a), 'Identifying Future Repeat Danger from Sexual Offenders Against Children: A Focus on those Convicted and those Strongly Suspected of Such Crime', 16 *Journal of Forensic Psychiatry and Psychology* 225.

—— (2005b), 'What is the Future Repeat Danger from Sexual Offenders Against Children? Implications for Policing', 78 *The Police Journal* 37.

Sorenson, T. and Snow, B. (1991), 'How Children Tell: The Process of Disclosure in Child Sexual Abuse', 70 *Child Welfare* 3.

Sparks, R. (2001), 'Degrees of Estrangement: The Cultural Theory of Risk and Comparative Penology', 5 *Theoretical Criminology* 159.

Spencer, J.R. (2004), 'The Sexual Offences Act 2003: (2) Child and Family Offences', *Criminal Law Review* 347.

Sproull, L. and Kiesler, S. (1986), 'Reducing Social Context Cues: Electronic Mail in Organizational Communication', 32 *Management Science* 1492.

Squires, D. (2006), 'The Problem with Entrapment', 26 *Oxford Journal of Legal Studies* 351.

Squires, P. (ed) (2008), *ASBO Nation: The Criminalization of Nuisance in Contemporary Britain* (Bristol: Policy Press).

Stafford, A., Parton, N., Vincent, S., and Smith, C. (2011), *Child Protection Systems in the United Kingdom: A Comparative Analysis* (London: Jessica Kingsley Publishers).

Stafford, A. and Vincent, S. (2008), *Safeguarding and Protecting Children and Young People* (Edinburgh: Dunedin Academic Press).

Stanley, N. (1999), *Institutional Abuse: Perspectives Across the Life Course* (London: Routledge).

Steen, C. (1993), *The Relapse Prevention Workbook for Youth in Treatment* (Brandon, VT: The Safer Society Press).

Stelzer, G.L. (1997), 'Chemical Castration and the Right to Generate Ideas: Does the First Amendment Protect the Fantasies of Convicted Paedophiles?', 81 *Minnesota Law Review* 1675.

Stephenson, P., McElearney, A., and Stead, J. (2011), *Keeping Safe: The Development of Effective Preventative Education in Primary Schools in Northern Ireland: Summary Report*, available at <http://www.nspcc.org.uk/inform> (accessed 7 May 2012).

Stoker, G. (2003), *Transforming Local Governance: From Thatcherism to New Labour* (Basingstoke: Palgrave Macmillan).

Stop it Now! (2010), *Stop it Now! Helpline Report 2005–2009*, available at <http://www.stopitnow.org.uk/files/Helpline%20Report%20 09%20SM.pdf> (accessed 23 April 2012).

Studer, L.H., Sribney, C., Aylwon, A.S., and Reddon, J.R. (2011), 'Just an Incest Offender?', in D.P. Boer, R. Eher, L.A. Craig, M.H. Miner, and F. Pfäfflin (eds), *International Perspectives on the Assessment and Treatment of Sexual Offenders: Theory, Practice and Research* (Chichester: Wiley-Blackwell).

Suchman, A.L., Markakis, K., Beckman, H.B., and Frankel, R. (1997), 'A Model of Emphatic Communication in the Medical Interview', 277 *Journal of the American Medical Association* 678.

Sullivan, H. (2002), *Working Across Boundaries: Collaboration in Public Services* (Basingstoke: Palgrave Macmillan).

Sullivan, J. and Beech, A. (2002), 'Professional Perpetrators', 11 *Child Abuse Review* 153.

—— (2003), 'Are Collectors of Child Abuse Images a Risk to Children?', in A. MacVean and P. Spindler (eds), *Policing Paedophiles on the Internet* (Bristol: John Grieve Centre for Policing and Community Safety).

—— (2004), 'A Comparative Study of Demographic Data Relating to Intra- and Extra-familial Child Sexual Abusers and Professional Perpetrators', 10 *Journal of Sexual Aggression* 39.

Sullivan, J., Beech, A.R., Craig, L.A., and Gannon, T.A. (2011), 'Comparing Intra-familial and Extra-familial Child Sexual Abusers with Professionals Who Have Sexually Abused Children With Whom They Work', 55 *International Journal of Offender Therapy and Comparative Criminology* 56.

Sullivan, J. and Quayle, E. (2012), 'Manipulation Styles of Abusers Who Work with Children', in M. Erooga (ed), *Creating Safer Organisations* (New York: John Wiley & Sons).

Sundgot-Borgen, J., Fasting K., Brackenridge, C.H., Klungland, M., and Bergland, B. (2003), 'Sexual Harassment and Eating Disorders in Female Elite Athletes—A Controlled Study', 13 *Scandinavian Journal of Medicine and Science in Sports* 330.

Sunstein, C. (2002), *Risk and Reason: Safety, Law and the Environment* (Cambridge: Cambridge University Press).

Sutton, D. and Jones, V. (2004), Save the Children Europe Group, *Position Paper on Child Pornography and Internet-related Sexual Exploitation of Children*, available at <http://www.popcenter.org/problems/child_ pornography/PDFs/Sutton&Jones_2004.pdf> (accessed 8 July 2011).

Swaffer, T., Hollin, C., Beech, A., Beckett, R., and Fisher, D. (2000), 'An Exploration of Child Sexual Abusers Sexual Fantasies Before and After Treatment', 12 *Sexual Abuse: A Journal of Research and Treatment* 61.

Sykes, G. and Matza, D. (1957), 'Techniques of Neutralization: A Theory of Delinquency', 22 *American Sociological Review* 664.

Tabachnick, J. and Chasan-Taber, L. (1999), 'Evaluation of a Child Sexual Abuse Prevention Program', 11 *Sexual Abuse: A Journal of Research and Treatment* 279.

Tabachnick, J., Chasan-Taber, L., and McMahon, P. (2001), 'Evaluation of a Child Sexual Abuse Prevention Program—Vermont, 1995–1999', 285 *Journal of the American Medical Association* 114.

Talamo, A. and Ligiorio, B. (2001), 'Strategic Identities in Cyberspace: Update for the 21st Century', 3 *CyberPsychology and Behaviour* 521.

Talbot, T., Gilligan, L., Carter, M., and Matson, S. (2002), *An Overview of Sex Offender Management* (Silver Spring, MD: United States Center for Sex Offender Management).

Tallon, J.A. and Terry, K.J. (2008), 'Analyzing Paraphilic Activity, Specialization, and Generalization in Priests who Sexually Abused Minors', 35 *Criminal Justice and Behaviour* 615.

Tamatea, A.J., Webb, M., and Boer, D.P. (2011), 'The Role of Culture in Sexual Offender Rehabilitation', in D.P. Boer, R. Eher, L.A. Craig, M.H. Miner, and F. Pfäfflin (eds), *International Perspectives on the Assessment and Treatment of Sexual Offenders* (Chichester: Wiley-Blackwell).

Tata, C. (2010), 'Sentencing and Penal Decision-Making: Is Scotland Losing Its Distinctive Character?', in H. Croall, G. Mooney, and M. Munro (eds), *Criminal Justice in Scotland* (Abingdon: Willan Publishing).

Tavuchis, N. (1991), *Mea Culpa: A Sociology of Apology and Reconciliation* (Stanford, CA: Stanford University Press).

Taylor, M. and Quayle, E. (2003), *Child Pornography: An Internet Crime* (London and New York: Routledge).

Taylor, P. and Chaplin, R. (ed) (2011), *Crimes Detected in England and Wales 2010/2011* (1st edn). Home Office Statistical Bulletin 11/11 (London: Home Office).

Terry, K.J. and Ackerman, A. (2008), 'Child Sexual Abuse in the Catholic Church: How Situational Crime Prevention Strategies Can Help Create Safe Environments', 35 *Criminal Justice and Behaviour* 643.

Terry, K.J. and Tallon, J. (2004), *Child Sexual Abuse: A Review of the Literature*, in John Jay College Research Team, *The Nature and Scope of Sexual Abuse of Minors by Catholic Priests and Deacons in the United States, 1950–2002* (Washington, DC; United States Conference of Catholic Bishops).

Tewksbury, R. (2007), 'Effects of Sexual Assaults on Men: Physical, Mental, and Sexual Consequences', 6 *International Journal of Men's Health* 22.

Thomas, T. (2005), *Sex Crime: Sex Offending and Society* (2nd edn) (Cullompton, Devon: Willan Publishing).

Thomas, T. (2003), 'Sex Offender Community Notification: Experiences from America', 42 *Howard Journal of Criminal Justice* 217.

Thomas, T., Katz, I., and Wattam, C. (2000), *CUPICSO: The Collection and Use of Personal Information on Child Sex Offenders* (London: NSPCC).

Thompson, B. and Williams, A. (2004), 'Virtual Offenders: The Other Side of Internet Allegations', in M.C. Calder (ed), *Child Sexual Abuse and the Internet: Tackling the New Frontier* (Dorset: Russell House Publishing).

Thornton, D. (2003), 'The Machiavellian Sex Offender', in A. Matravers (ed), *Sex Offenders in the Community: Managing and Reducing the Risks* (Cullompton, Devon: Willan Publishing, Cambridge Criminal Justice Series).

Toftegaard, J. (1998), 'Den Forbudte Zone' ('The Forbidden Zone'), unpublished PhD thesis, Institut for Idraet, Copenhagen, Denmark.

Tonry, M. (2001), 'Penal Developments in English-Speaking Countries', in M. Tonry (ed), *Penal Reform in Overcrowded Times* (Oxford: Oxford University Press).

——(2003), *Confronting Crime: Crime Control Policy Under New Labour* (Cullompton, Devon: Willan Publishing).

Tucker, S. (2011), 'Listening and Believing: An Examination of Young People's Perceptions of why they are not Believed by Professionals when they Report Abuse and Neglect', 25 *Children and Society* 458.

Utting, W. (1997), *People Like Us: The Report of the Review of the Safeguards for Children Living Away From Home* (London: HMSO).

Valier, C. (2005), *Memorial Laws: Victims, Law and Justice* (London: Cavendish).

van Dam, C. (2001), *Identifying Child Abusers: Preventing Child Sexual Abuse by Recognizing the Patterns of Offenders* (New York: The Haworth Press).

Vandiver, D. and Kercher, G. (2004), 'Offender and Victim Characteristics of Registered Female Sexual offenders in Texas: A Proposed Typology of Female Sexual Offenders', 16 *Sexual Abuse: A Journal of Research and Treatment* 121.

Vandiver, D.M. and Walker, J.T. (2002), 'Female Sex Offenders: An Overview and Analysis of 40 Cases', 27 *Criminal Justice Review* 284.

Vanhoeck, K. and van Daele, E. (2011), 'Denial of Sexual Crimes: A Therapeutic Exploration', in D.P. Boer, R. Eher, L.A. Craig, M.H. Miner, and F. Pfäfflin (eds), *International Perspectives on the Assessment and Treatment of Sexual Offenders* (Chichester: Wiley-Blackwell).

van Swaaningen, R. (1998), *Critical Criminology in Europe* (London: Sage).

van Wilsem, J. (2011), 'Worlds Tied Together? Online and Non-domestic Routine Activities and their Impact on Digital and Traditional Threat Victimisation', 8 *European Journal of Criminology* 115.

Virtual Global Task Force (VGT) (2006), available at <http://www.virtualglobaltaskforce.com/news/Dutch-study.html> (accessed on 28 November 2011).

Vogelstein, F., Kirkpatrick, D., Roth, D., Lashinsky, A., and Schlender, B., and Simons, J. (2005), '10 Tech Trends to Watch in 2005', 151 *Fortune* 43.

Volkwein, K., Schnell, F., Sherwood, D., and Livezey, A. (1997), 'Sexual Harassment in Sport: Perceptions and Experiences of American Female Student-Athletes', 23 *International Review for the Sociology of Sport* 283.

Wacquant, L. (2001), 'The Penalisation of Poverty and Neo-liberalism', 9 *European Journal on Criminal Policy and Research* 401.

Walden, I. and Wasik, M. (2011), 'The Internet: Access Controlled!', *Criminal Law Review* 377.

Walker, N. (1995), *Interpreting Crime Statistics* (Oxford: Clarendon Press).

Walmsley, R. (2009), *World Prison Population List* (8th edn) (London: International Centre for Prison Studies, King's College London).

Walrath, C., Ybarra, M., and Holden, E.W. (2003), 'Children with Reported Histories of Sexual Abuse: Utilizing Multiple Perspectives to Understand Clinical and Psychosocial Profiles', 27 *Child Abuse and Neglect* 509.

Walsh, D. (2011), 'Police Cooperation Across the Irish Border: Familiarity Breeding Contempt for Transparency and Accountability', 38 *Journal of Law and Society* 301.

Ward, T. (2001), 'A Critique of Hall and Hirschman's Quadripartite Model of Child Sexual Abuse', 7 *Psychology, Public Policy, and Law* 333.

——(2002a), 'Good Lives and the Rehabilitation of Sexual Offenders: Promises and Problems', 7 *Aggression and Violent Behaviour* 513.

——(2002b), 'The Management of Risk and the Design of Good Lives', 37 *Australian Psychologist* 172.

Ward, T. and Gannon, T.A. (2006), 'Rehabilitation, Etiology, and Self-regulation: The Comprehensive Good Lives Model of Treatment for Sexual Offenders', 11 *Agression and Violent Behavior* 77.

Ward, T. and Hudson, S.M. (1998a), 'The Construction and Development of Theory in the Sexual Offending Area: A Metatheoretical Framework', 10 *Sexual Abuse: A Journal of Research and Treatment* 47.

——(1998b), 'A Model of the Relapse Process in Sexual Offenders', 13 *Journal of Interpersonal Violence* 700.

——(2000), 'Sexual Offenders' Implicit Planning: A Conceptual Model', 12 *Sexual Abuse: Journal of Research and Treatment* 189.

——(2001), 'Finkelhor's Precondition Model of Child Sexual Abuse: A Critique', 7 *Psychology, Crime and Law* 291.

Ward, T. and Keenan, T. (1999), 'Child Molesters' Implicit Theories', 14 *Journal of Interpersonal Violence* 821.

Ward, T., Louden, K., Hudson, S.M., and Marshall, W.L. (1995), 'A Descriptive Model of the Offense Chain for Child Molesters', 10 *Journal of Interpersonal Violence* 452.

Ward, T. and Maruna, S. (2007), *Rehabilitation: Beyond the Risk Assessment Paradigm* (London: Routledge).

Ward, T. and Siegert, R. (2002), 'Towards a Comprehensive Theory of Child Sexual Abuse: A Theory Knitting Perspective', 8 *Psychology, Crime and Law* 319.

Ward, T., Yates, P.M., and Long, C.A. (2006), *The Self-regulation Model of the Offence and Re-offence Process: Volume 2, Treatment* (Victoria BC: Pacific Psychological Assessment Corporation).

Wardle, C. (2007), 'Monsters and Angels: Visual Press Coverage of Child Murders in the USA and the UK, 1930–2000', 8 *Journalism* 263.

Warner, N. (1992), *Choosing With Care* (London: HMSO).

Warner, S. (2000), *Understanding Child Sexual Abuse: Making the Tactics Possible* (Gloucester: Handsell).

Warren, G. (2008), 'Interactive Online Services, Social Networking Sites and the Protection of Children', 19 *Entertainment Law Review* 165.

Waterhouse, R. (2000), *Lost In Care* (London: HMSO).

Watkins, B. and Bentovim, A. (1992), 'The Sexual Abuse of Male Children and Adolescents: A Review of Current Research', 33 *Journal of Child Psychology and Psychiatry* 197.

Weaver, B. and McNeill, F. (2010), 'Public Protection in Scotland: A Way Forward?', in A. Williams and M. Nash (eds), *Handbook of Public Protection* (Devon: Cullompton, Publishing).

Webster, S.D. (2005), 'Pathways to Sexual Offence Recidivism Following Treatment: An Examination of the Ward and Hudson Self Regulation Model of Relapse', 20 *Journal of Interpersonal Violence* 1175.

Webster, S., Davidson, J., Bifulco, A., Gottschalk, P., Caretti, V., Pham, T., Grove-Hills, J., Turley, C., Tompkins, C., Ciulla, S., Milazzo, V., Schimmenti, A., and Craparo, G. (2012), *European Online Grooming Project: Final Report* (March 2012), available at <http://www.europeanonlinegroomingproject.com/wp-content/file-uploads/European-Online-Grooming-Project-Final-Report.pdf> (accessed 30 April 2012).

Webwise (2006), *Survey of Children's Use of the Internet: Investigating Online Risk Behaviour*, available at <http://www.webwise.ie/article.aspx?id=4526> (accessed 15 March 2011).

Wells, M., Finkelhor, D., Wolak, J., and Mitchell, K.J. (2007), 'Defining Child Pornography: Law Enforcement Dilemmas in Investigations of Internet Child Pornography Possession', 8 *Police Practice and Research* 269.

Wells, M. and Mitchell, K.J. (2007), 'Youth Sexual Exploitation on the Internet: DSM-IV Diagnoses and Gender Differences in Co-occurring Mental Health Issues', 24 *Child and Adolescent Social Work Journal* 235.

Westcott, H. (1991), *Institutional Abuse of Children—From Research to Policy: A Review* (London: NSPCC).

Westcott, H. and Clement, M. (1992), *NSPCC Experience of Child Abuse in Residential Care and Educational Placements: Results of a Survey* (London: NSPCC).

White, I.A. and Hart, K. (1995), *Report of the Inquiry Into the Management of Child Care in the London Borough of Islington* (London: Islington Council).

White, K. (1973), Residential Child Care Past and Present. Unpublished MPhil Thesis, University of Edinburgh.

White, M.D. and Terry, K. (2008), 'Child Sexual Abuse in the Catholic Church: Revisiting the Rotten Apples Explanation', 35 *Criminal Justice and Behaviour* 658.

Whitty, M.T. (2002), 'Liar Liar! An Examination of How Open, Supportive and Honest People are in Chat Rooms', 18 *Computers in Human Behaviour* 343.

Whitty, M.T. and Joinson, A.N. (2009), *Truth, Lies and Trust on the Internet* (Hove and New York: Routledge).

Wigfall, V. and Moss, P. (2001), *More Than the Sum of Its Parts? A Study of a Multi-agency Child Care Network* (London: National Children's Bureau).

Williams, A. and Thompson, B. (2004a), 'Vigilance or Vigilantes: The Paulsgrove Riots and Policing Paedophiles in the Community: Part 1: The Long Slow Fuse', 77 *Police Journal* 99.

Williams, A. and Thompson, B. (2004b), 'Vigilance or Vigilantes: The Paulsgrove Riots and Policing Paedophiles in the Community: Part 2: The Lessons of Paulsgrove', 77 *Police Journal* 193.

Williams, G. and McCreadie, J. (1992), *Ty Mawr Community Home Inquiry* (Cwmbran: Gwent County Council).

Williams, K. (2004), 'Child Pornography Law: Does it Protect Children?', 26 *Journal of Social Welfare and Family Law* 245.

Willis, G.M., Levenson, J.S. and Ward, T. (2010), 'Desistance and Attitudes Towards Sex Offenders: Facilitation or Hindrance?', 25 *Journal of Family Violence* 545.

Wilson, C., Bates, A., and Völlm, B. (2010), 'Circles of Support and Accountability: An Innovative Approach to Manage High-Risk Sex Offenders in the Community', 3 *The Open Criminology Journal* 48.

Wilson, D. and Jones, T. (2008), '"In My Own World": A Case Study of a Paedophile's Thinking and Doing and His Use of the Internet', 47 *Howard Journal of Criminal Justice* 107.

Wilson, R.J. (1999), 'Emotional Congruence in Sex Offenders Against Children', 11 *Sexual Abuse: Journal of Research and Treatment* 33.

Wilson, R.J., Picheca, J.E., and Prinzo, M. (2007a), 'Evaluating the Effectiveness of Professionally-Facilitated Volunteerism in the Community-Based Management of High-Risk Sexual Offenders: Part One—Effects on Participants and Stakeholders', 46 *The Howard Journal* 289.

Wilson, R.J., Pichea, J.E., and Prinzo, M. (2007b), 'Evaluating the Effectiveness of Professionally-Facilitated Volunteerism in the Community-Based Management of High-Risk Sex Offenders: Part Two—A Comparison of Recidivism Rates', 46 *The Howard Journal* 327.

Wolak, J., Finkelhor, D., and Mitchell, K.J. (2004), 'Internet-initiated Sex Crimes Against Minors: Implications for Prevention Based on Findings From a National Study', 35 *Journal of Adolescent Health* 424.e1.

——(2005), *Child-pornography Possessors Arrested in Internet-related Crime: Findings from the National Juvenile Online Victimisation Study* (Alexandria, VA: National Center for Missing and Exploited Children), available at <http://www.missingkids.com/en_US/publications/NC144.pdf> (accessed 31 March 2011).

Wolak, J., Finkelhor, D., Mitchell, K.J., and Ybarra, M.L. (2008), 'Online "Predators" and their Victms: Myths, Realities, and Implications for Prevention and Treatment', 63 *American Psychologist* 111.

Wolak, J., Mitchell, K.J., and Finkelhor, D. (2003), 'Escaping or Connecting? Characteristics of Youth who Form Close Online Relationships', 26 *Journal of Offender Adolescence* 105.

——(2006), *Online Victimisation of Youth: Five Years Later* (Alexandria, VA: National Center for Missing and Exploited Children), available at <http://www.missingkids.com/missingkids/servlet/ResourceServlet?PageId=2530> (accessed 29 March 2011).

Wolf, S.C. (1985), 'A MultiFactor Model of Deviant Sexuality', 10 *Victimology* 359.

Wortley, R. and Smallbone, S. (eds) (2006), *Situational Prevention of Child Sexual Abuse*, Crime Prevention Studies, vol 19 (Monsey, New York: Criminal Justice Press, and Cullompton, Devon: Willan Publishing).

Wykes, M. (2002), 'Evil Beast Meets Dangerous Stranger: Mediating Masculinities in News About Violent Crime', paper presented at The British Society of Criminology Conference, July (Keele).

Wyre, R. (2000), 'Paedophile Characteristics and Patterns of Behaviour', in C. Itzin (ed), *Home Truths About Sexual Abuse Influencing Policy and Practice: A Reader* (London: Routledge).

Yates, P.M. and Kingston, D.A. (2006), 'The Self Regulation Model of Sex Offending. The Relationship between Offence Pathways and Static and Dynamic Sexual Offence Risk', 18 *Sexual Abuse: A Journal of Research and Treatment* 259.

Ybarra, M.L., Espelage, D.L., and Mitchell, K.J. (2007), 'The Co-occurrence of Internet Harassment and Unwanted Sexual Solicitation Victimization and Perpetration: Associations with Psychosocial Indicators', 41 *Journal of Adolescent Health* 1.

Yorganci, I. (1993), 'Preliminary Findings from A Survey of Gender Relationships and Sexual Harassment in Sport', in C. Brackenridge (ed), *Body Matters: Leisure Images and Lifestyles* (Brighton: Leisure Studies Association).

Young, J. (1991), 'Left Realism and the Priorities of Crime Control', in K. Stenson and D. Cowell (eds), *The Politics of Crime Control* (London: Sage).

Zedner, L. (1995), 'In Pursuit of the Vernacular: Comparing Law and Order Discourse in Britain and Germany', 4 *Social and Legal Studies* 517.

—— (2002), 'Victims', in M. Maguire, R. Morgan, and R. Reiner (eds), *The Oxford Handbook of Criminology* (3rd edn) (Oxford: Oxford University Press).

—— (2009), 'Fixing the Future? The Pre-emptive Turn in Criminal Justice', in B. McSherry, A. Norrie, and S. Bronitt (eds), *Regulating Deviance: The Redirection of Criminalisation and the Futures of Criminal Law* (Oxford: Hart Publishing).

Index